Understanding Creative Business

To Joanne Naylor

Understanding Creative Business

Values, Networks and Innovation

JIM SHORTHOSE
and
NEIL MAYCROFT

Routledge
Taylor & Francis Group

LONDON AND NEW YORK

First published 2012 by Gower Publishing

Published 2016 by Routledge
2 Park Square, Milton Park, Abingdon, Oxfordshire OX14 4RN
711 Third Avenue, New York, NY 10017, USA

First issued in paperback 2016

Routledge is an imprint of the Taylor & Francis Group, an informa business

Gower Applied Business Research
Our programme provides leaders, practitioners, scholars and researchers with thought provoking, cutting edge books that combine conceptual insights, interdisciplinary rigour and practical relevance in key areas of business and management.

British Library Cataloguing in Publication Data
Shorthose, Jim.
  Understanding creative business : values, networks and
  innovation.
  1. Creative ability in business. 2. Business enterprises.
  I. Title II. Maycroft, Neil.
  658.3'14-dc23

Library of Congress Cataloging-in-Publication Data
Shorthose, Jim.
  Understanding creative business : values, networks, and innovation / by
Jim Shorthose and Neil Maycroft.
     p. cm.
  Includes bibliographical references and index.
  ISBN 978-1-4094-0714-0 (hardback)
  1. Creative ability in business. I. Maycroft, Neil. II. Title.
  HD53.S556 2012
  658.4'094--dc23

                                                              2012012324

ISBN 13: 978-1-138-25574-6 (pbk)
ISBN 13: 978-1-4094-0714-0 (hbk)

Contents

List of Figures

List of Tables

Introduction

It might not be immediately obvious why the three themes of this book – values, networks and innovation – are connected. So we start with this quotation because our book is above all else about *relationships* and the key role that they play in creativity and business. Getting to be good at relationships is necessary for getting to be good at creative business, and Theodore Roszak expresses better than anything we could come up what good relationships *could be* about.

In his book *Flow: the Psychology of Optimal Experience*, Mihályi Csíkszentmihályi expresses this intimate link between creativity and relationships by enshrining each facet within a broader concept of flow. This is something we will come back to a few times in subsequent chapters. But for now we can see this link in Csíkszentmihályi's definition of flow '... joy, creativity, the total involvement with life I call flow'.

Flow is a modern version of a much older idea – that of a fulfilling sense of happiness and well-being; creative self-expression; and a developed engagement with the world, and by extension with socio-ethical life all interconnected. And it is these interconnections that form the underlying logic of our book.

Values, and the ethical thinking that can help animate and improve them means nothing unless it is played out in and through real relationships to inform the *If* and *Why* of creative business. Networks for creativity are based upon the forming and maintenance of relationships that can help with the *How* and *With Whom* of creative business. Innovation comes from the flow of ideas between people to help with the *What* and *When* of creative business.

So these are our three themes. But we would prefer if you did not see them in isolation from each, because we see them as interconnected:

- Values can inform better ways of interacting in creative networks and help with decisions about the actual content of your innovation.
- Creative networks often seem to animate a new set of values-oriented economic relationships and stimulate concrete innovations.

- Innovation is usually based upon researching the relationships within your creative networks and with the wider public realm, which thus needs some value-oriented thinking to it.

So whilst we break down the book into relatively three themes containing relatively short chapters that concentrate upon, hopefully clear and direct, statements, we still hope you will take this book as a more coherent argument that that.

But this then brings us to …

Our Tone of Voice

We have deliberately tried to make our tone of voice open and playful. We think our book is academically informed enough to 'hold water' as we go through some of the often quite complex philosophical debates and concepts. But at the same we did not want it to be 'academicist' – another one of those books that uses overly academic language just for the sake of it. We are bored with reading that stuff too, and we come from that world.

So we wrote this book in a different way, by trying to present ideas so that they can be easily understood and digested, and then *used* in ways that contribute to actual concrete creative and business thinking. That is – we wanted to keeps things simple, whilst not being simplistic; keep things practical, whilst at the same time being conceptually thoughtful. This is why we have used lots of small stories, case studies, thinkpieces and exercises.

This is also why you will find a fairly broad-ranging account of relevant debates and discussions across the three themes, rather than any particularly deep inquiry into any one of them. We will leave the academicist kind of writing that shows great erudition but practical disconnection and linguistic mystification to others on this occasion.

We wanted to write something more like the way we would talk to someone in a bar or cafe, because that seemed much more appropriate to the themes we are covering and the people we wanted this book to speak to.

And these people are …

Three Overlapping Constituencies

It is always good when writing something to have an idea about whom you are writing it for. Who is your audience?

The book you are holding comes out of lots of university teaching, quite a bit of cultural activism and project organizing designed to support creative business; and some cultural policy consultation and research with/for professionals working in the cultural public sector. Given these experiences, we have written this book in a way that tries to navigate across this mixed cultural economy to offer useful ideas for:

- established or emerging creative businesses operating in the commercial sector;
- independent creative networks and other DiY cultural spaces that want to do the 'cultural business' but are not necessarily interested in the out and out commercial

sector as such; our experience suggest there are a lot of those people out there within such self-organized creative networks;

- cultural professionals who work in, with and for more formal cultural organizations in receipt of public investment that have a remit to support creativity and business in some way.

This implies another key distinction.

The 'Being in ...' and 'Doing ...' of Creative Business

The title of this book, *Understanding Creative Business*, can be read in at least two different ways. You have our permission.

Understanding Creative *Business* suggests that it is a 'business studies' book that offers ideas for 'Being in Business' and achieving success. It is partly that, and we try to offer useful stuff for business and organizational success.

But you could also read the title as Understanding *Creative* Business, and so approach the book as being about 'doing the business' of being creative. As you will see if you keep reading, we have used the creative voices and deeds of artists as much as those of the commercial side of things. So we hope we have offered ideas about the creativity thing as much as the business thing, and have achieved a balance dialogue across the two.

But enough preliminary comment. Let's get on with it.

Values

1 New Spectacles for Juliette?

Story

In his book *An Intimate History of Humanity*, Theodore Zeldin tells the story of Juliette, who sees her life as a failure. This is because of the neglectful and dismissive attitude people have always had towards her. Whilst she carries herself with dignity, Juliette is now very hesitant and guarded in her dealings with people. Only rarely does she feel able to open up to others because she has been made to feel rather worthless by their years of shouting.

At the age of 16 Juliette met a man she loved and became pregnant. At first their marriage went well, but gradually he came to treat her badly, having affairs with other women and finally beating her. Juliette was too ashamed to tell anyone about this and instead blamed herself for her plight. She became more and more cut off from her family as her husband prevented her from having friends and going out. In the end, her child was taken into care and Juliette's humiliation was complete and she felt her life was over.

After many years she managed to get away from her abusive husband, but she was too frightened to live alone. So she took up with another man so as not to be alone at night. When she gets home from work her only pleasure is to sit quietly alone and rest. Her only dream is to afford her own flat so that she can feel safe in her own space.

Juliette is now 51 years old and works as a domestic servant. Over the years she has mastered the art of cooking and cleaning for others. Her services are in demand and many people want Juliette to work for them, but not enough to treat her well. Even though many of them are highly educated and affluent, they have not shown her any warmth or treated her with dignity. Even the doctor she cleans for shows no interest in her. Perhaps Juliette's life could have been better if the people she had met along the way had not been so 'silent, superficial and routine'. If they had not been 'restrained by the ghosts which continue to influence what employers and strangers and even people who live together may or may not say to each other'.

Zeldin asks us how we might make sense of Juliette's plight:

One can say: that is what life is like, and there are many reasons why it is so. Or one can hope that if the knots into which humanity ties itself could be untied, and its crazy institutions made more sensible, that life could be changed, and poverty could be abolished … Or one can hate life for being so cruel and try to bear it by making fun of it … all the while protecting oneself against disappointment by refusing to suggest solutions to problems, and by condemning all such efforts as naïve … Juliette is not a slave: nobody owns her. She is not a serf: nobody has a right to her labor. But to think one's life is finished, or that it is a failure, is to suffer from the same sort of despair which afflicted people in the days when the world believed it could not do without slaves … The conclusion I draw from the history of slavery is that freedom is not just a matter of rights, to be enshrined by law. The right to express yourself still leaves you with the need to decide what to say, to find someone to listen, and to make your words beautiful; these are skills to be acquired ... I want to show how priorities are changing today, and what sort of spectacles are needed to observe them. In the course of history, humans have changed the spectacles through which they have looked at the world and themselves ...

(from *An Intimate History of Humanity*, by T. Zeldin)

Juliette needs new spectacles. And maybe we do too, to find better perspectives for our relationships with our selves, with each other, our creativity, our business ideas and Nature. We very much agree with Theodore Zeldin, and we want to contribute to his call for these changed spectacles, along with the acquisition of skills for more beautiful speaking to each other.

So maybe we need to talk about:

- having trust in each other
- not shouting
- overcoming any unnecessary sense of shame and failure
- ridding ourselves of the fear of others
- grasping our collective abilities to express ourselves
- switching attention to be less silent, superficial and routine with each other
- taking moments to exchange thoughts about our shared humanity
- giving up the desire for conquest
- making life better in a practical sense for as many people as we can.

This question of new spectacles suggests that one way or another the question of values and ethics within life and creativity is necessary and urgent. Whilst some of this might just 'come' – from the kind of person you, from your parents and friends, from how you have been brought up – to really get hold of the question of values and ethics in a way that gives them shape and practical application, it is necessary to consciously reflect upon them and develop skills in them.

But before we go any further, we should note ...

Three Difficulties When Talking About Values

The two people writing this book cannot claim to be offering a complete basis for any choice about values within creative business. We have inevitably made choices about *our* values, and ethics, the ones that motivate us to say what we say. Given this, there will always be some immediate difficulties:

- There will never be agreement about ethical ideas, moral standards and their consequent implications.
- It can all too easily get rather 'preachy' and 'holier than thou'.
- Creative people tend to be motivated by values and ethics anyway.

We are very aware of the last difficulty and, indeed, we refer to lots of case studies in our book from creative people who are doing fantastically proactive ethical work that takes its cue from concerns with social responsibility, usefulness and justice. But nevertheless we think what we have to say is worthwhile in terms of broadening and deepening understanding and encouraging other to do likewise.

We will try to avoid the second of the above difficulties by simply offering ideas for your consideration without any heavy-duty finger pointing.

Dealing with the first difficulty entails providing a balanced view of competing ethical ideas. But we have to write about something if we are to write this book! Inevitably this will involve us choosing to write about some things and, therefore, not others. Ultimately there is not an awful lot we can do about this. All books suffer from the same problem. We hope you find looking through the particular spectacles we have chosen for Section 1 useful. If you do not you can always read something else!

We do not mean that to sound grumpy!

As we finish writing this book in early 2011, lots of things are being said about ethics and the lack of them – the continued ethical bankruptcy of bankers and 'fat cat' chief executives; the need for corporate social responsibility; the ethics of environmentalism and sustainability; the current obsession of professional politicians with 'fairness' as they cut the public services that the poorest in society rely upon the most. A lot of these pronouncements seem pretty flimsy to us, lacking real meaning and certainly do not seem to go very far in practice – creative or business practice. This is annoying, but being annoyed only gets you so far. We are interested in exploring ideas that might make creative business practices less flimsy when it comes to ethical considerations. We feel this is a necessary and timely theme for thinking about our joint futures.

This involves:

- **Theory** – translating some of the difficult scientific, philosophical and theoretical *debates* about values and ethics into something directly useful for creative business.
- **Planning** – exploring relationship-based spaces between creative producers, audiences, users and organizations that might lead to expanded mutual care within creative business *thinking*.
- **Actions** – considering example of concrete creative business *practices* that have been about building a better public future.

We believe that writing within this cross-over space is a good place from which to explore questions like:

- Why is my creativity as it is?
- Can I make it better by asking what it is *for*, rather than simply what it *is*?
- What broad social values motivate it?
- Are there better ones?
- How do I turn values and ethical beliefs into regular business attitudes and concrete creative actions?
- How can I expand my capacity for care towards the World through my creative practice?

It might even make you happy(er)!

Happiness and Purpose

Many philosophers have suggested that a happy life comes from a sense of duty and commitment to something bigger than your own life. They suggest that it is futile to always seek an *arrival at the state we call happiness*. If you are always asking yourself whether you are happy or not it is likely you will always be unhappy, because you will always want the next thing, the thing you feel is missing. You are likely to become one of those 'glass half empty' people.

On the other hand, you could concentrate on the things outside yourself, put yourself into something you believe in – your creative work, your business, your service to others, your creative purpose.

And at the end of one of those working days when you lose yourself in your creative work you can reflect upon how happy this sense of purpose has made you.

> ## Quotation
>
> *Happiness is not a goal, it is a by-product.*
>
> (Eleanor Roosevelt)

In *Creativity: Flow and the Psychology of Discovery and Invention*, Csíkszentmihályi shows how people who experience creative *flow* do so by experiencing 'standing beside something', or 'going beyond normal routines'. He sees flow as being about:

- having a complete involvement in what you are doing – being focused and concentrated;
- gaining a sense of ecstasy – of being outside everyday reality;
- having great inner clarity – knowing what needs to be done;
- knowing that the creative flow activity is do-able – having the skills to pull it off;
- having a sense of serenity – of leaving one's worries behind;
- timeless-ness – of being in the moment;
- having an intrinsic motivation – such that the flow activity is its own reward.

Flow seems to bring creativity activity and a sense of happiness together to stimulate an intensity of experience that enables us to go beyond out egocentric human tendencies. As we will discuss in more detail below, this is the link between the creativity-happiness thing and being good at ethics. Going beyond one's ego, one's appetites, one's self-centred interests have been central to discussions of ethical skill for centuries, in both philosophy and religion. When all three aspects creativity-happiness-ethics are brought together, they seem to speak to and revitalize each other. Csíkszentmihályi speaks of flow as the joining of the first two sides of the coin, we want to suggest that the third adds greater depth and meaning because it adds relationships with others to creativity and happiness, which deepens the experience. So rather than seeing ethics as a break upon our natural selfish tendencies, we can argue that it is in fact an aspect of self-fulfilment and a source of great pleasure. And heaven knows we need more ethics in a public and professional lives these days.

And, anyway, being in creative business often means that your sense of yourself is intimately intertwined with what you do. Because *you are what you do* it will be good to do what you think is the right thing. You might as well go with a sense of creative purpose that you really believe in. This is the ethical parallel to the idea that *you are what you eat.* It is likely to make you happy as well as healthy.

So it might be that as with happiness so with creative purpose, some counter-intuitive thinking is needed. You might find these things by not looking inwards at what you want, but by looking outwards towards what you can give to the World:

- Don't look for happiness – do some work and you will *feel happy.*
- Don't try to define the meaning of your creativity – offer some service to others and it will *feel meaningful.*
- Don't try to stick to your creative purpose – look to other people and *act with purposeful-ness* in those situations.

For instance …

Thinkpiece
AVOIDING UNHAPPINESS

I believe unhappiness to be very largely due to mistaken views of the world, mistaken ethics, mistaken habits of life, leading to the destruction of that natural zest and appetite for possible things upon which all happiness … ultimately depends … Happiness is best achieved by those who do not directly seek it … I came to centre my attention increasingly on external objects: the state of the world, various branches of knowledge, individuals for whom I felt affection.

(from *The Conquest of Happiness,* by B. Russell)

For Bertrand Russell, one of the main barriers to happiness is the self-absorption that can come in various guises:

- **'The Sinner'** – the habit of believing too often and too strongly that you are always doing wrong, always disapproving of yourself. Carrying around an overt and visceral sense of your guilt –the kind that religion and overbearing parents often inculcate within people– is not good for your happiness, creativity or sense of purpose. Give yourself a day off. Then take the rest of your life off.
- **Narcissism** – the habit of admiring yourself and always wishing to be admired. We all need some positive feedback from the World but an overriding desire to always be admired can get in the way of creative purpose and leads you down ethical cul-de-sacs to become less of a person than you are capable of being.
- **The Megalomaniac** – rather than wishing to be admired, the habit of wanting to be feared and obeyed. We all like to get our own way sometimes but for the megalomaniac this desire is excessive, central to their identity and associated with their insufficiently developed sense of the 'real world' as it is experienced by other people. This leads to a lack of emotional intelligence which is not good for anything.

None of these personalities are useful for creative business if it is to have any sense of ethical purpose. These attitudes will only get in the way of your creative business.

- Do you need to get rid of any of these traits within your business?
- From within yourself?
- From within your business colleagues?
- From within your creative business 'personality?

Value-Based Happiness and Purpose

<table>
<tr><td>

Quotation

In *Flow: The Psychology of Optimal Experience*, Csíkszentmihályi writes about creative purpose thus:

In the lives of many people it is possible to find a unifying purpose that justifies that things they do day in, day out – a goal that like a magnetic field attracts their psychic energy, a goal upon which all lesser goals depend. This goal will define the challenges that a person needs to face in order to transform his or her life into a flow activity. Without such a purpose, even the best-ordered consciousness lacks meaning.

(from *Flow: The Psychology of Optimal Experience*, by M. Csíkszentmihályi)

</td></tr>
</table>

To take the discussion of happiness and purpose further, we need to make the distinction between 'feel good happiness' and 'value-based happiness'.

'Feeling good happiness' stems from the satisfaction of basic needs such as those for food, shelter and sex. The problem with feeling good happiness is the 'law of diminishing returns'. Some food, shelter or sex when you have not had any for ages is very satisfying and makes you happy. But the same amount when you are already satisfied will not produce the same amount of happiness – sometimes you get stuffed with food, have been in the house for ages and want to go out, just want to cuddle up in bed together and watch telly.

Being a bit more philosophical about this, we can see the behaviour geared towards getting the 'feeling good' stuff as 'resource acquisition' behaviour. The happiness you might get from this resource acquisition goes down the more you have the stuff it is directed toward. This is probably why people, in general, seem to feel less happy as levels of affluence go up. That new car, house, coat and so on you have been after for six months does not actually make you as happy as you thought it would when you actually get it.

'Value-based happiness' comes from a different place, is much less subject to the 'law of diminishing returns' and is much more important for a sense of purpose directing behaviour. As we will see in Chapter 3 it probably comes from a deeper need to demonstrate mutual recognition, reciprocity and kinship with *other people*. Easily recognizable sources of 'value-based happiness' are found in the sense of love and commitment we have to our kids (probably all kids when we get down to it), the sense of charitable-ness to the people around us, altruism. The satisfactions we get from it never 'run out' the more we do it. It can, therefore, be the basis for a sustained creative purpose.

And this is the fundamental point. Developing better value-based and ethical spectacles for creative purpose might satisfy an intrinsic human need to show commitment and reciprocity to others so that we can get a more developed sense of ourselves and our creative potential. It is possible that making value-based ethical behaviour part of your creative purpose will create happiness for both yourself and for others. Because …

<table>
<tr><td>

Quotation

… to live an ethical life is not self-sacrifice, but self-fulfillment.

(from *How Are We to Live?* by P. Singer)

</td></tr>
</table>

As with happiness so with creative purpose. We don't always find purpose by looking for it, especially looking for it within ourselves. We find creative purpose through our relationships with other people.

Doing Your Best so that You Can Do Your Best

Having noted difficulties associated with discussing values and ethics in the Introduction, we could also note that such discussions sometimes feel like they are closing in on you, reducing everything to a bigger and bigger set of pronouncements. 'Do this', 'don't do that', 'be ethical in your practice', 'be ethical in your business', 'be an ethical consumer', 'be a vegetarian', 'don't do air travel', and so on.

To discuss ethics in this way is unnecessary. Ethics is not a series of barriers but, rather, a map to better destinations. Values that underpin ethical thinking can be the way to explore new routes and new destinations for your creativity in a manner which may overcome the supposedly normal, and therefore 'only' way of living in this society – the 'Market', competition, selfishness and treating strangers as threats, dogs eating dogs, and so on.

There is no need to beat yourself up if you cannot find 'ethical purity', because it does not exist. Doing your best for a more ethical creative purpose is more about constant thinking and practical doing than sitting in a 'ethical arm chair' and trying to dream up a position that will suffice for all situations. It is more about:

- Using your innate capacity for Reason so as to develop your ability to act reasonably.
- Articulating yourself and your human feelings towards others in search of ethically skilful daily contact.
- Developing your ability to do/be the best you can do/become in and through concrete and practical examples of care towards others.

Thinkpiece
PRAXIS

Praxis is a philosophical term that talks about combining theory – abstraction or conceptual thinking, on the one hand, with regular practice on the other, in search of a coherent whole.

Praxis is the process by which a theory, lesson, or skill is enacted or practiced, embodied and/or realized. "Praxis" may also refer to the act of engaging, applying, exercising, realizing, or practicing ideas. This has been a popular topic in the field of philosophy, as Plato, Aristotle, St Augustine, Immanuel Kant, Karl Marx, Martin Heidegger, Hannah Arendt, and many others, have written about this topic …

It has meaning in political, educational, and spiritual realms.

(from Wikipedia)

There is no off-the-shelf handbook for how to think or act ethically. All you can do is try to bring these dimensions into your everyday life as often and as thoroughly as you can. Ethics needs to be played out actively in and through particular situations for it to really come alive and be a part of everyday creative purpose.

And it is not easy.

Metaphor
IT DEPENDS ON HOW CLOSE YOU ARE

It might seem relatively simple exercise to see the length of a coastline. Use Google Earth to hover 50,000 feet up in the air and you can see the whole of the coastline of Britain and how long it is.

Get a little closer and you begin to see more and more of the in and out detail making the coastline considerable longer.

Get a bit closer still and even more detail appears.

Eventually you see each individual stone on the beach, lengthening it so much it is now impossible to measure. It becomes impossible to say with any certainty where the coastline ends and the sea begins. Our relatively simple task appears more and more impossible the closer we get to it.

The same applies to the minutiae of particular ethical dilemmas. The closer we get to them the more intractable they can become.

This is especially the case when we consider another facet of closer-ness and distance – the closeness and distance we have to the person in question. If we are considering the fate of a loved one it is likely that we will use different lenses and levels of ethical urgency than if the person in question is a stranger.

Instead of all the ethical dilemma games that books on ethics often use, ask yourself a simple question – who is the person whose fate I am being asked to decide?

I know that if it is my daughter or son whose life was in the balance in a particular ethical dilemma game I would choose their survival every time. Sorry.

There is no ready-made solution to this, the coastline metaphor simply warns us that the issues of closeness/distance has an impact and suggests that we should be wary of assumptions that ethical certainties can be arrived at.

It is a weird one. You might think that what you see depends upon your ethical lens, but actually your ethical lens often depends where we are seeing things from.

And because of this it may be more useful to see creative purpose as an on-going *journey* rather than something to be *arrived at*. Do your best. And doing your best (ethically) will probably mean that you can do your best (creatively). And then by doing your best you to get to *being* your best. Do your best so that you can do your best. If you see what we mean. Which will probably entail …

Judgement

Making ethical choices requires active judgement. In his book *The Craftsman*, Richard Sennett refers to a long standing distinction between:

- *animal laborens* – the work humans often need to engage in without much thinking, and
- *homo faber* – our human capacity to combine thought and action within self-directed work that goes beyond our own immediate needs and wants.

The capacity to be *homo faber* is represented by the *demioergoi* that speaks to our responsibility to be the judge of what we do and why.

For instance …

Case Study

LINUX AS THE DEMIOERGOI

The Greek God Hephaestus is a good candidate to be the patron saint of creative practitioners because he stands for the image of using of tools for the public good. Hephaestus represents the spirit of the demioergoi, who in Ancient Greek society.

… included, in addition to skilled manual workers like potters, also doctors and lower magistrates, and professional singers and heralds who served as in ancient times as news broadcasters. This slice of ordinary citizens lived in between the relatively few, leisured aristocracy (today that would be the celebrity parts of the cultural economy who are overly wealthy-for-no-good-reason), *and the mass of slaves who did all the work.*

The demioergoi get their name from a combination of the Greek word demos – meaning the public; and ergon – meaning productive.

To understand the living presence of Hephaestus, I ask the reader to make a large mental jump. People who participate in 'open source' computer software, particularly in the Linux operating system, are craftsmen who embody some of the elements first celebrated in the hymn to Hephaestus … The Linux system is a public craft. The underlying software kernel in Linux code is available to anyone, it can be employed and adapted by anyone; people donate time to improve it … Eric Raymond usefully distinguishes between two types of free software: the 'cathedral' model, in which a closed group of programmers develop the code and then make it available to anyone, and the 'bazaar' model, in which anyone can participate via the Internet to produce code. Linux draws on craftsmen in an electronic bazaar … This, then, is a community of craftsmen to whom the ancient appellation demioergoi can be applied. It is focused on achieving quality, on doing good work, which is the craftsman's primordial mark of identity.

(from *The Craftsman*, by Richard Sennett)

Our common image of the craftsman (and maybe creative practitioner) tends to involve someone who is committed to the perfection of the object they are striving to create as an end-in-itself. But this can be ethically 'ambiguous'.

The distinction between *the absolutist* and *the practitioner* continues the point about doing your best in terms of the practical consequences of your creative purpose. Craftsmanship embodying *homo faber*, Hephaestus and the *demioergoi* suggests the need for constant ethical judgement concerning:

- what you are making says about you;
- the degree to which your creative work is allowed to embody proactive personal awareness of necessary ethical skill;

- the extent to which your tools, techniques, processes, aims and the objectives lead you towards or away from the public good.

... no matter what level of technical perfection you are seeking within your work.

Is the work for you to satisfy your own need for perfection? Or is it for another reason that might entail something for other people? Does it treat others as the point of the exercise? For the *demioergoi* there is no end-in-itself, there is no point in chasing perfection divorced from broader public consequences.

To develop good judgement we need to start deeper thinking about what business is for, not is be *is for*. It might be that an ethical discussion of creative business needs to go as far as to reclaim the very idea of 'business' back from the macho-Alan-Sugar-Dragon's-Den people, whose view is rather limited.

The Business Lens

Already you might have surmised that our particular spectacles are giving us an 'alternative' perspective on business. There is nothing inherently wrong with some of the traditional spectacles for looking at how ethics relates to business. But the traditional business agenda does tend to see itself as the *only way* of looking at how we might live together and organize ourselves to meet our collective needs. The traditional business lens tends to start and finish with certain pre-set assumptions that we need to recognize as *assumptions* before we can go further. These include:

- **Business is Business** – this is the traditional business community's 'fundamentalism'. It holds as sacrosanct competition between firms, the profit motive, traditional relationships between management and workers and when necessary satisfying the shareholders regardless of the human implications. These assumptions always come first for the traditional business lens because of even more fundamental assumptions about human nature that suggests that we are hardwired into selfishness. That is ...
- **Economic Man** – underpinning the business is business thing is the (in)famous economic man version of events which suggests that the only motivation is the competition associated with the maximization of our own individual economic benefit – 'looking after number one', personal profit, acquisition, maximized consumption. This lens occludes other views concerning what it is to be human before the evidence is in. By focusing upon what divides us all within this economic competition, and sticking to a limited view of human nature, the traditional business lens is unable to see what connects us all.
- **Let the Market Decide** – the 'amorality' and 'impersonal' nature of the Market is held up as the guarantor of fairness because it allows individual freedom and choice. It can therefore become the arbiter of everything, every social and political decision – from education and health care to scientific and culture developments. But this traditional business lens encourages *commodification* – turning every human interaction into a money-based transaction, and *individualism* – suggesting that we are all only concerned with our own self-interest. The outcomes resulting from the over-adherence to markets are not good for asking yourself broader and deeper

philosophical questions about the values and ethics you want within your (creative) business life.

The Big Business agenda that is usually underpinned by some version of these assumptions – the macho kind in which people get off on all the competitive stuff – is one of the few areas of human endeavour that comes with such ready-made, off-the-peg internal justifications. So it is easy to get sucked into it as the only sensible way of thinking and living. 'Business is business' tends to also come with the 'all is fair in love and war' thing which involves the:

- 'We can do whatever we want, it doesn't really matter if we are bad, because we are doing 'Business' thing.
- 'We are not really being bad, look at all the things we contribute to economic growth whilst we are being bad' thing.
- 'To say anything against our traditional business view of the World is pointless, because it is just the way things are. We've been to the 'University of Life' thing.

Well the 'University of Life' is a limited university. Experiences are great, but to really learn we need to go beyond simply *having them* to understand deeper and broader questions. Experience in the present does not mean *understanding* the present, and sticking at all costs to how things *are now* is not a good place from which to grow an *imagination* for the future. Lacking this understanding and imagination is good for neither creativity nor business, or much else come to that.

This is why the traditional business lens often has a fairly limited approach to ethics and, by the way, why it does not always get the creativity bit of creative business very well either. As you will see if you keep reading, we intend to go beyond this traditional business lens.

There is no point denying that there is a big, often harsh and competitive business world out there. But there have been some very major changes taking place lately:

- the global, post-crash, economic context;
- the ethical, political and cultural bankruptcy of many Establishment institutions;
- the continued Western neglect of the needs of people in the Developing World;
- the on-going ecological crisis and the abject failure of Big Institutions to respond adequately;
- embryonic changes to the way that the cultural economy is working and trading and the consequent forging of new values.

Given these big global changes, which we are only now starting to live through, we firmly believe that exploring issues of values and ethics for creative business is not an 'added extra' to be thought about later but an urgent need to make creativity more creative, innovation more innovative and business success mean bigger and better things. Values for creative business can be reviewed as something more than a *reactive* 'ethical wash' aimed at doing less 'bad' in business and become motivated by *proactive improvements* concerning how we relate to each other and the World so as to be more 'good' though creative business.

We need bigger specs! Those really big ones that Elton John used to wear. Or maybe not, but you get the point.

For instance …

Story
BECOMING A CITIZEN OF TOLEDO

After his story about Juliette, Theodore Zeldin tells us another story in *An Intimate History of Humanity*. This one is about Domenicos Theotocopoulos, an obscure Greek artist who painted rather conventionally. But he travelled abroad to paint and eventually settled in Toledo. It was here, in this 'frontier town' that he felt free from conventions and petty rivalries, and learned how to connect to the humanity of those who were thought to have none.

At the time Toledo was a place of both toleration and persecution. Where once Christians, Muslims and Jews had lived side by side and one of its kings had proudly accepted the title to *Emperor of the Three Religions*, now Domenicos Theotocopoulos saw supposed heretics tried before the local Inquisition.

He became:

… stimulated to try the seemingly irreconcilable. To paint the divine and the human intertwined, to have the courage to put his colours directly on the canvas … It takes a long time for people to recognise their soul-mates when they have too limited an idea of who they are themselves … (but) Today, the whole of humanity can see something of itself in the paintings of Domenicos Theotocopoulos, who came to be known as El Greco, who died owning only one spare suit, two shirts and a beloved library of books on every subject. Because of him, everybody can feel, to a certain extent, a citizen of Toledo. He is an example of a person who discovers what humans have in common.

(from *An Intimate History of Humanity*, by T. Zeldin)

Traditional and Organic Creativity in Business

How would you decide to creatively 'travel abroad', live in a 'frontier city' so as to 'put your (ethical) colours directly onto the canvas'? Before deciding, the philosopher Antonio Gramsci makes a useful distinction between 'traditional' and 'organic' intellectuals:

- **Traditional** – the academic who has become institution-bound, self-serving and too divorced from the reality of people's lives. The phrase 'it is just academic' – meaning that is of no real, practical importance points to the problem of the 'traditional' intellectual.
- **Organic** – the intellectual who tries to interpret and understand some aspect of the World in the way it is experienced by real people, can be understood by the majority and works to actually do something concrete about their felt experiences.

The mindset of the organic intellectual can be summed up with …

Global Lesson

SHAMANISM

Shamanism is the oldest form of mind/body healing known to humankind. It involves the use of altered states of consciousness for the purpose of restoring well-being to those who are experiencing ill health or helplessness. Shamanism is estimated by archeologists to be at least forty thousand years old. It's been practiced perennially – or continuously – by virtually all indigenous peoples up to today. Only in the West were its practices essentially eradicated, because of the so-called Enlightenment.

(from *Shamanic Counseling and Ecopsychology*, by L. Gray, in *Ecopsychology*, ed. T. Roszak.

(They) are intermediaries … (who) according to believers … can treat illnesses and are capable of entering supernatural realms to provide answers for humans … Resources for human consumption are easily depleted in tropical rainforests. In some rainforests cultures, such as the Tucano, a sophisticated system exists for the management of resources for avoiding depletion through overhunting … As symbolic teachers of tribal symbolism, the Shaman may have a leading role in ecological management, actively restricting hunting and fishing.

Shamanism involves:

Healing – *Shamanism may be based closely on the soul concept of the belief system … It may consist of retrieving the lost souls of the ill person …*

Knowledge – *Really, the Shaman is a person who is an expert in keeping together multiple codes … and has a comprehensive view on it in their mind with a certainty of knowledge …*

Art – *Shamans express meaning in many ways: verbally, musically, artistically and in dance … the Shaman knows the culture of his or her community well, and acts accordingly … .*

(from Wikipedia)

The distinction between traditional and organic intellectuals asks you to consider the degree to which your creative business is connected to the social and cultural world of the people around you, as they understand and experience it. This is likely to have a bearing upon its values and ethical abilities. There are many examples of organic intellectuals working in the Developing World that show how people have managed to keep hold of an 'organic consistency' between ethics and concrete ways of living everyday life. These lessons from organic intellectuals all share bigger spectacles focused on the relationships between values and:

- the organization of social, cultural and economic life
- the imaginative use of scarce resources
- solve practical issues so that the 'good' is shared.

We will look at other concrete examples of the organic consistency within organic intellectualism in the chapters below.

But first the question of the *organic* brings us to the facet that we are most familiar with, the question of everyday personal conduct within the context of creative business networks, what we explore in Section 2 as the *creative ecology*.

Personal Conduct and the Creative Ecology

As we will see below, the over-academic specialization of some ethical philosophy has tended to separate thinking about values and ethics from the people's everyday lives.

But often the everyday life of creative business takes place in relatively close-knit networks of interdependence that often means they can be as more like a natural world ecology of mutual species interdependence than competitive economy if isolated entities. A key feature of creative ecologies therefore is daily, intimate, intensive and trusting face-to-face interactions. This therefore might become an immediate and important factor in developing bigger creative business spectacles, because it requires your everyday personal conduct to also be part of your 'business skills'.

How are you going to get good at developing your personal conduct and sustaining relationships with the 'natural environment' of the creative ecology? How do you want the relationships that make up your network connections to be experienced by you and others?

It may well require everyday personal skills in:

- grace
- empathy
- humility
- dignity
- emotional intelligence
- non-egoistic friendliness and conviviality
- simplicity.

For instance ...

Quotation

... ethics only exists in practice, in the fine grain of everyday decisions. For instance, an environmental ethic will have arrived when most people see a large automobile and think first of the air pollution it causes rather than the social status it conveys, or the frustration it will cause them when they get stuck in traffic or spend precious time hunting for a parking place, rather than the convenience of personal transportation.

For those who choose to live simply, the goal is not ascetic self-denial, but a sort of unadorned grace. Some come to feel, for example, that clothes lines, window shades, and bicycles have a functional elegance that clothes dryers, air conditioners, and automobiles lack. These modern devices are silent, manually operated, fireproof, ozone and climate-friendly, easily repaired and inexpensive ...

In the final analysis, accepting and living by sufficiency rather than excess offers a return to what is, culturally speaking, the human home: to the ancient order of family, community, good work, and good life; to a reverence for skill, creativity, and creation; to a daily cadence slow enough to let us watch the sunset and stroll by the water's edge; to communities worth spending a lifetime in; and to local places pregnant with the memories of generations.

(from *Are We Happy Yet?* by A. Durning, in *Ecospychology*, ed. T. Roszak)

Not what you usually get within traditional discussion of business ethics but nevertheless very real, and found in other real social and economic settings all over the World.

For instance ...

Global Lesson
DAMA: THE GIFT ECONOMY OF MALI

Mali is a very cash poor country, but it is rich in other ways. Dama is the name they give to an informal gift economy, often made up of strong networks between Malian women that form solidarity, generosity and care for the whole of society. Dama is the spirit of solidarity that sustains community and culture and 'spins a rich web of relationships' of care.

Dama might provide a meal for a hungry stranger, give you change for the bus, or provide all the needs of women for 40 days after they have given birth. Dama means that you can give to some and receive from others, so that everyone's needs are attended to. Dama is a reflection of Mali's belief that generosity is the highest of human values. It reflects what Malians refer to as 'human-ness'. They believe that only by providing for all can anyone achieve dignity.

The spirit of Dama has existed for thousands of years, and Malians are working to protect it against the encroachment of globalization and market forces.

We will return to the issue of personal conduct below.

The issue of value-based purpose has raised some initial questions for thinking about what we want our creativity to be for and how we might develop better spectacles and case studies such as *Dama* hint at how other people from around the World have organized themselves around particular values for particular purposes.

But how can we pursue these broad and deep questions in a way that really helps with the specifics of creative business? Do you even want to bother thinking about this ethical stuff when the rest of the World seems to be only out for themselves?

We think you should bother because it makes sense. The idea of the *expansion of care* within your creative business is a good place to start thinking about both these questions. About the 'why' and 'if' questions of your creative business, and why bothering with such questions might help to make it both more ethical and more creative.

In the next chapter we will tell you why we think this.

2 *Why Bother? The Expansion of Care*

Story

ARE YOU STUPID?

A true 'it fell of the back of a truck' story occurred some years ago in the United States when a man of limited means found a sack of money that had fallen from a Brinks' truck. He returned the money to Brinks, who had not yet discovered the loss. The media made him a hero – but he received scores of letters and phone calls telling him he was a fool, and should look out for himself in the future.

This story illustrates how far our society has gone towards the assumption that 'looking out for number one' is the one sensible thing to do, and getting more money is the only way to do it. If we accept these assumptions, we are not making the ultimate choice about how we are to live. Our culture makes it for us. It limits the range of possible ways of living that seem to be worth taking seriously.

The story also suggests why some people hesitate to do what they know is right, if they can get more money., or something else they want, by doing what they know to be wrong. Absurd as it may sound, they don't want to do what is right because they think that by doing so they will look bad in the eyes of their friends. Their worry is not, of course, about looking morally bad, but looking stupid. Behind this response lies the idea that ethics is some kind of fraud. Since, according to this line of thinking, everyone does put herself or himself first, and this includes those who keep preaching to us about ethics and self-sacrifice, you'd have to be a fool not to do the same.

(from *How Are We to Live?* by P. Singer)

So why should you bother being ethical? What's in it for you?

The short answer is that this is the wrong question.

The slightly longer answer is that it makes sense. It contributes to your life, your creativity and your business because you will have better and more trusting *relationships*.

The even longer answer is that it is the way you are made and it will make you happy. To be greedy, selfish, intolerant and non-attentive to the needs of others is dumb and has been likened to a form of quasi-metal illness. And hardly anyone really wants that in their life.

As we will argue in detail below, thinking and acting ethically is the same as taking part in the real existence of your human nature and the relationships that make life interesting and beautiful. What else is there? Do you really want to develop your creativity in a way that deludes yourself and other people? In a way that just uses it as a way to earn a little bit of money? In a way that treats other people as some 'thing' to be ripped-off? Being graceful, kind and convivial through your creative work is just more interesting, fruitful and creative because it is usually more fertile, beautiful, socially responsible and useful.

Which brings us to ...

The Expansion of Care

Before we get into concrete details in subsequent chapters, let's try to lay out some basic parameters. Developing understanding and imagination for a value-based creative purpose implies the expansion of care-ful-ness for your ethical creative business. But what does this mean? What kind of expansion? What kind of care?

An expansion of care within creative business might involve:

Expansion – a broadening out beyond what your creative business already is and the way it has always been up to this point. An *expansion* of your creativity towards your:

* personal capacity for being good
* social capacity for doing right by others
* business capacity for developing new ways of interacting with(in) the broader social, economic and political contexts we live within
* creative capacity for developing new ways of interacting with(in) the natural world.

Care – nurturing, tending to, paying attention to. An expansion of *care* so that your creative business can be a more clear, self-reflexive and sustained articulation of:

* care for yourself through an awareness of your own personal conduct
* tending towards the needs of others through an attitude of looking after, providing respect for, and expressed within creative business relationships
* awareness towards broader social responsibility, social usefulness, justice and sustainable futures
* a 'cautionary principle' (care-fulness) about the consequences of your creative business actions.

An expansion of care entails being more responsive to all the different aspects of the World(s) you are part of, that you help to make and that help to make you.

For instance ...

Metaphor
LIFE-JACKETS

The designer Sergio Pellegrino talks about how he feels his life in a comfortable, affluent Western lifestyle is a bit like being in the eye of a storm. Things seem quite calm, but we know that the bad stuff is on the way, and we need to get ready.

In all sorts of ways, through spreading the word, designing a more responsible future, envisioning new ways of thinking and interrelating, creative business can be seen as creating the life-jackets for when the storm gets really serious – which is kind of now!

The expansion of care might get played out across one or more of the following broad facets:

- **Practical** - the potential contribution that your creative business wants to make to satisfying genuine human and social needs identified through direct relationships between producers and users – *integrity*.
- **Material** – the use of tools, materials and processes within your creative business that is less damaging to the natural environment – *prudence*.
- **Economic** – the degree to which your creative business increases human happiness and quality of life rather than reproducing unnecessary stuff – *humane-ness*.
- **Social** – the extent to which your creative business actively creates spaces for people to come together in trusting experimentation - *tolerance towards festivity and playfulness by acting with more love*.
- **Political** – using your creativity to engage in debates about new purposes for business – *wholehearted compassion and respect*.
- **Personal** – whether you want to explore your innate creative capacity to deepen the meanings that motivate your work – *self-awareness*.
- **Spiritual** – seeing creative business of producing beauty, inspiration and an articulation of peoples felt needs and innermost desires – *faith in our collective capacities to make a better, shared future*.

Ethics, Morality and the Social

This idea of the expansion of care suggests a very broad range of abstract thinking, practical concrete actions and conscience firmly located within the realm of *social relationships*. It suggests a combination of:

- **Ethics** – philosophies or theories about what is good and bad, right and wrong and so on – *thinking things*.
- **Morality** – the concrete judgements and actions that people and businesses make, or don't make – *deciding upon things*.
- **Social Responsibility** – relating one's ethical thinking and moral deciding to the society that you are living in, specific to the way you and your creative business impacts upon others. As we will see below some professions have a 'code of ethics' to articulate what they perceive as their responsibilities to the rest of society. Some professions do not declare what they perceive as their responsibilities to society so clearly. You might need to develop this for yourself.
- **Social Usefulness** – professional declarations of social responsibility can sometimes descend into the 'lowest common denominator' of ethical-ness. They can become corporate declarations about not getting into regular bad-ness. Ideas about social usefulness try to take ethical debates into areas concerned with proactively creating more good-ness. A creative business can be entirely responsible but still in the business of producing tat. A creative business seeking social usefulness might use ethical principles and moral judgements to stop the tat and work to meet the more urgent and pressing needs of the World.

- **Social Justice** – this asks for more focus upon what a genuinely just society would look like and, for our purposes what creative business can do to bring that about as part of a wider range of social, economic and political endeavours that aim to redistribute fairness. This might be about a drive to a more equality or a society that has a more equal distribution of opportunity so that people can (*re*)*make themselves* as an experiment in their own freedom. Either way, it will probably mean a redistribution of material resources (including, but not exclusively money) so that the quality of peoples' real lives can be improved.

You, Others and Nature

The expansion of care will almost always come from a mixture of care towards:

- Yourself and your own capacity for *flourishing* – becoming more than you are at the moment.
- Other people and the ethics necessitated by relationships – probably the most fertile place in which to construct ethical thinking and play out moral decisions for the expansion of creative business care.
- All sentient animals – this is more controversial. Some people would make a big distinction between human rights and animal rights, and they would see the use of animals as resources for human ends as unproblematic. Others take the view that the way we treat animals is a symbolic marker for how ethical we are as a society.
- Nature as a whole – more controversial still. As with animals, it might be difficult to talk of the rights of Nature. Clearly human history up to this point has been about treating Nature as a resource to be exploited. But this probably needs to stop. The unsustainability of this approach becomes clearer by the day and developing a more ethical approach towards Nature is probably part of the necessary change in mind-set we all need to go through.

Right and Responsibilities

In most democratic societies each individual person is a legal entity and has certain rights enshrined by law – the rights to freedom of speech, assembly and so on. And with such legally enshrined rights come certain responsibilities. The basic position being that because we expect certain treatment from other people and institutions we need to uphold the resulting responsibilities that other people and institutions expect from us.

However, it is useful when thinking about values and ethics to recognize that rights and responsibilities enshrined by law can be a rather crude and mechanistic way of doing things. As we will see below it can only ever be at best a back-stop. There is nothing inherently wrong with this, but without a more proactive *culture of responsibility* on the part of individuals and businesses who are motivated by a felt experience then the whole language of rights and responsibilities can become a little dry and dead. Which it has done.

For this culture of responsibility to become more alive, responsibilities such as those invoked by the expansion of care probably needs to express something beyond purely legalistic and institutional parameters. A culture of responsibility for yourself, towards others and Nature probably needs to become a chosen expression of *all* your creative capacities to act more humanely. In short, growing ethical skills towards *feeling* responsible and *living* responsibly in broader and stronger ways.

Global Lesson
'MANY LITTLE FINGERS'

Jogjami is a system of local co-operation that ensures informal networks of people both receive and provide what we would call 'services' such as letter and parcel delivery. Even though they never meet and no money ever changes hands they assume that the favor will be returned some time later. It is an example of an economy based upon genuine trusting relationships.

In a light and sustainable economy we will share resources – such as time, skill, software and food – using networked communications. Sunil Abraham, an internet advisor to NGOs, (in India) told us in Bangalore that local systems of barter and non-monetary exchange, such as Jogjami, have existed in India for at least 500 years. A cooperative distribution system called Angadia, or 'many little fingers' enables people to send goods over sometimes vast distances without paying.

(by John Thackara. To find out more go to www.doorsofperception.com)

Whatever legal rights and responsibilities we may or may not have, an expansion of care comes, at least in part from avoiding the oftentimes philosophical *cul de sac* of trying to say ahead of time what counts as ethical and *getting on with it in a more practical sense*. And as a creative business you are in a good place to do this.

An Applied Ethics for Creative Business?

Quotation

It might be thought odd by some; and a scandal by others, that a new venture calling itself 'applied ethics' ... had to come into existence at all, for it marks the abandonment of responsibility by these moral philosophers who disclaim all but theoretical interests in the question of ethics.

(from *What is Good?* by A.C. Grayling)

The very need to think about 'applied ethics' for creative business is perhaps a facet of a wider detachment of ethical questions from the real world. Ethics has become a rather 'traditional academic' concern that neglects urgently practical issues of social usefulness and justice.

But does creative business have particularly novel potential to:

- Explore human need, emotion, meaning, pleasure and pain?
- Give voice to the real lives and felt experiences of real people as they live their lives and culture(s)?

- Inspire humanity through music, film, literature, and all the rest, to feel their common heritage and act accordingly?

If so, then some very specific questions concerning creative businesses perhaps need to be posed:

- Is it possible to develop a specific creative business ethics for such a wide and diverse field of activity as art, design and creativity? If so, is it necessary for creative business to develop a *particular* ethical debate within itself, for itself?
- Can the specific nature of creative business contribute something *distinctive* to the expansion of care? What is it, if anything, that the artist can teach the philosopher about the inter-relationships between reason and emotion; between the human spirit and logic, between freedom and responsibility?
- Is it enough for creative business to adopt a reactive ethics that merely seeks to avoid doing their kind of 'bad'? Does it need a more proactive ethics that searches for specific ways of doing new kinds of *practical* creative good?

Many of the case studies offered for your consideration in subsequent chapters suggest that creative businesses are coming to novel answers to these kinds of creative business questions.

For instance ...

Exercise

ETHICAL MEANS AND ENDS IN ARCHITECTURE

In the context of architecture, Wasserman et al. ask the following ethical questions of creative business:

- Is there a significant ethical dimension to your particular creative acts or situations?
- How can you inform specific creative business choices, plans and strategies with ethical reasoning?
- To what extent is your creative business decision-making based upon compliance to professional codes of practice?
- Does your creative business attempt to actively articulate new ethical choices rather than simply adhere to existing precepts or codes of conduct?
- To what extent is your creative business guided by social usefulness, the needs of others and the forging of new relationship between creative producers and 'end users'?

(from *Ethics and the Practice of Architecture*, by B. Wasserman et. al)

Whichever it might be, the specific practices at the heart of many creative businesses, and their particular ways of joining thought and action, at least indicates some fertile terrain. Creativity often involves the 'fiction that can tell great truths'. Maybe it can add stronger emotional content, more vivid metaphors or more nuanced articulations of ethical life. Maybe it can add a more holistic exploration of the human condition and its sufferings that adds greater feeling to areas of life that are losing touch with any ethical groundings – the Catholic Church, bankers and Professional Politicians.

Or is creativity …

Quotation

… a simple, unanalysable property, just as a primary colour is – and that just as we cannot explain what (say) yellow is by means of a classification, but only by showing someone an example, so we can only explain goodness likewise.

(from *What is Good?* by A.C. Grayling)

Should creativity be left to its own devices above the fray of social, economic and political squabbles?

Which brings us to the thorny issue of …

An Obsession with the Creative Self?

Some types of creative practice often seem to be focused upon the *personal identity* of *The Creative Self* as a source of motivation. This can easily become an obsession with one's 'artist-ness' and a particular facet of an attitude which Jean-Paul Sartre has called 'bad faith'. We will come back to this in more detail in Chapter 4 but we will say now that bad faith is not good. There is also an overly reverential obsession with the *Artistic Object* due to internally self-validating propositions about what 'Art' does and is for. Herbert Marcuse has called this kind of self-referential logic 'one-dimensional thought', which is not good either. One-dimensional thought is found within the Big Art World when it celebrates artistic disconnected-ness from everyday life and deliberately mystifies the idea of art and creativity so that only the initiated can take part. It too often avoids plain speaking about what is going on and insufficiently engages with the everyday lives and needs of people.

And these attitudes have entered, however quietly by the back door, broader cultural perceptions. Current cultural assumptions about artistic and creative work being the product of a lone 'genius' descending from Heaven to reveal Universal Truths are often tied in with self-granted permission on the part of artist to avoid the ethical or moral codes that 'ordinary people' live by. Friedrich Nietzsche represents this tradition of thought and criticizes such 'ordinary people' for trying to constraint the 'genius' by imposing 'slave morality' upon them. Such 'genius' is given permission by Nietzsche to transcend this 'slave morality' and cultural stereotypes of the 'artist' or 'creative' are still sometimes affected by this rather elitist and patronizing attitude. We remember that we are living through the high tide of celebrity culture that suggests that fame and fortune are the only things that really count as cultural 'success'. Some forms of creativity have become rather indistinguishable from this celebrity culture and the circus performances it encourages. If the very being-ness of The Creative Self is presented as creativity it can end up as all creative mouth and no real creative trousers. It talks the talk but does not walk the walk. The Emperor has no clothes and so on.

We don't want to suggest that creativity should be devoid of self-exploration. It could never be anyway, and even if we did suggest it, who are we? But seeking to expand care for others through creativity is also good for the exploration of The Creative Self because such interaction with the real world(s) of other people is necessary for a fuller creative and professional development. To put it bluntly, an obsession with The Creative Self can be a starting point but it can never be a particularly interesting end point. As with most things a balance between exploring The Creative Self, on the one hand, and developing a creative practice that speaks to/for the needs of others on the other hand, is a more vibrant approach. So whilst we will say things in subsequent chapters about developing self-awareness and self-fulfilment we do not think these things truly come about through self-obsession.

To put it even more bluntly, we think that an obsession with The Creative Self might end up getting a bit boring for everyone else, whereas an expansion of care towards others might make you feel happy and cry with joy on the inside little bit.

Having a more authentic relationship with others is probably necessary.

Public Authenticity

We have witnessed improvements in the public understanding of science in recent years. This has tended to involve:

- articulating a coherent 'story' of science;
- developing a greater public understanding of the basic characteristics of scientific knowledge creation and methodology;
- ensuring the process of becoming a scientist is a relatively transparent process which people can join if they learn enough;
- encouraging a public appreciation of the broader contribution of the sciences to social, cultural and economic life.

Improvements in the public understanding of science have been about explaining what science has done for the public good. It could perhaps be summarized by a sentiment that says 'we know science is complicated, but we will pay particular attention to explaining it to everyone, because it is important to us all'. As a result, the public story of science is perceived through its practical benefits and tangible technological progress. We need look no further than medicine science for examples of its grandeur.

By contrast, the 'Arts' are perceived as increasingly arcane and disconnected from the general public even as its designs, images, sounds and experiences surround us more and more. A greater understanding of the creative professions and their potential contribution to the public good is needed, because:

- the public story of 'the Arts' is under-explored and incoherent;
- too much attention is placed upon the intuitive exploration of The Creative Self and a celebration of mysterious 'Art Objects';
- the processes and methods of creative origination are under-discussed and there is too little public reflection upon who gets to say what counts as 'Art';
- the contribution of the creative professions to broader social, cultural and economic life is too often tied to an overly economic agenda that conflates consumer culture with the public good.

This kind of 'Artistic' creativity is often about what it can do for an individualistic 'me'. It could perhaps be summarized by a sentiment that says 'I know my work is quite difficult to understand, but it is about me and if you don't understand it, then that is a problem with you, the viewer'. Too often people are heard to say 'I don't really understand art', fail to take up invitations to engage in public architecture, are given no recourse but to accept bad design.

And because a relatively closed, opaque process dominates, idea that 'Artistic' creativity is a potential site for ethical relationships is damaged. Whilst there are clearly pockets of great work out there within architecture, community arts and educational work using various creative disciplines as their vehicle, lots of opportunities for broader authentic public engagement are left underdeveloped. The outputs of the more commercially minded creative businesses are often nothing but a response to markets and consequently approach the public realm as being made up of passive consumers rather than active cultural citizens. So the potential contribution of creative business to actively improving quality of life, personal well-being, effective cultural communication and a beautiful public realm is too often left to a minority.

It might be time for 'the Arts' and the Big Business of Culture to get over itself, learn from the public engagements of science and look for more authentic spectacles for the future.

For instance …

Analogy
PUBLIC HEALTH

There is a useful analogy between ethical creativity and public health, in that ethical creative business might strive to provide a space to promote the co-development of public creativity.

A public health version (of creativity) *would entail dealing with the problems that the greatest number of people, especially the greatest number of poor people face in their daily lives … as Jesus knew well, giving of our time and talent to those most in need will have a transformative effect on us as well as them.*

(from *Architectural Design and Ethics*, by T. Fisher)

These are controversial points, and we have deliberately put them in a rather pointed way. It is part of the grandeur of 'Artistic' creativity that it *can* be about the unexplainable and ineffable. But to be truly authentic creative businesses might need to go beyond the celebration of objects and open up its processes to a wider public. If this kind of critical self-reflection and a breadth of public vision are neglected it damages the idea that all people can consider creativity as part of their life and lead to practical social change. In *Being and Nothingness*, Jean-Paul Sartre links our human capacity for authentic choice back to the possibilities of practical intention for envisaging a different state of affairs that we might call the public good.

Quotation

We should observe first that an action is in principle intentional … It is on the day that we can conceive of a different state of affairs that a new light falls on our troubles and our suffering and that we decide that these are unbearable … it is after he has formed the project of changing the situation that it will appear intolerable to him …

(from *Being and Nothingness*, by J.-P. Sartre)

Some ethical creative businesses have found ways to be more open to this public authenticity. For instance, Victor Papanek, in *Design for the Real World and The Green Imperative* has outlined the following key features of the socially responsible and publicly authentic creativity that motivated his own design practice:

- Can it make life easier for some group that has been marginalized by existing social, political and economic organization?
- Can it ease pain (in all its forms)?
- Will it significantly aid the sustainability of the environment?
- Will it save energy or? Or better still help to gain renewable energies?
- Can it save irreplaceable resources?

Quotation

A positive answer to these or similar questions does not make the design visibly spiritual. But the performance of such services to our fellow human beings and the planet will help us inwardly. It will nourish our soul and help it to grow. That's where spiritual values enter design ...

The job of the designer is to provide choices for people. These choices should be real and meaningful, allowing people to participate more fully in their own decisions, and enabling them to communicate with designers and architects in finding solutions to their own problems, even – whether they want to or not – become their own designers ... Any attempt to separate design, to make it a thing-by-itself, works counter to the inherent value of design as the primary, underlying matrix of life.

(from *The Green Imperative*, by V. Papanek)

And in practice ...

Case Study

URBAN DESIGN AND PUBLIC AUTHENTICITY

With specific reference to urban design, Papanek argues that the 'good life' entails the satisfaction of four public 'desires':

- Conviviality
- Spirituality
- Artistic and intellectual growth
- Politics.

To respond to the public realm with practical Reason urban design should provide:

- Informal social and cultural places
- Arts and sporting arenas
- Places for spirituality
- Places for intellectual growth (libraries, museums, networking spaces, and so on)
- Political meeting places for joint decision-making
- Economic places that support these social and cultural functions (the original conception of the 'Market').

Too often public squalor amidst private affluence characterizes our public realm and raises specific challenges for creative business. Because urban centres today do not always fulfil public needs Papanek advocates a more authentic approach to urban re-design around the following:

- Provision of the above six points
- A 'people not traffic' agenda
- An 'aesthetics of site'
- A 'sense of location'
- An 'ideal size of community' and adherence to simple design principles to shape it
- 'Learning the lessons of vernacular architecture'
- Developing a self-reflexively, ecologically responsible, consciousness to patterns of living, producing and consuming.

(from *The Green Imperative*, by V. Papanek)

But becoming skilled in spotting opportunities to take part in agendas that might flow from public authenticity is likely to require reflection upon one's basic motivations.

Motivations

Some philosophers have argued that the world of 'facts' arrived at through 'sciences' such as economics have no relationship with the human creation of the world of 'values' that speak about what ought to be. This view tends to argue that connecting these two worlds is merely a psychological defence mechanism that helps us deal with the scary 'real world'. For this view, values and ethics that contest this world of 'facts' are only fictions that we use to justify our own emotional wishes. The 'real world' of economics and business just doesn't work like that. Traditional business economics separates the 'facts' of how the market economy currently *is* from the values inherent in imagining how things *could be*. This encourages us all to think that the World as it is already organized can only ever be that way. History that gets hijacked to 'prove' that the way we are now is how we have always been. So imagining different social and economic futures is held to be futile by those who have been the 'University of Life'. This broad tendency has impacted upon recent debates about the creative industries that have largely neglected considerations about the motivation within creative business in favour of oversimplified assumptions of the ubiquity of markets and the 'economic man' idea.

But this is a highly questionable assumption. As we will explore in detail in Section 2 creative businesses are devising alternative, collaborative and non-proprietary ways of organizing their DiY economies. More generally, thinking about values and ethics for creative business encourages a more questioning attitude towards what could be, and as such it tends towards thinking about what *ought to be*. We will come back to this later chapters, but as creative businesses most of you already know that simple profit-maximization is not what motivates you and that the traditional businessman-in-suit view of the World is rather limited compared to the myriad motivations behind creativity. Nevertheless, thinking about what *could be* and what *ought to be* can help to provide even more new spectacles for creative business.

Even if ethical ideas are subjective creations that have no basis in hard fact, ideas about trying to 'do good' are still important because they motivate actual behaviour. Even if ethics is 'only' about feelings it can still inform us as to how we can strive to *live better*, together. Trying to demonstrate some proven scientific basis for ethics is just not an important question. What actually happens is more important. This gets us into the 'Pragmatist' idea of ethics explored in more detail in Chapter 4. This view suggests that you can be relaxed about not having a universal ethical basis for creative business motivations so long as you genuinely use your creativity to pursue what you believe is right. But this will be up to other people as much as it will be up to you and will probably involve treating other people as ends in their own right and not means to your ends, as in Immanuel Kant's famous maxim:

Quotation

Always recognize that human individuals are ends, and do not use them as means to your end.

(from *Groundwork of the Metaphysic of Morals*, by Immanuel Kant)

The fact that there can be no universal ethical agreement can be a good thing for creative business because it puts the onus on what we actually do in concrete terms. But this suggests the need for constant ethical debate between people about our motivations and their underlying values so as to co-evolve more care-ful relationships. And, because of this, we see that ethics can be both an end in itself to guide personal conduct, and a set of tools, what Ivan Ilich has called 'tools for conviviality', for making more specific decisions about the practical content of your creative journeys. And this tends to come out best in and through the actual *practices* of creative business.

Practising Care-ful Relationships

It might at first sight seem contradictory, but we are firmly of the opinion that you can sometimes find your own creative motivations through a sense of service to others, find your own creative voice through conviviality towards others. You can sometimes find your Creative Self through better relationships beyond yourself.

Any Big Philosophy of ethics worth its salt involves in some way or other to the idea of going beyond one's own creative 'appetites' and becoming aware of the broader *consequences* your actions have on others. But, as we will explore in the chapters that follow these are choices to be made, and they are your choices. You can work on expanding your ability to respond to others through care-ful relationships in lots of ways.

Global Lesson
COMIDA AND IMPOSTURA: SOUL FOOD FROM SOUTH AMERICA

To contrast the individual self ... from the 'we' of comida, we find ourselves remembering the beautiful small town of San Andreas Chicahuaxlta (Mexico) ... We remember when we first met dona Refugio, the mother of a friend of ours ... The fire is at the centre of the warmest room in the house. And dona Refugio is there, every day, at the very centre, surrounded by her whole family, talking with her husband, children and grandchildren; discussing personal difficulties or the predicament of the community … The whole community's life is in fact organized around such fires, the centre of kitchens, the source of comida …

There is no English word for comida. It is not easy to explain why. While 'feast' comes closest in its implications of eating together, it refers only to a special occasion, while comida is eaten by the 'social majorities' in the 'normal' course of every day. Perhaps we need to recall that the Anglo-Saxon world was the cultural space in which the industrial mode of production was established first and foremost. There, vernacular activities related to comida have been suffocated and suppressed … To eat, to care for comida, to generate it, to cook it, to assimilate it: all these are the activities that do not belong to industrial eaters.

IMPOSTURA

In the Dominican Republic's Monte Bonito, a beautiful small town in the northwestern part of the country, Erik Duus, a Norwegian, has been recording an extensive practice of the local women called impostura. (Both) comida and impostura create 'we's' in and through the communion of food embedded in soil (agri)culture … an informal contractual relationship, where the partners make an implicit promise to each other to exchange part of their meal with each other.

(from *Grassroots Post-Modernism: Remaking the Soil of Culture*, by G. Esteva and M. S. Prakash)

Thinking about practising care-ful relationships starts to show the practical benefits of co-operation for our creative lives.

Avoiding Prison and Getting Home Through the Snow at a Reasonable Time: The Benefits of Co-operation

Thinkpiece
THE PRISONER'S DILEMMA

In *The Evolution of Co-operation*, Robert Axelrod uses the Prisoner's Dilemma game to establish the long-term practical benefits of choosing co-operation.

In this game we imagine that two blokes have been brought in for questioning by the police. Each prisoner has to decide whether to break ranks and grass-up the other prisoner. But they are in separate rooms, so they must make their choice without any knowledge of what the other prisoner is going to decide.

So their dilemma is this:

- If they decide to grass on the other person they will get a lighter sentence for their crime.
- If they both keep quite they both get away with it.
- But if they do keep quiet but the other person grasses on them, they will get a harsher sentence.

What should they do? What would you do in this situation? Would you go it alone and give up on the other person? Would you assume that is what they would be doing to you? Or would you try to keep faith in the mutual co-operation?

The Prisoner's Dilemma shows that the immediate temptation is to go it alone and look after yourself. But if either one of them, or both give and break ranks then they both fail to get the best possible reward – freedom.

An assumption of co-operation and mutual support is the only way each individual can get the best outcome. Co-operation makes the best sense but is often the hardest thing to see and stick to.

But we also have …

Thinkpiece

THE SNOWDRIFT GAME

Whilst the Prisoner's Dilemma game is commonly used for talking about why co-operation makes sense, other thinkers have recently turned to the Snowdrift Game because they think it more realistically reflects how and why human co-operation comes about.

In The Snowdrift Game, two drivers are trapped at opposite ends of a big snowdrift blocking the road. Each driver could either:

- Stay in the car and wait for the other person to clear the road, or
- Start to shovel the snow and clear the road themselves.

Letting the opponent do all the work to clear the road has the highest pay-off in the work-to-reward ratio (no work at all – road cleared). Doing all the work to clear the road whilst the other driver does nothing to help has the lowest pay-off in the work-to-reward ratio (all the work – road cleared). Both people co-operating to clear the road has a medium pay-off in the work-to-reward ratio (some of the work – road cleared).

The Prisoner's Dilemma highlights the danger of being exploited in your co-operation (not grassing on the other whilst the other grasses on you) so you end up with zero reward. Indeed you go to prison so things actually get worse. In The Snowdrift Game whatever you do you benefit, even if you have to do all the work yourself at least the road gets cleared and you can get home at a reasonable time.

So when thinking about whether it makes sense to co-operate with others or not, the Snowdrift Game might be more useful because it better reflects the real situations you are likely to find yourself in. Whatever you might think about the possibilities of co-operation with real people in real situations, it is never a very good strategy for very long to just sit there in your metaphorical car waiting for someone else to come to your rescue.

But whatever, the fundamental and over-riding point that both the Prisoner's Dilemma and the Snowdrift Game show is this – if you want to stay out of prison and get home through the snow in a reasonable time then co-operation is usually the best strategy. Especially if everyone else thinks the same; you may have been through these types of events several times and have come to trust each other, which often happens in good creative networks with healthy working relationships.

Co-operation makes sense. And the more you do it the more it makes sense.

But the Prisoner's Dilemma and the Snowdrift Game are more than just abstract bits of thinking for avoiding the police and getting home through the snow. If you allow a co-operative attitude to inform your creative business approach it can bring real practical benefits.

For instance ...

Quotation

DEVELOPING MOBILE PHONES

Motorola, a success story, developed what it called the 'technology shelf', created by a small group of engineers, on which were placed technical solutions that other teams might use in the future; rather than trying to solve the problem outright, it developed tools whose immediate value was not clear. Nokia grappled with the problem in another way, creating an open-ended conversation among its engineers in which salespeople and designers were often included. The boundaries among business units in Nokia were deliberately ambiguous, because more than technical information was needed to get a feeling for the problem ... By contrast Ericsson proceeded with more seeming clarity and discipline, dividing the problem into its parts. The birth of the new switch was intended to occur through 'the exchange of information' among offices' rather than the cultivation of an interpretative community. Rigidly organized, Ericsson fell away. It did eventually solve the switching technology problem, but with greater difficulty; different offices protecting their turf. In any organization, individuals or teams that compete and are rewarded for doing better than others will hoard information. In technology firms, hoarding information particularly disables good work.

(from *The Craftsman*, by R. Sennett)

We will come back to these organizational questions of information flows for creativity and innovation in Sections 2 and 3.

For now, we need to consider ...

The Ultimate Choice

So when thinking about your value-based creative purpose and the possibility of an expansion of care it might be good to remember that Socrates is famous for saying that *'an unexamined life is not worth living'*, which suggests the need for a clear-sighted vision.

But, as we saw earlier, Bertrand Russell is famous for saying *'Happiness is best achieved by those who do not directly seek it'* which suggests that you might find something by not looking for it!

Albert Camus is just as famous for saying *'Judging whether life is or is not worth living amounts to the fundamental question of philosophy'*. He suggests that clear-sightedness, happiness or purpose cannot be found through abstract ideas alone. Only through consciously chosen and actively pursued engagements with the World of other people can we judge whether our creativity has purpose and a care.

And this brings the fundamental aspects of *choice* to centre stage. Philosophers usually emphasize that we are free to make our own decisions about how we are to live because we are our own end and not a means to some other end. So we are faced with a choice between narrow self-interest on the one hand – the World of 'economic man' that motivates the Raiders of Corporate Greed – and the search for more enlightened relationships with the World on the other – the case studies presented throughout this book.

You can be what you want to be. But this freedom to choose is not an ethical blank cheque! The freedom to make choices about how and why your life is going to be comes with responsibility to try to make it wisely on the basis of bigger ethical spectacles. This is another reason why you should bother. It is possibly the main reason why you should bother because it is the ultimate thing to bother about. It is what A.C. Grayling has called the *Ultimate Choice*.

Now we have introduced Juliette, raised some possible signposts for developing spectacles to see value-based creative purpose and suggested general reasons why you should bother to care with them, we can get into details.

First, we want to bust a myth. Rather than being contrary to our purportedly aggressive human nature, we will suggest in the next chapter that these new spectacles for Juliette actually fit well with our basic needs for fairness, co-operation, reciprocity and human kinship. After that, we will explore how ethical philosophy has developed particular concepts for a deeper and more intricate inquiry into how we might think and act ethically. We will then try to pin things down even further to concrete aspects of personal conduct and creative business activities.

3 Taking Part in the Existence of Things: An Ecological Lens

Story

If you were to curl up with any issue of a journal that publishes studies in social psychology, you would not get a very pretty picture of humanity. Racism, Aggression, Mindless Conformity. Failure to come to the aid of someone in distress. An inflated sense of self-worth. Prejudice against anyone who doesn't belong top your ethnic, religious, or socio-economic group ... Darkening the picture even further is that, social psychologists, who study how people behave and interact, are remarkably adept at spinning explanations of why these less-than-noble traits are natural to the point of near inevitability and universality.

(from *The Plastic Mind: New Science Reveals Our Extraordinary Potential to Transform Our Lives*, by S. Begley)

This view of humanity rests upon a fundamental separation between us all. But on the other hand, the Ancient Greek philosopher Thales, sometimes referred to as the father of philosophy suggested in around 580 BC that water is the fundamental 'principle of the universe'. Thales observed that water – the seas, rivers, the sap of the trees, the vapor in your every breath and in the blood your veins – was everywhere. This led him to see that everything's connection to everything else was the basic shape from which the World flows.

2,500 years later Roger Deakin wrote:

For a year I traveled amphibiously about the country, swimming in the wild, literally immersing myself in the landscape and in the elements, in particular the primal element of water, in an attempt to discover for myself that 'third thing' D. H. Lawrence puzzled about in his poem of that title. Water, he wrote, is something more than the sum of its parts, something more than two parts hydrogen and one part oxygen. In writing Waterlog, the account of my meanderings, swimming was a metaphor for what Keats called 'taking part in the existence of things'

(from *Wildwood*, by R. Deakin)

The water metaphor helps us to recognize the interconnectedness of all things and that 'taking part in the existence of things' entails immersing ourselves in already existing connections with other people and Nature. It asks us to see that we are part of something bigger than ourselves. It suggests that we have responsibilities to this bigger thing as much as to satisfying our own appetites.

Human Nature

Ourselves, we wary of ideas that suggest 'human nature' is fixed in some way, but we will now stop putting it in inverted commas, as that will get tiresome. The question of human nature often comes up when two or more people discuss values and ethics. We are not really going to claim that we know what human nature is. That would only make us look silly. But that goes for anyone else too. Whenever anyone tells you that they know what human nature is, you should go to talk to someone else because they are probably trying to tell you what they *want* it to be at that particular time, so they can justify something bad.

Scientific studies of the Natural World and human consciousness have interesting things to say concerning human nature. Perhaps the most necessary implications of these studies for our general concerns in this book is the debunking of the idea that human nature somehow hardwires us into being fundamentally aggressive, selfish and competitive. It might be that the thing we call human nature is actually defined by our ability to respond differently to different situations and reflect on how we are behaving whilst we are doing that behaviour. This capacity for *self-reflexivity* means that human consciousness is constantly moving around due to the choices we are constantly making. Whilst there might be human propensities towards selfish aggression in certain circumstances, there is plenty of evidence to suggest that Natural World of which we are part also involves basic drives towards mutual recognition and reciprocal behaviour to foster co-operative relationships of fairness, trust and kinship too.

It might just be that we are built to be ethical if we want to refocus our spectacles on this basic interconnectedness.

Let's take a closer look at some of the evidence.

The Dark Side

Some interpretations of evolutionary biology suggest that the more brutal impulses towards aggression and cruelty are instinctive drives of all animals geared towards survival and reproduction, and as such are fundamental aspects of Nature. And in the wrong hands this has taken social and economic forms. This Dark Side perpetuates a view of human existence that is characterized by:

- **Individualistic immunity** – they don't care about me, so I am not going to care about them.
- **Self-perpetuating denial** – although I know other people will suffer if I carry on like this, I have to do it because there is no alternative. There is no other way that I can look after myself and my own survival. Moral judgements are all very well inside emotional life, but I need to get what I need to get.

These tendencies have taken cultural forms that come from making fixed distinctions between your group and another group, between 'us' and 'them'. In the cultural world this process has been called *otherization* and might lie behind fundamental human experiences of fear and cautiousness towards the unknown, along with feelings of anger or disgust when dealing with the 'danger' of these unknown others. This seems to have led to all sorts of people giving themselves permission to be disrespectful and neglectful towards others as they work to convince themselves that they 'don't really count', 'are not really human'; 'deserve it'; 'don't really feel the same way towards their kids as we do'. Blah, Blah, Blah.

A less 'fundamentalist' view allows for the interplay between a basic impulses towards aggression and competition on the one hand, and reciprocal fairness on the other – what Jedi's might call *The Force*. This view suggests that the tension between instinctive drives towards cruelty and fairness, competition and co-operation, aggression and love is fundamental to human nature.

Quotation

'Nature red in tooth and claw', wrote Lord Tennyson in the 1830s. 'No man is an island' wrote John Dunne, about 150 years earlier. Both are right. War and peace are threads that run through all of life, from the cradle to the grave, from the seed to the compost heap. Everything we do reflects the tension between conflict and cooperation.

(from *The Secret Life of Trees: How They Live and Why They Matter*, by C. Tudge)

This applies to the world of economic and business too.

Quotation

The biological necessity for morality arises because, for the species to survive, any animal must have, on the one hand, some egoism – a strong urge to get food for himself and to defend his means of livelihood; also – extending egoism from the individual to the family – to fight for the interests of his mate and his young.

On the other hand, social life is impossible unless the pursuit of self-interest is mitigated by respect and compassion for others. A society of unmitigated egoists would knock itself to pieces: a perfectly altruistic individual would soon starve. There is a necessary conflict between counter tendencies, each of which is necessary to existence, and there must be a set of rules to reconcile them. Moreover, there must be some mechanism to make an individual keep the rules when they conflict with their immediate advantage

(from *Economic Philosophy*, by J. Robinson)

Likewise with creative business. It is not the pen, the brush or the software programme that produces good or ill but the character and intentions of the person using them. We tend to agree with Marcel Duchamp when he said 'I don't believe in art, I believe in artists'.

For instance …

Proverb

If the water of a pool is drunk by a poisonous snake, it is changed into poison, if the water of the same pool is drunk by a cow, it is changed into milk to feed a child.

It is not the water that produces good or ill, but the character of the creature using it.

Brain Plasticity and Evolution for Fairness?

The Dark Side perpetuates a view of human nature premised upon the idea that we are hardwired into certain types of behaviour. But a more developed view, with growing scientific back-up form neuroscience is showing that we are so non-hardwired that it makes more sense to refer to the brain as plastic. For instance, in *The Plastic Mind: New Science Reveals Our Extraordinary Potential to Transform Ourselves*, with which we started this chapter, Sharon Begley sees brain plasticity as the ability to constantly form so many new inner connections and novel pathways that it can be conceived of as being infinitely changeable and malleable. Not much hardwired here. Brain plasticity is the neurological version of the broader philosophical idea that it is self-reflexivity that defines us. Human consciousness can be ever reshaped and chosen. The brain seems to be reshaped on the basis of constant interactions with the world of experience, and experiences of the world. So at a basic level, brain plasticity is the neurological facet of ethics as something we can choose as an active aspect of our lives. If the brain wasn't so plastic and we were really hardwired, I would not be able to conceive of anything else. I would not have been able to conceive of the sentence about brain plasticity and ethical choice. And I did, just there. See?

Moreover, there is also evidence to suggest that the evolution of human nature which brain plasticity allows has led us to adopt fairness and co-operation for competitive advantage in the evolutionary stakes, and it is our current social and economic context that causes us to unlearn this basic co-operative nature. It might be that we can choose to return to this lens to overcome the Dark Side.

For instance …

Case Study

THE ULTIMATUM GAME 2.0

There is a relatively new research discipline called neuro-economics which entails economists working with neurologists to map brain functions of people as they make economic choices. They are beginning to 'prove' what more socially oriented theorists have assumed all along, but economists have tended to ignore – that we make decisions for social reasons as much as, or actually for more than rational economic (economic man) reasons.

The Ultimatum Game entails two players. £100 is placed upon a table and Player 1 has to make an offer to Player 2 as to how they should split the money. If they can both agree to Player 1's offer they both get to keep their share of the money. If they cannot agree to Player 1's offer then no one gets to keep any money.

After many studies it has been shown that offers from Player 1 to Player 2 below £30 are usually rejected. But this offer of £30 or less is clear profit for Player 2, so why not accept it?

Mapping the brain responses of Player 2 during the game have shown that their responses do not come from the Frontal Lobe that is supposedly where rational decision-making takes place. Instead it is the Lymbic System that seems to be active. It is thought that this part of the brain deals with more basic felt experiences that come as it where 'before' rational thinking.

It is suggested that Player 2 is responding to a more basic sense of injustice and disrespect, which suggests we may be hardwired to adhere to a sense of fairness and reject its transgression.

It may be that other more developed forms of fairness such as altruism, charity and protectiveness stem from this basic drive towards fairness.

The Science of Happiness

Complementing some initial points we made in Chapter 1, recent research in the neuroscience of happiness is suggesting more objective measurements of subjective experiences of happiness. Whilst the pleasures we get from the satisfaction of basic wants and needs (food, shelter, security and sex) produces certain feelings of satisfaction, recent research seems to be suggesting that happiness comes from a 'variety of pleasures'. Happiness is not created by the satisfaction of the same limited bodily pleasure over and over again because happiness is more complex than satisfaction, and it comes from more complex pleasures.

Maybe not that surprising if we stand back from the details and remember that human life is a complex mixture of basic human nature, individual personality, learned social and cultural behaviour, memories and expectations and an ability to think about different futures. So clearly not everyone will get the same experiences of happiness from the same complex pleasures (art, music, relationships, self-expression). There are personal differences here according to our individual personality, social expectations and cultural upbringing. Being satisfied in terms of basic human needs is not being happy as living, thinking human beings. For that we probably need to experience ourselves through our capacity for self-expression and demonstrate our particular feelings.

And it is highly probable that this will fundamentally entail forming relationships with others. The potential for happiness as a fundamental aspect of what it is to be human, 'human nature' if we want to call it that, seems to hinge upon what we choose to focus upon, the extent to which these interests become motivations that we are able to turn into concerted and viable actions in the real world, and the extent to which we are able to use this to connect to the lives of other people. This is what Aristotle seemed to have meant all those years ago with the concept of *eudemonia*. Happiness comes from a 'life well lived' not from simply getting more stuff for yourself.

So rather than seeing happiness laying in an obsession with the Self supposedly at the heart of human nature, this recent neuro-scientific research points to the centrality of what we might call a creative intelligence to engage with the World. In other words, we might be wired up to get happiness from the expansion of care for others beings beyond our Self. We see this all the time within creative practice or business. Creative people seem to be motivated by the deferral of the gratification of their own personal appetites in favour of articulating something deeper and broader about the World, to the World of others. We only need to look at the question of money to see this in action. If personal gain were the main motivation then why would the people who engage in creative work do it? As we all know, if we were into this for the money alone then most of us would be disappointed most of the time. But we are not. Creative people have always known what the Big Business agenda does not, that money and personal gain is not what it is about.

The idea of human nature underpinned by the concept of 'economic man', that we are all inherently selfish is shown to be incorrect at a deep level. Neuro-science is beginning to catch up with this idea and 'prove' it. It is time that the politicians, business economists and other advocates of the Dark Side caught up too.

Instead of believing in the Dark Side of human nature, you could allow yourself the social and psychological time to creatively engage in such happiness-producing activity because '… you're worth it'. And so is Juliette, and everyone else.

Self-Reflexivity for the Ultimate Choice

But whichever way the tension between selfishness and fairness, competition and co-operation gets played out there is a more fundamental problem with the claiming selfishness as to human nature. Because evolutionary biology tends to overemphasizes a hardwiring conception of the human condition they ultimately end by presenting *what we are* as *the way we need to be* as the final description of our one true human nature. They are scientists and as such tend to want those kinds of Big Answers. As a result they tend to extrapolate too many 'answers' from fairly limited evidence of the complex areas of human consciousness, motivation and decision-making. The truth is probably that human behaviour is *over-determined* whereby lots of different causes come together to produce one bit of actual behaviour. But this suggests that it can be very different next time as another combination of causes produce other bits of behaviour.

To ignore this is to underestimate the complexity of the human condition and the clearly demonstrable capacity for self-reflexivity. We clearly have the ability to reflect on ourselves and our actions as we are being/doing it. So evolutionary fundamentalism tends to underplay our ability to make choices. Most significant of which might be the Ultimate Choice of ethical spectacles. Choose for yourself.

Quotation

What makes the theory of evolution so remarkable is the enormous simplification and unification it imposes on the panorama of life on Earth. But a gap remains. We are not just another species. Our ability to reason, our ingenuity, and our linguistic skills place us so far above any competing animal species that many of us feel that something beyond the mechanisms of evolution must have occurred to produce homo sapiens. Or perhaps a unique mutation freed our brains from the constraints of instinct and gave us a mind. The sociobiologist Edward O. Wilson dubbed it the Promethean gene.

What distinguishes us more than anything else, however, is our acute awareness of a self, and a mental preoccupation with our own being that goes far beyond the kind of self-preserving behavior that all animals exhibit.

(from *The Creative Loop: How the Brain Makes a Mind*, by E. Harth)

Because we have the ability for self-reflexivity we are not at the mercy of our instinctual drives, nor are we locked into making the same choices every time we are faced with a particular situation.

Which raises certain questions:

- Should you remember that aggression and selfishness were self-defence mechanisms that no longer so necessary? Are they fitted to a society that no longer exists? Should you stop using this to justify a negative attitude to others, anger towards strangers, worries about safety, fear of the unknown?
- Have aggression and selfishness thus ceased to be a competitive advantage within the evolution of humanity and so mean that you might 'die out' if you insist upon sticking to it?
- If self-reflexivity means you can choose to be fair and good, should you try to unlearn the social and cultural influences that are getting in the way of your goodness and turning you bad – selfishness, greedy over-consumption, neglect and intolerance towards others?

Let's evolve. As Bill Hicks once said 'It's kind of our role'.

When it comes to culture, the evolutionary hardwiring thing finds it particularly difficult to explain why human creativity is so often deliberately playful, 'use-less' or expressive of the ineffable, especially when it has so little value in the evolutionary survival race. The universalizing nature of evolutionary theory as to what counts as human nature in relation to creativity is just not very good at explaining the complex particularities of culture(s). In John Carey's words it is like 'doing a jigsaw with a forklift truck'.

Clearly something else is at work within the overarching evolutionary process. And it is likely that constant self-reflectivity at the heart of creativity is part of this. Again this returns us to our ability to make choices, and maybe Ultimate Choices.

And this probably involves …

The Creative Brain: Tools, Technology and Culture

Less fundamentalist representatives of evolutionary biology emphasize the capacity for human nature to exhibit self-reflexivity as the basis for the *creative loop*. This creative capacity brings the ability to think about how we are thinking, devise abstract plans and then to act upon such plans.

It gives us a view of …

Quotation

… A subject who not only sees and hears but also perceives what he or she sees and hears, who recalls, projects, associates, imagines, invents, and creates. He or she also feels – is happy or sad, hopeful or despairing, elated or depressed, angry or in love … Toolmaking is the oldest creative activity, and still one of the most spectacular. To create a tool, even one as primitive as a paleolithic handax, requires more than serendipity, although accidents surely have played a role in many inventions. Concepts of need, of sharpness, of application, must have been in the mind of the creator before he started chipping away at the rock. There was memory also of the type of stone that chipped best and held its edge. The end had to be envisioned before the creation could be caused. Intentionality must precede creativity.

(from *The Creative Loop: How the Brain Makes a Mind*, by E. Harth)

Whilst evolutionary change is frozen within our DNA and is always part of the present, the creative loop allows for the purposive, intentional acts found in the development of tools, technology and culture that differ from this slow trial-and-error mutation.

Let's recap. The characteristics of the creative brain include:

- self-awareness
- perception
- imagination
- association
- projection
- vision
- invention
- intelligence geared towards an abstract plan
- memory
- intentionality
- application
- evolution of logical steps
- need
- purpose
- function.

The real existence of things is found in the creative brain that gives us a large degree of freedom from the constraints of our instincts, whatever they might be. Rather than being hardwired to act in any particular way every time it is more probable that the evolution of the brain gives us the creative ability to reflect back upon situations, ideas, strategies and plans *before, during and after* we choose a particular bit of behaviour. In his book *Consciousness Explained* Daniel Dennett talks about our capacity to choose between the 'multiple drafts of reality' that guide our personal conduct. It is this ability that offers us the possibility to be both creative and ethical because it allows us to understand the consequences of our creativity before we carry it out. This ability for abstract thinking suggests that creativity and ethical reflection inhabit a similar place in our human consciousness.

Which brings us to further complexities. Neuroscience tends to see human beings in terms of an isolated Self. Rather than looking at human nature in this way, a more realistic view of human-ness and creativity might be found in the here and now *contexts* that motivate particular acts. And this takes us back to the water metaphor we started this chapter with. If everything is connected to everything else, we are again involved in the realm of intimate and sustained relationships.

Beyond the Self: Back to Co-operation

We suggested earlier that co-operation makes sense. But it might be that it is just natural to the way we are and how Nature works. The competitiveness inherent within the individualism that right-wing interpretations of the human condition hold to be the 'natural state of affairs' contrasts with more contemporary and sophisticated emphasis on the fundamentally co-operative and collaborative character of Nature. And human nature cannot be something separate that 'stands above' this Nature. Human nature is *in* Nature. Where else is it going to be?

For instance …

Metaphor

NATURE IS CO-OPERATION

The very cells that we are all made of are eukaryotic cells, and are themselves an example of the inherent collaborative-ness within the Natural world.

The eukaryotic cell … is a coalition. It was formed initially be a combination of several different bacteria and archaes which hitherto had led separate lives (and others are probably involved, besides the protobacteria and cyanobacteria). Over the past 2 billion years or so the eukroytic cell, innately cooperative, has proved to be one of nature's most successful and versatile creations. There could be no clearer demonstration that co-operation is at least and much a part of nature's order as is competition. They are two sides of a coin.

(from *The Secret Life of Trees: How They Live and Why They Matter*, by C. Tudge)

If co-operation is so fundamental to Nature can it be so far removed from human nature?

Howard Becker, one of the godfathers of modern sociology has defined his discipline as the study of 'what people do, together'. And this inherent *togetherness* suggests that felt experiences underpinning co-operation – love, respect, trust, reciprocity and a capacity to use self-reflexivity for the expansion of care of others – are not only rational in a practical sense but also central to our 'natural intelligence'. It might be that acting ethically through mutual beneficial relationships is synonymous with taking part in the real existence of things.

Another more social example …

Case Study

SEX IS GOOD, AND GOODNESS

For sex to work, each creature must find a mate … Yet relationships between creatures of the same species – parents and offspring, friends and rivals, males and females – are only a part of life's complexities. Each creature must perforce interact with all the other species that share its environment … Sociology merges with ecology. It is not true (as Tennyson implies) that each individual or each species in inevitably in conflict with all the others. No species, to extend Donne's metaphor, can ever be an island. Co-operation is often the best survival tactic, as Darwin himself emphasized – and so it is that many pairs and groups of different species are locked in mutualistic relationships that are vital to all participants … Co-operativeness and amity are at least as much part of us as viciousness. The point is not to override our own nature, but simply to give the positives a chance.

(from The Secret Life of Trees: How They Live and Why They Matter, by C. Tudge)

Give the positives a chance. Do sex more often with someone you love. Put this book down right now and get on with it. It's much more interesting.

Now that you are back, let's repeat the optimistic last sentence from Colin Tudge. To develop new ethical spectacles we do not need to override some deeply intrinsic aggressive selfishness within our very nature. Rather we need to re-see that we have an in-built capacity for co-operation and mutual relationships. We just need to devise ways for such positive relationships to blossom. And humanity has been busy evolving words and concepts to express this potential for a long time now.

Global Lesson
THE WORDS FOR THINGS

Although there is no direct translation of Plato's concept of sophrosyne it involves ideas of temperance (moderation in all things), self-restraint and striving towards wisdom about the world as the basis for an attentive expansion of care. Plato's use of the concept amartiai means 'bad shots' to talk about getting things ethically 'wrong'.

In the Hebrew language of the Book of Genesis, nature is referred to through words such as *kabash* – to 'subdue', and *radah* – to 'have dominion over' whilst Jainism is premised upon care for all living things and refers to Nature though the concept of ahimsa – 'non-violence'.

The Latin root of the word 'Religion' is *religio*. The literal meaning of this is 'to connect' – not subdue or divide yourself from others.

In Greek the words 'economy' and 'ecology' share the same root, which is *oikos*. This means 'house' and implies a co-operative system of mutual benefit, not impersonalized markets or hardwired nastiness.

So,

Exercise

Which is the best mind-set for your creative business:

- Sophrosyne or Amartiai?
- Ahimsa or Kabash or Radah?
- Connect or Subdue?
- House or Market?

It seems that good is within us all. We need to let it come out through *reciprocal co-evolution*.

The Evolution of Social Reciprocity

To automatically see other people as some kind of enemy to be avoided, defeated or manipulated is a kind of social and economic madness. Sometimes it is a consequence of personal psychopathology. David Hare has developed the *Psychopathology Checklist* to assess the degree to which any person is psychopathic. The psychopath has high level of the following:

Factor 1: Personality 'Aggressive Narcissism':
- glibness/superficial charm

- grandiose sense of self-worth
- pathological lying
- cunning/manipulative
- lack of remorse or guilt
- shallow affect (genuine emotions are short-lived and egocentric)
- callousness, lack of empathy
- failure to accept responsibility for own actions.

Factor 2: Case History 'Socially Deviant Lifestyle':
- need for stimulation/proneness to boredom
- parasitic lifestyle
- poor behavioural control
- lack of realistic long-term goals
- impulsivity
- irresponsibility
- juvenile delinquency
- early behavioural problems
- revocation of conditional release (lack of response to experience).

Traits not correlated with either factor:

- promiscuous sexual behaviour
- many short-term marital partners
- criminal versatility
- acquired behavioural sociopathy/sociological conditioning (this is a newly identified trait concerning the psychopath's reliance on sociological tricks and strategies).

Brain scans have linked this kind of psychopathological behaviour to a lack of connection between the amygdala (the part of the brain already mentioned in the neuro-economics example) and the temporal cortex that deals with cognitive decision-making. It appears that this connection doesn't work very well in the brain of the psychopath, which means that they simply do not do empathy very well. They would not be very good at the neuro-economics game.

But these psychopaths need not be overtly 'insane' or 'psycho'. They often have highly successful careers where their natural abilities to avoid compassion and empathy, their skills in superficial charm, manipulative-ness, lack of remorse and shallow emotional life, and their grandiose sense of self-worth are all advantages. If Professor Hare's Psychopathology Checklist sounded to you like a description of corporate leaders, bankers and professional politicians then that was very perceptive of you. Research is beginning to show that people who score high on the Psychopathology Checklist do indeed occupy a disproportionate number of places in those walks of life.

It is putting it slightly crudely perhaps, but nonetheless it is accurate to suggest that the aggressiveness, competitiveness and selfishness that we are told is the basic character of human beings are actually only the characteristics of some of us. Unfortunately they tend to be our 'leaders' who have the loudest voices to perpetuate the myths of the Dark Side, which is not the real existence of things.

But there are other voices. As we have briefly touched upon so far, we are currently living through an amazing period of discovery:

- Neuroscience is beginning to map the inner workings of the human brain.
- Psychology continues to work with neuroscience to describe human consciousness.
- Evolutionary theory and allied trades show in ever more detail how and why humanity evolved all the amazing abilities it has.
- Archaeology is showing that these amazing abilities go back much further than we once thought.

But significantly for our debate in this chapter, they all appear to be under-going what we might call a 'social turn'.

By this we mean that the previous individualized focus upon the 'human machine' in isolation from others is being complemented by the view that it is relationships between humans that guide our neurological reactions, transforms our consciousness into conscience and gives us evolutionary advantage by forming groups. We are made successful by *forming and sustaining networks of social relationships* and much as by being good at reaching individual satisfactions through competition.

We evolved reciprocity.

Quotation

CO-EVOLUTION AND SYNECOLOGY

The Gaia theory (of James Lovelock), as well as the earlier work by Lynne Margulis in microbiology, has exposed the fallacy of the narrow Darwinian concept of adaptation. Throughout the living world evolution cannot be limited to the adaptation of organisms to their environment, because the environment itself is shaped by a network of living systems capable of adaptation and creativity. So, which adapts to which? Each to the other – they co-evolve. As James Lovelock put it, 'So closely coupled is the evolution of living organisms with the evolution of the environment that together they constitute a single evolutionary process …'. So the driving force of evolution, according to the emerging new theory, is not to be found in the chance events of random mutations but in life's inherent tendency to create novelty, in the spontaneous emergence of increasingly complexity and order. Once this fundamental new insight has been understood, we can then ask: What are the avenues in which evolution's creativity expresses itself?

(from *The Web of Life*, by F. Capra)

And this biology has a social facet. As David Brookes puts it in his book *The Social Animal: A Story of How Success Happens*, we are indeed social animals. It becomes ever more clear (for some perspectives it was never really in question) that general social and economic success, and more particular success in creativity, innovation and happiness is about being socially sophisticated, which is pretty much the same as being ethically sophisticated. In describing such people David Brookes writes:

Quotation

First they had good character. They were energetic, honest and dependable. They were persistent after setbacks and acknowledge their mistakes. They possessed enough confidence to take risks and enough integrity to live up to their commitments. They tried to recognize their weaknesses, atone for their sins, and control their worst impulses. Just as important, they had street smarts. They knew how to read people, situations, and ideas ... The skills a master seaman has to navigate the oceans, they had to navigate the world.

(from *The Social Animal: A Story of How Success Happens,* by D. Brookes)

This view of social evolution through reciprocity asks us to re-view:

- an awareness that we are all made from our relationships with others
- that human life is lived in and through a sense of emotional proximity
- feelings of responsibility towards the fate of others therefore make us what we are, or at least could be.

A reciprocal view of the social world:

Quotation

... recognizes that the whole process of human success has developed precisely upon the ability of our species to create and to keep intact large communal institutions through sustained mutual aid and co-operation ... (it) questions how it is possible for people to function as isolated atoms ... (this) Firstly places emphasis on the civic bonds established via participation in the social, economic and political life of the community, rather than on the impersonal market relationships. Secondly, it considers mutual co-operation for the common good as the fundamental norm of social behavior, rather than the pursuit of individual interest. Of paramount importance for our endeavor is that, since each person-in-community is aware of being constantly interrelated with others, then it will be possible for a moral culture assuming universal responsibilities for the well-being of others to take place ... the notion of mutual co-operation has long been considered as one of the decisive driving forces for the improvement of humankind ... (numerous philosophers and scientists) have demonstrated that it has been through reciprocal co-operation and not through the struggle for life that humanity has evolved.

(from *The Value of Reciprocity,* by C. Orsi)

To be wholehearted in life is to be true to your human nature and not so distracted by the fallacy of individualism. Wholehearted-ness requires a sense of living with the whole of your heart, your capacity for humane-ness and feelings for others as an expression of what your heart can be. Or what you want it to be. It is your choice, remember, and it is still the Ultimate Choice. There is not much hardwiring here.

The concepts of reciprocity and co-evolution illuminate the deep roots of such human behaviour. The way whole ecologies of people, creative or otherwise come about, grow and change through complex and mutually interacting relationships emphasizes two-way reciprocal interaction between species and environments. Species (us) do not just adapt to our environment, but can also create and change it. This deep ecology hints at recasting the fundamental relationships between being human, being co-operative, being care-ful and being creative. As we will explore in Section 2 expanding your care within, or for the ecology of creative business networks so as to co-evolve more ethical working relationships with others seems like a good place to start thinking about how you would like your creative 'environment' to be. But envisaging this possibility of reciprocal ecologies asks us to be more imaginative about how we might design care-ful relationships with other people, in what sociologist often call the *public sphere* or *civil society*.

For instance ...

Case Study

ARTICLES OF ASSOCIATION BETWEEN DESIGNERS, HUMAN BEINGS AND TECHNOLOGY

Organizing a space for reciprocal creativity can help to form more care-ful relationships between the creator and the people who use it. John Thackara advocates the following principles:

Article 1 – We cherish the fact that people are innately curious, playful and creative. We therefore suspect that technology is not going away: it's too much fun.

Article 2 – We will deliver value to people – not deliver to systems. We will give priority to human agency and will not treat humans as 'factors' in some bigger picture.

Article 3 – We will not presume to design your experiences for you – but we will do so with you, if asked.

Article 4 – We do not believe in 'idiot-proof' technology – because we are not idiots and neither are you. We will use language with care, and will search for less patronizing words than 'user' and 'consumer'.

Article 5 – We will focus on services, not things. We will not flood the world with pointless devices.

Article 6 – We believe that 'content' is something you do – not something you are given by a person in a black T-Shirt.

Article 7 – We will consider material and energy flows in all systems we design, with the objective of ensuring their impact on the biosphere is neutral.

Article 8 – We will not pretend things are simple when they are complex. We value the fact that by acting inside a system, you will probably improve it.

Article 9 – We believe that place matters, and we will look after it.

Article 10 – We believe that speed and time matter, too – but that sometimes you need more, and sometimes you need less. We will not fill up all time with content.

(from *Icon Magazine Manifesto Issue*)

We will come back to such points of concrete creative practice in more detail throughout the rest of the book. But before that we should note that these rather deep points hint at something wider.

Human Kinship

Archaeological evidence suggests that cultural communication which creativity allows is itself part of the evolutionary advantage of *homo sapiens*, but is played out across a broader stage than the selfish interests of lone individuals. This is because it contributes to the development of a greater sense of shared *human kinship*. For instance, in his great work *The Golden Bough*, J. G. Frazer shows the purpose and function of shared myths lead to 'practical' stories that guide concrete conduct *between* people. Such early myth-making leads to established ideas about how humans need to live together, which enables necessary human co-operation to become more effective.

Quotation

Regarded as a system of natural law, that is, as a statement of the rules which determine the sequences of events throughout the world, it (early myth) *may be called Theoretical Magic: regarded as a set of precepts which human beings observe in order to compass their ends, it may be called Practical Magic.*

(from *The Golden Bough*, by J. G. Frazer)

Modern anthropology, such as Alfred Gell's *Art and Agency* explores how artistic production, circulation and reception creates a stronger sense of human kinship. In *Homo Aestheticus*, Ellen Dissanayake uses the idea of 'making special' to show that creativity can bring an added sense of tradition, ceremony and meaning to invite a more conscious reflection amongst groups of people as to how we are going to live together. This 'making special' helps communities of people form and stay together by making what is necessary for mutual survival into something shared and meaningful, thus helping to expand a sense of mutual care.

Quotation

… human communities that made things special survived better than those that did not, because the fact of taking pains convinced others as well as themselves that the activity – tool manufacturing, say – was worth doing. So arts function was to render socially important activities gratifying, physically and emotionally, and that is how it played a part in natural selection.

(from *What Good Are the Arts?* by J. Carey)

This anthropological lens places an emphasis upon:

- **Agency** – *what* creative people actually do.
- **Intentions** – *why* they do it.

- **Causation** – the effects their work has upon *other people*.
- **Results** – where it takes us all in our *collective journey*.
- **Transformation** – how it might make things *practically better*.

Again the evidence suggests that creative relationships are much more important for human evolution than selfish aggression. These anthropological ideas almost automatically draw our attention back to value-based creative purpose and the expansion of care – what are we actually going to say to our kin about new ways of expressing care for each other? This draws our attention to the way an expansion of care grows out of *ongoing relationship forming and maintenance*. Ethical awareness is perhaps stronger and more alive if it lives in and through the shared 'special' spaces of social and cultural dialogue.

And perhaps the urgent need for new ethical spectacles to develop human kinship and 'make special' is best highlighted through the forming of new relationships with Nature.

For instance …

Global Lesson

SOIL AND SOUL

Alastair McIntosh describes his involvement in a community-led campaign to resist ecologically damaging industrial development on the island of Eigg in the Inner Hebrides. An increased sense of community solidarity grew as the stories of shared heritage, connection to the land and joint social care developed through the campaign. This simultaneously led to a strengthening of the community's capacity to develop their joint stories through the 'myths' of the campaign. As the myths led to stronger community and this stronger community-led to stronger myths, the art and culture of the campaign strengthened its inner sense of shared kinship.

People's very sense of who they were, what their human worth was, and what values they espoused was transmitted through legendary genealogy, myth, poetry the pibroch (piobaireachd) of classical bagpipe-playing and harp-accompanied song … Normality proceeds from the mytho-poetic rather than the other way round. The mytho-poetic is more fundamental … the bard's greatest gift lay in wisdom and eloquence joined together.

(from *Soil and Soul*, by A. McIntosh)

So why bother again? Because to not bother is to deny what you could fully *be* according to your nature, and *do* within communities of deep human kinship. And it's kind of important to hold onto those things

Don't let those miserable people from the University of Life tell you that everyone is inherently bad and should not be trusted. The 'Lecturers' at the University of Life have not done enough research. And don't let those pompous 'Business Leaders' dictate to you what human nature is. It is the attitudes of these people that have just screwed everything up. Your human nature can be an experiment in freedom to live through an innate capacity for fairness, co-operation, reciprocity and kinship with others. It is up to you to *become* the best that your human nature allows you to be. Your creative brain gives you that potential. And it is likely that this will benefit you along with others and the Nature. It is still your Ultimate Choice.

But although this chapter has tried to debunk the Dark Side account of human nature and offer an ecological lens to suggest an ethical life chimes with our human nature and our potential to be creative, it does not say enough about how this ethical life might be conceived of, shaped and played out in practice. For this, let's now turn to some developed philosophies of ethics and morality.

CHAPTER

4 Being Good and Doing Right: A Philosophical Lens

Story

A PERMANENT TESTAMENT TO THE SPIRIT

In twelfth-century Italy, Florence and Sienna were going through an early 'industrial revolution' as the textile trades expanded and thousands of people flocked to the cities.

This caused large wooden shantytowns to spring up on the edge of these cities and the inhabitants become largely disconnected from the cultural and religious life of the official city. The Franciscan order, followers of St Francis of Assisi saw this problem and started to build churches on the edge of the city rather than in the official centre. This was both a practical concern to better connect to the populace, and symbolic manifestation of their belief in the 'Poverty of the Church'.

About the same time, their religious iconography started to move away from very expensive mosaics that had characterized church art previously and towards the use of frescos. Frescos were seen as more appropriate for connecting to 'ordinary people' by expanding their chances to see and meditate upon visual manifestations of the Word of God. These churches and their interiors become a permanent testament of the spirit of kinship offering more open access to anyone as part of a public realm.

The early architectural and artistic responses of the Franciscan Order show them as using their creative energies to form and maintain ethical relationships – for being good and doing right.

Because it is the Ultimate Choice, and perhaps something basic to our human evolution, the ethical decisions we make as part of our creative business might also be a permanent testament to our spirit. But some aspects of modern life are encouraging us to unlearn this spirit, and are de-skilling us.

So although we have so far tried to set out some broad features about the idea of a value-based creative purpose and the expansion of care, about why you should bother and how ethics might simply be a facet of your human nature anyway – we need to get into some serious philosophy so as to tackle this modern day ethical de-skilling. Without this things could easily become a bit flimsy.

There is lots of ethical and moral philosophy out there and it comes from people smarter than us. So the philosophical lens in this chapter will have to be rather brief. But we hope it is not therefore superficial. Maybe we should start by looking at what has been said about practical elements within ethical philosophy. This seems a good place to start because it most immediately connects us to issues of creative business.

A 'This World' Reasonableness

Big Philosophizing sometimes becomes a mystified and mystifying activity using a specialized language that only the initiated can take part in. It can seem too disconnected from the lives and concerns of the majority of people.

We tend to agree with Peter Singer:

Quotation

... the way in which philosophy should be radical (is) *to get involved in practical issues and write about them in a way that reaches a lot of people.*

(from *How Are We to Live?* by P. Singer)

Since around AD 1500, the philosophical movement sometimes called *enlightened secular humanism* has been developing ideas about human development and welfare in a way that challenges to the 'other worldly' nature of religious dogma. Secular humanism roots its thinking within the human condition rather than accepting the universal ethical 'Truth' handed out by the representatives of god(s) and their various religious handbooks. The secular humanist tradition has made the simple but fundamental question 'How shall I live in order to achieve a good life?' possible and relevant for every person in the context of their own lives. The spectacles you use for Juliette and yourself are now *your* Ultimate Choice.

This calls on us all to put Reasonableness, that is practical human Reason at the centre of our live and decisions. A 'this worldly' Reasonableness can be:

- **Subjective** – being applied to your own chosen way of living and what you have decided is right/wrong for yourself, and/or
- **Objective** – that there are things that could, maybe should be taken on board by everyone because it encourages a shared sense of humanity. Obviously this has been difficult to agree upon, but something shared is precisely what we most urgently need for relationships between people.

Either way, a 'this worldly' Reasonableness puts our abilities in self-reflection at the centre of ethical philosophizing about *real-world stuff*.

For instance ...

Quotation

... suggesting an attitude of appreciation and mindfulness, especially mindful of beauty, as central to a life well lived ... in which the world and our experiences of it are good things in themselves, and in which, when life is lived with attentiveness and sensitivity – an intellectual as well as sensory attentiveness that can be educated by practice – it is rich and good ... it is not a long step from such an attitude to one in which attentiveness and sensitivity to others makes the life of the community good too; and it is hard to imagine such an attitude of mind being anything but tolerant and full of fellow feeling.

(From *What is Good?* by A.C. Grayling)

This takes us right back to Kant's central idea of treating the lives of others (as well as your own) as an end in itself and not as a means to an end that you might wish to impose upon them. Since the Ancient Greeks, a 'this worldly' Reasonableness has involved:

- developing freedom of thought that the ability to Reason offers you so as to become more as a person – trying to *be good*;
- respecting your ability to use your Reason to establish attentive judgements towards the World beyond yourself – *thinking about doing right*;
- combining Reason and judgements with practical attentiveness towards of the needs of others in the real World – *doing right*.

That is, thought and action combined for a real-world attentiveness.

However …

If you put two or more philosophers into a room and asked them to work something out they would first spend lots of time disagreeing about what the question means. Whilst this is a good pub game, we don't want to get into that kind of stuff here. As we said at the beginning, this section is not intended as a philosophical discussion of ethics as such but a discussion of some aspects of ethical thinking we feel might be useful for developing an ethical creative business. But having started to make the distinctions between 'being good' and 'doing right' it does become necessary to get into some of the developed philosophical debates about what this might actually mean.

On the one hand ideas about 'being good' tend to focus upon you as an individual person, your own internal character, personality and choices – your personal virtues, or lack of them. Hence the name *Virtue Ethics*.

On the other hand, ideas about 'doing right' tend to focus upon the way you interact with other people and the World. This is based, loosely or tightly upon shared social agreements that we learn so as to live ethical lives. For this reason it is referred to as *Social Contract Ethics* because it speaks of things like obligation and duty. Social Contract Ethics, found in philosophical traditions such as Utilitarianism and (sort-of) Pragmatism is a debate about ethics that focuses on the outward *consequences* of actions rather than the inward nature of goodness and virtue.

We shouldn't overdo this distinction because there is a lot of cross-over terrain between these various philosophical positions. Obviously 'being good' helps you to 'do right' and 'doing right' shows that you can 'be good'. But nevertheless it is a useful distinction to order our thoughts about devising new spectacles for Juliette.

Being Good: Virtue Ethics

A person's good character and conduct comes from sticking to things such as:

- **Classical Virtues** – justice, courage, temperance and prudence (some people think that prudence, as in being care-ful, as in the 'cautionary principle' is the most important, especially given the threat of impending eco-crises).

- **Theological Virtues** – faith, hope, charity and love.
- **Modern Virtues** – fidelity, humility, simplicity, honesty, compassion, tolerance, integrity and respect.

But then we get faced with the *paradox of virtue* in our everyday (creative businesses) lives:

- To be virtuous, we need to recognize our vice, so as to resist it.
- To be honest, we need to recognize our dishonesty, so as to resist it.
and so on.

So virtue comes from acting towards others as we would have them act towards us, rather than staying obsessed with how we as individuals are doing in isolation. Our own personal virtue is measured by how we are with and for others and it is this that can animate ethical creative business thinking. But it is a skill. We have already said that there is no ethical purity that we can arrive at in the comfort of our bedrooms. It comes into play when it comes *into play* (and work, creativity and business). The skills needed for developing ethical personal conduct is an issue we will come back to in Chapter 5, *but* for now we should recognize that Virtue Ethics form the basis for reflecting upon personal conduct for ethical creative business.

The downsides to Virtue Ethics are:

- They can only ever by loose guidelines about 'being good' and cannot give any definitive guide to the actual content of what 'being good' might entail in specific situations. As we will see below, developed 'codes of conduct' for professional conduct over and above the personal are more clear and definitive.
- There are always tensions between various virtues – for instance, being honest with a friend and being kind to a friend.
- Because virtues are general they are open to interpretation. This can mean they become something that people 'hide behind' and use to give themselves the 'blank cheque' of being 'true to their own beliefs' whilst neglecting broader consequences.
- Because of this, it can easily become an over-individualized focus upon one's interior beliefs at the expense of wider social responsibilities. This becomes a version of the '*i am just trying to make it better for everyone, so do what i tell you*' refrain.
- It can encourage a kind of 'straight line' ethical thinking that does not always exhibit a pragmatic real-world attentiveness towards more concrete situations.
- It works best when dealing with situations that are 'closest' to our emotional lives, when a sense of commitment is already there. Without this the personal and emotional basis of Virtue Ethics is perhaps not the best place to start and there more clearly defined codes of obligation and duty might be more useful.

Which brings us to …

Doing Right: Social Contract Ethics

This essentially flows from upholding a sense of duty to those around us, such that those around us do the same back – a 'contract'. A 'social' contract because it is about the way two or more people come together to *interact*, rather than focusing on the interior dynamics of an individual's virtuous beliefs.

For instance, Utilitarian philosophers such as Jeremy Bentham and John Stuart Mill used to talk about the 'Golden Rule'. This was the idea of basing political decisions on doing the greatest good for the greatest number of people. It embodies that idea of mutual obligation, duty and to care towards the happiness of others beyond the personal wants and desires of individuals themselves. Social Contract Ethics are useful for creative business in that they ask you to consider ways in which they can contribute to increasing happiness and avoiding pain.

Social Contract Ethics underpin the view that it is not so much about what we subjectively believe but the degree to which our actions adhere to externally agreed standards of behaviour. There are some obvious places where this works – Statutory Law, Civil Law, Common Law – all the legal precedents that have been established over the years that delineated right from wrong. You might not like them or agree with them but you generally stick to them because if you don't you will get into trouble. It helps to underpin professional codes of practice. Some of these have a formal legal aspect, such as medical ethics. But there is also a broader social contract element that professionals agree to on the basis of codes of good practice regardless of whether it is actually illegal or not. Most people don't get into producing pornography because of a wider decision about ethics rather than (un)lawfulness.

The main downside to Social Contract Ethics is their current institutionalized character, because:

- It has become rather hijacked by the maximization of material wealth and affluence as the arbiter of 'the greatest good for the greatest number' which is not always the increase of happiness it claims to be.
- This reduction of ethics to institutional economics and politics denudes our capacity to think about other dimensions of the 'good life' and forms of social justice. The rhetoric of economic growth and Big Democracy as inevitably about the public good neglects these alternatives.
- Social Contract Ethics perhaps too easily assume that it is possible to come up with social agreements and neglects the possibility that the loudest political and cultural voice claim general 'agreement' where it does not exist. For instance patriarchy – which is why feminism has felt it necessary to criticize such 'social contracts' and develop a specifically feminist ethics.
- Due to this, Social Contract Ethics do not always sufficiently respond to the felt experiences of the minority. Especially where the minority are the same people every time whose beliefs, needs and aspirations are *never* part of the majority view, resentment can be created.

- Social Contract Ethics do not necessarily require ethical thinking and belief per se, just a mechanical adherence to actions dictated by social norms. They can, therefore, lead to conformity to prescribed rules that is not the lived commitment that ethical behaviour probably needs to be.
- This implies a 'bureaucratization' of behaviour whereby an absence of a 'rule' can lead to an ethical void and a less than affective ability to deal with new issues and ideas as they arise. For instance, institutional ethics based upon social contract thinking have been woeful tardy at developing environmental ethics.

The institutional location of most Social Contract Ethics can lead to the adherence to prescribed social norms that are not the same as a genuine belief in social justice that might animate everyday creative lives. Ethical codes that social contract thinking tend to create might help to *reactively prevent* patently unethical behaviour, but they do not always help to inspire broader ethical sensibilities. It is likely that creative business behaviour for a better social and environmental future will need to *proactively encourage* a broader and deeper ethical sensibility, something we will come to in later chapters.

Professional Codes of Practice

As the most common public face of Social Contract Ethics, various professional codes of practice are devised within specific professional and institutional settings – the Geneva Convention, medical ethics, legal ethics and the other professional codes of conduct that specific industries have developed for themselves. Compliance with these rules and codes is accepted as a condition of entering the profession or getting a job within a particular institution. They often exist to comply with legal statute – health and safety, equal opportunities, non-discrimination policy, employment law and duty of care towards employees, a commitment to confidentiality and offering staff development opportunities. They are also usually connected to public statements from a particular profession, institution or agency about what they stand for and against.

For instance ...

Case Study

AN ENGINEERING CODE OF PRACTICE

The *American Society of Civil Engineers'* code of professional practice states that engineers shall:

- Hold paramount the safety, health and welfare of the public and shall strive to comply with the principles of sustainable development in the performance of their professional duties.
- Perform services only in areas of their competence.

- Issue public statements only in an objective and truthful manner.
- Act in professional matters for each employer or client as faithful agents or trustees, and shall avoid conflicts of interest.
- Build their professional reputation on the merit of their services and shall not compete unfairly with others.
- Act in such a manner as to uphold and enhance the honour, integrity, and dignity of the engineering profession and shall act with zero-tolerance for bribery, fraud, and corruption.
- Continue their professional development throughout their careers, and shall provide opportunities for the professional development of those engineers under their supervision.

In a more specific sense such codes of practice can be useful in practical ways for developing your creative business because they offer:

- a clear, objective and impersonal base-line for ethical business thinking that can help in quick, immediate and practical ways;
- a reference point from which to respond to other business and agencies who are either disinterested or incapable of more genuine ethical dialogue;
- a basis for talking to suppliers, collaborators and customers;
- ways to make decisions when ethical issues are paradoxical and confusing, which they often are.

Broad public statements about the value-based commitments within your creative business can help to signal your ethical credentials.

For instance ...

Case Study

BELIEVE IT OR NOT ... ETHICAL BANKING

The UK's Co-operative Bank includes the following points within their statement on Ethical Policies:

- **Tackling Global Poverty** – we will not finance businesses that do not respect fundamental labour standards and we are committed to initiatives such as micro-finance that enable people to work their way out of poverty and become self-sufficient.
- **Combating Climate Change** – since 1992 we have refused £169 million worth of finance to organizations involved in the extraction or production of fossil fuels. We now extend our policy on climate change, refusing to finance businesses engaged in the distribution of fuels with a particularly high global warming impact, such as tar sands.
- **Human Rights** – we support the principle of the Universal Declaration of Human Rights and will challenge organizations that undermine basic human rights; benefit

from oppressive governments; manufacture or transfer armaments to oppressive regimes; manufacture torture equipment or other equipment that is used in the violation of human rights. The global arms trade is worth over $50 billion. Our policy excludes finance for the manufacture or transfer of armaments to oppressive regimes.

- **Animal Welfare** – our policy will not finance businesses involved in intensive farming methods, for example, caged egg production.
- **Social Enterprise** – we are the UK's largest provider of banking services in the credit union sector. Our policy seeks to support charities across the broad range of organizations involved in the Social Enterprise Sector, including co-operatives, credit unions and community finance initiatives.
- **Customer Consultation** – we will regularly reappraise customers' views on (our) Ethical Policy and other ethical issues through, for example, our campaigning activities.
- Influence for Change – we've joined together with other investors and are engaging directly with oil companies to highlight our concerns over this issue.
- **Trade and Labour Rights** – we will seek to protect workers from exploitation and oppose child labour; support poverty reduction by encouraging the adoption of Fair Trade and ethical trading principles; advocate the ending of trade which fuels conflict and undermines human rights, for example by displacing people from their land; and encourage the promotion of co-operative enterprises.

The downside to relying on formal codes of professional practice, and the 'rule compliance' they encourage is:

- Because codes of practice are specific and detailed statements for a particular professional situation they do not invite debate nor do much to encourage active ethics within everyday lives. They can descend into becoming 'ass-covering' exercises.
- The codification of ethics can lead to mistaking ethical 'means to ends' for 'ends in themselves' that can place a higher value upon abstract rules than on more authentic ethical thinking.
- Referring to professional codes of practice as too small a base-line can culminate in institutions referring to them in situations they do not adequately cover.
- An overly strong focus upon limited ethics fixed within the pre-established boundaries of an institution or profession risks closing off broader debates and ethical futures.

Exercise
ETHICS WITHIN YOUR BUSINESS

Having considered the *ins* and *outs* of Virtues Ethics, Social Contract Ethics and the value of professional codes of practice, now ask yourself the following questions:

- What are the relative degrees of importance that you attach to each of the virtues?

- Does their relative importance differ depending upon who and what you are dealing with?
- Which virtues do you most admire in others?
- Which makes you most satisfied about yourself?
- Which is most missing from your job, company, practice, work in general?
- Why is this? Who says this?
- Do you think other people see you as being ethical?
- What are the ethical lines you would not cross in your personal life? Are these the same lines you would not cross in your professional life? If they are different, how come?
- Do you know the content of Professional Codes of Conduct relevant to your work?
- Do you feel yourself making compromises between what you believe and what you do?

(from *Ethicability*, by R. Steare)

Getting On With It: Pragmatism and Emotivism

For Pragmatism the focus tends to be about the practicalities of actually doing stuff, the pragmatic consequences. Hence the name. So, there is a natural connection between Pragmatist ethics and the practical focus of creative work because both tend to be concerned with 'getting on with things' rather than chasing an abstract position that stands for all time.

Richard Rorty, one of the big hitters of Pragmatism, puts it like this. Firstly he makes a distinction between *philosophy* (with a small 'p') and *Philosophy* (with a Capital 'P'). He thinks Philosophy is too concerned with asking Big Questions and establishing Universal Answers. For him this is not the best way of addressing things:

Quotation
PRAGMATIST PHILOSOPHERS ...

... are in a position analogous to that of secularists who argue that research concerning the Will of God does not get us anywhere. Such secularists are not saying that God does not exist, exactly: they feel unclear about what it would mean to affirm His existence, and thus about the point of denying it. Nor do they have some special, funny, heretical view of God. They just doubt the vocabulary of theology is one we ought to be using ... They think it will not help to say something true to think about Truth, nor will it help to act well to think about Goodness, nor will it help to be rational to think about Rationality ...

They would simply like to change the subject.

(from *Consequences of Pragmatism*, by R. Rorty)

Pragmatism wants to focus upon what actually happens rather than upon the search for the universals of being good and doing right which are probably not achievable nor agreeable to everyone for all situations for all times. They want to get on with thinking about the 'why' and 'if' of what we actually do by bringing an ethical lens to bear upon the consequences of those actions, and let the lens refocus as the action develops.

For instance …

Global Lesson

AN IMMUNE SYSTEM

Majid Rahnema describes pragmatic interdependencies that make up local ways of interacting in some developing societies. Decisions about economic and technological issues are genuinely set against their social, cultural and ecological consequences. These vernacular economies form an 'immune system' with which people can mutually protect each other from the ups and downs of the Big Global Economy.

Rahnema describes a vernacular economy as having:

- An 'organic consistency' to ways of living together that is a 'living tissue of social and cultural relations defining the activities of their members'. These ways of living together embody an ethic that helps to make human solidarities that preserve community. There is a holistic and multi-dimensional approach to life and an organic linking between the social and cultural on the one hand, and the 'economic' on the other.
- An approach to 'economic' questions about what should be produced and who should get it that is thoroughly embedded in social and cultural values. 'Economic' relationships are not abstracted or depersonalized away from the values that guide personal relationships. 'Economic' issues are situated against values such as reciprocity and the collective good.
- A practical perception of community need and definition of what is essential to produce that emanates from traditions of voluntary simplicity that rejects the culture of unlimited growth, unlimited needs and the maximization of consumption.
- An awareness of the community's collective capacity to meet its needs that is situated against its environmental capacity. There is an ecological vigilance informed by a sense of harmony and dialogue with Nature, rather than seeing it simply as resources to be exploited.
- A minimization of risk that seeks to sustain the community rather than pursue growth in ways that might endanger the sustainability of the whole. There is a diversification of strategies and approaches to resources which tries to ensure a greater capacity for self-protection rather than to rely upon one strategy or resource for survival.
- A 'prudent attitude towards innovation' whereby new ways are only sought if they are needed. That is, innovation is not fetishized or pursued for its own sake.

(from *The Post-Development Ready*, by M. Rahnema and V. Bawtree)

When outside investment, usually in the form of 'Aid' comes it usually comes with strings attached that often mess up local economies. Because of this Aid too often works like 'AIDS'. These vernacular forms of solidarity work to re-form the 'antibodies' that fights against this potential damage to the health of the local community and its ecology of social and cultural relations.

Whether these vernacular economies are 'ethical' or not is not an issue that seems to occupy the minds of the people who develop them. They work because they already embody pragmatic forms of solidarity, mutual commitment and the value of reciprocal care. Trying to devise an 'ethical position' is less important that getting on with it and demonstrating one's values and ethics through *pursuing* practical relationships that have mutually beneficial consequences.

The downsides of Pragmatist ethics are:

- The outcome-centeredness of Pragmatism can easily get hijacked by the rhetoric of 'the end justifying the means'. Fetishizing economic growth and expanding consumerism at all costs is a case in point. We will still probably need some ethical baselines 'behind' Pragmatism.
- At the other end of the spectrum Pragmatism can leave us unable to demarcate one consequence as better/worse than another. Any old tosh can stand as 'ethical' if someone shouts loud enough that it works for them. This starts to throw the ethical baby out with the philosophical bath water.
- This potential collision with Emotivist ethics, the 'ethics' of having a personally meaningful emotional reaction to something. This can end up as self-obsession dressed up as an 'ethical' argument which is not very good. We are probably going to need a more shared notion of ethics if we are to be saved from the bankers and professional politicians.

The value of Pragmatism lies in the way it draws our attention to a 'this Worldy' attentiveness and the issue of practical consequences when we are thinking about values and ethics for creative business. The problem with a purely consequence-centredness lies in ethical debate getting hijacked by those with a loud enough voice to draw attention to certain consequences (that suit them) and therefore divert attention from other consequences. The attempt of the Coalition Government in 2011 to hijack 'fairness' by focusing on some selected consequences of their policy is an example of this ethical bad faith.

This starts to get us into the idea that ethics needs to be a social dialogue, played out through real-World ethical encounters rather than technical Philosophy. And this itself starts to raise the idea that ethical differences have to be taken into account, because such differences, around which ethical dialogue revolves, carry heartfelt meanings for all people. Emotion is implicit, and possibly necessary within ethical debate. Which brings us to Emotivism.

An Emotivist idea of ethics is something that creative practitioners might feel drawn too given that they are often concerned with visceral, emotional reactions rather than purely logical ones. Emotivism might chime with creative business more easily given that it leaves room for the *feeling* of ethical-ness rather than focusing upon the dry technicalities of Big Philosophizing. It may also chime with creative practice because it is quite relaxed about the idea that ethical values are a kind of *fictional truth*. For instance, most creative practitioners are probably used to the idea that great literature, whilst being entirely fictional can reveal great truths about the human condition. No amount of rational Philosophy can 'prove' Shakespeare but it can still speak to us in very profound ways. If ethics, like music, art, film and all the other things we use to speak to each other, is capable of moving us to feel for the other person and become better people ourselves then it is doing its job. It perhaps does not need the technical authentication of Big Philosophy. Indeed we may need to resist Big Philosophy if it is emptying out ethical debate of all fellow feeling.

Emotivist ethics suggests that there is no objectively 'factual' basis for ethics but nevertheless felt experiences, wholehearted-ness and fellow feeling within ethical life are a necessity; it warns us that the best any of us can probably do in our concrete creative business is not get things *too wrong*. We can never get them universally *right* because there is no 'right' to get, which suggests wariness about what you think as the normal, received ideas of ethical behaviour that 'everyone knows'. These are probably social conventions formed by groups. And this is not the same thing as 'real'. Other people will be felling different things just as strongly as you are feeling your feelings.

There are no universal truths about values and ethics.

So the best we can do here is see ethics as a dialogue between different groups as a fundamental aspect of social, cultural and political life. This is politics in its broadest, most sophisticated sense and might be the only real place where we can co-evolve and share ethical idea and develop new ones. At the very least, Emotivist ethics suggests the need for a good balance between an emotional response to specific situations and broader principles that are bigger than your own emotional response.

And this is especially the case with creative work. Virtue Ethics, Social Contract Ethics and Pragmatism are fundamentally based upon Reason. Whilst it would be silly to argue against this, Human Reason is not always the thing that creative people turn to first. Indeed, it might be that referring to Reason holds the danger of 'improving' ethical behaviour at the expense of creativity. Sometimes creativity might need a space away from ethical conventions to take its first breath.

As A.C Grayling puts it:

Quotation

Established ethical positions might be,

... too middle-aged, middlebrow and middle-class, suggesting a rather limited individual prone to pomposity, who, in shunning the extremes of passion, love, anguish and like states, cannot know the value of them as sources of insight and creativity.

(from *What is Good?* by A.C. Grayling)

But we still think you should bother!

It is pretty obvious that Emotivist ethics needs to be treated with some caution. Your emotional responses are themselves likely to be coloured by your cultural background and subsequent ideas about what is 'right' and 'wrong'. There is an obvious danger in sticking to ethical beliefs just because you like the way that they make you feel. This can easily become the opposite of ethical skill because it ends up in a deep sense of selfishness and helps to reproduce the obsession with the Creative Self we have already discussed as potentially unhelpful. This is because purely individualistic emotional thinking can lead to fairly arbitrary ethical ideas that you alone have, and that don't necessarily make any sense to others. You can't expect everyone else to act upon your ideas just because you have them. Within ethical creative business you will probably need some firmer back up or more rational argument. This is where Pragmatism's focus upon the consequence of any suggested behaviour comes back in a purely Emotivist ethics opens up the possibility of all sorts of 'bad faith' whereby people use 'ethical' arguments to get their own way by convincing others that 'their way is how it (ethically) *should* be'.

We have mentioned bad faith a few times now so let's pay some attention to it directly: emotions and feelings can be dangerous sources of self-delusion and ethical inauthenticity.

Bad Faith, Collusion and Alienation

Being an existentialist, Jean-Paul Sartre argued that each one of us is fundamentally free to make choices about how we will be and live. When he wrote that we are 'condemned to be free' he meant we have an unavoidable responsibility to face this freedom. This often brings with it a sense of psychological discomfort but to not live our lives as an experiment in freedom is to willingly turn ourselves into an inert object.

Clearly circumstances limit what any of us can practically do. But when we work to convince ourselves to *believe in* the things that are happening to us or others due to these external circumstances then we are in 'bad faith'. Thinking ethically is an exercise in avoiding such bad faith. The example that Sartre famously uses to describe bad faith is the rather pompous, stuffy and overly 'waiter-esque' cafe waiter living through his 'waiter-ness'.

Quotation

His voice oozes with an eagerness to please; he carries food rigidly and ostentatiously. His exaggerated behavior illustrates that he is play acting as a waiter, as an object in the world: an automaton whose essence is to be a waiter. But that he is obviously acting belies that he is aware that he is not merely a waiter, but is rather consciously deceiving himself.

(from *Being and Nothingness*, by J.-P. Sartre)

In his books *Self and Others* and *Knots*, R. D. Laing has shown how our capacity for freedom can be complicated by our relationships with those around us. He shows us how something like Sartre's bad faith can occur in the space between two or more people due to what he call *collusion*. By this he means the process whereby two or more people agree to play false roles and maintain each other's chosen illusions – *I will pretend for you if you pretend for me, and together we can mutually avoid facing what we need to do.*

Bad faith and collusion can culminate in very unnerving and rather weird situations.

Case Study

THE STOCKHOLM SYNDROME

The Stockholm Syndrome is a psychological response sometimes seen in abducted hostages, in which the hostage shows signs of loyalty to the hostage-taker, regardless of the danger or risk in which they have been placed. The syndrome is named after the 1973 Nommalmstorg Robbery of The Kreditbanken in Stockholm, hence the name. The bank robbers held bank employees hostage from August 23rd to August 28th during which the victims became emotionally attached to their victimizers and even defended their captors after they were freed from their six-day ordeal.

The millionaire heiress Patty Hearst was kidnapped by the Symbionese Liberation Army (SLA) and after two months in captivity she actively took part in a robbery they were orchestrating. Her unsuccessful legal defense was that she suffered from Stockholm Syndrome and was coerced into aiding the SLA.

During 2002 in Missouri, Shawn Hombeck was kidnapped at age 11 and held for four years by Michael J. Devlin. Shawn started using Devlin's last name and despite talking to police on two separate occasions about other unrelated matters, he did not seek their assistance. There have been many cases including victims of sexual abuse and kidnapping who have expressed their understanding and support for Shawn's decisions not to make an attempt to escape.

(from Wikipedia)

Other philosophers such as Erich Fromm and Paulo Freire have discussed the 'fear of freedom' implicit within bad faith and collusion when we avoid our ethical responsibilities by over-conforming to the security of wider social, political and cultural conventions.

Quotation

Fear of freedom, of which its possessor is not necessarily aware, makes him see ghosts. Such an individual is actually taking refuge in an attempt to achieve security, which he prefers to the risks of liberty … the conflict lies in the choice between being wholly themselves or being divided; between ejecting the oppressor within or not ejecting him; between human solidarity or alienation; between following prescriptions or having choices; between being spectators or actors; between acting or having the illusion of acting through the action of the oppressors; between speaking out of being silent.

(from *The Pedagogy of the Oppressed*, by P. Freire)

But of course the conditions we are forced to live in impact upon this – meaninglessness and powerlessness within work for the vast majority, non-Reasonable attitudes within Big Economics, Big Politics and Big Business, non-social Social Institutions present which encourage us to 'believe in' that which stands above us. We are left with little option other than to rage against the machine.

So as with bad faith and collusion, we often actively embody ourselves in an 'alien power' that 'stands over us' in various ways that involve us reneging on our capacities for expanded care.

You can be alienated:

- **from yourself** – by embodying yourself into something that is less than meaningful to you (for instance an 'identity' as a 'fashion-head', Macho-guy, banker);
- **from others** – by treating them as a means to your ends rather than as someone who wants to flourish (for instance approaching people through relationships coloured only by money);
- **from Nature** – same thing. By treating Nature as a means to your ends rather than as something that wants to live as an end in itself. For instance treating Nature only as a resource there for you to use. A relationship still often coloured by money.

Alienation makes ethical creative business difficult. Actually it makes it impossible. Virtue Ethics, Social Contract Ethics, Pragmatism and Emotivism are useful and informative because they can help you to develop your ethical thinking for being good and doing right. But to go beyond thinking about ethical creative business and go 'out there' to expand your capacity for care also requires more basic questions about the way the institutions of economic power and cultural influence are set up. And ethical creative business is as good a place as anywhere to start this critical re-questioning for the development of bigger spectacles.

But living through an awareness of freedom to make ethical choices and live out moral judgements with strong commitment is not easy. We are all prey to self-delusions such as bad faith, collusion and alienation in order to make the often harsh World out there more psychologically palatable. But developing a value-based creative purpose for the expansion of care within creative business involves being aware of these tendencies to become what we think others want us to be, as well as facing the responsibility to embrace out freedom and make choices. It is still the Ultimate Choice.

Sartre, Laing, Fromm and Freire also start to bring us to a Critical Theory of ethics. But before we think about this idea of ethics in detail, we need to note a more general philosophical point.

Idealism and Materialism

There has never been a resolution to this deep philosophical debate and we are not going to give you one here. But a problem with a lot of ethical philosophy is its tendency to focus just upon the realm of ideas. For many this is not a problem at all because they believe that the concrete World out there is a manifestation or these of ideas. This is an *idealist* position – ideas come first and create the World. For instance, the idea that language determines what we have the capacity to think and therefore do in the World.

On the other hand there is *materialism*. This position sees the concrete, material World of economics, industry, power and poverty as coming first and the World of ideas and culture as being a manifestation of that. Real economic power enables the powerful to decide 'what counts' as Culture because they also have the loudest cultural voice.

For instance, many of the pronouncements about how art and culture connects with ethics and what it can do in terms of 'moral improvement' has been coloured by an idealist philosophy. And as a result they have been a bit limited.

For instance …

Quotation

In the nineteenth century it became a widespread cultural assumption that the mission of the arts was to improve people and that public access to art galleries would affect this. It was felt in particular that if the poor could be persuaded to take an interest in high art it would help them to transcend their material limitations, reconciling them to their lot, rendering them less likely to covert or purloin or agitate for a share in the possessions of their superiors.

(from *What Good Are the Arts?* by J. Carey)

Trying to 'improve' people's conditions of life through ideas without changing their material conditions – better incomes, working conditions, housing and so on – is a deeply unsatisfactory ethical position. And this is when idealism becomes ideology that uses culture to reproduce existing social and economic divisions. Moral improvement such as the ones mentioned above – not coveting your neighbour's possessions, not stealing stuff– are far more likely to come about if people have a decent income, job and house, some might say. But idealism is not an old nineteenth-century idea. It is still with us and too much debate about art, culture and creativity is still disconnected to the social and economic realities of the vast majority of people. It is often still geared towards creating 'social tranquility' and disconnects the potential of creative businesses to improve the *material conditions* of life for a greater number of people and as a route to an expanded sense of care.

Whilst ethical creative business might need to offer more than just ideas this does not mean you have to choose materialism alone and forget the realm of ideas. That would be kind of hard and probably counter-productive for creative business. But the practical possibilities within ethical creative business to expand care towards the lives of more people are high. Ethical creative business needs at least one eye on material questions as part of the basis for an ethical agenda.

The next two chapters will explore concrete examples of this. For now this brings us to ...

Flourishing

Aristotle's concept of the *eudemonic* nature of human life suggests that striving for a greater sense of flourishing, to become more than we currently are, is a central impulse. Already we see the good news, a view shared with Buddhism that we all have the capability get closer to what we want to be, and, ethics in and through a value-based creative purpose can be a vehicle for this.

There are many ideas about what this flourishing might involve. Maria Nussbaum's list is one of the most recent and best for thinking about the relationship between idealist and materialist facets for a value-based creative purpose and the expansion of care within creative business,

Nussbaum suggests that flourishing for yourself and others requires:

- **Life** – being able to lead a full life.
- **Bodily Health** – being able to have good health.
- **Bodily Integrity** – being able to have physical security, sexual satisfaction and choice about reproduction.
- **Senses, Imagination and Thought** – being able to use the senses in a truly human way through education and guarantees about free expression.
- **Emotions** – being able to develop our emotions of love, grieving, longing and gratitude.
- **Practical Reason** – being able to form a conception of the good and to plan one's own life.
- **Affiliation** – being able to live with and for others. Being free from discrimination on the basis of race, sex, sexual orientation, ethnicity, caste, religion or national origin.

- **Other Species** – being able to live with concern for animals, plants, and the world of Nature.
- **Play** – being able to laugh and play.
- **Control Over One's Environment** – being able to participate politically, being able to hold property on an equal basis with others, and being able to work with meaningful relationships of recognition with other workers.

It needs to be made clear that you don't *have* to do these things. That's up to you and Nussbaum wouldn't want to tell you off. She means that we all need these material opportunities so we can live more meaningful, flourishing lives. These material conditions form the basis for social justice because they form the basis for an equalization of social and cultural opportunity that is needed before the call to the realm of ideas can have any real purchase upon people's lives.

For instance ...

Global Lesson

NEW SPECTACLES FOR BANKERS: GRAMEEN BANK

Founded by Professor Muhammad Yunus, Grammen Bank (GB) in India challenged traditional banking practices by doing away with the need for collateral for loans, so as to make them more available to the people who really needed them – the poor. This was their way of encouraging self-development and expanding peoples' capabilities, as a way of tackling poverty. Professor Yunus argues that if such loans are made available to the poor then *'these millions of small people with their millions of small pursuits can add up to create the biggest development wonder'*.

The GB project sought to:

- extend banking to the poor;
- end the exploitation by money lenders;
- create opportunities for rural self-employment;
- encourage the poorest households to organize and manage things for themselves;
- change the vicious circle of *'low income, low saving and low investment'*, into a virtuous circle of *'low income, injection of credit, investment, more income, more savings, more investment, more income'*.

By 2009, GB had grown to have 7.80 million borrowers, 97 per cent of whom are women, 2,548 branches, servicing 84,096 villages. In 1996 GB won the Nobel Peace Prize. It has gone through problems in recent years as the Dark Side has interfered, but it still hints at another way of thinking about and doing banking, which we sorely need today.

(for more information go to www.grameen-info.org)

So we have now suggested that being fair, co-operative and reciprocal is part of the human condition and that it is rather dumb to pretend it is not. And we have briefly explored some developed philosophical ideas about how this inherent capacity for an expanded care for yourself, others and Nature could be thought about.

But all this is still rather abstract and a bit difficult to 'carry around' with you as you go through your everyday creative life. The next two chapters try to pin all this science and philosophy down to some ideas for everyday personal conduct and concrete creative engagements.

5 Everyday Skills in Care: Contact Lenses

Story

A DIFFICULT WEEK FILLED WITH LONG HOURS

It's 6.30 p.m. on a Friday evening in the early spring, and Scott, who recently celebrated his fortieth birthday is about to leave work. Scott has had a difficult week filled with long hours and hair-raising stress. Scott, who is single, is now preparing to go out with some male friends to unwind and share war stories about the week that was. They plan to go to a Japanese restaurant for sushi and sake. As always, Scott and his friends will spend much of their time talking about career goals. All of them will complain about not making enough money; at least one will brag about a recent business coup. They will also compare notes on personal relationships. Afterwards, the men will stop by a club in the hope of meeting some women.

Scott and his friends do the same thing almost every week. On one level, they think of it as networking; on another it's male camaraderie. Tonight at about 2.00 a.m. Scott follows his typical pattern and starts to head home, alone, a little bit drunk, worrying about whether he is going to have a headache in the morning and if he has spent too much money. He will probably also feel a little bit depressed, a little bit lonely, and he'll have an overriding sense that the night was a waste of time – in fact, that much of what he does is a waste of time. Scott would like to change. But how? And in what direction?

It's as it always is, week in and week out. But this night, although he is thinking his usual thoughts something amazing happens: As Scott walks down a dimly lit street searching for his car, he taps the sensor button on his key chain and waits for the flashing light to lead him to his vehicle. But instead of seeing car lights, he hears the sound of low chanting and immediately becomes aware of an unusual sight. A yellow robed man is sitting in the lotus position under one visible streetlight, meditating and chanting. It's the Buddha. What is the Enlightened One doing here, and what is the wisdom that he can impart to Scott?

'Instead of wandering around in this dangerous jungle seeking a woman and some money, wouldn't it be far better to seek your true self?' asks the Buddha.

(from *Awaking the Buddha Within*, by Lama Surya Das)

In fact, this is a modern version of the famous 2,500 year old tale about the origins of Buddhism. In the original story, the Buddha was sitting in the forest when a band of villagers came along looking for a woman who had stolen money from one of them. But the Buddha's question has as much meaning today as it did then. Should we be searching for meaning instead of chasing after temporary economic or sexual conquests within a repeating cycle of behaviour?

But how do any of us actually achieve this kind of change in our everyday personal conduct? Whilst the Big Ideas we have looked at so far might be interesting and useful, how do we find effective ways of bringing these ideas into the practicalities of our daily creative business lives? As we suggested at various points so far, this is your choice. We cannot tell you how to do this. Instead we will use this chapter to suggest some 'intermediate' concepts that will hopefully help you to join the Big Ideas to everyday practice.

We will suggest intermediate ideas as part of the thinking about new spectacles for Juliette, as new contact points between yourself, your creativity, your business and other people – as *new contacts lenses*.

In that sense, this chapter is about personal and professional development.

The Quest for Grace

For Gregory Bateson the *quest for grace* comes from practical responses to lived experiences. It is a life long journey full of wrong turns and failures, involving the rejection of the self-delusions, self-created ghosts and fears we touched upon in the last chapter. It is akin to a quest in the literary sense of the word. It involves the coming together of being good and doing right, of a Pragmatic concern with consequences and a felt experience of other people.

Quotation

In *Steps to an Ecology of Mind*, he describes it thus:

... for the attainment of grace, the reasons of the Heart must be integrated with the reasons of Reason.

(from *Steps to an Ecology of Mind*, by G. Bateson)

In his book *The Courage to Be*, Paul Tillich shows how courage is at least in part a moral choice to re-affirm yourself and what you want to be, for yourself and loved ones. The idea of *eutrapelia* (translated as graceful playfulness) is linked to courage in a broader embrace of value-based creative purpose as it links graceful virtues to concrete creative action. This requires what Ivan Illich and Amartya Sen amongst others have called *practical Reason*.

Grace and courage as everyday facets of a value-based creative purpose and the expansion of care require that practice and Reason, action and thought combine.

Practical Reason: Lost and Re-Seen

But grace and practical Reason, that combine the reasons of the heart and the reasons of Reason, are in short supply today. It may be that we need to reinvent practical Reason as we devise our new spectacles.

Writing in the fourteenth century, Ibn Khaldun wrote of *asabiyya* to refer to the spirit of human kinship and witnessed the growing decadence within the Institutions of power and control of the time as the denial of *asabiyya*.

Quotation

Whoever takes someone's property, or uses him for forced labour, or presses an unjustified claim upon him, it should be known that this is what the Lawgiver had in mind when he forbade injustice.

(by Ibn Khaldun)

The recent dramatic failings of the Big Institutions – banks, the Catholic Church, MPs, National Governments during the Copenhagen Conference on Climate Change, and industry's continued neglect of environmental responsibility show that some things have not changed that much.

Quotation

... the experts are knaves and fakers, the promise of unlimited material progress and universal affluence is a lie, the economy is an inhuman machine operated by rogues and blunderers ... the system is running out of control ... (we need to) *expand our conception of human personhood.*

(from *Person/Planet: The Creative Destruction of Industrial Society*, by T. Roszak)

In terms of practical Reason, what is the role of creative business in reproducing this 'fakery'? In the future will creative businesses continue to be motivated by Celebrity Culture and celebrations of acquisitiveness? Will it be about creating 'objects of desire' to be passively consumed? Or will it strive to design encounters to encourage more active participation for all? Will it embrace the practical Reason of serving broader social and environmental needs within a more caring public sphere? That is, will creative businesses approach people as consumers, or will they strive to relate to people as citizens?

These are very big questions, and we do not claim to have any universal answers but we do believe that asking questions concerning practical applications of creative Reason can help.

The history of humanity's attempt to attain Reason is a very long one, but, as we draw ever closer to the ecological limits of our Planet, renewing this sense of practical Reason becomes an increasingly urgent aspect of ethical creative business.

Practical Reason might involve:

- **practical *Reason*** – new wisdom and attitudes for our current circumstances as human beings and members of society. Learning a new grammar of life is an urgent necessity.
- ***Practical* reason** – artists, designers, writers and other creative professionals have the particular skills to create encounters that can help provide practical resources for a new public realm animated by ethical relationships.

For instance ...

Thinkpiece

For the Medieval mind, practical Reason is embodied in the Seven Work of Corporeal Mercy, which were:

Feeding the hungry

Give drink to the thirsty

Clothing the naked

Sheltering the homeless

Visiting the sick

Visiting the prisoner

Burying the dead.

And the accompanying Seven Works of Spiritual Mercy were:

Instructing the ignorant

Counselling the doubtful

Admonishing the sinner

Bearing wrongs patiently

Forgiving offences willingly

Comforting the sorrowful

Praying for the living and the dead.

Professional Self-Reflection for Practical Reason

In an attempt to pin this down a little more, we can borrow and slightly change Sandy Fraser's three overlapping aspects of professional self-reflection for developing practical Reason within creative business. Laid out in her book *The Critical Practitioner in Social Work and Health Care* they are:

- **Critical Analysis** – evaluating broad social, political and economic contexts leading to a recognition of broad social needs.
- **Critical Reflexivity** – questioning personal assumptions and values to engage the self more fully and negotiate new forms of active engagement with things.
- **Critical Action** – applying analysis and reflection to the practical possibilities of growing ethical standards and building them into on-going creative business strategies.

This kind of professional self-reflection might help specific creative businesses to arrive at practical Reason as they develop:

- **Imagination within Critical Analysis** – imagine new possible reactions to broad critical evaluations.

- **Awareness out of Critical Reflection** – finding new ways to relate one's creative motivations to the needs of others and Nature.
- **Engagements through Critical Action** – providing practical ideas and resources for a just distribution of self-determination.

Such professional self-reflection for practical Reason might help create a situation whereby:

Quotation

Technique would then tend to become art, and art would tend to become reality: the opposition between imagination and reason, higher and lower faculties, poetic and scientific thought, would be invalidated.

(from *Essay on Liberation*, by H. Marcuse)

... the basis of practical reasoning must include ways of judging how to reduce injustice and advance justice, rather than aiming only at the (abstract) characterization of perfectly just societies.

(from *The Idea of Justice*, by A. Sen)

Practical Reason requires personal awareness for better contact lenses.

Personal Awareness

In *Towards a Theory of Creativity* Carl Rogers highlights the complicated interplay between various personal motivations that aim at the public good and the outcomes of such intentions. For practical Reason to be played out through smart engagements with the World, good intentions are not always enough. Skills in understanding yourself and others are also needed.

Quotation

Many, perhaps most, of the creations and discoveries which have proved to have great social value have been motivated by purposes having more to do with personal interests than wider social value; while on the other hand history records a somewhat sorry outcome for many of those creations (various Utopias, Prohibitions and so on) which had as their avowed purpose the achievement of a social good ... (if) the individual is denying (an) awareness ... larger than areas of his experience, then his creative formings may be pathological or socially evil, or both. To the degree to which the individual is open to all aspects of his experience and has available to his awareness all the varied sensings and perceivings which are going on within his organism, then the novel products of his interaction with his environment will tend to be constructive both for himself and others.

(from *Towards a Theory of Creativity*, by C. Rogers)

Pierre Teilhard de Chardin's discusses such interactions between what he calls *the within* of personal spirit and the *without* of the concrete material World. He suggests that the practical Reason of engaging with the material World and ethical judgements within it should be mutually informative as they both flow from and simultaneously lead to greater personal awareness if they combine effectively. The World makes you, and you make the World, better, if you get it right. In *The Phenomenon of Man*, he writes:

Quotation

Nowhere ... is the need more urgent for building a bridge between the two banks of our experience – the physical and the moral – if we wish the material and spiritual sides of our activities to be mutually enlivened.

(from *The Phenomenon of Man*, by P. Teilhard de Chardin)

Too often traditional ideas of business encourage professionals to become stuck within self-oriented ways of thinking and working that deny this capacity for personal awareness. This can easily encourage a thoroughly bureaucratized attitude to the World such that an impersonalized professional mind-set becomes an end-in-itself and fails to deliver practical Reason. This calls on us all to recognize that personal and creative ways of seeing are also simultaneously ways of 'not seeing' other things.

It is easy for any of us to become individually prey to this creative business 'psychosis' and avoid personal awareness of the possibilities of practical Reason in our creative business life. Back to the question of new spectacles for Juliette, Freudian psychology has a number of ways of accounting for personal ways of not seeing:

Exercise

CREATIVE BUSINESS PSYCHOSIS

Are you sure that your creativity and business is not suffering from the following?

- **Repression** – burying thoughts, ideas and revelations.
- **Denial** – a failure to admit.
- **Displacement** – inappropriately transferring hostility and frustrations onto something or someone else.
- **Fixation** – an over-adherence to one's own idea or view.
- **Projection** – inappropriately directing feelings for oneself onto others.
- **Introjection** – inappropriately directing feelings for others onto oneself.
- **Rationalizations** – re-writing false accounts of the situation after the event.
- **Reactive Formation** – changing an emotion into its opposite to avoid the consequences of that emotion.
- **Regression** – adopting childish behaviour.
- **Sublimation** – changing basic impulses into socially acceptable or 'respectable' reactions.
- **Idealization** – working to convince oneself that the best possible conditions already pertain in order to avoid the discomfort of recognition.
- **Splitting** – falsely isolating elements that are really connected.

Buddhism can also help with personal awareness.

Quotation

We want success so much that we give up our real lives; we want beautiful things so much that we only see the imperfections in what we have; we become so attached to others that we try to control or own them; we become so attached to something or somebody that we become totally dependent on them and forget who we are … Purifying oneself of pride and jealousy is essential in loosening and diminishing our ego-centred and incorrect view of reality …

(from *Awakening the Buddha Within*, by Lama Surya Das)

Western civilization has only relatively recently come to appreciate what Buddhism can add to any thinking about the personal awareness needed at the heart of everyday ethical skill. It is way beyond our capabilities to give a full account of its practical relevance and beauty. But we couldn't ignore it. So with a large degree of humility, we wanted to say something about Buddhism.

Firstly, let's recognize that we don't have time to become Buddhist monks. But central to Buddhism are daily practices designed to bring greater personal awareness about the *what*, *why*, *how* and, indeed *if* questions of our lives. It is a way of being more constant in our ability to see the nature of our reality and to critically examine what we are thinking, experiencing and doing. When your breathe, experience yourself breathing. When your walk through a doorway, experience yourself walking through a doorway. Then maybe expand this, don't be worried *because* you are worried, upset *because* you are upset, jealous *because* you are jealous. These are just fleeting emotions and they will change. You can choose more useful and enjoyable emotions by more clearly seeing the negative impact of *The Three Poisons* or *Three Fires*:

- **Ignorance** – in its common forms of self-perpetuating delusions, confusions, fantasies and denials, ignorance is the fundamental barriers to personal awareness and the cause of the suffering you feel and that you sometimes cause others. Overcoming ignorance entails overcoming the false stories we tell ourselves.
- **Attachment** – the only thing you can truly rely on is unpredictability. The only thing that truly stays constant is change. There is not point moaning about change because it will happen. Moaning about change because you are too attached to the way things currently are will only mean you end up being annoyed *because* you are annoyed. Don't get stuck within your attachments.
- **Aversion** – ignorance and attachments tend to create frustrations that become anger, dislike, contempt and disgust towards bits of the World that we feel have let you down. We all do it – 'I hate him/her because …'; 'He/she/they make me sick because …'. Aversion only means that you focus upon emotions from the Dark Side when you could spend your time much more positively with bright emotions.

Overcoming these *Three Poisons* is likely to lead to improving everyday skills in engaging with the public spaces of other people's lives. It is likely that developing personal awareness will enable more effective recognition and empathy.

Which brings us to …

Recognition and Empathy

Human beings have developed a sophisticated capacity for mutual recognition as part of a system of rewards (for being good and doing right) and sanctions (for being bad and doing wrong). On-going mutual recognition between people is needed for regular contact to occur, is a basic necessity for things like trust and respect to work, motivates voluntary restraints upon unnecessary competition and allows selfless behaviour such as altruism to become meaningful.

Mutual recognition is necessary for agreements about the common good to co-develop.

However, we might be in danger of losing it if the Dark Side takes hold and we lose our capacity for mutual practical Reason. For instance, Michael Sandel has argued that recognition is becoming rather watered down into passive concern to avoid the other person – to respect someone's space has too often come to mean leaving them well alone; to respect someone's rights has too often come to mean no engagement with them at all. Recognition and respect are becoming a passive lack of authentic relationship with other people. Hence all the stuff we hear about people bemoaning the 'loss of community'.

This is not good for proactive ethically skilfulness. It might be that we need a more active sense of the other person and how we as individuals can be better ourselves through relationships – because as we have mentioned already ethics is best when it is based upon the recognition of relationships between people.

Perhaps we need a more active sense of *empathy*. In *I and Thou*, Martin Buber shows that to treat the other as 'Thou' is to recognize their full person-hood. To treat the other as 'It' is to lack true fellow feeling, And by choosing one or the other you say something about your own capacity for full humane-ness.

Quotation

If Thou is said, the I of the combination I-Thou is said along with it.

If It is said, the I of the combination I-It is said along with it.

The primary word I-Thou can only be spoken with the whole being.

The primary word I-It can never be spoken with the whole being …

If I face a human being as my Thou he is not a thing among things … The Thou meets me through grace.

(from *I and Thou*, by M. Buber)

Carl Rogers takes up this theme in *A Way of Being*, and suggests three elements to empathy:

- congruence
- caring
- understanding.

Quotation

In the ordinary circumstances of life – between marital and sex partners, between teachers and students, employers and employees, colleagues and friends – congruence is probably the most important element. Congruence, or genuineness, involves letting the other person know 'where you are' emotionally. It may involve confrontation and straightforward expression of personally owned feelings – both negative and positive. Thus, congruence is a basis for living together in a climate of realness.

But in certain other special situations, caring, or prizing, may turn out to be a significant element. Such situations include nonverbal relationships – between parents and infants, therapists and the mute psychotic, physicians and very ill patients – a nurturing climate in which delicate, tentative new thoughts and productive processes can emerge.

Then, in my experience, there are other situations in which the empathetic way of being has the highest priority. When the other person is hurting, confused, troubled, anxious, alienated, terrified, or when he or she is doubtful of self-worth, uncertain as to identity – then understanding is called for. The gentle and sensitive companionship offered by an empathetic person (who must of course, possess the other two attitudes) provides illumination and healing. In such situations deep understanding is, I believe, the most precious gift one can give to another.

(from *A Way of Being*, by C. Rogers)

Laziness, short-term thinking and self-obsession are the opposites of empathy. For James Fynn emotional intelligence that underpins being better at empathy stems from concentrating upon 'the right habits of mind' devoted to both *understanding* and living out *obligations* beyond our own desires. There is a resonance between this emotional intelligence and broader ethical issues so far discussed in that both ask us to be more personally aware when dealing with real situations in real, practical, friendly and wholehearted ways.

For instance …

Story

A murderer condemned to life in prison saved a man's life, was rewarded with a pardon and returned home. But he found his wife living with another man and a son who did not know him. He decided to end his life, but whilst he sat preparing himself to die a monk came along. The monk asked if he was OK, and the man told his story.

'I gave up all my wealth and possessions and have nothing to give you', said the monk. 'You want to die, but before you kill yourself, come and help me with my work. There is something I want you to do for me. Afterwards, you can do whatever you want'.

These words changed the murderer's world. At last he was no longer disposable. He agreed to help and later said to the monk:

'If you had given me money, or some other charity, I would have restarted my life of crime and killed myself, or someone else. But you asked me for something. You needed me'.

When faced with this person in distress, the monk gave nothing but asked for something instead. This is how Abbe Pierre's Emmaus Movement works.

How can empathy be taken into creative business? Aldo van Eyck shows one way:

Case Study
'BLIND SPOTS' OR EMPATHY IN ARCHITECTURE – IN-BETWEENING

The dominant approach to urban redesign is often based upon large-scale master plans that create 'blind spots' which forget the spaces that people have related to for generations.

In contrast to this approach the architectural work of Aldo van Eyck was inspired by the idea of 'in-betweening' borrowed from the ethical philosophy of Martin Buber. Buber believed that dialogue between people, and the 'between' realm was the key to developing the common good.

It is perhaps not surprising given van Eyck's commitment that he put these ideas into practice most effectively by constructing children's playgrounds – 734 of them in left-over bomb-sites in immediate post-War Amsterdam. He was very conscious of the parallels between effectively using these 'blind spots' for his in-betweening architecture and the lack of voice that children all too often have.

Van Eyck worked to put into physical form a collective empathy rooted in the 'everydayness' of people's lives. Rather than insisting on abstract plans, van Eyck's work took its cue from, in his own words 'ordinary language', 'real circumstances', 'lived-in conditions', 'experienced cases' and 'immediate contexts'.

Dignity and Humility

Witness the person returning home from a Florida holiday which a hurricane had hit – 'My holiday was completely ruined. I am not happy about this, I want to know what the Government is going to do about it!'

No, it was a hurricane! And anyway it doesn't work like that.

In contemporary society, this culture of 'entitlement' – the whole '… you are worth it …' thing is a facet of the more general consumerist culture of acquisition that chips away at more a dignified and humble attitude towards the World. Constant clamouring for what we can individualistically 'get' intrudes into everyday ethical skill. It is perhaps in our care-less relationship towards Nature that we have most clearly demonstrated our common neglect of dignity and humility.

In *To Have or To Be*, Erich Fromm recounts the differing reactions of two poets towards a flower in order to describe the acquisitiveness that lacks dignity and humility in favour of acquisitiveness.

Thinkpiece

Tennyson writes:

Flower in a crannied wall,

I pluck you out of the crannies,

I hold you here, root and all, in my hand …

Basho's haiku poem is,

When I look carefully

I see the nazuna blooming

By the hedge

Of this Fromm writes:

Tennyson reacts to the flower by wanting to have it. He plucks it 'roots and all' ... The flower itself is killed as a result of his interaction with it. Basho ... does not even touch it. All he does is 'look carefully' to 'see' it.

(from *To Have or To Be*, by E. Fromm)

The process of 'otherization', whereby certain groups create an identity out of differences creates distance and disparagements between groups is a common social form of indignity and false pride. It is rife within the creative and cultural world. In *What Good Are the Arts?* John Carey exposes the lack of dignity and humility too often found in the World of creative people.

Quotation

... persuad(ing) yourself that other people – because of their low tastes or their lack of education or their racial origins or their transformation into androids by the mass media – are not fully human, or not in the elevated sense that you are fully human yourself.

(from *What Good Are the Arts?* by J. Carey)

Overcoming the ludicrous self-obsession of our Florida holiday-maker involves overcoming the common tendency to put ourselves and our personal woes at the centre of the Universe. To treat others with authenticity, awareness, recognition and empathy involves lessening the importance one attaches to oneself. This is not easy but it is perhaps useful for developing effective contact lenses. This is close to the original meaning of *stoicism*, developed by the Stoic philosophers of ancient Greece. Epictetus speaks of this when he writes:

Quotation

The proper goal of our activity is to practice how to remove from one's life ... cries of 'alas' and 'poor me'.

(from *Discourses: Book 1*, by Epictetus)

Stoic philosophers made a distinction between what is *within* and what is *beyond* our power to influence. They believed that we should learn to accept with 'fortitude' what is beyond our power to change and things beyond this should not be used as a platform for blame of our selves or others when things go wrong. Striving to overcome feelings of anger, guilt or failure about things over which we have no influence is part of dignified personal conduct. But this does not mean they advocated a fatalistic acceptance of the ways things were. They believed that dignified acceptance of what is beyond our power to change helped to redirect attention towards that which we can change. This encourages us to develop a sense of 'orderliness' from which to develop our ethical creativity.

For instance, the postscript to *If This Is a Man*, by Primo Levi includes the following encounter:

Thinkpiece

Question – In (your) books there are no expressions of hate for the Germans. No desire for revenge. Have you forgiven them?

Answer – I believe in Reason and in discussion as supreme instruments of progress ... I prefer justice. Precisely for this reason, when describing the terrible events of Auschwitz, I have deliberately assumed the calm, sober language of the witness ... I have not forgiven any of the culprits, nor am I willing to forgive, unless he has shown that he has become conscious of his crimes ... an enemy who sees the error of his ways ceases to be an enemy.

(from *If This Is a Man*, by P. Levi)

And this brings us to ...

Less Ego: Friendship, Solidarity and Conviviality

For Aristotle 'genuine friendship' is central to an ethical relationship because it is 'grounded in good' and goes deeper into mutual responsibility than that the 'shallow' convenience of less wholehearted forms of associations. Aristotle thought of genuine friendships as 'completed' because their '... goal is wholly within the relationship itself' and not 'merely an instrument for some other or further end' situated somewhere within the individual ego. Echoing this, and some of the ecological evidence we looked at in Chapter 3, Bertrand Russell sees our capacity to love and the need to be beloved as an urgent and felt human need.

Quotation

... love is able to break down the hard shell of the ego, since it is a form of biological co-operation in which the emotions of each are necessary to the fulfilment of the other's instinctive purposes.

(from *The Conquest of Happiness*, by B. Russell)

The felt experiences of love central to human existence highlight the weaknesses of the more mainstream theories of ethics that hold out the possibility that everyday ethical skill will stem from the internal dynamic of the isolated individual.

Quotation

In the sense that the good is supposed to be something realizable in each separate person ... All such views, to my mind, are false, and not only in ethical theory, but as expressions of the better part of our instincts. Man depends upon co-operation, and has been provided by nature, somewhat inadequately, it is true, with the instinctive apparatus out of which the friendliness required for co-operation can spring. Love is the first and commonest form of emotion leading to co-operation ...

(from *The Conquest of Happiness*, by B. Russell)

Authenticity, personal awareness, empathy, dignity and humility do not reside in *individual bearing* but in *personal conduct in and through relationships*. These personal quests for grace can only truly succeed if others have dignity too. As Andre Gorz once said, 'your dignity rests upon the dignity of others'.

For ethical creative business motivated by an expansion of care, humble actions designed to bring dignity to others within the public realm are probably needed. For instance, Richard Rogers' discussion of urban re-design in *Cities for a Small Planet* and *Cities for a Small World* include the call for urban design to enshrine the possibility for a more dignified urban environment for all.

Global Lesson

CURITIBA: THE CITY AND QUALITY OF LIFE

Curitiba is a Brazilian city that once had the endemic problems of rapid expansion and shantytown dwelling that plague many cities in the developing world. But when the architect Jamie Lerner became mayor it made citizen participation the centre of its approach towards daily life and environmental policy.

The shantytown dwelling were mostly along the river bank and were plighted by uncollected rubbish and raw sewage in the river, so Lerner introduced a scheme to encourage public participation in the clean up by exchanging bags f rubbish for travel tokens, children's books and food. The mostly unemployed shantytown dwellers were offered opportunities to sell their own crafts and produce within specially built, non-corporate shopping centres. They can exchange their work time for rent and health care. The show piece of Lerner's re-development of Curitiba if the transformation of the city's disused quarry into a landscaped cultural centre that includes a 'university of the environment' built by the community from reclaimed telegraph poles. This approach espouses a view of the city as a place to meet our social, cultural and environmental needs as well as our economic needs.

It reminds us of the multiple facets of city life:

- **A Just City** – where justice, food, shelter, education, health and hope are fairly distributed and where all people participate in government.
- **A Beautiful City** – where art, architecture and landscape spark the imagination and move the spirit.
- **A Creative City** – where open-mindedness and experimentation mobilize the full potential of its human resources and allows a fast response to change.
- **An Ecological City** – which minimizes its ecological impact, where landscape and built form are balanced and where buildings and infrastructure are safe and resource-efficient.

- **A City of Easy Contact** – where the public realm encourages community and mobility and where information is exchanged both face-to-face and electronically.
- **A Compact and Polycentric City** – which protects the countryside, focuses and integrates communities within neighbourhoods and maximizes proximity.
- **A Diverse City** – where a broad range of overlapping activities create animation, inspiration and foster a vital public life.

(from *Cities for a Small Planet*, by R. Rogers)

If the capacity for everyday ethical skills is tied in some way to relationships then how can we develop a heightened sense of them by establishing spaces of attentiveness and sensitivity in and through *solidarity*?

In *What is Good?*, A.C. Grayling suggests that the creative spirit tends to be naturally open to an attitude of solidarity that comes from a sense of fellow feeling:

Quotation

... an attitude of appreciation and mindfulness, especially mindful of beauty, as central to a life well lived ... in which the World and our experiences of it are good things in themselves, and in which, when life is lived with attentiveness and sensitivity – an intellectual as well as sensory attentiveness that can be educated by practice ... it is not a long step from such an attitude to one in which attentiveness and sensitivity to others makes the life of the community good too; and it is hard to imagine such an attitude of mind being anything but tolerant and full of fellow feeling.

(from *What is Good?* by A. C. Grayling)

It is important that friendship, solidarity and conviviality can be *practised*. By 'practised', we mean both repeat attempts until we become good at it, and the bringing of solidarity and conviviality into the centre of on-going creative business based upon practical Reason, public authenticity and personal awareness. The contact lenses of solidarity and conviviality help us to re-see:

Quotation

... what we must do to use mankind's power to create the humanity, the dignity and the joyfulness of each one of us ... We can only live these changes: we cannot think our way to humanity. Every one of us, and every group with which we live and work, must become the model of the era which we desire to create.

(from *Tools for Conviviality*, by I. Illich)

Housing is one of the biggest material problems we all face. If we can do housing through becoming models of solidarity and conviviality, we could probably do most other things.

For instance ...

Case Study

CONVIVIAL HOUSING

The name of the late Walter Segal is now synonymous with self-build housing. Whenever people meet to discuss what they could do to house themselves, someone mentions the Segal system of quickly built, timber-framed dwellings which are environmentally friendly, and seem to generate friendship among the self-build groups that have succeeded in housing themselves this way. The attraction increases when we learn that they include men and women with every kind of background, and they often say that the experience changed their lives.

The heartbreaks and delays that self-builders experience are not to do with the process of building itself, but, as Walter Segal used to observe, are the result of the inflated price of land, the rigidities of planning and building controls, and the difficulty of getting mortgage loans for anything out of the ordinary. They are all made worse by the assumption of both regulatory authorities and providers of finance, that a house should be a full-finished product right from the start, rather than a simple basic structure that grows over time as needs grow and as labour and income can be spared. Segal's achievement was to devise a way of simplifying the process of building so that it could be undertaken by anyone, cheaply and quickly. He insisted that his was an approach, not a system, and he made no claims for originality or patents.

(from *Talking to Architects*, by C. Ward)

And this case study brings us to ...

Simplicity

The idea of simplicity as a lack, as an absence of plenty, as austerity, has taken a cultural hold. However, when discussing 'voluntary simplicity' in *Tools for Conviviality*, Ivan Illich exposes the inadequacy of this current view:

Quotation

'Austerity' ... has been degraded and has acquired a bitter taste ... (but Thomas Aquinas) *defines 'austerity' as a virtue which does not exclude all enjoyments, but only those which are distracting of personal relatedness. For Thomas 'austerity' is a complementary part of a more embracing virtue which he calls friendship ... it is the fruit of an apprehension that things or tools could destroy rather than enhance eutrapelia* (graceful playfulness) *in personal relations.*

(from *Tools for Conviviality*, by I. Illich)

Far from leaving a 'bitter taste', a reflection upon simplicity suggests a component for our broader everyday ethical skills. As Ernst Schumacher suggests in *Buddhist Economics*:

Quotation

It is not wealth that stands in the way of liberation but the attachment to wealth; not the enjoyment of pleasurable things but the craving for them. The keynote of Buddhist economics, therefore, is simplicity and non-violence. From an economist's point of view, the marvel of the Buddhist way of life is the utter rationality of its pattern – amazingly small means leading to extraordinary satisfying results.

(from *Buddhist Economics*, by E.F. Schumacher)

In *Stone Age Economics*, Marshall Sahlins contrasts the un-Reason of Western acquisition-based cultures with the practical Reason of more 'primitive' *gift economies* that ensure an intimate intertwining of material exchange and solidarity. He highlights the 'affluence without abundance' simplicity of these lives based upon movement and the portability of possessions. For these people an 'abundance' of material possessions are experienced as lack of freedom, as figuratively and literally a 'burden' to be carried. Simplicity-based gift economies are animated by a 'Want Not, Need Not' ethic of convivial solidarity where the Western ghosts of 'scarcity' and individualism have less purchase.

Quotation

... it was not until culture neared the height of its material achievements that it erected a shrine to the Unattainable: Infinite Needs ... The transfer of things that are in some degree persons and of persons in some degree treated as things, such is the consent at the base of organized society. The gift (on the other hand) *is alliance, solidarity, communion – in brief peace.*

(from *Stone Age Economics*, by M. Sahlins)

And we are beginning to witness all manner of experiments in sustainable simplicity within more contemporary creative business.

For instance ...

Case Study

SUSTAINABLE PARTYING

The average nightclub, with sound systems pumping and lights blazing three times a week, consumes 150 times more energy than a four-person family every year, according to Enviu, an environmental non-profit organization that's bringing green design to the dance floor—literally. The Netherlands-based group's research into sustainable partying has yielded plans for the world's first eco-club, which will use some fancy physics footwork to pump its dancers' energy back in to the house.

When clubbers press down on the spring-loaded floor, it dips about 2 cm and activates a flywheel, which starts to capture the kinetic energy of their bumping and grinding and convert it to electricity, similar to the electro-mechanical process of a handcrank or bicycle-back LED light. In fact, an early version of the floor used the stored power to light LEDs under tiles of the glass surface (at least 11 watts each) and let testers see sustainability in action. But the ultimate goal is to lose that gimmick and feed the main power grid of a club, says Michel Smit, general director of the Sustainable Dance Club project. Although the floor may never be able to power an entire club by itself, he added, its design could pave the way for the power-sucking nightlife industry to shore up its heating and cooling systems. Enviu even wants to convert dancer's sweat so it can flush a club's toilets.

These contact lenses, building on the ecological and philosophical discussions in the previous chapters suggest some 'intermediate' concepts that begin to link Big Theory to personal and public conduct. But now let's turn to even more practical, concrete thinking and look at how some of these ideas might be pinned down into professional attitudes and creative business actions.

The ideas we have offered so far about values and ethics for creative business can be taken up by individuals, informal and independent creative groups, established creative businesses or by larger cultural organizations. But cultural organizations and the professionals that run them, often on the basis of public investment do occupy a particular place within the cultural economy precisely because of this public investment. They often have a different set of public agendas and different demands placed upon them by politicians and policy-makers. Let's now turn to the question of values and ethics for the specifics of cultural professionals.

CHAPTER

6 *Seeing the Right Priorities: A Professional Lens*

Story

THE BED OF PROCRUSTES

Procrustes, in Greek mythology, was the cruel owner of a small estate in Corydalus in Atttica on the way between Athens and Eleusis ... (he) had a peculiar sense of hospitality; he abducted travellers, provided them with a generous meal, then invited them to spend the night in a rather special bed. He wanted the bed to fit the traveller to perfection. Those who were too tall had their legs chopped off with a sharp hatchet; those who were too short were stretched ...

... we humans, facing the limits of knowledge, resolve tensions by squeezing life and the world into crisp commoditized ideas, reductive categories, specific vocabularies, and prepackaged narratives, which on occasion have explosive consequences. Further, we seem unaware of this backwards fitting, much like tailors who take great pride in delivering the perfectly fitting suit – but do so by surgically altering the limbs of their customers ... The metaphor of the Procrustean Bed isn't just about putting something in the wrong box, it's mostly the inverse operation of changing the wrong variable, here the person rather than the bed ...

(from *The Bed of Procrustes*, by N. Taleb)

In *'Cultural Value and the Crisis of Legitimacy'*, John Holden has argued that the 'cultural system' is made up of:

- **Politicians and cultural policy-makers** – those at 'the top' who make strategic decisions about public investment and set out policies and plans for cultural organizations to implement.
- **Cultural professionals** – those in 'the middle' who run these cultural organizations who initiate and deliver upon either commercial or publicly funded cultural agendas.
- **The public** – those 'outside' who make up the cultural citizenry and participate in the cultural opportunities offered by cultural professionals.

This chapter considers values and ethics within the context of this 'cultural system' and what it might contribute to the key cultural role played by professionals running cultural organizations. It considers some practical ideas that might help cultural professionals working within the world of formal organizations *be good* and *do right* express public authenticity and expanded a sense of care from inside this organizational setting.

But we also consider some of the external issues that can affect what organizations are able and required to do. And often the most problematic of these external issues is the priorities, plans and agendas set by politicians and cultural policy-makers at 'the top' that make up the context within which cultural professionals work.

So let's start by considering this broad context and the particular turn it has taken over recent years.

Valuations Rather than Values: The Economic Lens

The lens that focuses upon economic valuations and impact of cultural organizations has come to the fore over recent years and is now the predominant conception of value within many aspects of the 'cultural system'. There are understandable reasons why advocacy for increased national public spending on the basis of the 'rise of the creative industries' was taken up at the organizational level by cultural professionals who advocate for local public investment on the grounds of the business support that their organizations could offer. A lot of people benefited from this. I am one of them.

There is nothing *inherently* problematic about this. The rhetoric of economic impact – job creation, business growth, the attraction of inward investment and cultural tourist spend – may be a useful component in national cultural policy advocacy. But when considering the more ethical *if* and *why* questions, cultural professionals might reflect that:

- Despite success in advocacy on the basis of economic impact over the past 10 years or so, the tap has been turned off almost immediately. The economic growth case does not seem to have really convinced the politicians and reliance on it can now be seen bringing inherent 'organizational risks' to sustainability.
- The economic lens undervalues what we are best at in favour of what we are less good at. Advocacy is best when it comes from strength rather than relative weakness. Whilst economic impact through culture may have general public benefits, constant overemphasis on it within the cultural arena puts the economic cart before the creative horse.
- The methodology behind the economic impact lens is shaky to say the least.
- It does little to address broader issues of public culture. If cultural organizations view things through the economic lens too often they risk being implicated in a broader 'democratic deficit' within the 'cultural system' and may miss opportunities for organizational innovation in their relationships with a broader constituency of creative practitioners and the public.

As the Bed of Procrustes story at the beginning of this chapter suggests, there is an inherent danger associated with a focus upon the wrong variables if this means that the 'system' requires that the people have their creative 'legs chopped off'.

Other Wrong Variables?

But as well as the over-economization of the 'cultural system', it perhaps focuses upon the wrong variable in other ways:

- It sponsors the growing 'cult of the expert' and 'cultural leadership' which does a disservice to any sophisticated idea of what public culture is and where it comes from.

- It drifts into the bureaucratization of cultural policy and governance processes so that it seems most concerned most with its own institutional survival rather than with organizational and cultural innovation.
- It consequently neglects the growing 'democratic deficit' within cultural policy that is periodically expressed within (often localized) 'crises of legitimacy' when cultural organizations could be contributing to the re-vitalization of democratic processes.

We are not alone in suspecting values analogous to the Bed of Procrustes have come characterize the 'cultural system' within which cultural professionals often work.

Quotation

Cultural policy is a closed conversation among experts. What culture needs is a democratic mandate from the public … cultural professionals have focused on satisfying the policy demands of their funders in an attempt to gain the same unquestioning support for culture that exists for health and education; but the truth is that politicians will never be able to give that support until there exists as more broadly based and better articulated democratic consensus.

(from '*Cultural Value and the Crisis of Legitimacy*', by John Holden)

Which can lead to …

Thinkpiece
ORGANIZATIONAL PATHOLOGIES

Apraxia is characterized by loss of the ability to execute or carry out learned purposeful movements … despite having the desire and the physical ability to perform the movements. It is a disorder of motor planning … (it is not caused by) in-coordination, sensory loss, or failure to comprehend simple commands.

Aphasia from the Greek root word 'aphatos', meaning speechless, is an acquired language disorder in which there is an impairment of any language modality. This may include difficulty in producing or comprehending spoken or written language.

(from *Wikipedia*)

Organizations can suffer from these pathologies:

- an organizational apraxia given loss of the ability to carry out purposes despite having the desire and organizational ability to perform these movements;
- an organizational aphasia given impairments in the ability to produce and understand spoken and written language from within itself or from the outside.

Questions of finding ways to relate to the public in an authentic way never really went away for many cultural professionals. Their work does a lot to direct our attention to the question of values in myriad ways that inspire us and teach our kids. A Procrustean Bed within the 'cultural system' is the opposite of expanded care and public authenticity. It suggests a loss of care-ful purpose in relation to the public that the 'system' is meant to serve. As we enter the 'age of austerity' cultural professionals might seek better ways to articulate what cultural and creative production and dissemination can do in terms of this broader idea of public culture.

And for this a sharper lens to re-envision more care-ful relationships might be useful for considering broader and deeper issues of values and ethics that go beyond the Procrustean Bed.

So Which Values? Whose Values?

Holden argues that three overlapping but distinct value orientations exist within the 'cultural system':

- **Instrumental values** – oriented towards '… the ancillary effects of culture', where culture is used to achieve social and economic purposes.
- **Institutional values** – the relative degree to which organizations value to 'in here' of institutional imperative and 'out there' of connections to the public realm.

Quotation

Institutional value is created (or destroyed) by how these (cultural) organizations engage with the public; it flows from their working practices and attitudes, and is rooted in the ethos of public service … Through its concern for the public an institution can achieve such public goods as creating trust and mutual respect amongst citizens, enhancing the public realm, and providing a context for sociability and the engagement of shared experiences.

(from '*Cultural Value and the Crisis of Legitimacy*', by John Holden)

- **Intrinsic value** – the values that are stimulated, reinforced, created anew through the subjective experiences and self-learning that cultural and creative works themselves can give rise to.

It is worth repeating the values other than economic valuation declared here:

- engagement with the public
- working practices and attitudes
- rooted in an ethos of public service
- creating trust and mutual respect
- enhancing the public realm
- sociability and shared experiences
- creating (self)-learning experiences.

It is perhaps something of a generalization, but according to Holden:

- politicians and policy-makers are primarily concerned with instrumental values;
- cultural professionals are primarily concerned with institutional values;

- the public are primarily concerned with the intrinsic values.

Because the cultural professionals are often required, often incentivized, often dragged into attending to the instrumental values of the politicians and policy-makers at 'the top', open and innovative conversations with the public at 'out there' are often neglected. What in an ideal, democratic situation would be an authentic *three-cornered dialogue* (in Martin Buber's sense) between all aspects of the 'cultural system' has become a *technical dialogue* (in Buber's sense) between instrumental and institutional values. This is why the word 'Institution' has become synonymous with 'bureaucracy' for many in the cultural sector, especially those who operate within loose creative networks that have come to mistrust the dead hand of Officialdom.

Cultural professionals interested in the expansion of care through their cultural organizations are then faced with three (at least) questions:

- How are *alternatives conversations* with 'the top' initiated?
- How do cultural organizations initiate *innovative processes* for more thorough-going public authenticity within 'the middle' of themselves?
- How can cultural organizations broaden their portfolio of partnership with creative practitioners and community voices 'out there'?

Organizational Reasonableness

In previous chapters we tried to draw out relationships between values and ethics and a 'this world Reasonableness' that encapsulates broader issues of practical Reason. This dimension also has implications for thinking about values and ethics within cultural organizations.

The instrumental valuation of culture exhibits the features of what the famous German sociologist Max Weber called *formal rationality* – a mind-set that tries to produce organization means to suit all ends. Formal rationality is an attitude that has strong echoes with the Bed of Procrustes. This is because it promotes a view of the (cultural) organizational task as:

- a series of abstract variables to be managed;
- a series of mechanistic relationships between 'inputs and outputs';
- a series of targets and 'impacts' conceived in purely quantitative terms;
- as something amenable to pre-set organizational tools and priorities.

This formal rationality mind-set tends to transform the organizational lens from one which pursues authentic, empathetic and simple *means to an end* into a situation whereby the organizational 'system' becomes *end in itself*. This approach tends to give us the everyday notion of 'bureaucracy' as an over-obsession with internally self-validating systems that are experienced as red-tape. And this usually has negative consequences, such as:

- **Ritualism** – insisting upon acting through pre-established organizational processes and performing ritualized tasks as an end in itself.

- **Goal-displacement** – mistaking pre-set processes and plans as the ultimate organizational goal.
- **Role displacement** – mis-appreciating one's professional role within the organization as enhancing one's professional position within the organization.

If managing the abstract variables, pursuing abstract 'inputs and outputs', measuring abstracted impacts and obsessing about pre-set strategies becomes the dominant mind-set of cultural organizations then it is likely that they are doing instrumental values rather than culture. Weber himself saw these 'dysfunctions'' as culminating in the 'iron cage of bureaucracy' and the 'disenchantment of the World', which cannot be good for cultural organizations.

In contrast to formal rationality, Weber defines *substantive rationality* as a course of action guided by 'a given set of ultimate values'. Whilst formal rationality might be organizationally 'unambiguous' – clear, predictable and routinized and substantive rationality might be 'full of difficulties' because it is inherently unpredictable, it is nevertheless an organizational mind-set that is 'oriented to ultimate ends'. As such it fosters an organizational approach better able to embrace flexibility of response capable of growing processes that can grow out of a wholehearted expression of the intrinsic values.

Organizational Tasks and Tools

This distinction between underlying organizational 'logic' raises issues concerning the relationships between organizational tasks and tools. Formal rationality is a means-orientation which tries to establish organizational tools *before* any particular task is considered. It sponsors a view that seeks to create a universal tool for suit all organizational tasks. Substantive rationality is an ends-orientation which allows the particular task to suggest the particular organizational tool as the task is *being considered*. If your organization is working in a highly predictable and routine environment and so values doing the same thing in the same way every time – running a bus service say, then a universal organizational tool might be a very good thing. But cultural organizations do not work in such environments. If cultural organizations try use universal organizational tools it is likely that they will be using the wrong tool most of the time. In contrast, substantive rationality suggests that you should use a hammer for nails and a screwdriver for screws.

There is no one best way to organize. In Section 2 we hope to make this abundantly clear when we consider the very informal, open-ended and highly networked nature of much of the cultural economy which most cultural organization relate too. It is more Reasonable to make a choice as to your organizational rationality when dealing with the public because it enables:

- a more nuanced conception of culture that is related to the intrinsic values of the quality of cultural life as the *end in itself*;
- graceful and dignified responses to the diverse, vernacular cultural values of different public voices;
- an organizational humility towards to the informal and temporary aspects of cultural life, creative production and non-official aspects of the cultural economy;
- an organizational simplicity that allows for evolution and growth through a symbiotic relationships with other organizations, creative businesses and the public who are no longer so much 'out there'.

Rather than obsessions with universal tools, a substantively rational approach to cultural organization tools suggests ...

Organizational Self-Awareness

We have already suggested in previous chapters that an expanded capacity for care relates as much to personal awareness as it does to the Big Philosophy of ethics. Ethical behaviour can be chosen, indeed for it to be real it needs to be chosen as the Ultimate Choice.

Organizational *being good and doing right* might also involve less 'ego' and:

- enough self-aware to reject seeing itself, its current structures, processes and priorities as the ultimate point of the organization;
- avoiding the adherence to 'extra' organizational meanings, which may be formally rational but not Reasonable for dealing with the changing world;
- avoiding organizational 'attack' and 'defence' positions within an unnecessary competition with the world 'out there.

A common problem with organizations is their tendency to become rather ossified spaces where the organizational goal becomes ensuring the organization gets what the organization wants. Relationships are the basis for expanded care-fulness and ethical behaviour and these always suffer in some way when there is too much ego. Like individual people, organizations might also need to 'get over themselves' so as to develop better *contact lenses*.

For instance ...

Exercise

ORGANIZATIONAL MEDITATION FOR GREATER SELF-KNOWLEDGE

We have already considered Buddhism for developing greater personal awareness and better contact lenses. It might also be useful for greater organizational self-awareness, and then perhaps greater public authenticity. It can help with organizational questions such as:

- **Who Are We?** – the basic question behind all meditative practice. Does the organization have enough self-knowledge?
- **Ignorance** – does the organization know itself well enough to allow itself to change? In what ways does it need to change? Is this something for public input and reflection rather than one based upon purely internal, practical and technical consideration?
- **Attachments** – are organizational attachments in the form of pre-set agendas, systems, priorities, plans and personalities blocking necessary change? Has the organization become an end in itself when it should perhaps be a means-to-a-bigger-end?
- **Aversions?** – are attachments within the organizational creating hostilities to the World 'out there', preventing it from seeing other possibilities and ensuring that it avoids greater success?

It is all very well suggesting that the organization learns to meditate so it can 'find itself'. But organizations are complicated things with lots of internally competing views.

Shopfloor Politics: Competing Organizational Lenses

There is likely to be lots of different lenses within the organization with different views of what is going on and what needs to happen next.

Organizations are made up of:

- **Formal structures** – hierarchies and other systems of authority that make decisions and allocate resources. Power and influence can be an aspect of the organizational *structure*.
- **Informal situations** – cultural, technical or personal aspects of organizational life that often mean that some people can have certain types of influence at certain times and not at others. Power and influence can be situational because it sometimes depends on the particularities of what is going on at that moment.

Quotation

... the political metaphor can ... be used to unravel the politics of day-to-day organizational life. Most people working in an organization readily admit in private that they are surrounded by forms of 'wheeling and dealing' through which different people attempt to advance their specific interests.

(from *Images of Organizations*, by G. Morgan)

So there is probably going to be an *inevitable* divergence of opinion between:

- various individuals and personalities
- different informal cultural groups within the organization
- 'management' and 'workers'
- different departments and their departmental priorities and plans
- different professional specialisms and areas of technical expertise.

Traditionally, organizations have tended to use one or other of the following 'templates' for dealing with these tensions:

- **autocracy** – the absolute power of one person/small group at the top;
- **bureaucracy** – the abstract power of the pre-established rules and processes that determine what happens;
- **technocracy** – the power of the technical expert or specialist;
- **co-determination** – combinations of interests into mutually beneficial organizational coalitions;
- **representative democracy** – elected representatives to speak for different interest groups within the organizations;
- **direct democracy** – everyone has a direct say/vote.

Clearly these different 'templates' can have an impact upon the organizations ability to make decisions, carry them through to effective work and maintain a clear sense of purpose. And the situation is only made more complex when broader questions of values and ethics within the organization are considered.

For instance …

Thinkpiece

ADAPTIVE OPTICS: SEEING POWER GAMES

In astronomy, adaptive optics enables lenses to see with greater clarity by re-focusing the light rays that have been disrupted and scattered by the Earth's atmosphere. When thinking about organizations a similar cultural disruption and scattering due to informal power games can lead the organizational lens to lose focus.

In the classic study *Power in and around Organizations*, Henry Mintzberg highlights 13 types of power games that get played in organizations:

- **Games to Resist Authority** – 'insurgency games' that sabotage the intentions of formal superiors in charge of the organization.
- **Games to Counter Resistance** – 'counter-insurgency games' that formal superiors use by creating more rules and regulations or finding means to punish informal 'take overs' or 'invasions' of authority.
- **Games to Build Power Bases** – which takes various forms:
  - the sponsorship game to connect oneself to a sponsor with formal authority to 'get higher up' the pecking order and so on;
  - the alliance game to build groups for power reasons;
  - the empire game to build coalitions with subordinates to make one's power role 'indispensible';
  - the budgeting game to use the control of resources to get one's way;
  - the expertise game to use (real or imaginary) perceptions of one's technical expertise to get one's way;
  - the lording game to continually exhibit one's authority so that it becomes universally accepted, and therefore expected.
- **Games to Defeat Rivals** – building short-term alliances for particular power games to defeat current rivals.
- **Games to Change the Organization** – which can be about either:
  - The strategic candidates game to inform on rivals so as to influence strategic developments for the future of the organization (you have to be in early for success in this game).
  - The 'young turks' game to form rebel groups as the key groups for the alternative futures of the organization.

Recognizing these power games for what they are can lead to something analogous to adaptive optics for cultural organizations by highlighting the source of unnecessary disruption and help with organizational re-focus.

(from *Power in and around Organizations*, by H. Mintzberg)

But cultural 'disruption and scattering' need not always be negative. Competing ideas and plans can also be the source of organizational creativity and innovation; a source of greater understanding of the complex world of different cultures 'out there'; and a way to motivate professional to express new strategies in collaboration rather than competition. The ultimate removal of competing organizational lenses is probably a non-starter, and anyway, if an organization does appear to have no differences of opinion within it this is probably due to staff being:

- scared by too much 'macho management' to raise their voice, which is likely to mean that discontent is bubbling under the surface somewhere – not good for commitment, morale or effectiveness;
- so ingrained into the way the organization already does things that they cannot see any other way – not good for creativity or innovation;
- no longer that bothered – not good for proactive expansions of care or public authenticity.

The role of the (cultural) manager is in part about finding ways to create organizational spaces so that divergence of values and opinions can be *healthy* rather than destructive. Rather than thinking about organizational ways to achieve a sterile 'organizational consensus' through a negative removal of different lenses, better to think about ways to create positive spaces for adaptive optics.

Because:

- the expression of values and ethics *within* that organizations comes to a large extent through the way it deals with, takes account of and tries to resolve divergent views within it;
- being organizationally good at values and ethics internally will probably mean that the organization will bet better at understanding expressing its values and ethics *externally* in and through its relationships with the public.

Managing divergent views into health brings potential benefit because:

- it can be the way people express themselves, 'blow off steam' and 'clear the air';
- it can lead to challenging conventions and accepted ways of doing things and so lead to innovation;
- airing divergent voices within the organization, as well as between organizational partners can lead to mutual organizational recognition and empathy.

This will therefore probably mean some form of organizational co-determination or internal democracy that enables:

- members seek and find ways to expand their capacity for care;
- confidence in expressing organizational values and ethics to the people its wants to work with;
- more creativity and innovative, and therefore being better suited to work within the ever changing realm of culture.

We see another facet of the natural coincidence of creativity and ethics. We will return to some of these issues in Section 3.

For now …

Exercise

CREATING A CARE-FUL ORGANIZATIONAL ENVIRONMENT

What can your organization do in terms of the following list of factors?

The Qualities and Nature of Internal Relationships

- levels of confidence and openness with each other – or not;
- levels of full and genuine consultations amongst the organizational membership – or communication by predetermined 'consultation-ism';
- degrees to which information upon which different views are constructed gets shared – or secrecy used for power games;
- degrees to which views are accepted on basis of logic and Reason – or forced through by more irrational power games.

The Uses of Internal Value Competition

- extents to which competition between views stimulates healthy sharing of a intermediate joint objective – or becomes divisive;
- extents to which competition is used to establish greater clarity of broad organizational purpose – or allowed to be seen as 'victory' and 'defeat';
- extents to which getting your view accepted is used to innovate – or allowed to become an empire- or career-building oriented.

The danger is that healthy competition becomes damagingly ingrained conflict, if:

- communication and consultation is experienced as overbearing dictat by some towards others;
- group identifications within the organization become too strong and generate too much on-going inter-group hostility;
- interpersonal friction between two or more personalities get in the way;
- inter-organizational competition grows into 'defensive positions' that go up the hierarchy and become 'departmental policy';
- rules, regulations and routines are used to enshrine power games as everyday 'organizational reality' that head-off other voices before they can be articulated;
- a culture is initiated so that the organization never hears much from that person/ group again, apart from about how unhappy they are.

(from *Undertsanding Organizations*, by C. Handy)

It is not possible to give any 'solutions' here, the devil is in the detail' But cultural organizations wanting to expand its external capacity for care-fulness – its institutional values, and relate better to intrinsic values in its relationships with the public might attend to these internal features of its organizational culture.

So far we have focused upon what happens inside the organization. But what about the public?

A Public Lens

Values and ethics *are* relationships. The 'closed conversation' between policy-makers and professionals limit this. However good the cultural organization is at adaptive optics and fostering healthy internal dialogue, the intrinsic values of the communities, groups and individual cultural citizens, and the creative ecology of practitioners 'out there' also need to be part of the general dialogue. Sensitive and intrinsic relationships to 'the work' should be mirrored by sensitive and intrinsic relationships with the public. Opening up the organization to public lens can be an even greater source of the organizational Reasonableness and innovation discussed above, as well as almost 'automatically' bringing public authenticity, credibility and public loyalty. This also starts to suggest that cultural organizations might be the place where the 'democratic deficit' that characterizes the 'cultural system' can be overcome. Furthermore, when we recognize the 'crisis of legitimacy' that the Big Economy and Big Politics as a whole is currently going through, we can begin to suggest that cultural organizations might be a large part of the solution. There is a lot to play for.

Organizational innovation, authenticity and democratic credibility might flow from cultural organizations with a re-focus upon:

- hearing publicly valued ends rather than mistaking internal means for these public ends;
- organizational friendliness, solidarity and conviviality rather than mistaking a hard-edged and 'cold' approach as organizational efficiency;
- sensitivity to that what people can do for themselves through active cultural processes rather than seeing public cultural provision as participation in what the organization has decided is valuable;
- facilitating the choice that everyday people would make if they had the cultural resources to actively pursue them, rather over-concentrating upon the distinction between the 'inside' and 'outside' of the organization;
- adopting a strategy of 'intermediateness' and 'appropriateness' for sensitive public responses, rather than an organizational insistence on the Procrustean Bed of changing the 'wrong variable'.

Ultimately all this suggests the importance of attending to the quality of the cultural journey *with the* public rather than the arrival *of the* public at organizationally defined ideas of 'cultural participation' and 'audience opportunity'.

Exercise
WHO SHOULD DECIDE?

Who should decide upon the priorities and plans within your cultural organization?

- Elected politicians who allocate public expenditure for certain things based upon their overall policies and manifesto commitments?
- Professional cultural policy-makers based upon their expertise and working knowledge of the Arts and Culture sector as a whole?
- Cultural professionals and stakeholders who have a closer relationship with the customers and 'clients'?

- Creative practitioners who have an intimate relationship with the work and will actually produce it?
- Members of the public who live the culture of the region/town/city which the organization serves?
- More specific members of certain communities that are affected by specific plans and proposals?

The predominant underlying instrumental and institutional values often at work within the 'cultural system' are perhaps not the best for any search for organizational Reasonableness, self-awareness and better relationships with the public. As well as trying to reframe institutional values for expanded organizational care, it might also be time to consider some fundamentally different values.

Ecological Values: A New Organizational Lens?

There is obviously an enormous and still a growing body of work that discusses the ecological movement. The current scientific focus upon global warming, the manifest implications for industrial, economic and energy policies and various cultural exhortations to live more sustainable are at the more well-known end of things.

But the ecological movement in its current form is a manifestation of much deeper and more long-term philosophical concerns with questions of values and ethics. It raises the prospect that values other than those we have so far discussed can be considered as a point of departure for cultural professionals thinking about ways to expand their capacity for organizational care.

In his book *Rising Tides*, Sprowers contrasts the 'mechanical world-view' that characterizes our predominant Institutions with what he call a 'new world-view' of ecological values. At its heart, this new world-view has grown out of a rejection of humanity's attempts to gain *mastery over Nature*, which has historically involved:

- the scientific interrogation of Nature;
- continued attempts at the management of Nature given its reduction to a series of 'controllable' variables (more Procrustean Bed);
- consequent reduction of the Natural world to the status of resources to be exploited;
- the commercial exploitation of these 'Natural resources'.

But at a deeper level this mastery of Nature agenda has been reflected in broader cultural forms:

- **Scientism** – the organization of the social and cultural world into a series of variables to be studied in isolation from the context that connects them and gives them meaning. This has historically involved a 'scientific arrogance' that to this day insists upon itself as the only way to have knowledge which has led to the organization and management of knowledge inside cultural organizations as much as anywhere else. Witness the triumph of the 'science' of economics within the cultural realm. These are the deeper roots of the instrumental values espoused by politicians and cultural policy-makers discussed above.

- **Rationalism** – the reduction of thinking and knowing to the confines of what is pre-established as 'rational'. In the cultural world this culminated in the insistence upon the Institutions of Culture (with a Capital C) as the only place for rational decision-making. These are the deeper roots of institutional values that inform setting for the rise of the professionalized cultural policy-maker, manager, 'leader' or 'expert'.
- **Individualism** – the growth of an 'atomization' which has given us the underlying economic and cultural assumptions that the individual is the only site rational choice which is expressed through The Market. Witness the decline in ideas of the common cultural good and the rise of the Consumer which suggests that perhaps not all intrinsic cultural values are necessarily progressive.

This leads to a deep sense of ethical de-skilling. One of the fundamental hallmark of scientism is the separation of 'facts' from 'values' due to the insistence that questions of values are non-questions that cannot really be studied using scientific methods, which they have already themselves insisted is the only real form of knowing. This has led to all sorts of institutional remits becoming 'technical' issues that pride themselves on having 'overcome' such non-questions. This is part of the deep roots of the ethical de-skilling of economists, professional politicians and their assorted 'special advisers'. Anyone not coming at things from a scientistic direction, such as us and our argument about value and ethics in this book can have their arguments debunked not because of what the argument actually says, but be the very fact of its lack of scientific credentials. This approach to the World can be summed up as saying, '*We cannot hear your argument, not because we can't hear your voice, but because we just do not recognize you as someone speaking. Better to stick to rational ways of seeing the World and look after yourself as an individual.*'

This fosters a cultural *alienation*. Our potential to be creative human beings together through humane relationships gets invested into scientism, rationalism and individualism that become alien power that stand over deeper ideas of human Reasonableness.

But the new ecological world-view is connected in various ways to the rejection of these alienating and un-Reasonable values. It embodies a:

- **Holism** – a reassessment of the multiplicity of cultural traditions and ways of knowing that go beyond scientism. Science (useful and insightful though it can be) is one amongst many ways of understanding and experiencing the world.
- **Openness** – an articulation of a wider panoply of values through the possibilities of non-hierarchical forms of inter-action and exchange between the human world of social and economic institutional world and the Natural environment.
- **Collectivism** – a sense of shared values in a common culture, common interests and forms of co-operation with and through Nature, and by extension with and through each other.

The new ecological world-view moves through a fundamental sense of *interconnection* rather than separateness alienation. It rejects the separation of 'facts' from 'Values' at the heart of scientism, rationalism and market individualism and values a return to the 'Ultimate Value' of healing the unnecessary and unhelpful dualism between:

- the material and the spiritual
- the 'realm of necessity' and 'the realm of beauty'
- the self and others
- Humanity and Nature.

This is the ecological articulation of the Ultimate Choice, because it seeks to overcome the false dualism between what 'is' and what 'ought to be'.

So What?

Why it is useful for cultural professionals to spend time looking at the deep value of the new ecological world-view? What can it add to our understanding and professional practice cultural organizations?

The first, fairly prosaic point germane the recognition that all organizations exist within an environment, and adaptation to achieve a good 'fit' with that environment is a key task of all organizations. Too often nascent assumption about what an 'organization' looks like prevent organizations from making relevant choices about how they will design and structure themselves. Not enough organizational self-awareness. We will look at the environment, the creative ecology and issues about achieve a good fit between organization and environment in Section 2.

For now, we could note that, rather than drifting towards hierarchy and top down management because that is how organizations are 'supposed to be', more conscious choices can be made about the everyday detail of cultural organization in terms of this fit with the environment. Indeed, one might say that the issues of values and ethics, and ways of relating to the public realm to achieve a more holistic way of working *necessitates* the search for alternative organizational tools.

For instance ...

Exercise

THE QUANTUM ORGANIZATION: INDIVIDUALISM, COLLECTIVISM OR DANCING?

In their book *The Quantum Society* Zohar and Marshall argue that the mechanistic world-view is a facet of a more general cultural overemphasis on separation, competition and conflict. It becomes a denial of our capacity for care-fulness because it fails to adequately:

... give any account of where life and consciousness belong in the universe (and) *leaves human beings with no sense or our place in the scheme of things.* (it) *... denies the reality and importance of relationships, establishing a precedent for conflict and confrontation and the pursuit of limited self-interest. As a model, mechanism cannot account for why people ever act on behalf of others, nor for any sort of social cohesion.*

In contrast, the holism within the ecological world-view can be used to envision different values and strategies for cultural organizations working through greater public authenticity:

We can think of society as a milling crowd, millions of individuals each going his or her own way and managing somehow, to co-ordinate sometimes. This is the Western way.

We can think of society as a disciplined army, each member a soldier marching in tight, well-ordered step. Individual differences as suppressed for the sake of the uniform performance. This is now a discredited (Soviet) collectivist way.

Or, we can think of society as a free-form dance company, each member a soloist in his or her own right but moving creatively in harmony with the others ... (this offers a) *new emphasis on unity and integration ... a whole new framework for understanding and fulfilling our potential as social beings...*

(from *Quantum Society*, by D. Zohar and I. Marshall)

- Which is the value that most informs your cultural organization – Individualism, collectivism or a new dance with the public cultural realm?
- How can your cultural organization encourage more public cultural 'dances'?

The Value of Professional Awareness

Another lesson that the new ecological world-view offers, along with the more general ecological metaphor is the idea of organizations as 'open systems' – systems that are able to change and adapt given the multi-faceted relationships with the environment. This is something else we explore in more detail in Section 2.

Before that, we should recognize here that the idea of the organization as an open system requires an openness on the part of professionals themselves. But the everyday realities of organizational life often seem like they are squeezing out any space for openness. This can be detrimental to the organization if it encourages cultural professionals to become too 'risk averse'. In Chapter 5 we suggested that being able to expand our capacity for care involves personal awareness and a reflection upon personal conduct, what we called contact lenses. Risk aversion within organizational can easily close down the space for this personal awareness and scope to choose personal conduct. In normal language, people become too worried about covering their back that they can't see the jobs so well. More Procrustean Bed. So perhaps there is organizational value in reflecting upon aspects of personal conduct.

The professional of Social Work goes through periodic crises and so has done more self-reflection than most professions. Cultural professionals might learn from this attempt at professional self-awareness. For instance, in her book *Critical Thinking in Clinical Practice: Improving the Quality of Judgements and Decisions*, Eileen Gambrill has suggested the following points that might help with thinking about professional grace, recognition and empathy, humility, dignity and simplicity:

- **Uncertainty in Making Practical Decisions Is Inevitable** – overlooking the uncertainty associated with practice and policy decisions may have a number of unfortunate effects, such as encouraging over-confidence that could result in harming rather than helping the client and overlooking effective service methods.
- **We Can Decrease Uncertainty by Drawing on Practice-Related Research Findings** – we can decrease (or reveal) uncertainty by drawing on practice- and policy-related research as well as research concerning decision-making, problem-solving, and critical thinking.

- **Transparency Is Important** – the value of being honest about what is done to what effect, and on what criteria decisions are based (is important) ... Only if we know what we did and what effects it had can we improve our decisions in the future.
- **Understanding Other People Is a Fallible Process** – (professional practice) ... is a deeply interpersonal process with all the false paths that are possible in trying to understand other peoples' point of view ... Recognizing this is vital for avoiding premature assumptions about what people mean, for example not checking out whether your understanding is accurate or not.
- **We Learn through Our Mistakes** – mistakes provide important feedback about how to do better in the future.
- **Recognizing Our Ignorance Is Vital** – only if we recognize out ignorance (what we do not know), which is vast, are we likely to avoid common mistakes that may harm clients.
- **Being Aware of Our Personal Epistemology Is Important** – only if you examine your beliefs about what knowledge is and how we can get it can you candidly examine your views about important (practical) topics.
- **Being a Professional Calls for Lifelong Learning Skills** – one of the joys and challenges of being a professional is continuing to learn.
- **Understanding Ourselves Is a Fallible Process** – (increasing self-awareness is important because) ... just as it is easy to misunderstand others, misunderstanding ourselves is an everyday experience that requires attention if we want to maximize opportunities to avoid harming clients and opportunities to help clients.
- **The Courage to Question the Obvious or the Accepted Is Vital** – what seems obvious or popular or exciting or new may by wrong, as shown by the (organizational) history of harming people in the name of helping them.

We started this section by talking about spectacles, so let's end in the same way with an example of ethical creative business case that encapsulates all that we have tried to say.

Global Lesson

HELPING 1BN OF THE WORLD'S POOREST SEE BETTER

It was a chance conversation on March 23 1985 ... that first started Josh Silver on his quest to make the World's poor see. A professor of physics at Oxford University, Silver was idly discussing optical lenses with a colleague, wondering whether they might be adjusted without the need for expensive specialist equipment, when the light bulb of inspiration first flickered above his head.

What if it were possible, he thought, to make a pair of glasses which, instead of requiring an optician, could be 'tuned' by the wearer to correct his or her own vision? Might it be possible to bring affordable spectacles to millions who would never otherwise have them?

More than two decades after posing that question, Silver now feels he has the answer. The British inventor has embarked on a quest that is breathtakingly ambitious, but which he insists is achievable – to offer glasses to a billion of the world's poorest people by 2020.

Some 30,000 pairs of his spectacles have already been distributed in 15 countries, but to Silver that is very small beer. Within the next year the now-retired professor and his team plan to launch a trial in India which will, they hope, distribute 1 million pairs of glasses ...

If the scale of his ambition is dazzling, at the heart of his plan is an invention which is engagingly simple.

Silver has devised a pair of glasses which rely on the principle that the fatter a lens the more powerful it becomes. Inside the device's tough plastic lenses are two clear circular sacs filled with fluid, each of which is connected to a small syringe attached to either arm of the spectacles.

The wearer adjusts a dial on the syringe to add or reduce the amount of fluid in the membrane, thus changing the power of the lens. When the wearer is happy with the strength of each lens the membrane is sealed by twisting a small screw, and the syringes removed. The principle is so simple, the team has discovered, that with very little guidance people are perfectly capable of creating glasses to their own prescription ...

The implications of bringing glasses within the reach of poor communities are enormous, says the scientist. Literacy rates improve hugely, fishermen are able to mend their nets, women to weave clothing. During an early field trial, funded by the British government, in Ghana, Silver met a man called Henry Adjei-Mensah, whose sight had deteriorated with age, as all human sight does, and who had been forced to retire as a tailor because he could no longer see to thread the needle of his sewing machine. 'So he retires. He was about 35. He could have worked for at least another 20 years. We put these specs on him, and he smiled, and threaded his needle, and sped up with this sewing machine. He can work now. He can see ...'

(From *The Guardian*, 22nd December 2008)

But in the end there is no real *conclusion* to this section on values and ethics. It's just a choice. But it is your choice. It's the Ultimate Choice – a choice about attitudes towards creativity, business and organization that offer new spectacles for Juliette, and for you, and for the rest of the World.

Having used various lenses to raise issues of values and ethics to consider the *if and why* questions within creative business, let's now turn to questions of *how and with whom*. We hope that looking for new spectacles for Juliette has raised some useful and interesting ideas to help your thinking about what your creative business *to be for*. But this thinking does not help that much with how you are going to do it. So let's turn to some more practical issues.

A distinctive feature of the cultural economy and the daily lives of creative businesses is the relatively high significance of informal networks and the implications this has upon the thinking and doing of both the creative and business bits of creative business. The centrality of informal creative networks can brings great spaces for mutual creativity and provide very welcome resource to enable things to happen that would otherwise not. But their unplanned, haphazard and sometimes chaotic nature raises specific issues of understanding them, being able to work effectively within them and avoiding any dangers the informality and haphazardness brings.

Let's stop thinking about spectacles now, and consider fish, horses and other animals that inhabit the creative ecology of various networks.

Networks

7 *From a Competitive Economy to a Creative Ecology?*

> ### **Proverb**
>
> ### **THE LAST ANIMALS TO DISCOVER WATER WILL BE FISH**
>
> This Japanese proverb holds that because fish are totally surrounded and immersed within water, have constant contact with it, and have nowhere to be out of water, they are not able understand that which they are in. This is an intriguing notion. It is all too easy to misunderstand that which we are immersed in and think we know best, if we are insufficiently self-reflexive to get a handle on it.

In Part 1 we explored the question and values and ethics for creative business. We now turn to the question of creative networks. But how do these two themes relate to each other? We have already shown that a central assumption of this book is the idea that whatever you do in creative business, whichever strategy you adopt, whether you work with purely commercial motives, for the public sector of in a more independent way, you will be working in and through *relationships* with lots of other people – other businesses, organizations, customers, stakeholders, friends and colleagues.

Many discussions characterize businesses as isolated entities inevitably in competition with everyone around them. Whilst competition is a factor, so is collaboration and co-operation. Unless we recognize these network relationships of collaboration for what they are, we will be unable to understand them and utilize them for mutual creativity.

We will be like fish in water.

But more than this, it might be that the cultural and creative economy embodies embryonic changes that exhibit alternative forms of cultural and economic exchange that makes understanding and working within network collaboration increasingly important for business. This is what takes our general argument from one of values and ethics and into the theme of networks. It seems that the concerns with being good and doing right in creative business and with better contact lenses are connected to the creative concern of working within alternative relationships. The relationship building that is good for ethics appears to be good for creativity, and networks of like-minded people are combining in collaborative relationships that are, in places at least replacing the competitive economy as the general context for creative business. These networks of relationships can be seen as a key resource, perhaps even *the* resource for creativity and business. But they can be easy to miss, because we tend to be 'in them', like fish.

The New Cultural Economy

General context setting is always useful. It is always useful to stand back from the details so as to 'see the wood for the trees'. The general economic context within which creative business operates is characterized by some very broad changes:

- In recent years Western economies have shift towards the 'knowledge economy' or the 'weightless economy' given the relative rise in economic importance of *ideas* carried by cultural stuff such as images, experiences and meanings, in contrast to previous industrial eras that were defined by the production of *things*, such as ships and cars (that is 'heavy' industry).
- Industrial success based upon big-ness and mass production came from low *marginal unit costs* (how much it costs to make one more of the same thing) and therefore *economies of scale*. But because being able to respond quickly to changed conditions is now more of a competitive advantage for some businesses in the new cultural economy, e*conomies of scale* are being replaced by *economies of speed*. Big-ness is a positive disadvantage here and being small and flexible is often better for creative business. The dinosaur is being super-ceded by the shrew because it is more adaptable.
- This has brought quite a radical change in the experience of work for some people. Jobs with a capital 'J', the one thing you do all week for years and years of your working life is, for some people at least being replaced by a *portfolio career*, whereby people do different things at different times during their working week. This is an especially prevalent feature of creative business.
- This means new opportunities for creative self-employment are opening up. This brings the need for fairly constant skills development, such as being your own manager or 'marketing department', but it also brings new tensions. Dealing with all its demands of business can close down your 'head space' for the creativity bit. 'Investing' in the creativity bit is often as necessary as developing the business bit.
- The economy has globalized. It will probably be an increasingly common feature for businesses of all sorts to be working with overseas partners or customers. For many big and medium sized firms this has been the case for many years. It is likely to be the case for all of us before too much longer. This brings the need for new professional skills as creative business increasingly flows around the World; as technology increases global communications; as people come and go around the World much more frequently; and as images have an increasingly global reach.
- Technological will continue to have a fundamental impact upon how creative products, service, experiences and meanings are conceived of, produced and disseminated to the public. It is way beyond our knowledge and competence to say anything approaching exhaustiveness on this, but clearly the rise of peer-to-peer business models such as the Open Source Movement and edge-to-edge distribution networks such as YouTube are by-passing traditional centres of cultural production and distribution and changing things fundamentally.

All of which tends to mean ...

The Rise of Creative Networks

These broad contextual changes have meant that creative networks and network-based business relationships; flexible ways of organizing and working; temporary, informal or 'DiY' forms of trading; and non-proprietary ways of exchanging and disseminating output are increasingly necessary and viable business models for creative business. There is ample evidence out there that creative networks are increasingly self-reflexive and see themselves as simultaneously *alternative cultures* and *alternative business strategies* that articulate a wider range of choices about your business strategies. Many creative businesses seem intent on moving from an orthodox competitive economy towards a creative ecology of co-operation and collaborations. Many creative businesses seem intent on becoming creative *alt-repreneurs* (alternative creative entrepreneur) rather than orthodox business entrepreneurs.

So as these new network 'structures', attitudes and personal styles come to the fore getting a clear understanding of creative networks; building your stock of network connections; helping to mutually grow vibrant networks; and becoming skilled at engaging with others all become key points of development. In the rest of this section we will try to offer ideas to help with this *understanding, appreciation* and *practical engagement* with creative business networks.

A Creative Ecology

A way getting a handle on the way networks operate, and the different ways in which they might be important for creativity and business is found in the concept of the *creative ecology*. If one imagines a natural ecology, then one immediately sees that it is defined by an inter-dependence of different species, sometimes competing and sometimes co-operating, but always rely upon a relationship of some kind with other species. We also see that their success or failure is to a large extent dependent upon the degree to which they find the right 'fit' with their environment, and that the health of the ecology as a whole is a major factor effecting everyone's future.

We also see different 'species' which begins to suggest that within the creative ecology different strategies for creative business will be needed. Whilst fish might be a bit stupid and lack perspective; horses run on courses, and 'horses for courses' is a way of suggesting you will probably need different strategies for different objectives. But in the context of the creative ecology, we also talk below about lots of other creative business 'species'. Foxes and hedgehogs; ant colonies and slime mould; about avoiding sharks and snakes; polar bears and alligators. We also extend the ecological metaphor to consider 'droughts and 'Climate Change'; incubation and a creative business 'extended family'; symbiosis and migration; and organizing coral reefs.

The Mixed Cultural Economy

But the cultural economy is a particularly mixed economy. Each of the three sectors that make up the mixed cultural economy – the commercial sector, the public sector and the independent sector – will have inter-dependencies and networks *within* them. In that sense each will have its own *intra-ecology* (*intra* – as in within). But significantly the mixed cultural economy is also characterized by constant overlap and cross-fertilization *across* the three sectors. In this sense there is also an *inter-ecology* (*inter* – as in between). So being able to deal with these various aspects of this ecology of network relationships involves learning to understand the rationale and speak the language of each whichever species you belong to.

So by way of general contextual points about the cultural economy as a whole, let's start by briefly considering in a more systematic way the different relationships one might need to consider as part of the overall network of creative business relationships within the mixed cultural economy as a whole.

Let' start by looking at some broad contours of the creative ecology.

The Commercial Sectors

The commercial sector is made up of all those established individual businesses working and trading in the creative industries.

In its broadest sense the different phases a business needs to go through if it is to take an original idea and become sustainable business involves networks of relationships at all stages:

- **Origination** – the 'light bulb' moment, the original creative idea that will form the basis of the creative business. As we explore in detail below, this nearly always comes from the access to creativity and innovation that open networks can offer.
- **Research and Development** – this might be project planning, proto-typing or piloting the initial steps necessary to turn an original idea into something that 'works' and that someone will want to buy. Creative networks are often the best place to do this 'trying out' work'.
- **Production** – producing that which you have made 'work' so that you can take it to market. This could be a product that you get manufactured, a service that you get ready to deliver on a regular basis. Taking things from ideas to actualities will nearly always require being good at sustaining working relationships with other businesses or organizations.
- **Marketing and Distribution** – once you are ready, you need to tell everyone else what you have and what you can do for them, and then you need to get it to them how and when they want it. The word-of-mouth marketing that networks offers is often the best kind of marketing.
- **Customers and Consumption** – getting paid, and taking care of your customers. On-going relationships are again central.

But over and above these basic points, there are other general aspects of business relationships that run alongside and span all aspects of creative business.

These are:

- **Legal Protections for You** – intellectual property, trademarks, patents, registered design and copyright – relationships with the World 'out there'.
- **Legal Protections for Others** – regulations, health and safety, data-protection – relationships with the people 'in here'.

- **Contract Clarity** – a whole host of contracts which form the basis of creative business relationships – relationships with suppliers and customers.
- **Access to Finance** – for start-up, for growth, for reinvestment and dealing with depreciation – relationships with funders or the bank.
- **Management Accounts and Cash Flow** – once the money starts to come in, making sure you are getting paid, and you are paying your bills on time – relationships with those who owe you money.
- **Technology** – getting the right communications kit at the right time and thinking about e-business strategies – relationships with the work and the Web.
- **Infrastructure** – getting the right workspaces for production, accessing the right space (physical and virtual) for public dissemination and marketing – relationships with your workspace and the landlord and so on.
- **Employment** – employing other people, formally or informally – relationships, often complex and moving with the people who formally work for you, or who 'work' for you informally.

There are a lot of networks and relationships to think about!

The Public Sector

The public sector is made up of all those cultural institutions and agencies that invest public money into the arts, culture and creative industries. Sometimes they operate at a national level, and sometimes they have regional offices. The public sector also includes local government and universities who often fund or support arts, cultural and creative industry oriented projects.

It is probably true to say that the role of the public sector is more significant within the cultural economy than it is in most other industrial sectors. Their public expenditure on art and culture are seen as socially important for the same reason expenditure on other public services, such as health and education is important. This is because sole reliance upon market mechanisms and individual private spending often leads to 'market failure' culminating in an 'under-provision' of culture whose general quality would probably suffer. It is useful to understand this point, particularly if you are thinking of applying for public funding for a particular creative business project, because it is a fundamental to the public sector rationale. It is fundamental if you want to have a relationship with them.

Exercise

MARKET FAILURE

Imagine if street lighting was left to individual consumers to buy. If we had to directly pay for our own street lighting, we would only switch these lights on outside our own homes when we as individuals wanted to use them. We would not want other people to get free benefits from which we were paying for. As a result, streets would not get lit most of the time, even though the lights were actually there. The market would 'fail' to satisfy a public need, and as a result streets would be less safe at night, cars would crash and crime would increase.

We can make a similar argument when it comes to culture. There is a public good to be found in culture, in the ways we as a civilization speak to ourselves, make challenging art, innovative design and use culture for education. Reliance on commercial markets alone would likely mean that much of the art and culture that got produced would be the stuff that promised mass sales and a profitable return to the private companies that invested in it. Clearly some innovative work can come from this route, but equally clearly we cannot rely on markets and the profit motive alone. To do so would threaten us with art and culture of the lowest common denominator. We would end up with a 'MacDonaldized' culture. Without being overly sniffy about reality TV and soap operas, we need more than this!

With this background logic in mind, ask yourself what your work could do for the public next time you are thinking of making a grant application:

- Why should public institutions fund you to do what you want to do, if no one else is going to benefit?
- How can you translate what you want to say to the public sector into a language you are both happy with?
- How can your grant application be seen as an investment of public money into the public good?
- How does your grant application alleviate cultural 'market failure'?
- My mum is not that interested in the arts, so why should her tax contributions be spent on it?

There are plenty of good answers, but it is good if you know what they are as far as you are concerned.

The underlying rationale of the public sector tends to revolve around two inter-related agendas, one being *Cultural Development*, and the other being *Culture AND Development*.

The *Cultural Development* agenda is focused upon *artistic and cultural* developments to allow for more cultural stuff to be generally on offer, so getting more people to engage. Its focus is upon:

- developing high quality, innovative and challenging work;
- developing the cultural capacity of a particular region or city;
- increasing audience opportunities and creating more cultural participation;
- developing the cultural infrastructure.

The *Culture AND Development* agenda is related, but different. This tends to see the arts and culture as a vehicle for *other types of development*. It sees the arts and culture as being a useful tool to help foster *social and personal* development to:

- overcome disenfranchisement and social disaffection, and thereby fostering social inclusion;
- enable the articulation of greater cultural diversity;
- encourage health, well-being and 'quality of life';
- contribute to community development and urban regeneration in a broader sense;
- contribute to educational development.

But as we have already noted in broad outline, the *Culture AND Development* agenda is also heavily linked to using the arts and culture for *economic* development. The national government's economic lens on creative business is often mirrored at regional and local levels by the view that creative business can be a useful vehicle for local economic development because it contributes to:

- business start-up and growth;
- job creation;
- attracting inward economic investment into a region in the form of expenditures by cultural tourists;
- an economic multiplier effect, whereby cultural events stimulate lots of 'knock on' economic activities as suppliers, service providers, retailers, food and drink sellers get more work/customers as a direct, indirect and induced effect of the original cultural activity.

Being good at networking with public sector agencies and getting funding or investment from them for your particular creative project requires an understanding of these things, because this is what the public sector wants from the relationship. When you are talking to a public sector agency about funding, pretend that they have absolutely no interest in art and culture whatsoever. They do have such an interest, but pretend anyway. What else can you do for them other than give them the work that you already want to do anyway?

The Independent Sector

The independent sector is made up of freelancers, sole-traders, volunteers and a whole host of creative people who, whilst often producing high level work, are neither formally established as a business nor working for a public sector organization. These creative 'businesses' are often hidden from official statistics, and the people involved appear to formally work in lots of other industries (education, retail, hospitality). But they are nevertheless a key aspect of a vibrant cultural economy.

Whilst the commercial and public sectors operate within formally established business or organizational structures, the defining feature of the independent sector of the broader cultural economy is its *informality*. It is no one's 'job' to do this creative business stuff. Independents do things because they do things. Their informal ways of working and intimate relationship to the work tend to suggest it is a much more *organic* place. In this sense the independent sector are often at the very heart of vibrant local creative ecologies. We explore the nature of the independent sector and its self-organizing, organic nature in details in subsequent chapters in a way that tries to offer practical insights and advice about 'being good' at networks.

So wait a little while for that.

For now it is useful to recognize that the view of creative business relationships developed so far is rather 'orthodox'. It might be that the increased significance of the creative business sector in general, and the informal independent sector in particular is evidence of shifts in the nature of the cultural economy and our very conceptions of what 'work', 'business' and 'the economy' mean. It might also be that the embryonic changes represented by the organic nature of the independent sector's focus holds new lessons about where creativity and innovation are increasingly coming from. The informal networks of the creative ecology may be driving the transformative moment we have touched upon above, or might be a reflection of it and the development of a new value orientation. Either way it does seem that as the values and ethics that underpin creative business shift so do is motivations and 'structures'.

Let's briefly consider a couple of examples of this before we get into a deeper look at the creative ecology of networks and some more practical creative business issues in the next few chapters.

Social Capital Networks

Networking can be understood specifically as a resource for business. It can be understood as a stock of this resource, as something that you can 'invest' in for business reasons, as the 'deposit account' for your creativity and business and as something that you can 'draw upon' to develop your business.

We can grasp all this through the idea of *social capital*.

Resources and ways to access them can be broken down as follows:

- **Human Capital** – the resources you as an individual have access to simply on the basis of your own knowledge, training, education, experiences.
- **Physical Capital** – the resources you have access to on the basis of owning equipment, hardware, buildings and so on.
- **Financial Capital** – money in the bank and other financial assets for investment.

Over and above these resources, there is:

- **Social Capital** – access to a resource that comes from having contacts, knowing people, developing working relationships and collaborations.

This type of resource is often the way you can circumvent the all too common lack of the other three types of resource. This can develop into a kind of '*share market economy*' whereby knowledge, expertise, equipment and time for favours are traded.

However, social capital is a particular type of resource:

- It is relationship-based and so it requires the development of your stock of social capital through networking. You may need to 'invest' in building up this stock of social capital.
- The management of social capital resources requires attention and social skills. Social capital differs from other types of capital in that it does not just sit there until you want to use it, like money or equipment. Social capital can be summed up with the phrase 'if you don't use it, you lose it'. Relationships need to be nurtured and fertilized if they are to be useful and usable resources.

The Play Ethic

Pat Kane's book *The Play Ethic* offers a new view on the relationship between work, creativity and everyday life. His basic idea is that the 'play ethic' is replacing, or perhaps should replace the 'work ethic' as the defining feature of how we rethink the relationship between our life and our creative potential.

Our normal (Western) perception tends to suggest that all 'serious' activity needs to be focused upon identifiable ends authorized by some external 'proper' motive (being professional, making money, doing your 'Job'). But the play ethic suggests different directions. In the 'modern rhetoric', the play ethic can be about the expression of the self and the freedom to explore through the work-play thing. It can be understood as:

- **Play as Progress** – play in education, play for healthy self-development.
- **Play as Imagination** – play as art, as scientific hypothesis, as culture making.
- **Play as Selfhood** – play as the expression of identity.

But also, in the 'ancient rhetoric', the play ethic is about 'joining in and taking part'. It is more about how we come together as social beings to take part in social and cultural networks. So in this version of play, there is a sense that it is more about sharing and following the rules of the group, and less about the (modern) idea of the individual self. It can be understood as:

- **Play as Power** – the contest of players in sport, markets, law, war, even culture.
- **Play as Group Identity** – the play of the carnival and the binding rituals of community.
- **Play as Fate and Chaos** – the play of chance, risk and experiment.

To this, Kane wants to add 'play as frivolity'. From a 'puritan' (industrial business) perspective this common source of criticism sees play as, quite literally, a 'waste of time'. But puritans are not very well known for their creativity. The drag of the nineteenth century 'work ethic' tradition is still around. But maybe it is becoming an increasingly inappropriate social convention, especially for working in creative business. Are not the clear distinctions between 'work' and 'play'; work spaces and social spaces; work time and leisure time tending to get increasingly blurred?

Which brings us to ...

The Gift Economy

In *The Gift: How the Creative Spirit Transforms the World*, Lewis Hyde anthropological perspective highlights a different rationality underpinning possible economic exchange within the public realm. In his chapter on *The Gift Community*, he discusses how Gift exchanges occurs across broad cultural networks and between kinship groups in such a way that it becomes more significant than the exchanges between two individuals. It moves in a '... circulation wider than a binary give-and-take'. This broad idea of the Gift helps to create and sustain the sense of cohesion within networks that actually enables such networks to form and stay together. But there is also a personal motivation for people in Gift exchange. It enables people to demonstrate 'standing' as a network member through how much they are able to pass on to other network members so as to forge new relationships rather than pursue standing through how much they are able to accumulate and demonstrate difference and separation through conspicuous consumption or conspicuous leisure.

The Gift economy hints at a new economic vision of how individuals are able to demonstrate and establish something about ourselves in the eyes of neighbours by circulating out Gifts from the things they are able to control as their own resources. This might take the form of material things but can equally be time, ideas, knowledge and experience. As Lewis Hyde writes:

Quotation

When we say that someone made a name for himself, we think of Onassis or J. P. Morgan or H. L. Hunt, men who got rich. But Kwakiutl (a North American Indian tribe) names are ... meant to indicate social position. And here are some of them:

- *Whose Property is Eaten in Feasts*
- *Satiating*
- *Always Giving Blankets While Walking*
- *For Whom Property Flows*
- *The Dance of Throwing Away Property.*

(from *The Gift: How the Creative Spirit Transforms the World*, by L. Hyde)

This might seem a little exotic and not really connected to modern creative business. But Hyde also talks about modern scientific communities as Gift communities, where new ideas and knowledge are freely given out and circulated so that the whole of the community can benefit from the ensuing synergy of the joined-up thinking that becomes more possible. Gift exchange is guided by mutually creative situations that the Gift community finds itself in. He contrasts the Gift 'temperament' with the formal, contractual and money-related 'temperament'.

Quotation

One temperament assumes generosity while the other assumes a lust for power; for one our passions are social, for the other they are selfish.

(from *The Gift: How the Creative Spirit Transforms the World*, by L. Hyde)

And this might be the central point. The Gift economy is a way of forging, sustaining and growing the *social* relationships which can form a much more solid basis for business relationships. And creative ecologies seem to form and maintain these kinds of Gift networks all the time. It might be the Hyde's ideas of the Gift economy is a way of expressing the fundamental characteristics of new business models for creative business based upon the heightened creativity that comes from mutual, collaborative networks and organic relationships rather than the traditional business emphasis upon an overly competitive view and mechanical relationships between individuals. As we will explore in the rest of this section and in Section 3, networks do seem to be the places where a lot of creativity comes from, and they do simultaneously seem to be animated by a different value system.

This sense of Gift economy may increasingly emerge within creative business networks.

For instance ...

Case Study

THE OPEN SOURCE MOVEMENT

The Open Source Movement provides an interesting case study in that it highlights how ...

... groups of computer programmers (sometimes very large groups) made up of individuals separated by geography, corporate boundaries, culture, language, and other characteristics, and connected mainly by telecommunications bandwidth, manage to work together over time and build complex, sophisticated software systems outside the boundaries of a corporate structure and for no direct monetary compensation ... '.

The Open Source collaborations appears to be able to maintain a sense of itself as a 'culture'; it appears to somehow use social and cultural means, though on-line communication, to police itself and maintain quality control over the software it produces; ensure that the software that gets produced is made freely available to all; avoid, what it sees as the unnecessary duplication of work and the wasteful use of time and resources that commercial competition often means; motivate and incentivize Open Source members to take up the necessary tasks, not for financial gain but for creative fun and recognition; assign a division of labour of sorts across the community – all this through an informal and voluntary agreement to collaborate that is motivated by a belief in the values and 'politics' that underpin the Open Source processes.

It is also claimed that, for a variety of reasons Open Source represents a new and increasingly viable business model, in that it overcomes some of the problems of large, clumsy and overly rigid corporate entities that are holding to non-collaborative methods that are becoming increasingly inappropriate within these fluid and ever changing markets.

(from *The Success of Open Source*, by S. Weber)

Exercise

'THE GIFT MUST STAY IN MOTION': PAY-IT-FORWARD

Is the Gift economy a useful source of:

- business network building
- creativity and inspiration
- on-going business sustenance.

for your creative business and the relationships it will need?

For instance:

So long as the Gift is not withheld, the creative spirit will remain a stranger to the economics of scarcity ... the Gift is not used up in use. To have painted a painting does not empty the vessel out of which the painting came. On the contrary, it is the talent which is not in use that is lost or atrophies, and to bestow our creations is the surest way to invoke the next.

(from *The Gift: How the Creative Spirit Transforms the World*, by L. Hyde)

Pay-it-Forward is the opposite of the often unspoken assumptions inherent in doing favours for each other. That is, I do something for you on the assumption that you will somehow 'pay it back'. Pay-it-Forward rests on the idea that you do something for someone else without any other strings other than they agree to Pay-it-Forward out to someone else, by doing something for a further random stranger, who passes it on again … and (hopefully) so on. Remember the Open Source Movement that created Linux that now rivals Microsoft Windows? This way, the favour gets paid forward through an ever increasing circuit of people, rather than being locked up within a relationship between the original favour giver and favour receiver. Pay-it-Forward keeps the Gift in motion.

Pay-it-Forward for creative business is a slightly different version of this basic model in that it cannot be so general and deliberately anonymous. But the process remains essentially the same. Learn to spot opportunities whereby you can do a random, unrequested favour for another business and/or collaborator, on the basis that they will pay-forward a favour for someone else.

And just see what happens.

But why would you want to do this? What is in it for you? Well, firstly that is not really the point, it is just good for your creative soul. But there is potentially a lot in it for you, because potentially everyone benefits, and you are part of everyone.

Apart from these reasons, it is good fun, makes you feel good about yourself and so is far from the completely selfless act it might at first appear.

So if you have the time, energy and you think it would be useful for your creative business, maybe you should give Pay-it-Forward a try.

Give yourself:

- A **'Timeframe'** – decide how many times per week you want to do a Pay-it-Forward. Once a week, once a month?
- A **'Budget'** – this could mean any resource you control and can afford to give away – ideas, knowledge, advice, time, work in progress.

Remember, it is about a play ethic, but it can have serious, profound and sometimes quite beautiful outcomes.

The idea of the Play ethic and the Gift economy brings us to …

The Creativity of the Creative Ecology

The ecological metaphor underpinning the idea of the creative ecology is also useful for drawing our attention to the constant rebirth and renewal necessary for creativity and innovation. The Natural World is characterized by movement – the only thing that is certain is uncertainty; the only thing that is constant is change. Life is best characterized as *a journey* rather than *arrival points* that will last forever. Networks are a great source of new ideas and insights that can bring the creativity that helps us to deal with change and uncertainty and turn them into opportunities. Creative business success may ultimately come from how one copes with the *reproduction* of your creative business 'DNA', and how it is passed on from one 'generation' within your creative career to another. Such reproduction might be a vital component for an overall creative business strategy because *adapting* to ever changing environments are not only basic survival strategies, but is key to creative business *health* and *growth*.

As we explore in lots of different ways below, creative networks are often the best place to find the new information, insights and ideas upon which this adaptation, health and growth rests. Creative networks are not just networks made up of creative people. They are in and of themselves creative places. Their collective minds, possibilities for collaborative relationships and stores of easily accessed knowledge and information means that they can sometime do what individual businesses or organizations cannot do. For a variety of reasons, creative networks embody the intriguing idea that best source of creativity is the co-operative space *between* individual human brains rather than the space *inside them*.

Let's test this proposition.

Asylums, Trains and a Superfly

Story

ARE YOU MENTALLY ILL?

In the 1960s two social psychologists named Rosenthal and Jacobsen decided to test the way mental health institutions diagnosed people. To carry out this test they recruited a number of post-graduate students from the university they worked at, for whom there was no reason to suspect, prior to the test, any reason for a diagnosis of mental health problems. Without informing the mental health institutions, they sent these people as 'ringers' in amongst all the other people who had been sent through more standard medical channels, to be diagnosed.

They found that a high percentage of the 'ringers' were getting diagnosed as being mentally ill! After the test, they informed the various institutions of the testing they had carried out. The institutions got a bit irritated with them for doing this kind of test, claiming it was sneaky and unprofessional.

OK, said Rosenthal and Jacobsen, we'll give you another chance. They informed the various institutions that they would be sending another group of 'ringers' over the next year, along with a challenge to pick them out from the rest of the people being diagnosed. After the year in question the mental health institutions presented the information about 'ringers' that they had found, and why they knew this time that they were 'ringers'.

But Rosenthal and Jacobsen had not sent anyone!

The institutions had picked out 'ringers' who had simply been people who had been sent through the normal mental health channels, who in the 'normal' course of events did have some signs of some mental health issues.

The test showed, in both directions, that simply by the fact of finding oneself in the 'diagnostic situation' one can get caught up in a whole institutional logic which often has no real bearing upon what one 'really is'. Other research allied to this has shown that whatever reaction or behaviour one exhibits within these 'diagnostic situations', it can get put down as 'problem behaviour'. If one complies with the institutional requirements and 'behaves oneself', it gets put down as apathy and resignation; if one resists and stands up for oneself, it gets put down as resistance, transference and self-hatred. Remember Jack Nicholson in *One Flew over the Cuckoo's Nest?* That is precisely what the book/film is about. Once he is there, there is no possible escape from the 'total institution'.

The point of all this is that it provides a warning about how easy it is to end up becoming absolutely defined by the situation you might find yourself in, in spite any particular person characteristics you might have.

This little story shows us that creativity might require strategies to resist a similar process. Remember, it is creative business we are talking about. It is easy to get defined by the 'diagnostic situation' of the *business bit* and neglect the *creative bit*. If your business becomes too much of a 'total institution' and you neglect the creative bit for too long, your creative business is likely to suffer because:

- morale, commitment and inspiration will suffer;
- you might start to miss opportunities and not keep up with the latest developments, trends, technologies and so on;
- you might start avoiding risk and trying out new creative things, processes, areas of business, because …
- you will have 'too much to lose'. For instance, life's financial commitments (mortgages and kids) that you were able to set up because of business successes will start to define you and become your 'diagnostic situation';
- things will start feeling like 'just a job'.

The 'opportunity costs' associated with doing things in a particular way comes from this inevitably precluding doing it another way and missing creative opportunity. If the 'costs' associated with doing business in one particular way or one particular area is greater that the benefits from carrying that through then it is unlikely to be good for business for very long. If being wedded to a particular creative process means that you have to miss out on a more creative process as a result, then it is unlikely to be very creative for very long.

You could start to turn into your own opposite, and business strategies that were once part of the solution will start to become part of the problem'. Fish may or may not be mentally ill, who knows, but they are definitely 'in'. But as Rosenthal and Jacobsen show it is easy to get submerged within a particular creative universe and become unaware of the 'water' you are in. So it is good for creative business to have regular *refresh* buttons, and to have strategies where you can protect your creativity. Networks are usually the solution to this potential problem. They are the place where the refresh button can be regularly pressed.

But how can you get a handle on this way of thinking? How can you think about what you haven't thought about yet? That's crazy. Lateral thinking exercises can sometimes be useful.

Seven Sources of Creativity
NO. 1: LATERAL THINKING

In his book *Serious Creativity*, Edward de Bono identifies seven key sources of creativity. For de Bono lateral thinking, a term he made famous is the most significant. This can be approached as a systematic creative technique that can be practised and learned. For de Bono, lateral thinking comes from an expanded perception of the tools (concepts, theories, ideas, ways of measuring) so as to be better at 'stepping sideways' beyond those particular tools to use other, perhaps better ones.

For instance …

Exercise
LATERAL THINKING

There are two trains travelling towards each other at 50 miles per hour.

Train 1	Train 2
50 mph	50 mph
>>>>>>>	<<<<<<<

And they are 100 miles apart.

There is a 'super fly'. This fly is very quick. As the trains are travelling towards each other to meet in the middle, it is flying from the front tip of Train 1 across to the front tip of Train 2, then back again and back again … all the time the two trains are travelling towards each other, the fly is constantly going back and forth as the two trains get closer to each other.

And the superfly is travelling at 967 miles per hour.

The question is this …

How far does the superfly fly until the 2 trains meet in the middle?

You have 2 minutes to work it out, and the answer is just below, so no cheating.

LATERAL THINKING ANSWER

The answer is really very easy once you have thought laterally.

Because the question is presented to you in terms of speeds (50 mph, 967 mph) and distances ('how far … ?' and 100 miles apart), you are encouraged to work out the answer using the same tools. But in this case they are not the best tools.

Instead …

The trains are 100 miles apart, travelling towards each other at 50 mph. So each train travels 50 miles and is going at 50 mph.

So the whole encounter takes 1 hour to happen.

The fly is travelling at 967 mph, and does so for the 1 hour it takes for the whole encounter to happen, so how far does the superfly fly? It travels 967 miles. Easy!

The point is ...

It is sometimes useful to step outside the parameters given to you by the question as it is originally presented. In this example you are given this original question in terms of speed and distances, once you introduce the element of time from outside the question, arriving at the answer becomes much, much easier.

And this is why it is lateral thinking. Step sideways rather than try to proceed in the direction you have been handed by the parameters of the question as it is originally set.

So lateral thinking exercises can sometimes be useful sources of creativity and innovation because they encourage you to step outside your normal way of doing things, outside your 'comfort zone' and come at things from completely different angles from those which you normally use to approach particular issues.

It is not possible for anyone to tell you what these different angles actually are, you will need to work that out for yourself, but stepping outside your usual ways of working is a good place to start – whether in terms of techniques, the use of technology, your usual collaborators, your usual motivations and definitions of success ... whichever, it will give you a new 'map reference' points for new navigation routes within the creative network.

Perhaps the fundamental reason that creative networks are so important for creative business is the way they can become sources of lateral thinking. They are made up of all sorts of other creative people, coming at similar issues to the ones you are struggling with from all sorts of different angles. These people offer great ways of helping your thinking to step sideways, to step 'out of the box' and find different angles from which to see things. Creative networks can help you find people who can help you to step beyond the parameters set by your 'question' and find other tools with which to think about things.

That is why it is so useful to understand, appreciate and become skilled in creative networks as the 'water' that your creativity is in. That is the benefit of seeing this 'water' for what it is that we intend to explore deeper into these issues of understanding and growing in the rest of this section.

So let's look at this in more detail.

CHAPTER 8 *How to Make Friends and Influence People*

Proverb

SAVING FOR THE FUTURE

There is a saying ...

The best place to store surplus food is in the stomach of a neighbour.

This protects you against the future, and means that both you and your neighbour have a better world to live in.

We have begun to set the broad context for thinking about and understanding creative networks, and the potential implications they have for creative business. Now let's think about some practical and concrete issues that might help with being good at networks and networking within one's daily creative business life.

A Non-Zero-Sum Game

A 'zero-sum' game is a contest that has finite rewards because there has to be a winner and a loser. In a 'non-zero-sum' game everyone can gain just by taking part, the rewards are not necessarily finite and the players can make a better context to live and work in just by playing together. Balancing the pursuit of one's individual ends against acting together with other people is a powerful idea if you, we, get the balance right and invest in our relationships with the people around us as well as ourselves.

Quotation

A 'non-zero-sum' sensibility is similar to what Ivan Illich called conviviality, which he defined as:

... the autonomous and creative intercourse between persons, and the intercourse of persons with their environment ... I consider conviviality to be individual freedom realised in personal interdependence and, as such, an intrinsic value.

(from *Tools for Conviviality*, by I. Illich)

As we have already touched upon, one of the great myths about business is that it has to be competitive and selfish. But creative people do networking all the time. It is just part of who we are and what we do. We tend to be constantly talking about our work, our new ideas and our plans. But if we fail to appreciate those processes for what they are, fail to get a handle on them, reflect back upon them and try to mutually grow them, they can elude us. It is useful to understand the value of creative business networks as potentially expandable spaces like the 'non-zero-sum' game.

In a practical sense:

- Good networking can mean you do not necessarily need to buy that new piece of kit, or learn that new skill right away as you know someone who can help you out in exchange for a return favour. This makes creativity and business quicker, cheaper and means you can compete for business across a wider field by getting and staying together when it is strategically smart to do so.
- Good networking inevitably brings greater capacity to work well in cross-disciplinary creativity, which is likely to be increasingly necessary in the future. Good networks can be a great R&D department for your business that can allow you access to great sources of mutual teaching, learning and informal professional development in all sorts of unforeseen ways.
- Broadening networks out, away from the usual networking with the usual suspects can open up new areas of development. Like its basis in lateral thinking, it is counter-intuitive but useful to remember that you do not know *who* you need to know, because you do not know them yet. Allowing for the spontaneous and unplanned aspects of networking to happen can bring things to creativity and business that fully worked out plans cannot.
- Deepening networks brings prolonged, intimate and trusting creative relationships that are often good for creativity, for business and for a whole host of other 'emotional' reasons.

Exercise

MAPPING YOUR NETWORKS NO. 1: 6 DEGREES OF SEPARATION

This well-known idea suggests that everyone can make contact with everyone else in the world through already existing contacts, through only five steps. If I asked you to contact an astrophysicist living in Chile, the '6 Degrees of Separation' game would require you to use your best existing contact (maybe you know another kind of scientist living in your home town), and then pass the task on to the next person, who might know another scientist living in South America, and so on. Together we get closer, until someone gets there.

This asks us to consider the notion that everyone is connected to everyone else through only six moves. A useful 'philosophical' notion for thinking about networks. If this applies to the whole world, surely you can make contact with other creative people within your own local business setting!

MAPPING YOUR NETWORKS NO. 2: KEEPING YOUR ACCOUNTS

- Keep a diary for one week of all your creative and business contacts. Then ask all these people to give you six other contacts they have networked with, then get six contacts from these six contacts – to begin drawing your own '6 Degrees of Separation' map.

> • Try setting yourself a local 6 Degrees of Separation task to take you somewhere you have not been to yet, but would like to go. Then use your existing networks and contacts to get there.

All this suggests that good networks include an element of *breadth* (knowing lots of people a little), and *depth* (knowing a few people who you might work with more intensively). Both aspects of networks can be very useful. Networks can be about contacts you have with people over many years who are fundamental to what you do and how you do it (creative collaborators, joint authors, members of a creative group); or they can be quite fleeting relationships that come and go, are not necessarily experienced as meaningful but are vital to business nonetheless (with suppliers and service providers, and perhaps with customers).

The Creative Ecology: Some Basic Biology

In the previous chapter we first raised the notion of the creative ecology. Let's start to explore this biological metaphor in more detail.

As we touched upon earlier, if one thinks about the Natural world we see a very complex, diverse and rich network of intimate and moving relationships of mutual interaction that supports different 'species'. Some feed off others, some create the right environment for others, and some have symbiotic relationships with others. Most importantly of all perhaps, all species rely upon the mutually created and sustained health of the ecology as a whole for their continued survival, health and growth. In unpacking the ecology metaphor for a more detailed understanding, we would like to suggest a few ideas that might seem at first glance a little strange and exotic and perhaps not immediately relevant. But if you give them a little time they can be quite revealing.

Auto-poesis and Self-organization

Firstly the concept of 'autopoiesis' elucidates something about how 'structures' like informal networks come about.

The traditional workplace is usually a professional organization devised and structured prior to any one individual becoming involved within it. It is 'organized' from the outside and run by managers, strategists or policy makers who have the authority to make decisions about what occurs within it. One the other hand, creative ecologies tend to be characterized by high levels of informality, flexibility, and openness. This suggests an 'organizational structure' which is very different, one that is difficult to grasp if we use traditional notions of the workplace, business, organizational structures and management.

The concept of autopoiesis refers to:

- 'Auto' = 'self ...'
- 'Poiesis' = 'the making of ...'

It is a way of talking about entities that are self-creating, that grow out of themselves according to an internal dynamic, that emerge from the processes that actually make the entity itself. Autopoietic structures are *specifically not* the result of any external organization or management.

They are self-organizing.

In the biological sciences the concept of autopoiesis is used to describe how a cell is formed. Internal cellular processes (chemical messages between nuclei, mitochondria and so on) can only take place once the cell boundary is formed. But it is these internal cellular processes which themselves create the cell boundary. In this strange world the internal processes create the structure, whilst simultaneously the structure allows the internal processes to happen. To ask which comes first in a uni-linear (orthodox business planning) way is to ask the wrong question, it cannot be understood in that way because the structure and the internal processes co-create each other from the inside, rather than being the result of decisions or plans made from the outside.

The same might be true of the creative ecology. Particular internal network processes and emerging collaborations often create a sense of cultural place or 'structure', which other network members can then recognize and come into. Once these cultural 'structures' get recognized as the places to be, people congregate to create more internal network processes. As with the biology of the cells origins, internal processes create the 'structure' and the 'structure' allows internal processes, and the intertwining of these two factors enables organic growth of the creative ecology.

What all this shows is that creative ecologies emerge out of the activities of the people involved in making them for themselves. The 'structure' *is* the process, which *is* the 'structure'. Such networks are inherently 'do it yourself' (DiY) born of the *doing* of creativity and business by the *selves* in the network, rather than being formed on the say-so of someone outside them. The fact that creative networks are self-organizing, DiY spaces suggests that you can build them yourselves, just by doing them. They can emerge out of themselves.

Examples for the Natural world provide case studies in this *emergence* that does not require central organization. For instance …

Case Studies

In August 2000 a Japanese scientist named Toshiyuki Nakagaki announced that he had trained an amoeba-like organism called slime mold to find the shortest route through a maze … Despite its being an incredibly primitive organism (a close relative of ordinary fungi) with no centralised brain whatsoever, the slime mold managed to plot the most efficient route to the food … Without any apparent cognitive resources, the slime mold had 'solved' the maze puzzle.

Local turns out to be the key term in understanding the power of swarm logic. We see emergent behaviour in systems like ant colonies when individual agents in the system pay attention to their immediate neighbours rather than waiting for orders from above. They think and act locally, but their collective actions produce global behaviour.

(from *Emergence*, by Steven Johnson)

Slime mould and ant colonies are not unified organisms in the traditional sense. They are completely lacking in centralized co-ordination mechanism (management) or unified plans. However, they can form something that looks like a unified whole, respond to their environments and reach effective solutions through an internal network of small, internal micro-messages.

But how do you get good at doing this? If creative ecologies can be understood as emergent, what constitutes a creative business attitude that fits with working in the ecology?

We need to look at *emergent behaviour*.

Emergent Behaviour as Professional Development for the Creative Ecology

Given this somewhat strange ecological discussion of autopoiesis, slime mould and ant colonies, it might be useful to recap that this is just a series of ecological metaphors which are useful for understanding the internal characteristics of creative networks. But these metaphors do also suggest a different mind-set, and that a particular professional attitude for developing new everyday skills may be useful.

In his book *Emergence: The Connected Lives of Ants, Brains and Cities*, Steven Johnson has provided a check list of the key features of emergent behaviour that can also be a check list of ways to think about engaging with creative networks. Treat these points as an exercise, and test yourself to see how good you are at these things. It is professional development!

- **More is Different** – so the more micro-difference involved in a creative network, the livelier they will be. Look for diversity in your networks. The higher the levels of difference among the creative people who come together, the more everyone can draw upon. Be an ambassador for difference; be a DiY 'dating agency' to bring creative people together and maybe everyone will benefit.
- **Ignorance is Useful** – as we touched upon above, you never know what you need to know, because de facto, you do not know about it yet. As Bertrand Russell once said, there is no such thing as 'useless knowledge'. Be open to new learning experiences that may not seem directly connected to your own creative work, you never know. Fish think they know all about everything, but they don't even know about water yet!
- **Encourage Random Encounters** – because networks are highly decentralized systems they rely heavily on random interactions. Without these haphazard encounters you will not stumble over new and innovative ideas, new collaborators and new possibilities so often. Without random encounters you will not get the usefulness from difference and 'ignorance'. Not everything needs to be planned, if it is you might 'plan out' innovation and adaptation to new environmental conditions.
- **Look for Patterns in the Signs** – stand back from the detail and look for common patterns across the network. Pattern detection is a sure sign of intelligence and a learning business, and it also encourages collaboration. It is useful to recognize that you and potential collaborators may be working on similar issues, even though the overt and substantive content of each creative business might at first appear very different.

- **Pay Attention to Your Neighbours** – The most important one. Local information leads to global wisdom. Paying attention to the micro-communications coming from your neighbours encourages joint understanding and mutual growth. Be convivial, take time for each other, have a coffee and a chat, it is work!

Seven Sources of Creativity

NO. 2: CHANCE, ACCIDENT, MISTAKE AND MADNESS

For Edward de Bono, the history of ideas is characterized by accident, mistake and wrong turns that led someone down new avenues that turn out to lead to success. These accidents, mistakes and wrong turns are significant for creativity because they take people outside their normal ways of working and thinking.

Business Practice within the Creative Ecology

Zooming back out we can see how emergent behaviour might help with the wider issues of working with the creative ecology, Issues such as:

- **Natural Selection and Adaptation** – since Darwin we have known that adaptation is the key to species survival. The orthodox business world has known this for many years. 'Diversification', being a 'learning organization', 'managing change', getting the right fit with your 'business environment' have been the various ways in which big business has talked about this to itself. Emergent behaviour may be an appropriate way for creative businesses working within networks to recognize this. We will return to these issues below.
- **Preparing for 'Climate Change'** – within the creative business ecology the scope and speed of environmental change is increasing – globalization and technological change are two of the more fundamental facets of this. So whilst you need to adapt to change as ever, you might also increasingly need to adapt to ever more fundamental changes in the very nature of the game. This is analogous to 'Climate Change' in its more usual articulation – that we will need to think more often about doing things in a qualitatively different way. So spotting the nature of the changes and 'believing the science', and then finding good response will likely be needed more often. Economies of speed will only come if you are ready for this as an opportunity, otherwise it will become a threat.
- **More Migration, More Often** – creative businesses with a portfolio career need to constantly be 'on the move' in and around the various parts of the creative business landscape. Again economies of speed are replacing economies of scale as a successful business strategy only for those who can travel easily.
- **Symbiosis** – creativity is increasing about inter-disciplinarity and bringing people together from different backgrounds with complementary skills. So creative businesses can grow and develop together through symbiosis. Networks are good places to do this and emergent behaviour is of the 'business plan' for achieving it.
- **Exploring Natural Habitats** – different 'species' within the creative ecology can only thrive if a suitable, shared and sustainable 'natural habitat' is there. Different

creative networks tend to inhabit certain key places (physical or virtual) that form this 'natural habitat' or 'watering holes'. These spaces allow the creative ecology to become itself. Emergent behaviour helps to find out where these autopoietic places are and so you know where congregate and get 'plugged in'.

- **Knowing the Keystone Species** – in the Natural world, keystone species form the basis for a sustainable ecology. They are usually what the other species feed off. In the cultural world however, things are not always so predatory and 'feeding off' each other can be a more collaborative, symbiotic thing. So in creative ecology the keystone species may be groups, events or organizations that allow lots of other things to grow around them and survive. Again, use emergent behaviour to find out which autopoietic spaces work for you and get 'plugged in'.

Game

THE KEVIN BACON GAME

In 1941 the American movie actor Eddie Albert appeared in The Wagons Roll at Night, which starred Humphrey Bogart. Little known today outside the United States, Albert was never a major star, although he was nominated for an Oscar for his role in Roman Holiday (1953), alongside Audrey Hepburn and Gregory Peck … . But Albert was still acting in Hollywood films fifty years after The Wagons rolled. In 1989 he appeared in The Big Picture, with Kevin Bacon.

Albert is thus the crucial link which gives several famous actors of yesteryear a low 'Bacon Number'. The Bacon Number is the smallest number of movies that link the actor in question to Kevin Bacon, where each movie brings two actors along the path. Albert has a Bacon Number of 1, because he has actually appeared in a movie with Bacon. Bogart has a Bacon Number of 2; he appeared in a movie with Albert, who appeared in a movie with Bacon. James Dean and Ronald Reagan also have Bacon Numbers of 2 thanks to Albert, who starred with them both in the TV drama I'm a Fool (1953). Errol Flynn is linked to Bacon via Albert, who shared the screen with Flynn in The Sun Also Rises (1957) … .

The aim (of the Kevin Bacon Game) is to find the shortest route to Kevin Bacon – the lowest Bacon Number – for any movie star. But why Bacon? Like Eddie Albert, he became renowned for appearing in a large number of films in which he was not the star. In this way he links many bigger and lesser names in a network of movie relationships. Kevin Bacon, it was ironically suggested, was the real centre of the Hollywood industry.

The surprising aspect of this game is just how densely connected the network is. Something like 15,000 distributed films have been made since motion pictures began, together featuring about 300,000 different actors as named cast members. And yet nearly all of these can be assigned a Bacon Number (BN) of 3 or less. The last time I checked there were 1,686 actors with a BN of 1 (that is, those who have appeared in a film with Bacon), 133,856 with a BN of 2 (those who have appeared with someone who has appeared with Bacon), and a phenomenal 364,066 with a BN of 3. As of October 2003, the average BN for all movie actors is 2.946.

(from *Critical Mass: How One Thing Leads to Another*, by Phillip Ball)

The Kevin Bacon game shows us two key things – firstly seemingly large and disconnected networks are actually densely interconnected; and secondly certain people (Eddie Albert and Kevin Bacon) seem to find a place at the centre of such networks. So …

> - **Exercise 1** – Play this game with a few friends – identify someone from within your creative network to replace Kevin Bacon and together work out your various 'Bacon Numbers'.
> - **Exercise 2** – Who do you want to work with most? What is your 'Bacon Number' with this person/organization? How can you actively reduce this 'Bacon Number' number?

- **Critical Mass** – in the Natural world, this refers to the size that an ecology has to be in order to be sustainable. It highlights the need for the ecology to be large and fertile enough so that the 'birth' rate (creativity, innovation) that replaces different species is greater than the 'death' rate (personal burn-out, movement back into the formal system, retirement). If Natural world ecologies are not at or above critical mass, the death rate is higher than the birth rate and eventually the health and viability of the ecology spirals down. In the creative ecology a similar point can be made. If the creative ecology is at or above critical mass then there will be enough going on to keep people engaged and attract new generations. If it is below critical mass then people will look for other places to be and the creative ecology will not be sustainable. Emergent behaviour suggests that you look to bring new generations of people into the ecology to achieve 'critical mass' as part of your 'ambassadorial duties' to the network you have benefited from.

Business Clusters

The more traditional end of business studies has recently begun to talk more about 'business clusters'. But this is subtly different from that which we are discussing here. The key difference between a creative ecology one the one hand and a business cluster on the other seems to be the intensity of creative business interaction. Creative ecologies as discussed above are often about quite intensive and sometimes prolonged creative collaboration. The idea of business clusters on the other hand is often used to describe how and why businesses congregate together around a pool of skilled labour or a transport network. Silicon Valley would be a good example of a classic business cluster. This may or may not lead to intimate creative collaboration, but such features are not the driving force behind their development in the same auto-poietic way that creative ecologies seem to develop. This is not to say however that business clusters are not a potentially important feature. There may be formal business networks that can add to your stock of social capital if you get involved:

- Whilst creative networks are often informal and stem from just knowing friends of friends, formally organized business networks, trade associations and the like run by various business support projects may also offer tangible benefits for training, research and professional development.
- Whilst creative networks are often about practitioner-to-practitioner interaction, business clusters that aid networking between businesses and customers are equally useful.

- Whilst creative networks that help bring together different sectors of the creative industries are useful, so are those that bring together creative industries and other industries in wider 'networks of networks'.
- Creative networks have a tendency to be very local and specific to a place, whereas more formal business networks often have a much more ready-made (inter)national reach.

It is sometime useful to approach these broader business clusters and the broader networking encounters they offer.

But this does imply a different idea of networks and networking.

Networking as Business

Everything so far in this chapter has tried to present some ideas about that anatomy of creative networks. This has assumed that there is a degree of shared passion in something that two or more people have in common and can immediately 'trade notes' on to form the basis of further talking and maybe creative collaboration.

But this is not always the case.

Sometimes networking involves standing in a room with a group of strangers with whom you have absolutely nothing in common, drinking free white wine paid for by an organization which has put on a 'networking event'. Sometimes it can become 'speed dating' where you are asked to say something about yourself for two minutes so that you can 'get to know people'. Whilst there are benefits in these (potential) encounters, they will not be especially useful for developing your creativity or business if you cannot engage in the situation fully. Good contacts for your business will not come from standing on the edge of the room. Networking for business is best understood as something you *do*, rather than something you are *in*.

Some people just seem to be good at this kind of networking and others seem to find it difficult. So maybe learning some 'networking skills' for specifically business networking could be useful. I am not always that sure about these 'skills'. They can appear a little Machiavellian at times, and some people do seem to approach networking as a kind of military campaign. But they might be useful nonetheless, as there are different ways of doing networking and different reasons for doing it. Because networking cannot always come from a 'natural' encounter you may need to prepare for other types of network situations so at least you can go into these encounters with some confidence. Having some clear ideas about what you want from the encounter can help with this. Think of it as business, it is not your whole identity that is on show.

The more mechanical end of networking skill involves things like:

- Identify the person in the room you most want to talk to as early as possible.
- Be aware of your body language (make eye contact, smile and so on).
- Always say something complimentary about them and their work first, before talking about yourself, even if it just 'that is a nice sweater!'
- Don't over complicate things and try to tell them the story of your whole life. If you fall in love with each other, you can tell them that later.

- Always leave knowing that you have left them with one clear idea of who you are, what you do and what you can do for them.
- Leave them with a business card.
- Make contact with them over the next day or so to reconfirm the contact.

Foxes and Hedgehogs Know All about Water: Planning and Competitive Advantage

When starting a business the advice and support one can get usually revolves around having a business planning. In essence the business plan is about having a clear view of how you are going to deal with the various stages your creative business needs to go through from origination to taking it to market, and how you are going to make money.

But business planning is not something one does only for business start-up, nor should it be a document that sits on a shelf once you have convinced the bank manager to give you a business loan. A good plan can lead to business growth as much as it can help with initial start-up. Even if you have successfully been in business for a number of years you still can usefully go back to the plans you initially made to measure the extent to which you are hitting your 'success' targets, sticking to your milestones, reinvesting. Or maybe you need to be thinking about a new business plan given changed circumstances and new opportunities.

Throughout this section we have highlighted the value of networking and collaboration for creative business. This all rests upon the assumption that people co-operate and that there are mutually advantageous network relationships that people can build. But obviously this is not always the case. The Dark Side that we touch upon below, and return to in others chapters, hints at the need to sometimes balance this *co-operative mutualism* with a more *competitive individualism*, so that you can deal with what will sometimes be a competitive environment. Back to the ecology metaphor, the Natural world is sometimes about symbiosis, but sometimes about fierce competition for scarce resources.

So, how are you going to compete? What is your *competitive advantage?* In short, why is it you that can do something for a client or customer better than anyone else? For instance:

- How are you going to deal with new businesses and competition coming into your market? Do you have competitive strategies to differentiate yourself from them and show you can do things your competitors cannot?
- How are you going to deal with 'substitution'? This is where customers can spend their money on things other than what you are selling, and substitute your product with something else. Are you failing to keep up with new developments? Have you missed the new *big thing* coming up that will substitute your creative product/service? This is a version of 'preparing for Climate Change' touched upon earlier.
- Are you good enough at dealing with your customers? Have you asked yourself the question 'What's in it for the customers?' sufficiently thoroughly? You cannot really answer this question sufficiently well by referring to the *internal workings* of your business. The customer wants to know what *they* get, not why you enjoy doing it! Try the 'market failure' exercise again.

Exercise

COMPETITIVE ADVANTAGE – THE FOX, THE HEDGEHOG OR ANOTHER ANIMAL?

The fox, renowned for his cunning, has many strategies for killing the hedgehog. On the other hand, the hedgehog has only one strategy for defending itself. Whenever the fox attacks, from whatever direction, the hedgehog rolls itself into a ball of spikes. It works every time. The hedgehog is supremely good at one thing, and it survives by sticking to its winning strategy.

(from *T-Shirts and Suits: A Guide to the Business of Creativity*, by D. Parrish)

So, does your business growth strategy come from being a fox or a hedgehog?

- Does your unique selling point come from having the 'cunning' to have a broad strategy that enables you to work across different fields of creativity; from making connections within the networks and be competitive by coming from different directions?
- Or is it better for you to adopt a 'hedgehog' strategy, where you become really, really good at doing one thing, and stick to it? Is it more appropriate for your creative business to develop a competitive advantage by showing just how 'supremely good', and therefore better than anyone else, you are at doing this one thing?

Do you develop your 'portfolio' or do you 'stick with it'?

- Or – play a game. Are there other animals with other characteristics that make more sense to you in summing up your business? Slime Mould? Ants? Pilot Fish? Homing Pigeons? Lions? Chameleon? Talking Parrot?

If 'the last animals to discover water will be fish' because they are immersed within it and so cannot see it for what it is, then you need to develop perspectives for creative business growth to avoid this trap. But developing a perspective so as to ask yourself better questions does not in itself provides actual answers. You still need to devise concrete business growth strategies.

That is, once you have decided not be a fish and have decided to be another animal, it likely that the best animal/strategies for competitive advantage will come from finding a good 'fit' between you, what you do and the environment you are working within. This will be key to the survival, the growth and 'health' of your creative business. When Charles Darwin talked of the 'survival of the fittest', it is this that he meant – that those species that had the best 'fit' to the conditions they were in would survive and prosper. The notion of 'fittest' does not necessarily mean the biggest, strongest or fastest. Lions are not always best. As has been noted already, there is no 'one best way' that works for all situations.

So deciding what 'species' of creative business you are to be is a metaphorical way of considering how you can arrive at this best 'fit' with your environment. As well as helping to grow your creative business, this 'fitness' will also help you to deal with the Dark Side in that it will:

- Move you to a more dominant position in the 'food chain'.
- Help to see off predators.

- Contribute to evolution, adaptation and sustainability.
- Help you avoid 'droughts'.
- Prepare you for 'Climate Change'.

In more orthodox business terms this amounts to highlighting your *unique selling point* to increase your competitive advantage. It is a useful exercise to list these things every so often, so that you can make clear strategic choices about current and future directions.

This will enable you to decide more clearly what your *core competencies* are – to decide what it is about you and your creative business that can make you the best there is, and help you to find better ways in which you can focus in on these core competencies.

The Dark Side

The ecological metaphor for discussing creative networks implicitly calls our attention of the 'Dark Side'. Ecologies are not always cosy places characterized by happy symbiosis. As we have touched upon in the previous section, nature is sometimes described as 'red in tooth and claw' because ecologies are also characterized by predators, by 'food chains', by the competition for scarce resources and by periodically harsh environmental conditions that kill off the weaker of the species to make room for new generations. Natural selection can be harsh.

Similarly in creative business, you will need to deal with 'natural selection'. Of course some members of any ecology will be out for themselves and will be looking for ways in which they can out-compete others to survive. You will also need to avoid 'sharks' and 'snakes', because there will be people who want to rip you off, something we talk about below. Avoiding 'droughts' and preparing for 'Climate Change' are also part of dealing with the Dark Side.

However, species at the top of food chains often live fairly solitary lives, sharks and tigers for instance. The obvious exceptions to this are human beings. We tend to be at the top of most food chains, maybe because, as we touched upon in Section 1 we have developed highly sophisticated ways of co-operating with each other (most of the time at least!). We have developed things like language, law and social conventions so that we are capable of dealing with competition in a co-operative way. In its most general, philosophical manifestation this has been described by Norbert Elias as the 'civilization process' whereby we are able to overcome our more base and aggressive impulses so as to behave in a mutually non-aggressive way. Freud made similar points.

We don't really, really act like the animal world and we have already tried to debunk the prevailing myth that we are all essentially selfish, greedy and in a constant battle everyone against everyone else. Some crazy people are, but values and ethics enable the more sophisticated of us to see beyond our own immediate impulses and try to see that there are consequences to our actions that we need to be accountable for. Of course the business world will involve competition at certain times, and much of what we say elsewhere in the rest of this book is designed to offer advice that we hope will enable you to be good at competing. However, at the very centre of the networks that seem so prevalent in the creative business world is reciprocity and mutualism rather than an overstate individualism. Despite the Dark Side, taking an active part in networking, going to people rather than waiting for them to come to you, offering them things rather than always thinking 'what's in it for me', can all be very useful for clear creative business reasons. This can lead you to previously unknown, interesting and beneficial places, and is really good fun sometimes. One might say that being around other creative people is actually the best think about being in creative business.

So yes, there is a Dark Side. But traditional business discourses overemphasizes competition and underemphasizes the importance of co-operation and collaboration. Even Darth Vader recognized the error of his ways eventually! So use the force.

So let's turn next to the nature of these co-operative and collaborative relationships, and the protection you might need from the Dark Side.

9 *Whom Do I Get into Bed With?*

Story

I REALLY LOVE YOU, BUT ...

There is a cautionary tale about new relationships.

- **Stage 1** – You spend lots of time and energy trying to find someone you find really attractive. You ask them out on the first date. It goes well. You meet them a few times more. You find that they share similar interests to you, that they make you laugh, they are warm and caring. There is just something about them that you find really appealing.
- **Stage 2** – You meet them a few times more and you find out that they feel the same way about you, and you feel really pleased. This relationship seems to be going somewhere! You both agree that you would like to carry it on, and before you know it you are 'in a relationship'. Great!
- **Stage 3** – After having found someone you find really attractive, you spend the rest of your time together trying to turn each other into someone else!
- **Stage 4** – It ends. You spend lots of time and energy trying to find someone you find really attractive.

Have you been there? I certainly have!

If creative business is about building and maintaining relationships, and if you choose for it to be about expanding care, then it also needs to entail being care-ful about *who* one gets into bed with. Remember the Dark Side. You do not want to become part of someone else's food chain in the predatory sense. So this chapter explores some of the issues involved in making and maintaining business relationships and other creative collaborations that takes account of the *how, why and when* of 'getting into bed' with someone, especially if you want to do it more than just once!

For instance:

- Do you do formal business with friends, family or loved ones? Are you sure this will not lead to personal and/or emotional complications down the road? The Chapman brothers have developed a highly successful artistic career by working with family members. Simon Pegg and Edgar Wright, who co-wrote *Shaun of the Dead* have been best friends for years and shared a flat together. So it can work, but you need to be sure.
- Are you good enough at saying 'no'? It is always quite flattering to be asked to get involved in something, but is it going to detract from what you really need to focus upon?

- Do you really need to get other people from your creative network involved now? Or is it better at this stage to work on your ideas alone, to keep things clear and maintain 'editorial control'? Maybe this means you need to 'get into bed' with someone later on, just not right now? As we all know, 'timing is everything'.
- Some people are just bad at keeping in contact. You may spend a lot of your time try to maintain creative network relationships with them, but no matter how hard you try they never get back to you. Maybe you need to let them go, and be with someone else rather than metaphorically being left '… hanging on the telephone'.
- Some people are more central to networks and can help you navigate more than others, but they may not be all that interesting. Back to the Kevin Bacon game, his central connectivity within the Hollywood network is to a large extent based upon the fact he has never been the star, but he has been in films with Jack Nicholson and Robert De Niro. Getting into bed with Kevin Bacon might be good for navigating to certain places, but it might be more fun to get into bed with Jack Nicholson straight away if you have the chance. It depends what you want.
- Not all creative business relationships are symmetrical. Sometimes you might be giving more than you are receiving. You end up talking about their stuff all the time, yours get overlooked and you feel you are not being taken seriously. What started out being about collaboration can end up feeling like you are 'doing all the house work'.

There are no universal answer to these questions. You need to be your own judge and trust your judgement. All one can say is that you need to be aware of the pitfalls as well as the benefits of 'getting into bed' with someone. Is it the right person, for the right reasons, at the right time? Do they really love you are will they try to change you into someone else?

Use Protection

As we have already suggested creative business will include relationships with (in no particular order of importance):

- customers
- official business partnerships
- more general stakeholders and partner organizations
- investors/funders, and those with equity rights
- franchisees
- creative network members
- business support agencies
- professional associations
- business service providers (lawyers, accountants, it support)
- creative collaborators
- existing and prospective clients/customers
- marketing outlets, retail spaces, public dissemination points
- creative service providers
- landlords and/or tenants
- staff.

Some of these will be experienced as deeply meaningful for you, your creativity, your business and your future. They will feel important. Some will be 'casual' relationships that sometimes feel quite mundane. But building and maintaining all these business relationships is likely to be important to success and in creative business you will often need to be your own *ambassador*. When it comes to actual working relationships, you may also need to be your own *diplomat*. Getting the relation right, and keeping it right with all these people will be important on a practical level as much as an ethical level. The contact lenses we suggested in Section 1 might help here.

It does not usually come easily when we are discussing the exciting, inspirational and passionate bit of creative business to be also thinking about establishing ground rules, clear roles and responsibilities. But it might be vital if the creative network relationship is going to work. If you start a creative business relationship and then spend your time trying to get the other person to 'be someone else' it will almost certainly end in tears. Even though you might really believe this 'someone else' is what they really should be, the other person is not likely to agree. Better to have those conversations, and maybe the contracts drawn up ahead of time.

So good decisions about 'getting into bed' with someone involves:

- Being able to spot for yourself what useful and interesting mixtures you need in your business when it comes to a 'division of labour', given the rapidly changing nature of the work you are likely to be involved in. If you are designing your own, specific 'division of labour', that might include employees, informal network contacts and formal business associates. This can become a new and quite tricky element to business. These are the '*who*' and '*why*' questions.
- But there are also the '*when*' questions. When do you get various types of collaborators involved? At what stage of the development of the business process? Maybe you want certain 'flighty' people involved at certain times, and definitely not involved at others. Similarly, you might want the 'grounded' people involved for certain discussions, but then you would need to go back to the 'flighty' types to see if that really was what you intended to create, and whether that will really 'fly'.

Which brings us to ...

When to Get Into Bed: Degrees of Collaboration

So, let's go back to the various stages of business:

- **Creative Origination** – the initial creative idea.
- **Research and Development** – turning ideas into something 'do-able'.
- **Production** – getting the thing made and out there.
- **Marketing and Distribution** – letting people know about you and what you are good at, and then about your product/service, then getting it to them.
- **Consumption** – building a relationship with your customers/clients and getting paid.

For each of these stages certain people with certain skills and interests will be more important to work with than others. You may need to prioritize certain people at certain stages. Nonetheless you will still need to maintain creative business relationships with the whole 'team'. This is especially the case if the people you are 'getting into bed with' are not formal employees but are collaborators from your creative network – remember the point about managing social capital? Certain contacts are good for certain things at certain times but they all need to be kept warm.

For instance ...

Exercise

DRIFTING APART: GETTING BACK TOGETHER – CLOSENESS, DISTANCE AND IMPORTANCE

When deciding 'who to get into bed with', you might not need to be monogamous. Without being too much of a 'tease', it might be useful to let certain creative relationships 'drift apart', and then 'get back together' later on when needed. This is about when to get into bed with someone at a particular creative business stage.

Think about whose input is important for a particular stage. Then think about the degree of closeness-distance each of your collaborators has at that particular stage.

So there are two scales here, for each distinct business stage:

- Degrees of input importance for each stage of business.
- Levels of closeness-distance for each stage of business.

Draw a quadrant diagram for a particular stage.

For instance ...

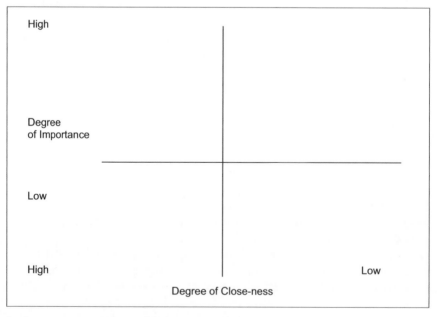

Figure 9.1 For creative origination

The object of this exercise is to make sure that each associate or collaborators is in the right quadrant for each stage:

- If their input importance is high for a particular stage, then their degree of closeness needs to be high for that stage too.
- If their input importance was felt in the last stage but is less so now, maybe they need to start taking more of a back seat for the new stage.
- If their degree of closeness is low but their possible degree of importance will soon be is high, then they need to be brought into the centre a little more for this particular stage.

The variation and placing of associates and collaborators needs to be contingent upon the particular stage you are thinking about and not just left to drift across the project as a whole. So the placing of people needs to move around as the project develops and you get to new inputs for new stages.

This might even need to apply to you. If you need to turn something over to an expert (for instance the proofreading, design, layout and printing of this book), then you (I) maybe need to stand back a little, trust them and let them do what they are good at.

Seven Sources of Creativity

NO. 3: EXPERIENCE

For de Bono, experience is an important source of creativity in that it enables us to know what works in particular situations. The creativity we get from experience is the low risk, reliable aspect you often need when finishing something off and taking it through to completion.

Which brings us to ...

How to Get into Bed with Someone

In stages 1 and 2 of 'I Really Love You, But ...' it would not be very romantic to start drawing quadrant diagrams about 'degrees of closeness' on the first date. Any further discussion would be a moot point, you would probably put him/her off because they would think you were just strange!

But nevertheless, stages 1 and 2 are about telling someone else about what and who you are and finding out about what and who they really are. They are about finding common ground so that both parties feel happy and interested in further collaboration.

So, again not very romantic, but the communication needs to be:

- clear and concise
- honest
- based upon something you can, and actually want to deliver on.

The same might be said of proper romantic relationships now we come to thinking about it!

This brings us to the issue of marketing. But marketing is often associated too closely with just advertising a particular product or service that you are trying to sell. Obviously this is part of it, but marketing as a whole is broader than this. How you describe yourself to the market is something we will return to below, but for now it can also be understood as how you communicate what you are all about to the World. And this is likely to be the basis from which you decide to 'get into bed' with someone, and whether they decide to 'get into bed' with you.

Given that many creative practitioners and businesses have a portfolio career comprising various facets, arriving at a description of what you do can be particularly difficult compared to some other professional practices. If someone describes himself or herself as 'an accountant', we generally have some idea about what that entails and roughly what they therefore do. This might not be especially accurate and our understanding of the actual details will probably be sketchy at best, but we have some idea. If however someone describes himself or herself as 'an artist', or 'a designer', or 'a creative practitioner' we generally are none the wiser about what they actually do. Such self-descriptions only lead to further questions – 'what kind of art?', 'what do you design?'

So arriving at a business description that is useful for all occasions is a useful thing for thinking about how to get into bed with someone.

It probably needs to be:

- Tight enough to not give the wrong idea about what you do, or want to do, so that you are not spending your time fielding non-appropriate enquiries.
- Open enough to include all the things you do, or could potentially do for a customer without being too open. There is often a temptation to say too much, and so you can end up saying nothing at all.
- Credible and providing of a clear demonstration that you can professionally deliver.
- Easily understood by a non-specialist.
- Coherent across all the different forms of communication – verbal, graphical, image-led, web-presence.

Exercise

WHOM DO I GET INTO BED WITH? – MATING CALLS

- **Exercise 1** – Tell the story about your creative business in just 26 words. The first word of this story needs to begin with the letter 'A', the second with 'B' and so on. This forces an economy and creative use of words. When you have played this game a few times you might be able to tell the story of your creative business in a clearer and more elegant way.
- **Exercise 2** – Mentally play a game whereby you are explaining what you are doing to someone you have never met before and who knows absolutely nothing about you and what you do. They have no interest in the arts or culture whatsoever, indeed they are quite grumpy. And you are not allowed to use phrase like '… know what I mean?' or 'kind of' in this exercise!
- **Exercise 3** – What colour and shape is your business? Is it 'male' or 'female'? What clothes does it wear? What car does it drive? What newspaper does it read? Does it like a drink and a cigarette, or is it more often found at the gym?

> - **Exercise 4** – You are in an elevator with David Bowie and Bill Gates. They ask you what you do because they are looking for new projects to get involved in, and you have the time it takes to get to the 14th floor to tell them.

People People

As we touched upon above, being good at creative networks often involves migration across the ecology. It involves developing skills for becoming a *people person* good at forming and maintaining relationships. Some might say it is increasingly inevitable as the rate of change in the creative business environment increases and people develop portfolio careers.

Remember:

- more is different
- ignorance is useful
- encourage random encounters
- look for patterns in the signs
- pay attention to your neighbours.

In the 'degrees of collaboration exercise' you might need to balance 'being sure' about getting into bed with someone against 'encouraging random encounters'.

Spotting something or someone that you love at first sight and just *need* to get involved in because it inspires you will probably be good for creativity and so it will probably be good for business too. We can try to plan relationships, and we can be careful about them once they happen, but sometimes we also need to just let them happen. We should not 'plan out' this love. But jumping between creative relationships to the extent that nothing ever gets completed, followed through with or developed further will not be good for business. You might need some 'lane discipline' (in the motorway driving sense) to compliment your manoeuvrability, otherwise you might confuse the people behind you, or worse still be involved in a 'crash' as you switch lanes too often. Being good at navigating creative networks sometimes requires these fine balancing acts.

For instance ...

Exercise

DOES THIS PLANE GO TO BARCELONA?

It is good to have a plan and 'stick to it', but it also good to spot new opportunities and 'go for it'. Working in flexible creative networks and having a portfolio career can open up all sorts of new avenues, but there are dangers associated with casting around and losing focus. Sometimes you need to balance the conflicting pulls that are trying to take your creative business in different directions.

When a plane takes off from London and flies to, for instance Barcelona, pilot error, turbulence and sideways drift of the plane mean that the direction of flight needs to be constantly re-adjusted so as to stay on course.

This can be visualized in the following way.

London

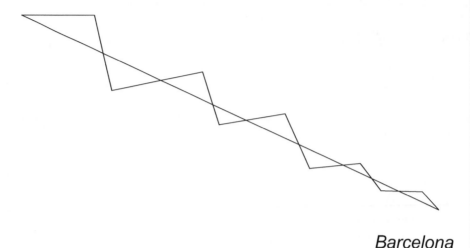

Barcelona

Figure 9.2   London to Barcelona

The straight line represents the intended flight (business) plan. The zig-zag line represents what actually happens.

This illustrates that:

- For the vast majority of the flight the plane (creative business) is actually flying in the wrong direction. Only just before it lands on the runway in 'Barcelona' is it actually flying in the right direction. But it does get there. And it will need to do the same on another flight tomorrow.
- The points where checking, corrections and re-alignment are made are more important and realistic for pilot of the plane (creative business) than an unreasonable obsession with being exactly on course all of the time.

This is a useful analogy for thinking about the tension between following a plan and allowing for emergent behaviour in creative networks. It may with thinking about balancing a clear plan for degrees of collaboration with encouraging random creative encounters. It might not be possible, or even desirable, to be exactly on course with your creative business plan all the time. You are supposed to learn new things along the way. But nevertheless you still need to 'get there'.

Put the other way around, it might be good for creativity and business to go with opportunities as they arise and allow your business to change and adapt, but you still need to get to 'Barcelona' and not end up crashing into a mountain range because you are lost or run out of fuel.

Journeys within the Creative Ecology

Story

THE CONSULTANT GOES ON HOLIDAY

A management consultant goes on holiday to a tropical island and encounters a local fisherman sitting on the beach one afternoon, just relaxing.

The management consultant asks, 'What do you do? How come you are not working today?'

'I am a fisherman. I have been out fishing this morning. I caught enough fish for my family and me. Really good fish', he replies.

'Why don't you fish all day? That way you could catch some extra fish and take them to market. You could sell them for a profit', says the management consultant.

'What do I do then?' asks the fisherman.

'Well, after a few years you will have enough money to buy another boat, and have people work for you. Then you will be able to catch even more fish and make even more money', replies the consultant.

'Yes, and then what?'

'Soon you could end up with a whole fleet of boats and lots of people working for you. Imagine how much money you could make.'

'And then?'

'After around 10 years you will have enough money to set up your own fishery plant to can fish, and you will be able to export fish all over the world. You could be a millionaire within 15 years!' is the management consultant's reply.

'What do I do then?' asks the fisherman

'Well then, after you have done the accounts in the morning, you can sit on the beach all afternoon and just relax.'

Seven Sources of Creativity

NO. 4: INNOCENCE

For de Bono, innocence is the facet of creativity that is opposite to experience. Innocence is the kind of creativity that kids often exhibit. Because they do not know the usual opinion, the usual perception, the usual approach to a question, they are free from inhibition t think whatever they want, and so often have greater imagination and novelty.

There is no incompatibility between running a business and being creative. But there are sometimes tensions between your creative 'soul' and 'selling' to the market. Without over doing it, it is probably true to say that this is a key difference between working in the creative industries and working in other industries. This is especially the case when you are self-employed and using your own, often heartfelt creative talent to also make a living. Professional and business development discussions of creative business often implicitly assume a purely commercial motivation for being in business. Obviously we all need to earn some money somehow, but many of us already know that the overtly commercial agenda for developing a career or business in creativity is by no means the only, or even the most important thing.

Whether you are just setting up a business, have been running a successful business for years, or are thinking of coming out of a successful business to do something else, tensions can be set up between pursuing one's creative inspiration on the one hand, and doing things to be successful in the commercial marketplace on the other. To deal with these potential tensions it helps to be clear about one's motivations. It helps to be as clear as possible what you are trying to achieve in creative business, what you want out of it, and how you are proposing to achieve these aims. Over time you might also need to recognize that your aims have changed and maybe your business strategy does not fit that well any more.

That is why we will raise the seemingly quite simple 'basic motivation questions'.

Exercise
BASIC MOTIVATIONS QUESTIONS

What am I into this for?

What do I want out of it?

Who am I doing this for?

What aspect of being in business gives me most enjoyment?

What are the things I would not do just for the money?

Why am I doing this and not something else?

Business Motivations

Because the orthodox picture of business planning often carries an implicit assumption of a commercial motivation, it tends to accept the 'economic man' view of the World we touched upon in Section 1. The assumption that we are all essentially selfish and greedy is translated by Business Economics into the more polite idea that we are 'self-interested economic maximizes' concerned with financial and material rewards alone. As we began to suggest in Section 1, not a very developed view of human nature can be, and also wrong. We all need to have some concern with earning a living and with financial reward, and there is nothing wrong with that, but for many the picture is much more complicated that these assumptions allow for.

Our creativity is motivated by more than this.

Because it operates in and through networks, creative business often *stems from* relationships as much as it is about growing and maintaining them. And these relationships are often as much social, cultural and emotional as they are simply economic. That is, there are often as much informal and friendship-based as they are formal and contract- or money-based. So unpacking the question of the motivations within creative business and its ecology of relationships can help with the avoidance of 'selling your soul' a little more, and with exploring the professional, business and technological spaces for creativity that are opening up a much wider range of choices for how creative business motivations can be understood and articulated.

Some of our research into the motivations behind creative business has revealed various business spectrums that people seem to migrate between (migration – more ecology!). This migration within and across various, moving positions depends upon competing and often contradictory aspects of creativity and business. In general terms, creative businesses inhabit different formal contracts, professional contexts and informal group collaborations at various times within their working week. This signals migration within and across the commercial, public and independent sectors of the cultural ecology as a whole. In a more detailed sense, however, it may be a better business strategy to think about how to constantly migrate across different business possibilities, organizational structures, marketing strategies, and so on, rather than trying to find the 'one best way' that doesn't exist. Horses for courses remember. You may need to migrate across different points at different times, to change rides for concrete reasons. For instance:

- A job comes in that you don't really want to do, but you really need the money?
- Someone offers you a Job with a capital J, working for them. Can you fit this in with your self-employed work to add some security that could help with risk taking creative business elsewhere?
- You are asked to do something you really want to do, but they can't afford to pay you much, so do you do it cheap because it is likely to lead to more work later that they will be able to pay for?
- Do you offer your services for free, for at least some of your time, to someone whose mission you believe in? Is there something you can get out of this that is worth more than money? Well-being? Creative credibility? Good, long-lasting contacts?
- Do you refuse a potentially well paid contract because you feel the work would end up damaging your credibility with the other creative business and potential collaborators you know?

You can probably imagine lots of other scenarios whereby your creative (and social, political and ethical) 'soul' needs to be balanced against what you have for sale.

Exercise

THE 'SUIT' AND THE 'NO COLLAR WORKPLACE'

The idea of the 'white' and 'blue' collar workplace is well known. The rise of the creative industries has brought with it the idea of the 'no collar' workplace – a lot of us wear T-shirts for work now. These things might seem quite peripheral, but if we see clothes as a 'social signal' or 'text' that other people read in the same way they read other texts, it starts to seem more interesting.

Big corporate identity manager say that all organizations have an internal culture and 'personality', whether they are aware of it or not. If you are a small business or a freelancer, then your 'corporate identity' is you. So getting the way you present yourself right for the right situation is important. So ...

- What do you wear for work?
- Is it the same every day?
- Are you getting this right?
- Does it need to change for different situations a bit more often?
- Does it signal more fundamental facets that you are migrating across for business reasons?

All we are really asking in this exercise is to see the clothes you wear for 'work' as a signifier of a wider point – the extent to which you migrate, or maybe need to migrate better, across different creative business ecologies. It also therefore signifies the need for different strategies to better deal with these different ecologies.

- You could do the same exercise with the language you find yourself using within work – do you speak different languages to different 'work tribes' at different times?
- Or work space – does 'work' take place in different spaces, some formal and some informal?
- Or work times – does your 'work' take place in non-standard work times depending upon the 'work tribe' you are dealing with?

The 'Suit' and the 'No Collar Workplace' exercise highlights wider social features of creative business and signals the need to be clear that you are getting the details right so as to migrate effectively. Perhaps more fundamentally for your creative soul:

- Do you need to migrate within your creative business to balance commercial success and your original creative inspiration, one that balances creative input from different professional disciplines in non-standard mixtures?
- Do you need to migrate between a degree of market success that 'pays' for the time for more autonomous, independent times and spaces away from formal industrial or business discipline?
- Is your work-life balance right? And if so, is your creativity-business balance right?

We cannot make any recommendations as to the 'correct' answer to these questions, but we do feel that they are good questions to be conscious of.

Migrations: Specific Journeys

Over and above business and more specifically related to creativity itself, some of our research suggests that people routinely migrate between a creative desire, inspiration and felt need to demonstrate *creativity for its own sake,* and at other times pursuing a clear and well defined *commercial orientation.* The specific journeys described by this migration includes:

- A creativity that is motivated by the intrinsic meanings of creative acts themselves – and other motivations stemming from more extrinsic meanings coming from other business and/or professionally oriented agendas.

- Creative motivations that place a high value upon creative autonomy – and other creative work that accepts orthodox contractual relationships, hierarchies and thoroughly managed creativity and institutional settings.
- Creative processes and outcomes that come from a proactive creativity where new experiences, services, objects and meanings are communicated to the World irrespective of external 'demand' – and creative business motivations that are reactive, that respond to demand and offer a corresponding 'supply'.
- Thoroughly personal motivations – and others that are geared much more towards an audience orientation. This might include migration between creativity that is geared towards a risk orientation offering deliberately difficult, shocking and challenging work – and a viability orientation geared towards more appealing outcomes.
- Creative ideas that are motivated by an exploration of the creative processes themselves and the cultural, educational and artistic knowledge gained from these processes – or a creative business that is outcome-based, geared towards the delivery of product or service.

Because your creative business will likely be motivated by a whole series of things such as these, and not just making money, your creative business strategy cannot come *just* from a business plan. Recognizing the important of motivation questions that comes from your 'soul' enables you to choose the right 'horse' for your particular 'course' in a more deliberate and self-reflexive way.

Are you migrating well across competing demands upon your work and creativity to get to the place(s) you want to get to as part on your on-going creative journey? It is central to the very idea of migration that it is a regular, on-going and periodic journey. It is not about the final, ultimate arrival at a particular finishing post. If you are not migrating well, do you have a plan for the future that will improve you room for manoeuvre? Do certain creative acts or business decisions move you from where you are to where you want to be? If you have to do something that moves you in one direction, what can you do next time to migrate back to where you want to be?

And sometimes this needs particular skill and attention.

Exercise

WHICH WAY INTO TOWN?: COUNTER-INTUITION FOR NAVIGATION

Central to effective and useful migration are navigation skills.

Secondly, as we will examine in detail in Section 3, a fairly well accepted idea within the philosophy of science is the notion that the types of questions you ask yourself will go a long way to determining the types of answers you will arrive at. There is a skill in learning to ask better questions rather than just staying within the conceptual framework one has 'always' worked within. Sometimes counter-intuition is needed. For instance …

A traveller goes to a foreign land of which she knows nothing other than the fact that there are two tribes living there. One tribe always tell the truth, and the other tribe always lie. The traveller comes to a fork in the road, and she does not know which path to take to get into town. A local comes along, but the traveller does not know which tribe she is from. How can she get accurate directions?

The traveller asks the local which path would be recommended to her if she were to ask directions from someone from the opposite tribe. And then she takes the opposite path. Why is this?

When the traveller is recommended to take the right-hand path, she is either talking to someone who is telling the truth about the lie the other tribe member would tell, or to someone who is lying about the truth the other tribe member would tell. Either way, the left-hand path is the correct path.

What use is this for navigation and migration? It suggests that sometimes it is useful to be counter-intuitive. Rather than just asking other peoples' advice about your already existing path and looking for a direct answer, it may sometimes be useful to question your questions. To use the potential dynamic between one set of ideas (yours) which you might think are the 'truth', and other ideas which you might think are the 'lies'. This dynamic might help in situating your existing views against other ways of seeing the world, and thus navigate it better.

A BUSINESS COMPASS?

So maybe get someone to be your counter-intuition, your 'business compass' to help you navigate. Is there someone who can help you with the conversation you need to have with yourself, to question your questions before you get to the 'truth'? If there is no 'one best way' or 'one size fits all' way to achieve your objectives, who is it that you feel would be most useful to talk to for the exploration of different paths 'into town'?

You may need to get someone who you know is a bit awkward and difficult to convince. It is not so much use getting someone too easy. This person can then be analogous to the 'road testing' of your creative ideas and business plans.

Navigating Success

Quotation

There is a growing trend whereby creative entrepreneurs are:

... construct(ing) their own professional destinations. They forge career paths by pursuing their own indicators of achievement, devising methods of realization, and defining their rewards.

(from *Making Contemporary Art: How Today's Artists Think and Work*, by L. Weintraub)

Different motivations for creative business bring different measures of success. All industries are 'creative' to some degree, but because people working within the creative industries always have at least one eye on the question of their own creative motivations, it is probably true to say that defining and measuring 'success' within the creative industries is a more open question than that it is for other industries. For example, because a relatively high percentage of creative practitioners work at portfolio career within creative networks, they are more often in a position to define their own creative meanings and futures simply because they do not work at formal jobs within formal organizations.

So as well as looking at basic motivations so as to be clear why you are in creative business, it is useful to have a clear idea of what counts as success for you so that you know with clarity what you want out of it and when you have got it.

But this might not be easy. You may for instance want to see your business grow and be employing 10 people within five years, but at the same want 'recognition'. You may want to do 'interesting work' for your own sense of satisfaction, but at the same time you want to 'give something back' to the community. All these measures of success are laudable aims. But because many creative practitioners have a portfolio career and mixed motivations, they also tend to have a portfolio notion of what counts as creative business success. So it might require a little more deliberate thought to be clear about what success is for you and how you are going to recognize it when it arrives. This suggests that the idea of 'business' is best understood is a *verb*, as something you *do*, rather than as a *noun*, as something that just exists outside what you want it to be. It is maybe clearer to understand yourself as '*doing* the business' rather than simply 'being *in* business'. That way, you can keep hold of the core reasons you are doing it, and that way you will probably do it better because your creative input will be that much more alive, fresh and vital.

Exercise

A MIGRATION CHECKLIST

Let's remind ourselves of our basic motivation question in the context of migration, navigation and success:

What am I into this for?

What do I want out of it?

Who am I doing this for?

What aspect of being in business gives me most enjoyment?

What are the things I would not do just for the money?

Why am I doing this and not something else?

Choosing Horses

Migration and navigation implies a fairly constant, on-going journey. Whilst it is easy to dismiss the myth of a universal way of achieving success in business (the Dragon's Den view of things), you can learn business skills in the same way you can learn lots of things. It is probably not true, however, that learning such business skills will answer all the questions that need to be raised for the specifics of your creative business. You need to arrive at these answers for yourself because they will be particular to you. The business is what *you do*, the 'Business' should not be in charge to the extent that it dictates the situation you are *in*! Remember Rosenthal and Jacobsen?

Some creative disciplines within the creative industries tend, almost naturally towards a *commercial orientation* whilst others tend more towards creativity *for its own sake*. Whilst these differences are in no way hard and fast, they suggest differences in business strategies and ways of working with others. For instance:

- Fashion tends to be more geared towards designing and selling clothes, whilst fine art is sometimes deliberately shocking or experimental. So fashion tends to be geared towards the commercial markets and sales, fine art more often relies upon public funding.
- Practitioners within the performing arts usually work within groups and constantly discuss their work with collaborators, whereas aspects of the computer games industry often feel the need to be much more secretive and protective of their ideas.
- Publishing tends to operate through fairly large and orthodox organizational structures that have employees, whereas the creative writers themselves have a much more independent creative career and tend to be freelancers.

There may be good reasons for these particular strategies, but there may mean missed opportunities if 'being in the business' in these ways is only a result of what one is 'supposed to do'. The last animals to discover water will be fish remember, because they can no longer see the thing that they are most *in*. Fashion could be more geared towards cross-experimentation with other art forms whilst fine artists could open up to business a bit more; performing artists could adopt a more streamlined approach and games designers could loosen up and get used to 'Open Source' working; publishers could downsize and writers could get together into networks more effectively. These are indeed 'stereotypes' that we are using only using to make a point, that the right 'horse' for your particular, ever changing 'course' should maybe come from '*doing* the business' in your way, and not simply from 'being *in* business' according to the orthodoxy.

Or if you are thinking about growing or redefining an existing business, what is the best strategy for getting that done? Is it simply employing more people within the existing organizational structure? Or is it better to work with new network partners on specific things at specific times? Maybe they can bring something new and fresh to your business? Are you at a stage where collaboration is better for business than competition? Are you in danger of losing your creative passion because you feel bogged down by the day-to-day pressures of running a business? Has the business you dreamt of when you started out become its own opposite, and you have turned into an accountant or personnel manager? Have you turned '*into* your business' and therefore stopped '*doing* the business'?

Which brings us back to the central theme running throughout this book, the question of relationships.

CHAPTER **10** *The Nature of Relationships*

STORY

THE CONSULTANT GOES ON ANOTHER HOLIDAY

A management consultant goes on holiday to a tropical island and encounters a local fisherman sitting on the beach one afternoon, just relaxing.

The management consultant asks, 'What do you do? How come you are not working today?'

'I am a fisherman. I have been out fishing this morning. I caught enough fish for me and my family, but ... ', he replies.

'Why don't you fish all day? That way you could catch some extra fish and take them to market. You could sell them for a profit', says the management consultant.

'That sounds interesting, what do I do then?' asks the fisherman.

'Well, after a few years you will have enough money to buy another boat, and have people work for you. Then you will be able to catch even more fish and make even more money', replies the consultant.

'Yes, and then what?'

'Soon you could end up with a whole fleet of boats and lots of people working for you. Imagine how much money you could make'

'And then?'

'After around 10 years you will have enough money to set up your own fish canning plant, and you will be able to export fish all over the world. You could be a millionaire within 15 years!' is the management consultant's reply.

'What do I do then?' asks the fisherman

'Well then, after you have met with business colleagues and decided upon the future business strategies and investments in the morning, perhaps taken care of your staff and generally made sure everything is running smoothly, you can sit on the beach all afternoon and just relax'.

'That's fantastic! I have been looking for ways to develop my career and make lots of money for years. It would be great for the village if I could create some jobs. That sounds really exciting. I am gonna get started right away!' replies the fisherman.

This chapter is about business growth, and about moving your creative business from a 'lifestyle' choice to a more sustainable business from which you can start to earn more money. By growth we mean increasing turnover, increasing profits and/or increasing the number of staff employed.

Seven Sources of Creativity

NO. 5: STYLE

For de Bono, working within a certain style is useful for creativity because it can provide an on-going practical guide to creative decisions. Your own particular style can be your source of creativity if you style is new and in demand. But style as creativity is likely to be of limited duration because it does not really include the generation of new thoughts and ideas as such.

The Ups and Downs of Growth for Creative Business

If you go down the business growth route with your creative business and you are successful it will bring its own particular points for further development, because it will put you into a position where you can start to do things you could not do before. But with these new possibilities come new issues to deal with. Such as …

Employing Other People

Business growth might mean that you can bring in new creative ideas and talent, give a livelihood to people and build a team to be proud of. Your business will be more creative if you get the right people, and you will be able to do things you cannot do now.

Our fisherman can employ others, and create jobs for the village. This is the up side, but it brings the need to deal with …

'… hell is other people' as Jean-Paul Sartre once said. Implicit within the main theme of this book is the notion that it is good to be around people, to network and collaborate. But as we have seen deciding upon *the who, why, how and when* of this requires deliberation. When it comes to employing other people, this can bring its own problems as well as its own benefits. There are a whole host of legal issues involved in employment law, from health and safety, minimum wage, insurance, confidentiality agreements and duty of care and so on. But these are only the formal legal issues. There are the other 'softer' issues such as trust, moral rights, personnel management issues, dealing with someone's absence from work because they have a really good reason and so on. You may even need to become deliberately unpopular with employees to get the job done, and perhaps need to sack someone

Our fisherman seems a cool, laid-back kind of guy, and the management consultant has not told him about this stuff yet! And he might not like doing this stuff.

Developing Investment Opportunities

If you successfully grow your business you can get into a position where you will be able to do creative work you could not before simply because you have more scope and more capacity. If it grows in *quantity* (as in size) then eventually the *quality* (as in the basic nature) of your creative business will change too.

Our fisherman can buy bigger boats, fish further out at sea and so catch bigger fish. But it does bring the need to deal with …

… being in debt and managing money. Taking advantage of business opportunities and growing your creative business will probably mean raising investment funds, and this will mean borrowing money from someone, usually the bank. Again there are a whole new range of skills associated with this that differ markedly from the creative skills you probably learnt to get into creative business. Are you good at numbers? Do you have the right methodical mind-set to be able to manage budgets, deal with spreadsheets of current and projected expenditure, invoices in and out and keep an eye on cash flow? There are also added pressures. Is the cash flow OK so that you can pay the staff wages at the end of the month? Will you be able to pay the bank loan this month?

Maybe our fisherman will not be able to relax all that much during his afternoons on the beach after all!

Expand Creatively

With the growth of a business and the shift from quantitative growth to qualitative change comes the potential shift of creativity. Creative business growth may not just mean that you can start to do more, different and bigger *business* things, but also different and bigger *creative* things. Business growth may mean you can start to pitch for bigger, more exciting and more creative jobs, work with more talented and creative people, work nationally and internationally. Standard economics talks of *extensive growth*, which is growth that comes from the quantitative expansion of activity that is your business – essentially doing more and more of the same thing. But they also talk of *intensive growth*, which is the growth that comes from doing things differently and better. Business growth can lead to expanded creativity in the sense of intensive growth.

Our fisherman is able to start exporting, and this involved him in lots of interesting foreign travel setting up the supply chain deals which lead to all sorts of other opportunities (I know because I invented the story!), but …

… other people get all the fun. The opportunities for more exciting creative work associated with business growth will happen if someone goes out there to make them happen. Even if something comes to you, someone will need to do the initial communication, pitching and client care during and after a project. Dealing with the scaling up of your operation, with contracts, clients, suppliers, service providers and sub-contractors might mean that whilst your creative business now deals with new and exciting *creative* work, someone else is now doing that creative work and getting all the fun

It is our fisherman's employees who get to go out fishing on the beautiful, sunny Caribbean mornings on brand new boats, whilst he is stuck in the office dealing with stuff.

So creative business growth might enable you to make more money, but it is not all easy. It involves learning new skills and getting into a whole new mind-set to deal with new and different pressures, and maybe giving up other aspects of the creative business that you once enjoyed. Horses for courses again. If going for growth is what you want, then great. If it is not, then maybe choose another strategy. If you are really more committed to other aspects of creativity, then maybe you should choose others paths and other tools. Like anything else, to be good at business growth will require you to put your real energies into it. It is not something that should be embarked upon just because that is what one is 'supposed to do' in business.

If you are not sure about your answer to these questions then maybe go back to the last chapter again. Or if you are sure but have started to think of new directions, maybe the next section on innovation will be more interesting.

An Extended Family: Incubation for Business Growth

Further to the ecological metaphor, it may be useful for you to consider *incubation* for your creative business. This is especially relevant for newly set-up or emerging creative businesses.

Incubation in the normal, biological sense is the *intensive care* you get in the early stages of life as a newly born member of the species. There are increasingly common creative business parallels to this on offer. Business incubation units can give vital time and space for creative business growth, to get to 'stand on its own two feet' and come to maturity so it can survive in the wider business world.

Specifically, business incubation offers access to:

- A safe *home environment* in the form of relatively cheap rents for creative business work space, usually with 'soft' terms and conditions and a flexible cut-off date for the time when it comes to *leave the nest*.
- Business support programmes, training and advice in lots of different areas. This brings creative business *mothers and fathers* in the sense that it provides some training in how to cope with the World.
- Ready-made creative business networks, given that other creative business will be occupying similar incubation spaces for similar reasons, at a similar stage of creative business growth. Business incubation centres usually bring access to creative business *brothers and sisters*.
- Mentoring with more experienced and established creative businesses. As well as a creative business *immediate family*, incubation can also bring creative business *uncles and aunties* or other members of an *extended family*.
- A *good neighbourhood address* for business profile and credibility, in that having a business address in a recognized and well established creative business centre can help with general business profiling and marketing.
- An introduction to *the neighbourhood* in the forms of a shop window facility. Good business incubation centres can often help in disseminating your creative business in

general, and creative work in particular, to a wider public. This can include providing networking events between creative business, or between creative businesses and potential customers.

Incubation support can be a key resource to help take you from creative business earning just 'beer money' to establishing something more than that.

Technology and Creative Business Growth

Clearly, technology is having an increasingly fundamental impact upon creativity and business growth. Writing about the implications of new hardware and/or software could be in itself another book. But someone else would need to write that one! For now questions of technology and business growth can be related to two generic issues:

- It is always changing and evolving, at an increasing speed, so keeping up with this change is increasingly a full time job. Knowing what technology to invest in for business growth, if indeed any at all, is increasingly difficult, especially if one's investment funds are limited.
- There is always the 'sex appeal' of new bits of technological equipment. There is the tendency to fetishize technology and therefore invest in it for less than clear business reasons.

So when it comes to investment in technology for business, it is useful to be clear and concise as to why you need a new piece of equipment. Once you have decided you need it, try working without it for another few weeks to see if you really do.

Or … try playing the 'Kevin Bacon' game (referred to in Chapter 3) specifically around the shortest distance between yourself and someone you know who already has the technological capacity in question. Maybe it makes good business sense (for both of you), that you negotiate access to their kit for a while and buy something else that you both can use for business growth?

Or … are you sure there is not a lateral thinking solution (discussed in the next chapter) to these questions?

Just don't jump into spending all your investment funds of a new piece of flash technology too soon, which is going to sit there unused whilst the business grows in a completely different direction. Lots of people have made this mistake before and regretted it! Being care-ful could save you some money. But more than that, it could be the difference between overall business success and failure if it means the money saved can be invested in something else that can become the springboard for further growth. And it can sometimes actually make you *more* creative. Maybe a pencil and paper is the best 'technology' for today's job? Horses for courses.

Marketing

We have previously touched upon the issue of marketing in the general sense of profiling yourself and your creative business in its broadest terms. But clearly there are other more specific issues within marketing that relate to creative business growth that revolve around advertising what you are supplying to the market. Creative marketing strategies and tactics are key to creative business growth in that they are key to how you commercialize your creativity, and networks are often key to this.

Successful marketing comes from having a clear and concise idea of who you want to reach, how you are going to reach them and what you want to say to them. It comes from having a clear view of why the thing you are saying is better than that which your immediate competitors are saying. It needs to be clear and well directed.

An effective way of doing this is to build relationships. For instance ...

Case Study

ANYFISH, ANYWHERE – E-MARKETING AS A WEB-CONVERSATION WITH YOUR CUSTOMERS

Anyfish, Anywhere broke the rules. They developed their marketing strategy before they had anything to sell. The orthodox business rules of supply and demand suggest that businesses supply something that the market demands. The general assumption within this is that production, maybe informed by some market research, comes first and then the marketing of that product or service comes next.

But this is why *Anyfish, Anywhere* broke the rules. They started their business with marketing.

Anyfish, Anywhere started as a small company designing sea-fishing clothing and gear. Their mission was to bring a kind of snow-boarding 'cool' into sea-fishing, which was seen as something of an 'old man's' thing. The guys developing Anyfish, Anywhere were sea-fisherman themselves, so they knew of what they were speaking.

They developed the company by setting up a website which was designed as a 'conversation with their audience'. This was specifically not just a 'shop window', informing potential customers what the company had already produced and had to sell. It was something different to that.

The conversation with the audience proceeded through asking simple, but clearly well informed questions about sea-fishing, such as 'Where do you want to fish today?'; 'Have you ever fished at ... ?' This then developed into showing on the website some loose ideas they had about different clothing designs they were working on, to get feedback from other sea-fishing people. This included both technical issues such as the functional aspects of the design as well as the look of the clothing.

Quite soon people were going into fishing tackle shops around the country asking for *Anyfish, Anywhere* products – because these guys obviously knew what they were talking about when it came to sea-fishing!

All this before they had produced a single garment!

Anyfish, Anywhere's marketing strategy was simultaneously their product development strategy and their business growth strategy. They had created their own market demand before any production had taken place by consolidating their networks connections.

Only then did they start actual production and supply to that market.

Cash Money and Getting Paid

Growing a creative business implies the development of strategies whereby your business is going to bring in more income from doing creative business. However, it is one thing doing lots more creative work, and sometimes quite another thing entirely ensuring that you get paid promptly for this work.

Cash flow is an important aspect of this. Late payments force around 25 per cent of companies to go out of business. So make sure you keep an eye on the following cash flow issues whenever possible.

The following points are useful guidelines:

- Try to check the creditworthiness of your customers before you start to offer them credit, in terms of your time and creative input.
- When agreeing on a contract with a customer, agree a schedule of staged payments to you throughout the project before committing to the job.
- Keep the customers informed and seek approval at all stages. The customer is more likely to pay promptly if they have been kept happy and informed. Or at least they cannot avoid payment by claiming you have delivered something at the end of the project that was not agreed upon, if you have been showing them work all the way through.
- Remember to use protection. Start any discussions around pitching ideas with a confidentiality agreement, use a written contract to define the brief and the working relationship, and include in this a retention clause so that the customer does not get ownership rights of your work until you have been paid.
- Watch out for 'mission creep', 'feature creep' or 'project creep', whereby the clients starts to add extra tasks that were not agreed upon and which they are now asking you to include for free. This is a difficult one, you may want to show some flexibility by way of showing 'good faith', but don't get ripped off by doing too much for free.
- Send invoices promptly, accurately and in good time so that your customers receive them before the end of the payment schedule period. That is, do not give any excuses for none/late payment by getting invoices wrong/late.
- Keep a record of payments and none-payments. Monitor your invoices closely and keep in contact with customers regularly about none/late payments.

But the question of money in the context of the nature of relationships inevitably brings to …

Don't Get Ripped Off

Story

FENCES AND THE COMMON LAND

There is a short story about a Russian peasant who works the common land to feed his family. But he has done a good deed, so in return he is given the opportunity to own some land of his own. He can have all the land he can walk around in one day.

So he sets off walking at sunrise the following day. A little way into his walk he starts to think about his route. 'I'll just take in a bit more' he says to himself.

And again later in the day, I'll just take in a bit more, I've still got lots of time.

After half a day of walking he thinks about how much land he is going to own. Then he remembers a beautiful area nearby and thinks 'I'll just take in a bit more'.

He is determined to get a big piece of land. He is feeling good and walking at a fast pace, thinking to himself how much the ownership of the land will mean to him and his family. He has had to work the common land for too long now. This will be his land and he will be able to do with it what he decides. He will not have to allow other people onto this land.

And so he goes on.

He returns to his starting point, just after dark. He is really pleased with himself, and how much land he has been able to take in.

But, so intent has the peasant been on thinking about what the ownership of the land means to him, it is only then that he realizes that he has not 'walked around' any land at all. Because he did not return to his starting point until after sunset he did not walk around any land within a day. He has not completed a circuit, he has not drawn a completed 'fence' around any land at all.

He has failed. He gets no land!

This story offers is obviously a morality tale warning about being greedy, but what else does it tell us?

Firstly, it highlights the need to 'draw one's fence' around what one has, or for our purposes what one has created. It is all too easy to focus on 'just a bit more' creativity to the neglect of the business administration dealing with protecting ownership, and so end up not owning anything. This is where issues of intellectual property, copyright and other legal protections, contracts and confidentiality agreements come in. You need to draw fences around what you do, what you own and what you want to be paid for. So in this chapter we will introduce some basic legal principles concerning ownership and what you need to do to protect yourself. This is especially necessary when considering the changing nature of creative business within creative network relationships. Whilst the flexibility and openness of creative networks are usually good for creativity, their informality sometimes means that a certain extra level of care and judgement is needed when considering 'fences' within the ecology.

But this brings us a secondly point. Our story about fences draws our attention back to values and ethics for the expansion of creative business care, as well as the idea of 'horses for courses'- different business strategies at different times for different things. It hints at the idea that an overemphasis on owning more and more, trying to take more and more in, might actually damage the thing you are trying to create and own. By not being satisfied with enough and by trying to own more so as to exclude others, the peasant ends up with nothing. This has particular relevance when discussing the relationship between ownership and authorship within the field of culture and creativity. The idea of creating culture based upon the exclusion of other people is really quite a strange one, if one steps back from the details. It has not always been this way. Sometimes culture has to be 'common land' for it to really be culture, because cultural artefacts only become 'culture' once it is shared. Things can happen when you have control and ownership that cannot happen otherwise, not the least of which is earning money. But equally things happen on 'common land' that cannot happen on privatized land. Protection does not *have to mean* exclusion! If the previous chapters on the creative ecology have said anything, it has been to advocate the value(s) of co-operation and collaboration, and has tried to provide some ideas about how the creative ecology works so as to aid people's 'right to roam' across the common cultural landscape. It makes little sense whilst working within this context to be putting up *unnecessary* 'Private Property: Keep Out' signs around your creative business. It might sometimes be a more enlightened strategy, both for creativity and for business to look for cultural 'nature reserves'; protected areas where creative work can be shared, mutually developed and where no one is excluded simply because of someone else's ownership. Copyleft and the Open Source Movement are have for many years now been developing new business and legal models that might be better tools for developing facets of this mutual 'common land' for various species within the creative ecology.

As has been suggested previously, there is no universal 'one best way' for creative business. This applies equally when it comes to legal protection. You need to devise the strategy that best fits your creative motivations and the business environment you are working in. That is, you need to think about which *type* of 'fence' you need within the context of your 'horses for courses' strategy building. Perhaps our peasant's basic failing was that he did not arrive at the right *balance* between taking in a big piece of land and ensuring he competed his circuit; the right balance between ownership and communality; between closed-ness (ensure ownership) and openness (overcoming his desire for exclusion and control).

In more orthodox business terms you might need to consider:

- Contracts and contract negotiations – establish clarity with collaborators and business partners and get proper contracts drawn up if necessary. As we have seen creative business will involve 'getting into bed' with a host of different people, for a variety of reasons. Clear contractual agreements are needed as the basis for most of these relationships, most of the time. Especially where money is involved.
- The dangers of 'project/mission creep' associated with getting sucked into doing more work for the clients than what was originally agreed and what you are being paid for. Again clear contracts are important here.
- Skills for ensuring you get paid promptly and maintain a good cash flow.

Exercise
BASIC PROTECTION QUESTIONS

Do I know what am I worth?

How can I ensure I get paid?

Who is paying me and are we all clear about what it is for?

What aspects of my creativity and business need legal protection?

Is my proof of original authorship in order?

EXERCISE

- Do a self-assessment of what you have that is worth someone else's money (ideas, skills, products, techniques, services and so on) – What can you charge for?
- Can you convince someone outside the business (a friend, collaborator) that they might, in principle, pay for something you have? If so it needs legal protection of some kind!

But there are more specific legal forms of protection that might become necessary for your creative business and its network relationships.

Intellectual Property[1]

Intellectual Property (IP) Rights are legal rights that were originally devised to enable those who invested time, effort and money expended into their creativity to benefit from the fruits of their labour. This entailed giving the creator the legal right to exclude others from using their creative work, or to gain from that use by granting permission on the basis of payment.

But IP is also about achieving a balance between entitling the creator to protection by giving them the right to exclude others on the one hand with restricting monopoly and keeping competition open. Often this means that IP Rights are time limited, allowing a period of reward for the creator followed by a period of open access after IP.

Different countries have different ways of doing this, so your rights to IP and ways to enforce them will depend upon which country you are in. If you have any seriously urgent IP issues that involve practicalities, you will need more than this book, and should probably talk to someone who is an expert in the details of the law that affects you. But the first step in protecting your creativity is identifying yourself and your rights as original creator. Without this basic identification as the original creator you will not be able to go much further in protecting your rights to be recognized as just within credits or references, or to get paid in any way and apply them to the specific legal protection most appropriate.

Realizing IP

IP Rights are intangible, but they can be bought and sold as a way of getting paid. You might sign over the rights to use your work to someone else (a client or customer) if that is what they are paying for. By IP Rights that enable you to exclude others from using your work also means that you can grant temporary permission to others to use it in exchange for payments, which can come in the form of a fee for a licence or as royalties. Licence can grant permission to others to use your their creative work for different media, in different markets and countries, for set periods of time or to particular people.

---

1   We are very grateful to Jill Tomsin of Gateley Wareing, who supplied some of this professional legal advice.

The right to control access to your creative work is also valuable for growing a competitive edge against those who cannot use the work. One of the most important aspects of benefiting from IP is appreciate how separate elements of separate IP Rights may give you more than one Right. For example, you might promote your creative business goods and services under a logo registered as a Registered Trade Mark, but which also might have copyright protection as well. It is appreciating and using this synergy that enhances the value of the IP Rights.

Managing IP

Often the most important aspect of managing IP is ensuring you have the relevant documentation and evidence to identify you as original creator, and keeping records of any agreement you have made about your IP Rights. This entails that you ensure that design documents of any type are dated, signed by the creator of the work and securely and safely stored. Again, you should check the details of the law that covers the country in which you are working to ensure you have sufficient documentary evidence.

A second aspect of good management of IP is regular reviewing and auditing what your business has created that might need new or renewed IP protection. These regular reviews become more important as a business grows and its portfolio of IP Rights becomes more complex.

The third aspect of good IP management is being able to handle infringements of your Rights effectively. The essentials of this are to:

- act early – matters only get worse, never better if you don't act now, whether you are enforcing or defending a claim;
- gather as much evidence as possible;
- clarify what you are doing in terms of the Right being alleged against you, or what you want from the Right which you are claiming against someone else.

If you do wish to bring a claim, you might need to set a budget or ask your legal representatives to provide you with a breakdown of the likely costs of enforcing your rights and what you might have to pay if you lose. Seeking legal advice on disputed cases is usually essential. The law also protects people from unjustified threats of legal actions which can backfire on people who hastily accuse others of infringement.

It is possible to insure your IP Rights and these insurance policies often cover some of the costs of defending or bringing infringement actions.

Finally, whilst infringement claims are usually dealt with in Court or formal arbitrations, another way to resolve dispute is mediation where an independent third party facilitates a discussion to hopefully resolve things. This method can be quicker, cheaper and keep the details more confidential.

Expert Advice

We have barely scratched the surface of IP issues in this small section. There is a lot more to say about the subject, but we don't have the space or proper expertise. If you have any detailed issues or an actual IP issues that you think might be a case, you should always get proper legal advice. It might be expensive but it may also be worth it. IP is a very complicated area of law, especially if you are working across international borders.

Why is Copyleft Interesting and Useful for Creative Business?

In contrast to copyright, a common form of orthodox IP protection, the 'Copyleft Movement', the 'Open Source Movement', or 'Open Content Licensing' are all various articulations of a growing movement that may have benefits for lots of creative businesses. Although there are some differences between these various aspects, they have something fundamental in common. They all share the idea of offering free access to creative work and a value system that encourages a collaborative effort to create something together within networks. So they all have something very different to traditional concepts of 'ownership' at their heart.

At first sight some aspects of this general movement appear quite strange and not at all connected to creative business. Why would people do creative work for free? Why would they give it away? In his book A *Guide to Open Licenses*, Lawrence Liang identifies the following motivations. You could for instance be:

- The creator of a website who wants it to be available indefinitely as a free, public resource. You would like to allow anyone to mirror your site or use its content for other projects without needing to obtain permission ... but at the same time you want to prevent someone downloading from this site and then copyrighting content that would prevent any further people using it in the future.
- A musician or part of a band that wants to make your music available to a larger audience, and you decide that making it available online would be a good idea. But yet you may want to ensure that no one makes any commercial use of your music without your permission.
- A part-time photographer who has no problem with any person using your work or sharing it with others as long as they acknowledge your authorship and give you proper credit for it whenever they use your work.
- A documentary filmmaker willing to share your footage with others, and allowing them to use portions while making their films.
- Someone looking at using existing images, music, videos, and so on, and mixing them with other content to create a remix or a new version, but who cannot afford to pay the high royalty, or be someone interested in having people from other backgrounds use your work, or incorporate it into theirs.
- An artist whose work fundamentally depends on the ability to use existing material to create parodies, spoofs or subversions.
- A designer looking at collaborating with either another designer or just someone from a completely different discipline, by incorporating their work.

So there are lots of people, for lots of different reasons, interested in the alternative type of ownership protection that Copyleft gives, such that it protects the ownership of your creativity whilst also allowing you to be open and make choices about the type of legal protection you can use.

Seven Sources of Creativity

NO. 6: RELEASE

Release from cautions, inhibitions and other breaks on thinking is for de Bono an important source of creativity because it shows us what might actually be possible. It is the psychological antidote to a self-limiting 'talking ourselves out of things', and is often the thing much in need within formal organizations that tend to value safety and routine rather than imaginative experiment. According to de Bono, release is often a necessary first step for creativity, but it will not be sufficient in itself.

There are some fundamental technical and legal differences between orthodox Copyright and Copyleft. However, for the general purposes of creative business it is useful to note that Copyleft:

- Still affords legal protection. It is not the opposite of copyright. It is more accurate to see Copyleft as a creative version of copyright more appropriate for creative network relationships because it affords different choices about what protection is used for and how it protects. Copyleft may be the simplest and best way to arrive at joint protection if your creative business genuinely involves jointly produced creative work. Traditional copyright may be appropriate to protect different aspects of joint creative work if there is a clear division of labour to which you can refer. But this may not be possible, so a Copyleft strategy that allows joint and open access for all parties may be a better tool – both for initial protection of ownership (nobody can out-flank your copyright if original authorship is not obvious and clear), and also for onward use (you can use these jointly authored pieces of creative work for further projects without further permission).

- Is potentially an important component of an *alternative* business model and represents the legal facet of the wider distinction made throughout this book between standard business models and commercial environments on the one hand, and alternative creative business motivations, more informal and networked creative practices within the creative ecology, and a more proactively ethical stance on the other. Copyleft helps articulate a key distinction between 'proprietary' (money-oriented) and 'non-proprietary' (non-money-oriented) creative business exchange that various creative businesses migrate between.

- Forms a component of getting the right 'fit' between your overall business strategy, your creative practice, the legal business tools you use to pursue this and the environment you are working within. The competitive individualism inherent within profit maximization strategies tends to necessitate copyright-based strategy to protect individual ownership within a competitive environment. A Copyleft-based creative business strategy is more coherent if one's creative business strategy is based upon a co-operative mutualism in that it provides a way to legally protect a creative space for shared content creation.

- Has a 'political' component to it, in that it challenges what some see as the increasingly restrictive use of copyright legislation that is closing down new forms of creativity, and is leading to an increased corporate ownership of culture. As many large corporations are increasingly 'buying up' bits of culture and turning what were commonly owned cultural artefacts into something we have to pay for, specific Copyleft solutions are helping to articulate a wider point about creativity, cultural politics and access to the shared heritage of our 'cultural commons'.

Back to the ecological metaphor, copyright is analogous to the way different species 'defend their territory' through *warning signals*, whereas Copyleft is analogous to the *symbiotic agreements* that certain species enter into so that they can share the same space. We have been suggesting throughout that there is no universal 'one best way' to start or grow a creative business. There are often complicated motivations at work, and so finding an appropriate business strategy from a wide range of choices to adapt to your environment is important. The debate between Copyright and Copyleft is another facet of this adaptation.

For more concrete information and advice, as well as some 'off the peg' and 'road tested' Copyleft agreements, go to the *Creative Commons* website, whose address is in the Further Reading section.

Case Study

GNU AND COPYLEFTING

In his book *The Wealth of Networks*, Yochai Benkler tells the story of the origins of The Open Source Movement.

In 1984 Richard Stallman started work on GNU, a non-proprietary operating system whilst he was at the Massachusetts Institute of Technology (MIT). Stallman's did not want people to have to seek permission to change their software to better fit their needs or share it with friends. But this was incompatible with mainstream business models for software production that rely on restrictive property rights. Markets for software can only work if software is unavailable unless one pays for it.

As well as writing his own software contributions to GNU, Stallman adopted an approach that has become an alternative business model. As well as releasing his bits of software themselves, he also made open the source code behind the software so that anyone could copy, share, and change it. He only insisted that the changed software coming from the modifiers was also then subsequently made openly available further downstream under the same conditions that he had distributed his original version. This was in effect an open invitation to all programmers to collaborate with him on the programme, on condition that they be as open with their contribution as he had been.

For added legal protection, Stallman retained copyright on his original software. Anyone sharing the software without modification or modifying it for their own use would not violate his copyright. But anyone wanting to share their modified software would have to include an open source code or they would be in violation of Stallman's original copyright. Stallman used his own copyright to force downstream users/modifiers to make their own contributions open.

This came to be known as the GNU General Public Licence, or GPL, which had the added benefit of ensuring that no one could take the collectively created work and copyright it themselves later, thus locking out the previous creators. This creative-legal alternative became known as *Copyleft* – a 'left-wing' alternative to traditional, market oriented 'right-wing' copyright which actively maintained and defended the openness.

In the last few chapters we have looked at some 'strategic' and 'tactical' issues about understanding, engaging with and being protected whilst operating within creative networks. Let's draw out now to return to broader issues useful for thinking about creative business.

Creative business is different from many other areas of business in the sense that the people involved often invest their heart and soul into the creativity as an expression of their identity and attempt to say something to the World beyond their own lives and interests. As we explored in Section 1, there is often a close link between creative business and the question of values. It creates the ideas, images, designs and spaces with which we live, expresses the meanings and aspirations that give our lives shape and reflects those underlying hopes and concerns. So creative business is closely tied to public culture.

But the informal creative networks and broad ecology of independent creative businesses and groups from which a large part of this public creativity emerges has a different shape and operates through different processes compared to the world of formal cultural organizations. So the interface between the formal organizational world and the independent network world of creative business can be a difficult one.

So let's now turn to look at this interface. At how the professionals who work within cultural organizations who are concerned with supporting public culture and creative businesses can gain from a better understanding and engagement with the creative ecology.

11 *Organizing Coral Reefs*

Story

In his book *Where Good Ideas Come From: A Natural History of Innovation*, Steven Johnson tells the story of Charles Darwin's discoveries on the Keeling Islands in the Indian Ocean.

In April 1838, Darwin found himself on the coral reefs that make up the Keeling Islands. All around him the coral reef teems with life and diversity. He sees butterfly fish, damselfish, parrotfish, Napoleon fish, angelfish, golden anthias, all feeding on the plankton above the coral itself. Sea urchins and anemones travel the sea bed in search of food this rich environment supplies.

Just a few feet away, the dry land of the Keeling Island is almost devoid of life, and Darwin already knows that further out in the middle of the Indian Ocean the inventory of life is similarly sparse. Only at the edges, the cross-over point does Darwin see this amazing richness and diversity.

Darwin's Paradox is why this should be. And it is a useful one for creative business:

When we want to answer a question like 'Why has the Web been so innovative?' we naturally invoke thoughts of its creators, and the workspaces, organisations, and information networks they used to build it. But it turns out that we can answer the question more comprehensively if we draw analogies to patterns of innovation we see in eco-systems like Darwin's coral reef ... Whether you're looking at the original innovations of carbon-based life, or the explosion of new software tools on the Web, the same shapes keep turning up. When life gets creative, it has a tendency to gravitate towards certain recurring patterns, whether these patterns are emergent or self-organising, or whether they are deliberately crafted by human agents

(from *Where Good Ideas Come From: A Natural History of Innovation*, by Steven Johnson)

These 'recurring patterns' are usually more like mutually supporting networks than the norm for professional Organization (with a capital O) run by Management (with a capital M). Because the work of cultural professionals tends to reside within *formal* organization, such organizations might need new ideas to better support the *informal* patterns of the creative ecology – the butterfly fish, damselfish, parrotfish, Napoleon fish, angelfish and golden anthias of the cultural coral reef.

In the most general sense this is because of:

- **A relative lack of understanding** – the formal organizational world does not always have sufficient knowledge to include what broader public ecology is thinking, doing and waiting for within their cultural policy-making and planning.
- **An obsession with centres** – the ecology around the edges of cultural organizations need to be re-assessed as more important than the organizational centre. The centre

of Darwin's atoll – the dry land – is relatively devoid of creativity, innovation and diversity. The life, the action, is where it is 'not supposed' to be. It is at the edges.

- **An anxiety rather than an embrace** – cultural organizations sometimes seem to find the chaotic world of emergence, self-organization and networked creative spaces found in the creative ecology to be a problem. It may require new professional skills and attitudes for formal cultural organizations to fully embrace patterns of creativity found within the creative ecology.

Too often the 'closed conversation' between cultural policy-makers and cultural professionals we touched upon in the previous section insists upon staying on the 'dry land' of the formal organizational spaces. Maybe cultural professionals need to get their feet wet as well as getting their hands dirty.

Let's consider some ways of getting your feet wet.

Make Love Not War: Creative Ecologies and Organizational Innovation

Standard theories of business organization tend to emphasize preparedness for competition by putting military metaphors of 'strategy' and' tactics' at the centre of organizational think about efficient and business-like approaches to organization. The history of management mirrors these military metaphors by seeing a hierarchical 'chain of command' as their basic tool. Cultural organizations have taken on these military metaphors, albeit in a 'weaken' form.

But the history of creativity and innovation suggests this might not be the best way forward. As we will explore in detail in Section 3, openness, connectivity and collaboration are the central characteristics of the 'recurring patterns' of innovation. Organizational life and professional management has for a long time popularized the idea that curtailing the flow of information and knowledge in the name of competition is the way to succeed. But cultural organizations and their management might be better served by a connective flow of ideas and information. Especially cultural organizations – this is after all what culture *is*.

Many successful commercial firms are embracing an 'open innovation' approach. Cultural professionals working in the public cultural sector could develop their own version of this open innovation approach by working in more effective and thorough-going collaborations with informal creative ecologies at work on the coral reefs at the edge of the organizational 'dry land'. This would entail proactively opening up the *processes* of cultural priority setting, planning, decision-making and governance to the informal creative networks. Organizing as a coral reef rather than through military metaphors might lead to mutual benefit in that the cultural organization can better support the creative ecology and at the same time gain internal organizational innovation.

A Natural History of Innovation

Steven Johnson's 'natural history of innovation' holds some clear lessons about how cultural organizations might organize as coral reefs. So before we go any further, let's set out clearly what Johnson sees as the hallmarks of this creative innovation, as we will be coming back to them throughout this chapter and during the next section. He identifies the following aspects of innovation,

- **The Adjacent Possible** – connecting to the ideas that are 'near' your ideas, in the 'next room' so that they can help your ideas to come to fruition in some way.
- **Liquid Networks** – the way networks are in and of themselves sources of creativity as their very flexible nature offer routes to various adjacent possibles.
- **The Slow Hunch** – the way certain ideas often take time to incubate and germinate, and often come to life after they are fertilized by new liquid network contacts.
- **Serendipity** – how chance and non-deliberate creative wanderings can lead you to unexpected ways to bring the slow hunch to actual creative outputs.
- **Error** – how accidents, mistakes and taking wrong turns can be the vehicle for serendipitous journeys.
- **Exaptation** – how creative ideas adapted for one reason get re-adapted for other reasons outside the original thinking.
- **Platforms** – how the building of creative environments upon which different creative species can rely is a key factor for growing all of the above.

All these factors have an 'organizational' character in that they are all in some way about inter-relationships, whether that is in the context of informal networks or formal organizations.

Let's look at some of these ideas in detail here, and some in the next section.

The Adjacent Possible: Organizing the Opening Doors

Originally devised by Stuart Kauffmann, the idea of the adjacent possible asks us to imagine the creative process as being like a house that magically expands every time we go from one room to another.

Being in Room A of this house gives us the choice of one of four doors, and whichever one we go through will take us into Room B, which in turn gives us another choice of three more doors of opportunity. These choices are only possible because we have travelled from Room A to the adjacent Room B. And once you have gone through one of the doors in Room B, you are faced with three more adjacent possibles in Room C. Creative options come through the process of travelling to more adjacent possibles. They are not all in Room A. Creativity comes from opening more doors, often unexpected ones rather than staying in the same room and if you have enough adjacent possibles you have a palaces of creativity.

Whilst the history of innovation seems to be full of practical explorations of adjacent possibles, organization and management has not grasped this all that well. Organizational spaces and everyday approaches to professional work that open as many doors as possible by building real, intense, vibrant creative relationships that support a 'myriad of livelihoods' inside, outside or 'at the edges' is possibly the best thing a cultural organization can do to build adjacent possibilities that support creative business networks. The 'cultural system' of cultural policy-makers and professionals we touched upon in Section 1 could perhaps forego their rather mechanical concerns with the

Procrustean Bed of strategy and tactics because there are big problems associated with designing cultural organizations like machines.

This starts to get us into a consideration of the basic nature, shape and qualities of organizations. And there is often some confusion about this. Words like 'bureaucracy' and 'institution' often get bandied around as shorthand to discuss what is wrong with cultural organizations when they become too ossified or fail to connect well with the fluid networks of the creative ecology. There are good reasons for this. The fundamental problem with 'bureaucracy' is its tendency to overemphasize the regularity and precision of a machine when a more organic approach to organization is needed. Whilst there is an 'upside' to bureaucracy the distinction between 'organizations as machines' and 'organizations as organisms' is a useful one.

Let's have a closer look.

Organizations as Organisms rather than Machines

Max Weber's discussion of bureaucracy is universally held to be the starting point for any discussion of its upside and downside. His describes bureaucracy as having the following features:

- **Rules** – '… administrative acts, decisions, and rules as formulated and recorded in writing, even in cases where oral discussion is the rule … (to ensure) a continuous organization of official functions bound by rules'.
- **Division of Labour** – '… a specified sphere of competence. This involves (a) a sphere of obligations to perform functions which has been marked off as a part of a systematic division of labour, (b) The provision of the incumbent (professional) with the necessary authority to carry out these functions, (c) That the necessary means of (managerial) compulsion is clearly defined and is subject to definite conditions.'
- **Hierarchy** – '… the organization of offices follows the principle of hierarchy; that is, each lower officer is under the control and supervision of a higher one'.
- **Rational Adherence to the Rules** – '… the rules (covering 'all eventualities) which regulate the conduct of an officer may be technical rules or norms. In both cases, if their application is to be fully rational, specialized training is necessary.'
- **Professional Objectivity** – '… in the rational type it is a matter of principle that the members of the administrative staff should be completely separated from ownership of means of production and administration … there is also a complete absence of appropriation of his official position by the incumbent'.
(from *Economy and Society*, by M. Weber).

The upside of this system of continuous, rational organization and professional conduct stems from:

- A continuous organization of official functions bound by rules is often better than short-term, haphazard organizations that 'make it up as they go along'.
- This allows for an organizational predictability and reproducibility which is usually better than a lack of transparency and continual organizational uncertainty.

- A fully rational professional context based upon specialized training is often better than amateurism and the personal whims of a particular person on a particular day.
- Professional objectivity that separates organizational conduct from personal interests is always better than the office being seen as an opportunity for personal gain.

But as we all know all too well from our personal and professional life, bureaucracy is never this *rational*. This can be because:

- individual professionals often fail to follow the rules and do act according to personal interests;
- the mechanical approach at the very heart of bureaucracy *encourages*, perhaps even *requires* organizational conduct that are ultimately irrational, because following the rules ceases to be the means to the an organizational ends and become the end-in-itself.

The first set of problems can dealt with through a more professional attitude, better management or the removal of bad professionals.

The second set of problems are much more difficult to deal if they are inherently due to the bureaucratic mind-set that tries to fix an organizational machine-ness that resists adaptation due to interaction with the cultural environment. We began to look at the practical implications of this fundamental problem in Section 1. They are laid out by Robert Merton in his classic study *Bureaucratic Structure and Personality*:

- **Trained Incapacity** – '… actions based upon training and skills which have been successfully applied in the past may result in inappropriate responses under changed conditions'.
- **Occupational Psychosis** – '… as a result of their day to day routines, people develop special preferences, antipathies, discriminations and emphases … A way of seeing is also a way of not seeing.'
- **Over-Conformity** – '… if the bureaucracy is to operate successfully, it must attain a high degree of reliability of behaviour … (and therefore) an unusual degree of conformity with pre-scribed patterns of action … (it) depends ultimately upon infusing group participants with appropriate attitudes and sentiments'.
(from *Bureaucratic Structure and Personality*, by R. Merton).

Too often organizational life descends into attending to the needs of the organization rather than the job in hand. This is the reason that people too often experience formal organizations, in the cultural world as much as anywhere else as systems that 'do not get it', or 'do not want to get it'. It is because they often have no 'reason to get it', indeed have a 'reason not to get it'. No real incentive to adapt. Why make the job more complicated for yourself?

But the problem for cultural professionals, especially when we consider this in the context of a values for an expansion of care and public authenticity, is how this can culminate in deeply irrational organizational mind-sets, in a situation whereby professionals have no 'REASON to get it'.

As in …

Quotation

Adherence to the rules, originally conceived as a means, becomes transformed into an end-in-itself, there occurs the familiar process of goal displacement whereby an instrumental value (following the rules to get a broader thing done) *becomes a terminal value* (the 'whole point' of the organization).

(from *Bureaucratic Structure and Personality*, by R. Merton)

It is rather too common for organizations simply to assume that 'being organized' somehow means taking on the characteristics of the machine. Whilst it has its upsides the mechanical approach is only one organizational tool in the toolbox. Moreover, organizations as machines are usually disastrous for working with openness and sensitivity in ever changing environment. Machines cannot relate to the fish of coral reefs. And just as importantly the fish cannot relate to machines. Developing more supportive relationships with the creative ecology around its 'edges' is usually better for connecting to the 'recurring patterns' we saw on Darwin's coral reef.

Organization theory has for many years proposed the alternative view that approaches organizations as organisms. Let's look at the details.

Quotation

Let's think about organizations as if they were organisms.

We find ourselves thinking about them as living systems, existing in a wider environment on which they depend for the satisfaction of various needs. And as we look around the organizational world we begin to see that it is possible to identify different species of organization in different kinds of environments. Just as we find polar bears in arctic regions, camels in deserts, and alligators in swamps, we notice that certain species of organization are better 'adapted' to specific environmental conditions that others ...

(from *Images of Organizations*, by G. Morgan)

This immediately raises new ways of considering organizations. Rather than 'machines' that are self-contained systems that only obey an internally set logic, organizations can be seen as systems that:

- adapt by choosing between different possible 'species-ness'.
- have internal needs and life cycles that can affect their health and development.
- can find smart ways to relate to other species within a broader ecology.
- Hopefully we can already see how this ecological view is much more germane view of organization and professional conduct for relating to the creative ecology of fluid networks. But in *Images of Organizations*, Gareth Morgan lays out very clearly some of the broad concepts taken from ecological thinking that also offers us smarter ways to think about, design and run organic organizations as an aspect of cultural professional life.

He offers us the following ways into ecological thinking:

- **The Concept of an Open System** – 'organic systems at the level of the cell, complex organisms, and populations of organisms exist in continuous exchange with their environment ... The idea of openness emphasizes the key relationships between the environment and the internal functioning of the system.'

Because organizations are better if they are open to the environment, a key aspect of professional life is relating to it effectively:

- **Homeostasis** – 'the concept of homeostasis refers to self-regulation and the ability to maintain a steady state ... (this) is achieved through homeostatic processes that relate to and control systems operation on the basis of what is now called 'negative feedback', where derivations from some standard or norm initiates action to correct the derivation'.

If the relationship between the organization and the environment is not one that enables a good fit to ensure internal balance then professional needs to 'regulate' to achieve this.

Thinkpiece
THE VALUE OF ORGANIZATIONAL HOMEOSTASIS

Homeostasis is achieved by an organism (organization) when it is able to maintain a state of equilibrium, stemming from:

- internal coherence and stability – each internal 'organ' (department, project, priority) is in harmony with the others;
- a fit with the environment – it is able to take the needed (cultural) resources and 'nourishment' from the environment (creative ecology) it is living within.

A lack of homeostasis stems from a state of internal conflict and tensions, caused by:

- various aspects of the whole in perpetual internal conflict with the other;
- being at odds with the (cultural) environment.

This suggests that healthy organizations will have a coherence between:

- means and ends;
- structures, internal culture and operational processes;
- a sense of purpose coming from leadership and everyday realities coming from management;
- clarity of purpose and the space for professional judgement and initiative;
- overall organization plans and strategies and the experiences of individual.

- **Entropy and Negative Entropy** – 'closed systems are entropic in that they have the tendency to deteriorate and run down. Open systems, on the other hand, attempt to sustain themselves by importing energy to try to offset entropic tendencies. It is thus said that they are characterized by negative entropy.'

Finding ways to 'take organizational energy' from the cultural environment to prevent cultural entropy is a key task for cultural professionals. The creative ecology 'at the edges' is often 'where it is at':

- **Structure, Function, Differentiation and Integration** – 'It is easy to see organisation as a structure of parts and to explain system behaviour in terms of relationships between parts, causes and effects, stimulus and response. Our understanding of living systems warns against such reduction, emphasising that structure, function, behaviour and all other features of systems operation are closely inter-twine ... complex organisms ... reflect increased differentiation and specialization of function (for example, with specialized organs performing specific functions) – which thus require more complex systems of integration to maintain the system as a whole (for example, though the operation of the brain).'

Cultural organizations may have different (differentiated) departmental structures that perform their own functions. Sometimes this is needed. But a more holistic approach to cultural organization requires someone to ensure a broader internal organizational coherence (integration). As we have already noted in the previous section, this inner coherence cannot always be assumed because of 'power games' and conscious attention may need to be paid to it.

- **Requisite Variety** – 'Related to the idea of differentiation and integration is the principle of requisite variety, which states that the internal regulatory mechanism of a system must be as diverse as the environment with which it is trying to deal ... Any system that insulates itself from diversity in the environment tends to atrophy and lose its complex and distinctive nature.'

If cultural organizations are dealing with a diverse, ever changing and fluid environment, which they are if they are dealing with culture, they need to themselves be diverse, ever changing and fluid. The voices within the cultural organization need to reflect the culture 'out there' and not only the (limited) knowledge of the various professional 'experts in here'.

- **Equifinity** – 'This principle captures the idea that in an open system there may be many different ways of arriving at a given end state ... Living systems have flexible patterns that allow the achievement of specific results from different starting points with different resources in different ways.'

The flexibility of response within the natural world is what makes it 'organic', and the fixed regularity of machines is what makes their responses to the world 'mechanical'. Cultural organizations that are open to a diverse environment will need professional equifinity if they are to mirror this flexibility and achieve desired end states in a smart and resourceful way:

- **Systems Evolution** – 'The capacity of a system to evolve depends on an ability to move to more complex forms of differentiation and integration, and greater variety in the system facilitating its ability to deal with challenges and opportunities posed

by the environment. This involves a cyclical process of variation, selection, and retention of selected characteristics.'
(from *Images of Organization*, by G. Morgan).

To allow the cultural organization to adapt and evolve requires internal change and movement away from already set processes and procedures and the adoption of new ways of thinking and seeing that stem from the integration of new relationships with the environment. A lack of evolution towards self-reflexivity is why fish cannot discover water. Don't be an organizational fish.

This final point starts to get us into the question of the 'intelligence feedback loops' and the spotting of patterns to enable an organizational self-reflection capable of doing the variation, selection and retention upon which the integration of new information into new knowledge rests. This is what organizational 'learning' or the idea or the 'organization as brain' entails. This is something we will come back later in this chapter.

For now, this ecological thinking can help to show that a flexibility of professional response is necessary because the creative ecologies are about as changeable an environment as it gets. Indeed they are so changeable they are 'liquid'.

Supporting *Liquid Networks*: The Most Direct Routes to New Adjacent Possibles

Thinking about organic organization so as to respond to the coral reef of creative fish making up the creative ecology involves considering what Johnson calls *liquid networks*. Such liquid networks are analogous to ...

Quotation

... a network of cells exploring the adjacent possible of connections that they can make in your mind. This is true whether the idea in question is a new way to solve a complex physics problem, or a closing line for a novel, or a feature for a software application.

(from Where Good Ideas Come From: A Natural History of Innovation, by Steven Johnson)

Creative networks are not just ways of bouncing out information that has already been determined and formed into marketing. They are potentially (self)organizing spaces whereby different creative 'species' can re-form existing information into new knowledge. But it is useful if someone organizes the myriad adjacent possibles into creative encounters. If networks are used to both give and receive in a way that mirrors the symbiotic relationships of the coral reef then they can help everyone to innovate.

Two common failings in the approach that cultural organizations adopt towards creative networks are:

- **Small-ness** – limiting the size of networking only to the preselected whose opinions have been sought in the past.
- **Wooden-ness** – restricting the range of debate to the pre-established boundaries so that it does not go beyond already agreed agendas.

Organizing to support liquid networks might need to:

- **Seek Bigness** – the bigger the better, up to certain dimensions. The more creative resources, skills and information networking contains, the more everyone has to draw upon. Finding ways to include as many people as possible gives potential access to more adjacent possibles.
- **Allow Plasticity** – capable of taking different forms in different situations by encouraging new combinations of creative people, agendas and open discussions. Finding ways to mix as many different creative species together as possible gives potential access to better adjacent possibles.

Organizations that are creative and innovative tend to resemble the large scope and plasticity of *brains* rather than the small-ness and wooden-ness of machines.

Organizations as Brains

Whilst we will explore the idea of 'organizations as brains' more fully in the next section when we consider 'learning organizations' we can begin this by recognizing that organizations are more learning when they:

- take in and use information from the environment, rather than avoiding new information because it makes things seem more complicated;
- circulate new information within and across the organization so that it can be used by the whole organization, rather than keeping organizational secrets to play power games;
- use new information effectively to make smarter organizational plans and decisions, rather than sticking to old ways of doing things;
- try to regularize information sharing within 'intelligence feedback loops', rather than organizationally 'hoping for the best' when it comes to new ideas;
- as we will see in the next section when we consider the theme of innovation and the research that it rests upon, the flow of ideas is central to effective cultural organization as much as it is to creative business success.

But as well as good information flows that characterize organizations as brains, creative networks also rely upon a *randomness* that formal organizations are often rather uncomfortable about. Management and organization tend to want more control, predictability and regularity. It is good to have routine, predictable organizational systems and well laid out managerial plans to initiate them. But if this means planning out organizational creativity and innovation, which it often does, then the tail is wagging the dog. Another animal.

Which brings us to ...

Snails rather than Hares: The Slow Hunch

The 'natural history' of innovation shows that it does not occur all at once as ready-formed ideas that can be taken straight to the Marketing Department. Creativity and innovation often take a long time to germinate and grow from a vague idea into something more concrete and viable. Johnson calls this the period of the *slow hunch*. The history of world-changing innovations is full of stories of incomplete ideas being left to one side for years; of false turns and mistakes that seemed astonishing afterwards; of years of inactivity on things that were to later become ground-breaking.

Quotation

... most great ideas first take shape in a partial, incomplete form. They have the seeds of something profound, but they lack a key element that can turn the hunch into something truly powerful. And more often than not, that missing element is somewhere else ...

(from *Where Good Ideas Come From: A Natural History of Innovation*, by Steven Johnson)

Creativity and innovation often comes about through the cultivation that bring two or more of these 'somewhere elses' together.

This has some key lessons for the cultural organizations interested in supporting creativity and innovation:

- **It Takes Time** – and therefore business support and 'incubation' needs to be devised as sustained relationships rather than one-off hits of 'business planning' advice. The creativity bit of creative business needs to be supported first. The business planning bit based upon the innovative idea is the relatively easy bit. Supporting creative networks needs to create supportive cultural environment.
- **It Requires Different Skills** – rather than the skills of the business economist, the cultural professional needs skills in spotting connections between two or more 'somewhere elses' to foster inter-creative relationships.

This is where the *liquid* bit of liquid networks comes to the fore.

Organization as Cultural Liquid

Many ideas of the origins of life have some notion 'primordial soup' at their heart. The idea of swirling possibilities of liquids allowing random, accidental collisions, and unexpected connection seems to be fundamental.

Liquids have a plasticity that might be similarly fundamental for organizational innovation. Organizations that have the plasticity of liquids and their connective power can be envisaged as encouraging an 'information spillover' whereby good ideas flow easily from one mind to another so that they can become new adjacent possibles. This kind of organizational liquidity highlights a meeting point between 'organization as brains' – that create internal information flows, with 'organizations as organisms' – that encourage information flows between itself and the environment.

This approach to cultural organization fosters productive spaces *between* various creative agents (businesses, independents creators and other organizations) rather than treating such creative agents as isolated recipients of organizational support. Finding ways to get individual creators to exchange deep knowledge and understanding to each other by supporting *inter-creative spaces* is as important for liquid organization as simply building the size of a creative network. Supporting inter-creative spaces allows the wisdom of the crowd to become the wisdom of *someone in the crowd by* creating a flow of specific information such that new adjacent possibles can grow into actual *innovative probables* or even *creative definites*.

Quotation

... large collectives are rarely capable of true creativity or innovation ... When the first market towns emerged in Italy, they didn't magically create some higher-level group consciousness. They simply widened the pool of minds that could come up with and share good ideas. This is not the wisdom of crowds, but the wisdom of someone in the crowd. It's not that the network itself is smart; it's that individuals get smarter because they're connected to the network.

(from *Where Good Ideas Come From: A Natural History of Innovation*, by Steven Johnson)

Simply 'having' a creative network within a town or city is not sufficient support for creative networks. Actual inter-creativity needs to be organized. Given that cultural organizations often occupy central positions within local creative ecologies they have better opportunities than most to proactively *help the flow* of liquid networks.

Which brings us to ...

Platform Gardening

On his trip to the Keeling Islands, Darwin's has somewhere to stand because one species, the coral reef has created a habitable platform for all the other species to find a sustainable livelihood.

The knowledge that the coral itself created a platform upon which Darwin was able to stand can be read as analogous to the idea that the creative ecology and the wider public create the platform upon which cultural organizations stand. It is not the other way around, despite what 'cultural leaders' and other self-selected cultural policy-makers might suggest. Darwin, along with cultural organizations, stands upon what was created *before they arrived*.

Secondly measuring the true creative diversity of the coral reef platform has proved impossible. This can be read as analogous to the paucity of dry obsession with economic impact measurement on the part of the cultural policy-makers. Supporting the sustained development of the creative coral reef *as a whole* is what is likely to have the real impact in terms of public value on the one hand and creative business on the other.

This suggests two points for cultural professionals:

* (re)building creative spaces upon which everyone can stand is a key organizational task – building platforms;
* supporting the whole is the way to do this – a holistic approach.

Coral polyps perform this role for the coral reef because it is the *keystone species*. The very existence of the coral polyps support the emergence of multiple other species within the ecology. Cultural organizations can perhaps adopt an analogous keystone role given their often central place within local creative ecologies. Platforms need to be created, but cultural professionals need to create them through holistic care for the whole ecology. This requires the mind-set of the gardener rather than the mechanic reordering isolated components. Cultural professionals could act as platform builders by:

- deepening knowledge of *what* creative networkers are doing, to go beyond a 'social media' attitude that sees networks as simply about sending out pre-established information;
- broadening scope of *who* creative networkers might be, to go beyond repeated, often 'closed conversations' amongst the already invited;
- lengthening ideas of *how long* creative networking last for, to go beyond minimal 'networking events' within formal, time limited business support projects.

The gardener knows about deep roots, broad cross-fertilization of species and has an innate relationship with seasonal time. Platform building requires a 'constant gardener', which brings us to …

Cross-Fertilization

The role of cultural professional as platform gardener can be unpacked further when we consider the potential for cross-fertilization:

- Cultural organizations tend to already have large amounts of cultural information access to technologies and skills and control physical spaces that could be re-envisaged resources for the growth of the creative network – the cultural organization fertilizes the creative ecology.
- Many 'ordinary' citizens are already committed to the cultural life of their place and could be re-envisaged as active participants who simply need to 'let them in' as part of the organization's 'R and D' effort – the creative ecology fertilizes the cultural organization.

In finding imaginative ways to expand this cross-fertilization with proactive support could enable cultural organizations to simultaneously support and receive support from the creative ecology. The cultural professional becomes a gardener by initiating a mutually supportive platform of joint support without the need for big shiny new projects that costs lots of new money. Most fertilizers used in the natural world are not what we might call 'precious metals'. As cultural organization enter an Ice Age of funding cuts we should remember that gardeners are great recyclers of waste products of all varieties, if you know what we mean.

So specific tasks for cultural professionals interested in working as platform gardeners involve:

- leaving the 'dry land' of the institutional world and dive below sea-level in search of symbiotic relationships;

- re-envisaging 'waste products' and identifying 'energy sources' beyond the traditional organizational resources and capacities;
- building discrete methods and opportunities to increase the total energy capture for the whole ecology;
- building 'tight nutrient cycles'.

Seven Sources of Creativity

NO. 7: MOTIVATION

For de Bono being motivated is a vital source of creativity because it gives it impetus and energy. Strong motivation means a person who is willing to keep working at something and seeking better alternatives, whilst everyone else is satisfied with how things are at the moment.

We started this section on networks with a little proverb about fish. So let's end with another one.

Story

THE BONES OF THE DEAD: THE KWAKIUTL AND THE SALMON

The Kwakiutl were an American Indian tribe living on the Northern Pacific coast.

They '... *depended upon the ocean to provide their primary sustenance – herring, eulachon (candlefish), whales, and most of all, the salmon that annually enter the coastal rivers to swim inland and spawn ... the North Pacific tribes developed a relationship to the natural abundance of their environment based upon a cycle of Gifts. It was the Indian belief that all animals lived as they themselves lived – in tribes – and that the salmon, in particular, dwelt in a huge lodge beneath the sea. According to this mythology, the salmon go about in human form while they are at home in their lodge, but once a year they change their bodies into fish bodies, dress themselves in robes of salmon skin, swim to the mouths of the rivers, and voluntarily sacrifice themselves that their brothers may have food for the winter ...*

The first salmon to appear in the rivers was always given an elaborate welcome ... The first fish was treated as is it were a high-ranking chief making a visit from a neighbouring tribe ... After a ceremony the priest gave everyone present a piece of fish to eat. Finally – and this is what makes it clearly a Gift cycle – the bones of the first salmon were returned to the sea. The belief was that salmon bones placed back into the water would reassemble once they had washed out to sea: the fish would then revive, return to his home, and revert to its human form ... part of the Gift is eaten and part is returned – and once again the myth declares that the object of the ritual will remain plentiful because they are treated as Gifts ... the first salmon ceremony establishes a Gift relationship with nature, a formal give-and-take that acknowledges our participation in, and dependence upon, natural increase. And where we have established such a relationship we tend to respond to nature as a part of ourselves, not as a stranger or alien available for exploitation.'

(from *The Gift: How the Creative Spirit Transforms the World*, by L. Hyde)

In previous chapters we heard two versions of the story about the fisherman that relied upon his individual skill and motivation. In the midst of all the competing demands on your time and energies when you are developing, running or growing a creative business, it is all too easy to lose sight of the water you are *in*. But understanding and engaging with creative networks asks us to recognize that our individual skills and motivations are a starting point but not an end point. Being good at creative networks entails remembering the relationships we can have with wider 'Nature', the creative ecology as a whole. It comes from co-creating similar Gift cycles over and above simply concentrating upon our own skills as individual fisherman to exploit the ecology as being made up of 'strangers available for exploitation'.

This section on networks has implied, or often explicitly stated that networks are the place to find the new ideas, insights and information that will help you to take your initial inspiration and creative talent forward into an actual innovation. And this ability to innovate is likely to be the basis for creative and business success. So in the next section we will explore this theme of innovation in more detail.

PART III

Innovation

CHAPTER

12 *Mozart and the Innovation Economy*

Story
MAKING A GOOD DISH OF IT

When I am, as it were, completely myself, entirely alone, and of good cheer – say, travelling in a carriage, or walking after a good meal, or during the night when I cannot sleep; it is on such occasions that my ideas flow best and most abundantly. Whence and how they come I know not; nor can I force them. Those pleasures that please me I retain in memory, and am accustomed, as I have been told, to hum them to myself. If I continue in this way, it soon occurs to me how I may turn this or that morsel to account, so as to make a good dish of it, that is to say, agreeably to the rules of counterpoint, to the peculiarities of the various instruments etc.

All this fires my soul, and, provided I am not disturbed, my subject enlarges itself, becomes methodized and defined, and the whole, though it be long, stands almost complete and finished in my mind, so that I can survey it ...

When I proceed to write down my ideas, I take out of the bag of memory, if I may use that phrase, what has been previously collected into it the way I mentioned.

(This is taken from a letter written in 1789 by Wolfgang Amadeus Mozart. Cited in *Creativity*, by A.J. Cropley)

Research and Innovation: Two Sides of the Same Creative Coin

People bandy around the term *research* all the time, in lots of different ways. *Innovation* is another term that is currently talked about a lot. These two terms are often talked about as if there is some mysterious route to these things that only a few people have access to. And you don't.

Innovation can be something that stems from rigorous, planned and prolonged inquiries into the world out there. Or it can be as simple as talking to someone, thinking about it in the bath and changing the way you do things. But fundamentally, it hinges upon two key things:

- How you can arrive at a better understanding of something and carry this through so that you can develop better ideas for your creativity.
- How your creativity can better apply these better ideas and do something with them.

Research and innovation are, or at least should be, two sides of the same coin. So what is all the fuss about?

Mozart implicitly suggests the following:

- People have been thinking about the way they do thinking for a long time.
- There are lots of different, often quite personal ways of doing research for creativity – that is, different methods – in a carriage, walking after a good meal and so on.
- Innovation can come from unknown places. This does not really matter, so long as they come somehow – that is, so long as the ideas flow.
- Creative people usually become aware very quickly that they are working within a particular tradition of creativity – for Mozart, these were the rules of counterpoint and the peculiarities of various instruments and so on.
- Making something happen as a result of creative inspiration entails embracing its unfinished nature and looking to develop it through applying associated skills – this involves seeing how the subject enlarges itself, and searching for effective ways to methodize it, define it and crystallize (write down) the ideas.
- The first creative flash will have to be developed and worked upon – to create a good dish.

We will explore all these issues in detail below, in terms of how initial creative inspiration and research connect to each other, and how the research useful for creativity connects to innovative applications for creative business. And innovative applications are as likely to bring creative business success as the creativity itself. Without going into any great detail, the general economic context of creative business implies the need for constant research and innovation within what Geoffrey Hodgson has called the *learning economy*.

For instance …

Quotation

… new growth theory … postulates that technological change and economic growth are intrinsically connected, since the wellspring of growth is innovation in products and processes, and new ways of combining inputs to generate new types of outputs. As economist Paul Romer puts it, 'Human history teaches us … that economic growth springs from better recipes, not just from cooking more.'

(from *Creative Economy*, by T. Flew)

Even back in 1789, Mozart knew you had to make a 'good dish'.

Intensive Growth and Innovation

We have touched upon the distinction between *extensive* and *intensive* growth already. Without overstating hard and fast binary distinctions, intensive business growth implies a shift from the 'old' to the 'new' economy. The general contours of this shift are as follows:

Case Study

Table 12.1 Economy wide issues

	Old economy	New economy
Economy wide issues		
Markets	Stable	Dynamic
Scope of competition	National	Global
Organizational form	Hierarchical, bureaucratic	Networked
Source of value	Raw materials, physical capital	Human and social capital (skills and contacts)
Business issues		
Organization of production	Mass production	Flexible production
Key drivers of growth	Capital/labour	Innovation/knowledge
Key technological drivers	Mechanization	Digitization
Source of competitive advantage	Lowering costs through scale	Innovation, quality, adaptive-ness
Importance of research/ innovation	Low-moderate	High
Relations to other firms	Go it alone	Collaboration, outsourcing
Customers/workers		
Tastes	Stable	Changing rapidly
Skills	Job-specific skills	Broad skills and adaptability
Educational needs	One-off craft training or degree	Lifelong learning
Nature of employment	Stable	Increasingly contract/project specific

(this is a slightly adapted version of an original table from *Getting the Measure of the New Economy*, by D. Coyle and D. Quah)

Everything within the new economy column is about change, movement and the need for a smart, flexible response to an ever-changing cultural and economic environment. Everything either states explicitly, or at the very least strongly implies the need to keep up with change. So it is fundamentally about research and innovation, whether that is within *what* you do with your creativity – the products, objects, services you provide;

why you do it – how you put your motivations into action; *for whom* you do it – which markets you engage in and how; and *how* you do it – the ways you work, organize your relationships with others and 'manage' the processes involved.

Theory

THEORIES OF CREATIVE INNOVATION: NO 1 – THE ECONOMIC VIEW

There has been a growing interest in the importance of creativity in the knowledge (or learning) *economy ... However* (some of this is) *... too often based upon a common but flawed understanding of creativity. The attribution of creativity to unique individual personalities loses sight of the extent to which creativity is best understood as being the outcome of a process* (of research) *rather than a personae, and how moments of creative discovery are characteristically the outcome of incremental processes undertaken as part of a team of people that possess diverse skills ...*

(from '*Creative Economy*', by T. Flew)

But enough of this general scene-setting, let's get into it.

Behind, In/Through, For and In Front Of: Research Starting Points

What? *Behind, In/Through, For and In Front Of?* What does that mean? Sounds a bit complicated!

Proverb

The questions you ask yourself will determine the answers you get.

At first glance, this might seem counter-intuitive, but it suggests something fairly straightforward. The direction you choose to travel in will determine where you end up.

It is always useful for creativity to go beyond one's usual way of doing things. Or, put another way if doing concerted research is new to you, it is useful to know about the different starting-points upon which research can be based. This then almost automatically asks you to think about the different research tools you can use, because certain research tools are only really appropriate for certain research agendas. Knowing these things will help you to create a *coherent research design and strategy*. This helps to ensure that the questions you are asking within your research, the basic conceptual position from which you set out, and the specific tools you are going to use, all relate to each other in a clear and focused way. We will come back to this later.

For now, the idea that the questions you ask yourself determine your answers stems from some fairly heavy-duty academic philosophy. But the practical benefits of such an idea lies in asking that you are sure that the basic trajectory of your creative journey is the one that will be most useful in the long run, because there are always alternative *directions* that could be better. A good way to start all this thinking about research and innovation is to question all the different, sometimes overlapping elements of your creativity and the research you might need to do within and for each element. That way, you can begin to outline various research starting-points relevant for each of these elements.

For example ...

Paul Ricoeur and Hermeneutics

Paul Ricoeur is a hermeneutical philosopher who formulated a particular method of interpreting written texts. We have borrowed some of his thinking as an analogy to outline various research starting-points.

He argued that any written text could be 'read' according to three different, overlapping levels of research, which are:

- behind the text
- in/through the text
- in front of the text.

For example, George Orwell's *1984* could be analysed in the following way:

- **Behind the Text** – what were the various economic, political, social and cultural contexts that framed the writing of this text? How did these find expression in the text? We would have to consider the Cold War, Soviet totalitarianism, the nuclear arms race, the institutional bastardization of language and so on. The stuff way beyond and outside the book itself.
- **In/Through the Text** – the writing process itself. Where did Orwell write the book? How? Longhand or by typewriter? What particular routines or processes did he follow in the editing and, how did all of these manifest themselves in the text as a whole? The way the book itself came together, how the interior dynamics of the writing process evolved.
- **In Front of the Text** – what were the reactions of the various audiences who read the text – editors, reviewers, critics, the general public and so on? How did all these reactions effect the production of the developing text and the various edits? What was the relationship between the book and what other people made of it in terms of how it impacted upon Orwell's creative process before, during and after? What have we done with the book since and how this 'in front of' might actually now be the 'official' version of the book?

To the Ricoeur's thing, we have added research:

- **For the Text** – this involves valuing the kind of research that 'runs alongside' the actual doing of the creative work itself. The value in knowing what is going on in the broader creative network, within other related disciplines and viewpoints as the work itself develops. Research 'for' creative practice takes account of these other perspectives and what they can add to 'your thing' itself.

These different research starting-points, their particular foci and different levels of generality start to show that different types of questions are going on within each. Being clear about the differences between these potential aspects of your research, using the right research tools within each and seeing the interconnection between and across them without getting them mixed up, are all good skills to have. Thinking about the *behind*, *in/through*, *for* and *in front of* elements in turn is also a useful way to clearly structure your research, understand what each element can potentially bring to your creativity and which you feel it is best to concentrate upon at any given time.

A Research Map: Boxes as Starting-Points, but also Arrows as Navigation

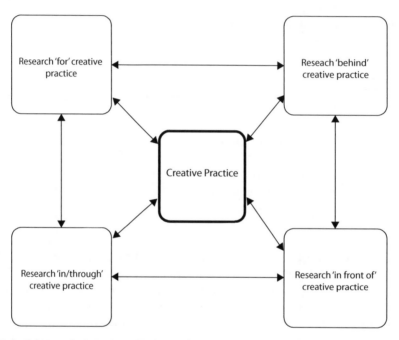

Figure 12.1 Research for creative practice

Putting these four starting-points into four boxes (your own creative practice being the fifth) on the 'map' can consolidate the order it can bring. This research map puts your creative practice at the centre, and asks you to think about how to navigate across the map to get the kind of 'better ideas' that you think might be useful for applications to get to innovation.

But it also suggests that the various research starting-points are not separate or mutually exclusive. The diagram involves as many *arrows* as *boxes*:

- boxes are about conceptual things – the starting-points and the different levels of research generality that this implies;
- arrows are about how these various starting-points link together, because research inevitably flows from one concern to another, and insights found at one level will inevitably have consequences for all of the other aspects.

This is why research can sometimes feel really uncomfortable, when everything feels like it's connected to everything else and you don't know where to start. It may feel uncomfortable, but that is a good thing. It is supposed to feel like that, at least at the start. If it feels too easy it is probably because it is not as broad or deep as it needs to be.

If your research does feel uncomfortable, try to remember the map as something you can move around in, looking for the research 'stop-off points' as well as starting-points. The map can also help you to visualize your research as something that you can approach from lots of directions. This is what maps do. They show you where things are, but they also show you how to get to them. They also give you an over-view of the whole terrain and show you how everything 'fits together', which can be really useful even though you don't necessarily want to 'go there' right now.

Research Leading to Innovation

In terms of how the *Behind, In/Through, For and In Front Of* model specifically relates to the innovation, we can make some brief points by way of introducing the basic model, before we return to the details of this in later chapters.

Research *Behind* Leading to Innovation – can lead to innovation in two ways:

- **Generic** – research into the various broad contexts against which the creative genre you work within is connected, and the other broad social, economic, political and cultural features that impact upon the possibilities for innovation.
- **Specific** – research that takes a similar cue but which focuses more upon how these contextual features impact upon the particular circumstances surrounding your creativity and potential for innovation.

Of the *Behind* aspects leading to innovation, the social context in its broadest sense can obviously mean all sorts of things. To say anything detailed on this would require a book in itself, because virtually any aspect of the context that surrounds you could become relevant for thinking about innovation. Researching people who have said and done innovative things within your field narrows this down a little, and such research can lead to innovation in terms of understanding the contextual features such as how history, politics or economics impact upon all our lives. Researching the history of your particular field of creative practice – not just as a survey of its internal features (though this is often useful), but rather as an exploration of the relationship between the particular historical context and the way it developed – can be specifically useful for innovation. Finally the objects, processes, artefacts and other creative outcomes that come from your particular creative field can be a fruitful kind of *Behind* research. Whatever forms these outcomes take, researching such objects can be a fruitful way of understanding the contexts behind your creative process and thus lead you to innovation.

Research *In/Through* Leading to Innovation – is concerned with the specific insights gained from the actual processes involved in your creativity. Simply put, innovation can come from this kind of research because you can *learn* from it as you are *doing* it. This is the other meaning of the phrase *creative practice*, what you learn from doing something over and over again. Innovations can come from the act of working with materials, techniques, processes and software which can feed back into your broader thinking about how you can develop and improve on what you do, how and why.

This can lead to creative innovation because it asks you to think about:

- questions concerning how you apply the insights emerging out of practice to develop better and more effective ways next time – researching technique and process to innovate new techniques and processes;
- relationships between developing your practice and broader ideas about new places to put innovations – researching techniques and process to innovate in new markets, new forms of dissemination, new collaborations with other industries.

And this can include a whole range of practical issues.

General

- What best gets you 'into the mood' for successful creative practice?
- Is there a specific working time you favour?
- Is there a specific working place you favour?
- Are there specific pieces of equipment that you favour?
- Who is most important within each part of the process if it is not you?
- What is liable to disrupt your creative practice? What is the biggest barrier?

Materials

- Is your relationship to the materials you most often used in your creative practice (paper, ink, paint, canvas, wood, metal, glass, clay, software, your body and so on) the best it could be?
- How do you react when faced with using a new material?
- How is your relationship to your materials 'mediated' (softened, explained by others, interfered with) by other things/people? Is this good or bad? If it is bad, how do you get a better relationship?

Tools

- What tools do you use in your creative practice?
- Which are used most often?
- Are these the same ones that you feel are central to your creative practice?
- Have you considered (or tried) using other tools?
- Are your tools experienced as extensions of your body or as obstacles between you and your practice?

Processes

- Do you regularly follow the same processes within your creative practice?

- Which stages cannot be left out without the effect being detrimental – networking, sketches, brainstorming, models, prototypes, computer simulations, and so on?
- Which stages of your individual practice do you enjoy and which do you find burdensome? Make a list.

Research *For* Leading to Innovation – many books concerning research for creative practice will start with the process itself, for example, *the design process*. The talk will immediately be about the 'search for ideas', 'searching for solutions', 'searching for understanding' and so on. It will then go on to suggest various techniques to achieve these ends – 'brainstorming', 'objectives trees', 'counter-planning', 'interaction matrices' and the like.

These techniques for developing innovations can be useful. But before that stage there are other issues to address. Research *For* creative innovation can simply be about the 'head space' that many people identify as a necessary part of their creativity. It can lead to innovation simply by being the time you give yourself to look around to see what is going on in creative fields that 'run alongside' your work; or remember that good idea you had, the thing you always meant to chase up; or time to work on how to bring to fruition the thing that has been on 'the drawing board' for a while.

Or it can be about innovation through enabling you to think about those generic skills that are often necessary for innovation but are not necessary 'inside' your creativity as such. Innovation does not always come from doing something new. It can come from doing the same thing in a better way, or telling people about it more effectively. So research *For* innovation can be about things like improved writing skills, better sourcing of materials, improving basic business acumen or organizing group creativity better. More on that stuff later.

Research *In Front Of* Leading to Innovation – creativity is never really a solely individual exercise. It always depends on other people, and is something that by its very nature needs to be communicated to others. So knowing about the people that your creativity is for is necessary if you are going to innovate within it. For innovation to really work, researching audiences, end-users or customers is clearly useful to assess their needs, reception of it, understanding and so on. So research *In Front Of* that can lead to innovation by enabling you to be better at speaking to these people.

But the link between you and your intended audience is not always direct. Rather, it is mediated by all manner of 'gatekeepers' who may provide opportunities and constraints as part of their role as cultural intermediaries. So innovation can also come from researching how these systems work.

For instance:

- How do the Press and TV pick up on stories?
- How do you write a good Press release?
- What hits the buttons of those who select pieces of culture and business for exhibition?
- How do you speak to potential investors or funders?

The *Behind, In/Through, For and In Front Of* research distinctions we have considered, and the ways in which they can lead to innovation are not clear-cut distinctions. These starting-points and routes to innovation can overlap in many unexpected and reciprocal ways. But this is a way of beginning to put some order to the different things that can, or need to happen within research.

And that is what the rest of the book is about.

What/Whom is Your Research and Innovation For?

As we have already noted creative business can be motivated by a multitude of things. Whichever research starting-point you feel is most immediately relevant and useful, finding a useful relationship between these basic motivations and the way you approach your research is something else that it is good to be clear about.

So consider the extent to which your creativity is motivated by one or more of the following:

- The attempt to say something about the world at large, to the world at large and the way this informs how and why you develop your creativity.
- The way the specifics of your own creativity are actually panning out in terms of your overall creative discipline, techniques, business agenda and so on, and how you might want to develop this, or even need to change it as you learn more.
- The meeting point between the first two points. This could be how understanding the world and developing the interior dynamics of your work bounce off or mutually influence each other.
- Specific business applications and the management of creative processes that enables you to develop new products and grow your creative business. This can sometimes be for quite instrumental reasons. Which might involve …
- Researching other people, such as suppliers, competitors, collaborators, business colleagues and staff, audiences.
- Research that critiques what someone else has done, or is a critical response to creative work already out there, because you feel this will inform your creative responses …

… or lots of other potential variations of these things.

Theory

THEORIES OF CREATIVE INNOVATION: NO. 2 – BEHAVIOURIST PSYCHOLOGY

Behaviourist psychology advances:

… a theory of creativity which is of the associative sort. (It) … defines creativity as involving the formation of associations between stimuli and responses which are characterized by the fact that the elements linked together are not normally associated. Thus, (it) suggests that divergent (creative) people tend to link stimuli with highly unlikely responses, whereas in most people any particular stimuli is usually linked with the response with which it has most frequently been paired in the past. In other words, highly divergent people are particularly skilful at linking together, in effective ways, aspects of their environment which, on the basis of experience, do not normally belong together. In most people, such happy stimulus-response linkages seldom occur, except perhaps by chance, whereas they are more or less commonplace among highly creative individuals.

(from *Creativity*, by A.J. Cropley)

Why is Your Research?

The various answers to 'What/Who?' questions have implications for this 'Why?' question of the research. In general terms research can be:

- **Descriptive** – an investigation into something that just seeks to describe an aspect of the world as it is. For instance, most surveys, opinion polls and market research will be descriptive in that it will show percentages of this opinion, that preference, and so on, without trying to explain *why* people think and act as they do. A lot of commercial and policy-oriented research is like this.
- **Explanatory** – research that aims to arrive at an explanation that addresses the *why* question. Why things are the way they are, why people think and act the way they do, or why one business process is better than another. Most academic research will have an element of this because it tends to go beyond the collection of data to develop an argument or theory.
- **Exploratory** – more open-ended investigations into something new, an aspect of the world or a new creative process or technique. This kind of research often develops with no especially fixed agenda other than having a look to see what is going on. This kind of research tends to look for the new rather than attempting to describe and/or explain what already is.

Added to this distinction of the types of research, there can be certain time scales. Research can involve:

- **A Pilot Stage** – a short look at something with a view to developing your research strategy and methods before you actually embark on the main thing. The warming up exercise before the match really gets going.
- **Interim Research Findings** – looking at the progress of the research as it is going along, to check progress, think about emerging trends and findings. Looking at things at 'half time'.
- **Longitudinal Research** – research that carries on over a long period of time, over and above the first look at something. This means repeating the same research agenda after a period of time to see how things are changing. Looking at things during extra time or having a replay.

Exercise

IT'S YOUR THING, DO WHAT YOU WANNA DO

So, at the very beginning of any thinking you might do about research for creativity, and whichever starting-point(s) you think best, it is good to ask yourself these very basic and simple questions:

- What is my research for?
- Whom is my research for?
- Why is my research?
- Is it about knowing more about the world out there? Or is it about the interior dynamics of me and my work?

- Do I need research to be able to convince someone else about my particular project or proposal? Or is it about researching bigger questions than that?
- Is it descriptive, explanatory or exploratory? Or a bit of each?

Once you have asked these kinds of questions, you can then start to think about:

- What different research tools are out there?
- Which research tools are the most appropriate for the kind(s) of research I want to do?
- How do I design my research to get me to where I want to be?

Whilst these questions might be useful, you will ultimately have to answer them yourself, because this depends upon the specific research agenda you need/want.

As The Isley Brothers once said …

It's your thing, do what you wanna do. I can't tell you who to sock it to.

Exercise

THE MODEL IN ACTION: DECIDING UPON BEHIND, IN/THROUGH, FOR AND IN FRONT OF

So, with all this in mind, place yourself at the centre of the research map.

Now ask yourself the following questions:

- What has my creativity been for in the past few years?
- Who has it been for?
- Why have I done it this way? Has this been my decision or someone else's?
- What do I want the future of my creativity to be?

So then …

- In what specific way(s) can research help me to get to these new places?
- Which research starting-points do I feel most drawn to?
- Which do I feel wary of?
- Which seem irrelevant to my concerns and plans?

With these questions and responses in mind, which one of the boxes on the research map are you now in? – Behind, In/Through, For, In Front Of?

All starting-points are reasonable, as are all the ambitions and rationales behind choosing them. This is just an initial exercise aimed at helping you clarify where you want to go, and therefore where it is best to start from.

However, this does brings us to …

Warning

WHAT A LOVELY VIEW: THE DANGER OF SOLIPSISM

Solipsism (Latin: solus, alone + ipse, self) is the philosophical idea that 'My mind is the only thing that I know exists'. Solipsism is an epistemological or metaphysical position that knowledge of anything outside the mind (one's own mind) *is unjustified* ... (It involves the presumption that) *my most certain knowledge is the contents of my own mind – my thoughts, experiences, affects, etc.*

(from Wikipedia)

Any of us can get so involved with our own creativity, and generally with our own view of the world that we can end up mistaking our own personal view of reality for the real thing. Everybody has the tendency to find evidence for their own personal view of the world simply from the fact that they have the view they have.

For instance ...

A SHORT PLAY ABOUT SOLIPSISM

Person 1 – How can you be so sure?

Person 2 – Well, I know I've been right all along and everybody else wrong all along, because otherwise I wouldn't have thought what I think. I would have thought something else, wouldn't I?

Person 1 – Oh, I see, and then thinking that 'something else' would have made you right all along and everyone else wrong all along, wouldn't it? I'm going over here now to talk to Jeff!

Unfortunately, having a view is not the same as having a fully worked out, well researched and well-rounded view. Solipsism is the worst kind of ignorance, because it is ignorance that stems from believing that one already knows everything one needs to know. It is ignorance that stems from self-congratulation and it is therefore very bad.

White is not cold, nor does it go swish-swish. The world is much more complicated than that, and sorry, but it will never conform to your view of it just because you have that view.

Say it one more time, the question you ask yourself will determine the answers you get! We will really drop that one now!

With the question of how to study white, the quotation from Mozart and the dangers of solipsism we start to enter thinking about the way to do thinking. And this entails entering the big, mysterious world of epistemology (it's not really that mysterious).

Epistemology

The name of this debate about the relative merits of different conceptual universes that can underpin research, and consequently the different grounds for knowledge that they offer is *epistemology*. The short play at the start of the chapter asks you to 'step outside' of the way you perceive the world as it is presented to you as a way of finding a more sophisticated sense of perspective on it. Epistemology is essentially about considering ways of questioning your questions in the search for better, firmer, more solid grounds upon which to develop your research.

All this sounds complicated, and sometimes it is. Epistemology often makes people feel a bit uncomfortable because it re-problematizes what they thought they could take for granted. It revolves around the basic question *how can we know ... ?* or indeed, *can we know anything for sure?* Some people believe that there are universals truths out there that we can discover through using established research methods that work for all situations. They sometimes get a bit irritated by epistemological debates. But creativity generally requires an open and exploratory approach to new ways of thinking and doing. So rather than holding a sense of trepidation, epistemology is something to be embraced and enjoyed. It is in and of itself a part of creative thinking, if you get beyond all the jargon and mystification that is.

C.P. Snow was once famous for talking about 'two cultures', the sciences and the arts, and about the lack of mutual understanding between them. The development of academic specialisms over the past century or two has meant that different languages of research have developed, and these languages have not always been very good at talking to each other. Very, very briefly, this history has involved:

- Modern science growing out of the idea that there is one way to do proper research, through proper unified scientific method based upon certain epistemological assumptions. And nothing else really counts.
- Some aspects of the social sciences and humanities have signed up to this, but others have not and are still debating epistemology. This has routinely involved prolonged debates about what can count as social science research and therefore as legitimate research methods. Some of which is very useful for creativity.
- Creative disciplines have not been too involved in this debate. Or if they have, they have tended to use another language. For instance, students of Art and Design courses often get told to 'go and do some research'. This can mean virtually anything, from going to a gallery to talking to your Mum. It is not always something that is particularly systematic. Nor is it something that always routinely involves self-reflexive debate about epistemological underpinnings and consolidated research methods.

Despite this, creative people often have a more immediate and visceral reason to be doing their own practical research, to inform their work and expand their creativity. So this chapter is conceived as a space where these different concepts and languages of research, creativity and innovation can be explored in a way that overcomes these 'two (or more) cultures'. When it comes to research, creativity and innovation, there is no reason why science and technology, business, the arts and the social sciences cannot learn from each other much more effectively. The examples and case-studies we include below are designed to show this potential for cross-fertilization leading to creativity and innovation.

Epistemology is such a good place to start all this because it involves recognizing the way in which becoming a sophisticated researcher requires a philosophical breadth to back up the depth of expertise you might have in something. Getting to know epistemology for doing research and creativity is like a carpenter getting to know his/her tool box, before getting to know the wood and doing any cutting or fixing together.

Jargon

Jargon and official terminology is always a problem, but you are likely to come across it when dealing with epistemology. And some of it is not actually that complicated.

Without going into massive detail, some useful epistemological terms to think about are listed below. They form the basis of a professional research language that can help to frame a research agenda.

- **Theory** – basic ideas and concepts shaped into an explanation, prediction, or basic handle on some aspect of the world. Useful for thinking and turning information into (albeit temporary) 'knowledge'.
- **Methods** – the way one constructs the basic game plan with which to go out there and collect information. (The term 'methodology' is sometimes used, but this term is more accurately used to describe the study of different methods. To keep things simple, and to signal a practical focus upon the actual doing of research, the term 'methods' is best here).
- **Truth** – science is built upon the idea that we can find universally true facts that are …
- **Objective** – they are not a matter of your opinion and how you would like things to be, objective facts exist out there and are independent of what anyone thinks. They are the opposite of opinions. But in the arts and humanities we cannot always be dealing with such hard facts. Truth with a capital T is sometimes not really that important, because we are often dealing with …
- **Interpretation** – despite what 'hard science' wants to say, Truth with a capital T does not really exist in the social or cultural world. Obviously there is a 'real world' out there, but the thing we call 'reality' in social and cultural life is largely constructed out of a whole series of social, cultural, economic, historical and personal processes. This is the social construction of reality position, which suggests that most views of the world have at least some component of the …
- **Subjective** – it is about what is going on inside your head rather than what exists out there, independently of you. So for your own research, you need to be clear about the degree to which you are interested in …
- **Quantitative or Qualitative Research** – quantitative research is about 'hard objective facts', often about putting a number to something. For instance, 48 per cent of people think this, or 76 per cent of people rated the event as 'excellent'. Some research questions however are about trying to find out the subjective – what people dream about or the history of their relationship with their dad and how they feel about that. This entails qualitative research. This is more about ways of studying the interior perceptions, meanings, motivations and desires of real people, as they exist for them. It is about a different quality (texture and flavour) of research, and not so bothered about quantities (numbers). Because these research trajectories are so fundamentally different, and because research for your creativity might involve both these kinds of research, you need to be aware of …
- **Commensurability** – the degree to which the research tools you use are appropriate for the type of research you have in mind. Once our carpenter has got to know his/her toolbox, there is no way they would try to hammer in a nail with a screwdriver. Similarly it's not good to try to research people's innermost thinking with a questionnaire.

There is more jargon, but we will come to that later.

Whichever research starting-point you might choose, and whatever motivates your engagement, there will always be 'more than one way to skin a cat'. That is, choosing between behind, in/through, for and in front of research starting-points will still require you to be clear about the underlying type knowledge you are after. You will need to make smart epistemological choices. So let's now look at the basic characteristics of some standard epistemological positions that underpin systematic research.

13 Thinking About the Way to Do Thinking: Epistemological Choices

---

Short Play

WHAT IS WHITE?

In his book *An End to Suffering* Pankaj Mishra tells the story of two blind guys sitting together one day discussing the colour white.

'I've heard that white is the colour of snow', said the first guy. 'So I asked my friend to take me up to the mountains to let me feel it. He put me into the snow, and I now realize that white is cold.'

'I've heard that white is the colour of swans' said the second guy. 'So I asked my friend to take me down to the river. He took me near to the swans, and I now realize that white goes 'swish-swish.'

White is cold and goes swish-swish?

In their attempts to research the colour white, the first guy used his sense of touch and the second guy used his sense of hearing. Because they used one particular sense only, their thinking about the way to do thinking was limited and so their research into what is white is less than complete answer. Actually, whilst not wanting to be unkind to them and their heartfelt attempts to understand white, what they came up with was so limited you could say it was 'wrong'. It is the same for all of us. Failure to think about the way to do thinking can all too often lead you to a less than fully developed answer. If you don't question your questions, you too could be 'blind' to other choices about ways to see.

So when you do research for innovation it is good to know that there are lots and lots of different ways to tackle any particular question. Because of this, you have to *choose* a particular way of approaching it. That is, you have to make an epistemological choice.

So choose wisely, young Jedi.

In the previous chapter we began to consider the basic distinction between *behind, in/ through, for and in front of* research starting-points, and the Research Map as an initial *practical consideration*. This is underpinning by *philosophical propositions*. Whichever research starting point and underlying conceptual universe you choose, being conscious that it is a *choice* of research outlook, in and of itself, already suggests that *other conceptual universes could be chosen.* We are already getting into the idea of making epistemological choices.

Two fundamental points about creativity flow from this:

- All possible choices could contribute to illuminating research and innovative breakthroughs. All conceptual universes and research starting-points have their relative practical merits.
- The very act of thinking about thinking, and thus thinking about thinking differently is creativity and innovation. It is possibly where one of the mainsprings of creativity actually comes from in the first place.

Theory

THEORIES OF CREATIVE INNOVATION: NO. 3 – COGNITIVE PSYCHOLOGY

... cognitive theorists are chiefly concerned with the ways in which people organize information received from the world. The individual is regarded as actively at grips with his/her environment, not merely the passive receptor of whatever it chances to offer him/her. Different people possess differing ways of 'taking hold of' the external world; they receive information in characteristic ways, interpret it idiosyncratically, and store it in terms of all the information processed in the past. Intellectual functioning is thus seen as a highly unified process so that the attempt to break it down into discrete fragments in the way stimulus-response (behaviourist) ways is bound to be inadequate. Hence, in accounting for the appearance or absence of creative thinking, cognitive psychologists are concerned with differences between highly creative and highly divergent individuals in the characteristic ways in which they come to grips with their environment.

Consequently, as far as cognitive theorists are concerned, creativity represents not differing systems of associational bonds, but differing ways of getting and handling information, and different ways of combining data in seeking effective solutions (different 'mind styles' if you like). Hence, the cognitive approach to creativity asks about the extent to which highly creative people are prepared to take risks in their thinking, about their willingness to take in large quantities of information the environment has to offer (rather than restrict themselves to a narrow, but safe, segment of it), about their capacity for quickly changing their point of view.

(from *Creativity*, by A.J. Cropley)

So let's take a closer, informed look at what our epistemological choices are.

Mista Know It All: Science and Positivism

In Western society at least, the thing that we call research changed after The Enlightenment. This started sometimes in the seventeenth century, but really got going in the eighteenth century when the approach to research that we now call *science* really came to the fore.

Immediately you might think, 'I am a creative practitioner and I don't do science, so what does that matter?' But that is not the point. The cultural weight of science, or more accurately *scientism* has tended to colour all subsequent epistemological debates. This is because science has become fundamentally connected to what we now call *Reason*, as opposed to *Metaphysics* (superstition, mysticism, the Spirit). As a creative practitioner, you might be really interested in superstition, mysticism, and the Spirit. And there is nothing wrong with that. But if you want to engage in research using those conceptual worlds you will be up against people who will reject your research because they reject your very starting point. Before they have even listened to what your research says scientism will reject it because of its metaphysical nature. This starts to get us into the ideological nature of scientism and the *politics of knowledge* as a facet of a broader cultural politics, but that debate is for another time. It also begins to suggest the need for epistemological nervousness, which we discuss towards the end of this chapter.

Given the rise of science, the predominant epistemological position underpinning quantitative research is *Positivism*, which is defined by the following features:

- A unified method that is applicable to all types of research questions. That is, a science that involves rigorous methodological principles. These can take various forms such as straightforward observational techniques through to more complex experimental models and other ways of collecting raw data through observation and measurement. But they are all essentially about collecting ...
- Facts-with-a-capital-F. Positivism is about collecting *positive knowledge*. Positivism sees it as less than adequate to be basing your research on opinion, hearsay and other things that are, as they see it, tainted by *values*.
- So, correspondingly, one of the key slogans of Positivism is the *separation of fact from value*. As a result, Positivism is very big on *value-freedom*, which is the hallmark of objectivity.
- As a result of the concern with objectivity, Positivism is about *measurement* rather than argument. If one is being objective then the 'facts' should (sometimes at least) speak for themselves. This is why the Positivist epistemology tends to have a very intimate relationship with *numbers*, the measurement tool par excellence.
- This has all been motivated by a scientific desire the find causation. That is, explanations that lay out how one thing causes another. This is seen as good because it enables things like the separation and control of variables, analysis, prediction, reproducibility (others can redo your research and test your findings) and therefore again Truth-with-a-capital-T, stemming from dealing with the aforementioned positive facts.

This is all very reasonable, and involves thinking that might help you design some of your research. Especially if your research is motivated by the need to convince someone else, you might want to construct some objective knowledge so that you can 'prove' something in a way that does not rely solely upon your own opinions. Sometimes it is good to let the 'Facts speak for themselves' because it can put you in a much stronger position to make *truth-claims* about your research when trying to speak to a potential investor, funder or decision-maker.

Theory

THEORIES OF CREATIVE INNOVATION: NO. 3 – A SCIENTIST'S VIEW

It seems clear that the creative development of science depends quite generally on the perception of the irrelevance of an already known set of fundamental differences and similarities. Psychologically speaking, this is the hardest step of all. But once it has taken place, it frees the mind to be attentive, alert, aware, and sensitive so it can discover a new order, and this creates new structures of ideas and concepts ... In order properly to understand the relationship between science and art, it is necessary to go into certain deeper questions that have to do with what underlies both these forms of human activity.

(from *On Creativity*, by D. Bohm)

So science and art do have some similarities, if we go back far enough.

However, science and scientific culture is based upon the notion that there is an ordered whole out there, and all we need to do is get better at researching it, so that one day we will arrive at the ultimate answer, once and for all, and know *everything*. But this is an epistemological assumption, and scientists do not have any proof for this assumption, nor for the idea that science is the best vehicle to get us there. It is not good to use the very existence of your epistemological choices to try to justify your epistemological choices!

We told you epistemology can sometimes get a bit complicated.

The downside of Positivism is its tendency to hold itself up as the *only* way to really know anything. Positivism tends to criticize other epistemological positions not so much in terms of what their research says, but in terms of their epistemological credential to even speak, if they do not measure up to Positivism's own standards of scientific rigour. It can be epistemologically quite self-obsessed, which is why it can sometimes be a little like Stevie Wonder's *Mista Know-it-All*.

Secondly, the desire to 'prove the Truth' is not always, and need not necessarily be, the point of cultural or artistic research. Because epistemological choices tend to already imply certain methods, it is not always relevant or indeed possible to apply Positivism to research for creativity. Meanings, internal personal motivations and histories, interactions between people and all the 'soft' stuff that creative people are often most interested in often has to be left out of the Positivist idea of research because it cannot ever really be measured with numbers. All too often one ends up 'talking at cross-purposes' with Positivists (investors, funders and decision-makers), and this is at the heart of the 'two cultures' thing touched upon above.

The Interpretative Tradition

There has been, maybe always, but certainly for a few hundred years now another basic epistemological tradition made up of various threads. It has developed sometimes outside, and sometimes through a direct challenge to Positivist epistemology.

This is usually referred to as the *Interpretative Tradition*. Because it is made up of various threads, it is less easy to sum up this tradition of research in a few bullet points. But let's try anyway.

The Interpretative Tradition:

- Does not have any self-referential sense of itself as the only way to do research, and there is little or no sense of a unified method that fits all occasions. Choosing the right research tool for the right job and particular time depending on what it is you are researching, is more of a hallmark of the Interpretative Tradition.
- Sees separating Facts from values, and being value-free as a bit of a non-starter. This is essentially because the Interpretative Tradition sees knowledge as being conditioned by the social and historical context that we live in. What we call 'the Truth' is always moving around and changing. We used to know that the human species was created by God in his own image, but now most people at least reckon it is something to do with Natural Selection. So the Interpretative Tradition is much more relaxed about the idea that all knowledge is probably a story coloured by the social, historical and cultural context we find ourselves in.
- Therefore tends to see knowledge as *contingent*. Like stories, narratives and debates, knowledge is not fixed for all time. If Positivism is generally about Truth-with-a-capital-T then the Interpretative Tradition is more plural truths-with-a-capital-S. There are many competing ideas about how the world is. This takes us back to ideology and the politics of knowledge. Who says what is 'True', is partly at least a question of economic and cultural power. But that still is another debate for another time.
- Is thus much more about argument, debate, and a contest of ideas (more politics of knowledge) than it is about measurement.
- Tends to also be more relaxed with the idea that we cannot always prove the relationships between cause and effect, and with the idea that things in the cultural world don't necessarily sit in such neat relationships with other things. The Interpretative Tradition tends to be more relaxed about the idea of over-determination. That is, lots of things (causes) happen at the same time in strange, interpenetrating relationships to produce something (an effect) in the real human and cultural world. We will come back to this when we look briefly at dialectics below.

So all in all, the Interpretative Tradition is often more useful for research for creativity, especially when this involves researching other people as they exist in *their worlds*. The Interpretative Tradition shows us that the epistemological problems arising from Positivism stem from the over-insistence that there is 'one best epistemological way'. Their way.

But there isn't one.

The distinction between Positivism and The Interpretative Tradition is the fundamental epistemological distinction. It underpins the distinction between quantitative and qualitative research, which is the fundamental distinction when we get to actual research methods. However, it needs to be said somewhere, so we might as well say it here, that not everyone will agree with the characterization we have just put forward. We have just been very quickly through a few hundred years of heavy-duty philosophical debate, so there will inevitably be some skating over details. Sorry.

Warning

SAY NO TO REDUCTIONISM

Despite the epistemological problems associated with Positivism and its over-focus upon supposedly Positive Facts, there is a clear and present danger in going too far to the other extreme and denying the evident nature of the 'real world' in favour of a partial view. As we saw with the dangers of solipsism, we are all subject to the tendency that we think we know best, and this is why we are all always a little bit wrong. Choosing one way of seeing the world means we have to forego the usefulness of seeing it in other ways.

When we insist too strongly that our own chosen (socially constructed) way of seeing and therefore understanding the world is the only way, we are in danger of unnecessarily reducing ways of doing research to a self-limited range of possibilities.

This is reductionism, and it is never going to be very good for any kind of research. But it is especially bad for creativity because closing down possibilities is not going to lead to open exploration nor innovation. And reductionism can take many forms, some of which we touched upon in Section 1. But it can also come as:

- **Economism** – Too often within cultural policy and planning discussions of the creative industries and their relationship to wider public culture, economic impact agendas becomes an overly privileged concern. Cultural and creative life is inappropriately reduced to economic measurements (job creation and business start-up statistics) and purportedly positive facts about it, which are at best very rough approximations of what is really going on, and at worst encourage a wilful misreading.
- **Gender Essentialism** – Whether from patriarchy or feminism, the reduction of all responses to an argument down to a reaction to the gender of the person making it is presented as a legitimate way of assessing its worth, when it is not.
- **Technological Determinism** – The idea that it is technology that orders the whole of society, and as a result the idea that technology always and already comes first and determines everything else. This is usually wrong because the technology we get is shaped by all sorts of other economic, political and cultural factors.

All such forms of reductionism are the enemy of creative thinking and good research, and should be resisted whenever encountered.

We mean it!

All this philosophy might be good for impressing people at parties, but it doesn't necessarily help you to construct your own structured research in any great details. So from now on, we will stop being so philosophical and try to pin things down a little more in terms of *doing something* with epistemological concepts.

This will include ideas from both the Positivist and Interpretative Traditions, because they both hold useful ideas and say things that are practically useful.

Empiricism, Induction and Deduction

Empiricism is kind of the public face of the Positivist Tradition. It is an epistemological position based upon the idea that research can simply be about using sensory experiences to observe things happening. At its heart this is common sense. You see something happening over and over again, and you work out that it is likely to happen again tomorrow. This is the basic way we respond to the world in our everyday lives, how we 'research' the cultural world around us simply by being part of it and seeing what is going on.

But it is not always that simple.

To do something with these observations – construct a proper theory that you might want to use to say something that you think other people should listen to, or predict something about the world, or convince a bank manager to loan you some money for investment in a new product line – you need to get into some of the technicalities of how an actual prediction or explanation, that is a *theory* can stem from simply observing something happen a few times.

This gets us into *induction* and *deduction*. These two philosophical ideas, which are about how collecting observations can enable you to construct a theory, involve one of two logical manoeuvres:

- Induction is the most straightforward. It is about constructing an explanation or prediction that something will happen in the future by collecting observations that it has happened that way in the past. If you observe the sun rising in the morning often enough, you can construct a theory that the sun rises *every* morning.
- Deduction is connected but different. If I observe something happening every time I enter a particular room, I can predict that that thing will happen to me again if I enter that room again, without the need to actually enter the room and observe anything. Deduction is what Sherlock Holmes was good at.

There are pitfalls within deductive logic because people 'jump to conclusions' on the basis of false premises. Deductive logic is based upon syllogisms, but that starts to get very technical and we don't really need to get into that.

More important is the famous *Problem of Induction*.

If we want to construct a theory based upon induction and the serial collection of observations, then how many observations are enough to conclusively 'prove the point'? Just because you observe something happening at lot does not actually provide logical proof that it will happen *next* time. Everything changes.

This can have important practical consequences for the quality of your research and business innovation plans based upon it. You might observe that the cultural trend you have spotted is 'definitely' happening, and so develop a new product line and sink all your new investment funds into meeting this new 'demand'. But you might have spotted it just as it is changing into something else. So it is useful to have a way of *testing* your creative or business hypotheses that is based upon something a little more solid than just observing what is going on around you.

This gets us into falsificationism.

The Colour of Swans: Falsificationism

You might not be convinced by what one of the two blind guys said about the colour of swans, and you might want to do some more proper research to see if white really is the colour of swans and their swish-swish.

According to induction, if you want to know the colour of swans you need to go out and collect observation of them. If you notice that every time you see a swan it is white, you might then construct a theory, based upon induction, that 'all swans are white'.

But back to the problem of induction. How many swans do you need to count before you can say that they are *all* white? You can never prove that all swans are white simply by observing swans, but you can *disprove* the theory 'all swans are white' just by observing *one* black swan. You can never conclusively prove something, but you can conclusively disprove something with only one observation that is contrary to your original idea. You can never conclusively *verify* but you can conclusively *falsify*.

And this is where falsificationism comes from. It is a really elegant solution to the problem of induction, devised by the famous philosopher Karl Popper who first used the swans thing. It provides firmer epistemological grounds upon which to build theories of the world and can be invaluable for your research into creativity and business innovation. As we shall see in below, experienced creative practitioners have various ways of testing their own creative output. For instance, writers often talk about 'murdering their darlings' by editing out of the novel their favourite characters because they don't fit. Being one's own harshest critic, or asking someone else to be, can be very useful.

Interestingly for creativity and the sometimes unknown and unexpected sources of inspiration we experience, Popper argued that it did not matter where scientific hypotheses come from. Their value is assessed according to the extent to which they stand up to *testing*. And testing lies in the attempt to disprove them. It might seem counter-intuitive, but according to this view good research lies in trying to destroy your own ideas, in 'testing them to destruction'. If you can't, then they are probably good ideas. This enables you to see if your creative or business plan really does stand up, or if you are kidding yourself. Which is always really useful.

Falsificationism is not something that comes very easily to creative practice. It is not so easy to set out to disprove or 'destroy' ideas, plans and work that you have invested so much of yourself in. But no matter how uncomfortable it is, it is good for your creative soul.

Game

AM I ON THE RIGHT TRACK? CONFIRMATION BIAS

We all have a deep-seated need to feel that we have some control over our immediate environment. To feel a lack of this control in a fundamental, Existential way is very destabilizing and scary. So we are often tempted into *The Illusion of Control*.

One of the ways this can play itself out is the way we feel the need to keep hold of our view of reality as the correct one. This is kind of the interior philosophical manoeuvres we go through to arrive at and sustain solipsism. It appears that people have a hardwired motivation to seek validation for the views they already hold.

So we all suffer from Confirmation Bias. And it can be very bad for research and creativity if we are constantly trying to reconfirm our existing views. Remember Krishnamurti? The best antidote to Confirmation Bias is to recognize it for what it is.

To help with this, Leonard Mlodinow introduces the following game in *The Drunkards Walk*.

He gives you three numbers – 2, 4, 6.

He has chosen these numbers because they confirm to a particular rule that he has in mind. And you have to work out what this rule is by asking if another three number sequences also conform to the rule.

So what three number sequence would you come up with to research what this rule is?

Did you say – 8, 10, 12? The next three even numbers ascending in order of size?

8, 10, 12 does adhere to the rule, but what is the rule?

How about 20, 30, 40? Yep, still conforms to the rule, but the rule is not 'even numbers ascending in order'.

What about 3, 5, 7? Maybe it is just numbers ascending by a factor of two? Yep 3, 5, 7 conforms, but what is the rule?

Are you trying to choose three numbers that conform to the rule, or three numbers that test the rule to find out what it is? That is, are you trying to get the particular answer to this specific question right, when getting it 'wrong' so that you could get better insight into what the rule is, the bigger question, what you are actually researching would be a better strategy? What the rule is!

If you are just trying to get the numbers right instead of trying to find out what the rule is, it is probably because of the Confirmation Bias. You are experiencing the need to get things 'right'.

The rule is the simplest one available, three ascending numbers. No evens or odds or factors of 2. But that doesn't really matter. The point is the need to try to disprove yourself so that you can get the answer right.

Exercise

CALL IN THE AWKWARD SQUAD

It is an old proverb, but still a good one …

You can learn more from failure than you can from success

This proverb implies a falsificationist position, in that learning from failure is akin to testing to destruction the things (concepts, theories, practices and techniques) you thought were your way forward.

And you can easily get help with this kind of research. A research technique that chimes with falsificationism is to deliberately seek out people you know are going to be difficult to convince, The Awkward Squad. And there is never a shortage of awkward people!

These are the people who just love asking those really difficult, Exocet questions. *Why are you doing it like that? Why is it blue, and not green? What is that character for?* You know the ones.

If you have answers that convince both you and them, then you are probably onto something. Whilst it doesn't really have to be as pompous as the Dragon's Den thing, it won't be comfortable, and it might get really irritating. But it will probably be really useful.

Case Study

TEST YOURSELF: FALSIFICATIONISM FOR CREATIVE BUSINESS

Yvon Chouinard once wrote:

Do your testing – testing your own ideas, no matter where they came from, is often the best way to conduct research for business …

Chouinard is the guy who set up Patagonia, the outdoor clothing firm. A very successful business as well as a very eco-credible label that seems to stand for something beyond its own profit motive. So maybe we should listen to him some more:

… Testing is an integral part of the Patagonia industrial design process, and it needs to be included in every part of the process. It involves testing competitors' products, 'quick and dirty' testing of new ideas to see if they are worth pursuing, fabric testing, 'living' with the new product to judge how 'hot' the sales may be, testing production samples for function and durability, and so on. and test marketing a product to see if people will buy it.

(From *Let My People Go Surfing*, by Y. Chouinard)

We will hear more from Chouinard later.

Stuck in the Middle with You: Paradigms Can Be Good and Bad

Karl Popper's work on falsificationism was the beginning of what some people now refer to as *post-Positivism*, where epistemological debate started to move away from the *naïve* Positivism described above. Another key milestone within this development is the work of Thomas Kuhn, whose discussion of *paradigms* became central to current epistemological debate.

A paradigm is made up of the shared assumptions that a particular research community gathers around. It tends to include a definition (tight or loose) of what count as good questions to be asking right now, and therefore what counts as good answers. It is the shared assumptions that are current within a particular discipline, the research *zeitgeist* of the day. Paradigms can be a good thing, but they can also be a bad thing. They can lead to you getting stuck within one particular position that then precludes you thinking in other ways.

Quotation

A paradigm is defined by Thomas Kuhn as follows:

Close historical investigation of a given speciality at a given time discloses a set of recurrent and quasi-standard illustrations of various theories in their conceptual, observational and instrumental applications. These are the community's paradigm, revealed in its textbooks, lectures and laboratory exercises. By studying them and by practicing with them, the members of the corresponding community learn their trade … discover what isolatable elements, explicit or implicit, the members of that community may have abstracted from their global paradigm and deployed as rules in their research. Anyone who has attempted to describe or analyse the evolution of a particular scientific (research) tradition will necessarily have sought accepted principles and rules of this sort.

(from *The Structure of Scientific Revolutions*, by T. Kuhn)

Creative disciplines, whether they are aware of it or not, also have paradigmatic assumptions underpinning them.

Paradigms can be *good* in that they:

- Indicate current best practice and what 'counts' as important research, current trends, 'cutting edge' and so on within your chosen creative field. It provides ready-made knowledge of what are the acceptable tools, concepts, current debates, urgent next issues and so on that need to be researched.
- Encourage the sharing of the knowledge generated within a particular field of research. This sharing is 'oxygen' of the paradigm. This also includes creating the social spaces for practitioners within a particular field to congregate in a broader sense, for example when you attend a conference, trade show, private view or festival.
- Provide the shared rituals of initiation into a particular creative discipline – the qualifications, memberships, accolades and so on.

Paradigms also tend to encourage 'revolutions' whereby people carve out a creative place on the edge of the accepted way of doing things by opening up new possibilities. This seems to be especially the case within creative disciplines. This can be good fun, and lead to fruitful forms of creativity and innovation that develop out of a critique of what went before. For instance, a history of Avant Garde art movements throughout the twentieth century could be couched in a history of 'paradigmatic reactions' – how Fauvism and Cubism reacted to the 'paradigm' of The Salon, how Dada and Surrealism reacted to Naturalism, how Expressionism reacted to all this by rejecting everything that went before, and so on. It is very useful for creativity to know what you are not, so that you can know what you are.

However, paradigms can be *bad* because they:

- Impose 'rules' on research and creativity that can easily lead to an agenda that is too 'closed off'. They can encourage the researcher (creative practitioner) to believe there really is 'one best way' to do research (creative practice), leading to a rather arrogant belief that other research can be dismissed as already wrong simply because of its paradigmatic starting point.
- Can discourage cross-disciplinary research and foreclose on such potential dialogue with someone else from a different paradigm. If you are both too wedded to your paradigmatic position you will just end up speaking different languages, at cross-purposes and maybe not at all. This entails too high an 'opportunity cost' (discussed below), which is the cost incurred by pursuing one research direction and therefore having to dismiss others that could be equally fruitful.
- Require 'revolutions' to carve out a creative place that doesn't conform to the accepted way of doing things. This can be wasteful and time consuming in terms of constantly debunking everything that went before. It can also be wasteful and time consuming to be arguing about basic concepts and tools. Carpenters tend not to have debates about hammers and screwdrivers when they are making tables.
- Can encourage a 'group mindedness' whereby people get together and mutually reinforce each other's partial view of the world, leading to a kind of irrationality and/ or creative short sightedness.

Paradigms and Opportunity Costs

The idea of 'opportunity cost' that we have touched on already also highlights the cost associated with choosing to do something in a particular way because you cannot therefore do it another way. You have inevitably closed off another opportunity. Being too wedded to a paradigm, whether you are aware of it or not, can encourage a high opportunity cost.

In *Steps in the Ecology of Mind*, Gregory Bateson has articulated this kind of thinking in the following way: Because of the basic rules of grammar and syntax (a very broad and powerful paradigm), if I choose to now write down the letter 'F', I have already, by that very act closed down my options for the next letter, because only certain letters can follow an 'F'. And if I choose to write the letter 'R' next, then my choice for the next letter is even more limited, it is going to have to be a vowel, and there are only five of them to choose from!

This is only a little game, but it does elucidate something more central to research for creativity and innovation. Every time you make a choice you are in danger of closing down the range of options you can choose for your next move, and then closing down even further the next set of options, and so on ...

So, two things:

- You need to be sure your basic starting point and general directions are right. If you are going in slightly the wrong direction with your research, it might not matter at first, but the more you go into it the further you will be off course.
- Avoiding too strong a link to any one paradigm and always having an awareness of the potential to borrow ideas from other disciplines can be a good compass to avoid the consequences of these wrong directions, the antidote to opportunity costs and the 'refresh button' on your potential for innovation.

So be self-aware of the existence of the paradigm you are currently in, and of its impact upon the way you do things. Paradigms can help, but at best probably only for a while. As we will see in various places below, there is a complex and intimate relationship between *problems* and *solutions*. All too easily the (creative) thing that you think is part of the solution can flip over to become part of the problem. If your paradigm encourages too strong a conformity to some spurious notion of the standard way of doing things, it is unlikely to be good for fruitful research and creative innovation for very long. It will certainly work against innovation eventually.

Mr Blue Sky: Epistemological Anarchism

Whilst you might be able to falsify a swan, and there is more than one way to skin a cat, it is also sometimes good to pull a rabbit out of the hat.

It is good to have a clear and precise idea about what and why you are researching, and for whom. But it is also good to be alive to what the weird and unusual can bring, and to be open and eclectic within your research and creativity.

Along with Karl Popper and Thomas Kuhn, Paul Feyerabend is usually held up as the third key representative of epistemological discussions that started to open things up in the 1960s and signalled the end of *naïve Positivism*. He advocates an *anarchistic* approach to epistemological issues which involves taking research methods, findings, directions, inspirations, insights and rabbits from anywhere and everywhere. Feyerabend's slogan for research is *anything goes*, because to do otherwise is to accept the stultifying dead-hand of official, authorized (paradigmatic) and supposedly credible approaches to doing research. If August Comte, who is the poster-boy of Positivism was *Mista Know-It-All*, then Paul Feyerabend is *Mr Blue Sky*, advocating much more 'blue sky thinking' for research.

Quotation

Feyerabend writes:

History generally, and the history of revolutions in particular, is always richer in content, more varied, more many-sided, more lively and subtle then even the best historian and the best methodologist can imagine. History is full of accidents and conjectures and curious juxtapositions of events, and it demonstrates to us the complexity of human change and (its) unpredictable character ... Are we really to believe that the naïve and single-minded rules which methodologists take as their guide are capable of accounting for such a maze of interactions? ...

Therefore ...

... anarchism, while perhaps not the most attractive political philosophy, is certainly excellent medicine for epistemology, and for the philosophy of science.

(from *Against Method*, by P. Feyerabend)

Dialectical Logic

At first sight dialectics can appear very weird and slightly unnatural. It is a discussion that does not often show up in the more orthodox discussions of research and business. But it does offer an interesting epistemological choice for creative research.

We cannot prove it, but we think this is partly to do with the generally cultural hangover of living in a Western scientific culture. Eastern philosophy and culture, especially Hinduism and Buddhism seem to think dialectically much more easily. Dialectical thinking can potentially be very useful for creativity and innovation because it is fundamentally about grasping movement and change, which is kind of what it is all about! So even though it can appear weird, abstract and counter-intuitive, give it a chance.

The place to start with dialectics is to recognize that it is a different form *of logic*. Since the ancient Greeks, we in the West have based the vast majority of our thinking upon *Formal Logic*, the type of thinking that we are all familiar with when we say that someone is being *logical*, argument that seems *internally consistent*. The type of thinking that Mr Spock is into. There are three laws of Formal Logic:

- **The Law of Identity** – a thing (a thought, argument or proposition) has a fixed identity and it equals its own thing-ness.
- **The Law of Non-Contradiction** – a thing's identity cannot be something else.

- **The Law of the Excluded Middle** – a thing must be either one thing or the other, it cannot be both at the same time.

And there is no doubt that we sometimes need this type of internally consistent logical thinking. But this does not necessarily mean it is the only route to logical thinking.

Dialectical logic is different from these laws of Formal Logic because it suggests that things:

- do not really have fixed identities, they come from somewhere and they go somewhere else, that is they evolve.
- are best understood in and through their contradictions. Sometimes the best way to understand something is to see it in its relationship with what it is not, through what is called the interpenetration of opposites.
- are always changing, they are always more than one thing at any one time, they are in *flux*.

Thinkpiece

DO YOU LIKE MY SHIRT? THE INTERPENETRATION OF OPPOSITES

I used to have a blue-and-white striped shirt. The blue stripes and the white stripes were the same thickness, so they were the same distance apart. I could never work out if it was a blue shirt with white stripes, or a white shirt with blue stripes.

But this is the wrong question. And finding the right question is key to good research as often as finding the right answer. If I had carried on researching whether my shirt was fundamentally blue with white adornment, or fundamentally white with blue adornment, I would have got precisely nowhere.

Because …

The essential character of the shirt was its stripey-ness and this was a result of the interpenetration of opposites, the blue and the white.

Its basic characteristic was a result of the relationship between its non-blueness and its non-whiteness as much as the blue and white. The movement from blue to non-blue, from white to non-white is what made it what it fundamentally was, striped. Whether it was fundamentally blue or fundamentally white could never have been answered.

Sometimes you can understand things better by understanding what they are not. We told you dialectics is a bit weird.

Thinkpiece

TWO RIVERS AND ONE BODY: RESEARCHING MOVEMENT

Rivers are often used as metaphors in dialectical philosophy. One proverb about rivers and dialectics, from Herodotus reminds us that:

… you can never step into the same river twice.

Whilst the whole river, its basic shape and course remains fairly constant for a while, it is also always changing because it is always flowing. Rivers are not ponds. So whilst you can step into the 'same' river again, the 'same' river is also a 'different' river.

In another river, this time a little faster flowing, the water rushes over a rock. As the water rushes over it, it causes a 'standing wave'. The water is so fast that the wave looks as if it is standing still. It is always there in its basic shape. But at the same time it is always different, always moving and made up of different water from higher up the river.

It is always the same and always at the same time different. Always standing still and at the same time always moving.

Your body is made up of a certain structure. But your cells are constantly reproducing themselves. We have heard various theories on this, but we are told that the cells that line your stomach take the longest to reproduce, 13 weeks. So 13 weeks from now, you will still be you, but you will also be made out of completely different stuff.

You are the same, but after every 13 weeks you are a completely different person.

So What?

It is all very well going on about shirts and rivers, but how can this dialectical stuff help in doing creative research? What good is all this dialectical philosophy?

Creative practice is best if it is aware of its own evolution, of its own movement and change. And this is the key point about dialectics. Recognizing the interpenetration of opposites and things as being in constant flux can help you to grasp how new things emerge out of older versions of themselves as a result of internal processes. Things might change a little, then a little more in terms of the internal *quantities*, but not really change their basic nature. But eventually this series of small incremental changes culminate in a fundamental change in *quality*, it becomes something completely different.

Applying this kind of dialectical thinking to the creative process raises the following kinds of questions:

- Does the inspiration behind your work come from inside you as a specific person, or does it come from your experiences of the world outside and beyond you?
- Is your creativity 'hardwired' into your personality, or does it come from the conversations you have had with other people?
- Does it come from shared ideas of how things should look, be put together and work which stem from the particular context you are working in now, or does it come from resonances and memories of when you were a child?
- Is your creative business about what you do, or what your customers want you to do? One or the other!
- Are you successful now? If so, is this a result of where you are now? Or perhaps it is a result of all the experiences you had when you were not so successful? Is your success due to your non-success?
- Is your creative work about you, or is it about the critique of what someone else has done before you that you are responding to? Is it about now, or is it about the things

that you are not yet, but would like to see, have and experience? Which actually is you, just not yet.

- What is your creative network? Is it something that has come about because you have done things for someone else? Or because they have done things for you? Or does it come from you doing things for them because they have done things for you because you have done things for them? And anyway, lots of other people have been involved and no one can remember any more, you all just live like that now?

And the best dialectical question of all for a creative person:

- What do you do? Is it this, or is it that?

According to *Formal Logic* the answer to each of these questions has to be one or the other, it cannot be both at the same time otherwise you are just confused, and *not logical*.

So answer now. Quickly!

You don't have to really, but Mr Spock would want you to. We will come back to this later.

Thinkpiece
HOW THINGS HAVE CHANGED

Most proper Shakespearian tragedies have a main character who already has within him, usually him, the seeds of his own downfall. King Lear, Macbeth, Othello, Hamlet and so on. It is not so much that some external event comes along to mess things up, rather that the behaviour that they have always exhibited eventually leads to the trouble when it really gets going.

As Joy Division have already said:

Love will tear us apart again.

The thing that was once the solution changes to become the problem.

This is an example of how change happens as far as dialectics is concerned. The thing that drives the change from A over to B is already within A all the time. In more technical language, the initial thing (A) is the thesis, the thing that is already within A and is it's opposite (not-A) is the anti-thesis. The interpenetration of these opposites causes change to happen from within, which eventually means we arrive at B, the synthesis.

For instance, Love (thesis), due to its internal dynamics, will tear us (the interpenetration of opposites – anti-thesis), so that we end up apart (an entirely new and different state of affairs – synthesis).

But it doesn't always have to be this upsetting. Understanding change through dialectics can also be used to think about good things, helping you to understand and get a grip on yourself and your creativity as a constant process of change. It is a good way to grasp how things evolve out of themselves, how things emerge, develop and grow.

This dimension of change is another important facet of having a proper stab at answering the dialectically oriented questions, asked above about your creative journey that Mr Spock would find so difficult to understand.

So hopefully the limitations of *Formal Logic* and the usefulness of dialectical thinking for creativity and innovation is a bit clearer. It allows you to think about things as a moving set of interpenetrating creative relationships between things that may at first sight seem like opposites, but which we know within our creative minds are often just facets of the same, interconnected ways of thinking and living. This is probably what innovation *is*.

Something like dialectics is the underlying logic needed for innovative lateral thinking and finding 'killer application' that we discuss in chapters below.

Phenomenology and Existentialism

At the most subjective end of the epistemological spectrum is phenomenology. This is an epistemological position that focuses upon consciousness and perception. It is the perceptions of phenomena as they appear to us as individuals, as distinct from the idea of the real world *out there* that is phenomenology's focus. As we will see in the next chapter, it forms the epistemological basis for specific research methods that try to engage with people's beliefs, assumptions and expectations as they articulate them for themselves within the context of their own lives.

But phenomenological epistemology is in no way an exact science precisely because it tries to get to the heart of ways in which individuals experience the world in their own terms. When we try to understand other peoples' perceptions, we soon realize that we can never be sure about them, will probably never really be able to share and mutually understand them in a complete way. We can only approximate them within our discussions and attempts to articulate them. Max Weber, who is big in the historical development of the Interpretative Tradition of epistemology, although not an out-and-out phenomenologist, called this *verstehen*, because he was German. Verstehen is one of those words for which we do not have a direct equivalent in English. The closest we can come up with is *interpretative understanding*.

However, if we apply this epistemology to our own reflective creative practice and become the object of our own research, which research for creative innovation often is, we can see that there are some important resonances between phenomenology and the individual creative act. Both are very much about understanding the subjective aspects of life.

Phenomenology, along with the related world of Existentialism also focuses our attention upon the *choices* that we can make as to what our perceptions are to be, as a never-ending series of movable possibilities. These choices need not be tied to anything in the world in any really fundamental way. This then highlights a greater self-awareness as to the Existential choices being made, or that are capable of being made. This in turn raises all sorts of political and ethical dimensions and issues concerning personal tastes and sensibilities. This brings us to big questions of *ethics* and *authenticity*. Again there are very close relationships between this epistemology for studying individual choice and the creative act.

We say more about the specifics of the ethical dimensions to research and innovation below, but for now it is good to recognize that Phenomenological and Existential epistemology can be an established basis for researching your creative self and who you are to be in the future. Standing as they do at the subjective end of epistemological discussions, Phenomenology and Existentialism are potentially part of the epistemological underpinnings for a truly open approach to creativity, the basis for *reflective practice* discussed in the next chapter.

Theory

THEORIES OF CREATIVE INNOVATION: NO. 4 – THE PHENOMENOLOGICAL TRADITION

… modern psychology and phenomenology use the term 'perceptive ambiguity', which indicates the availability of new cognitive positions (creative perceptions) *that fall short of conventional epistemological stances and that allow the observer to conceive the world in a fresh dynamic of potentiality before the fixative process of habit and familiarity comes into play.*

(from *The Open Work*, by U. Eco)

Epistemological Openness: Be a Little Bit Nervous

Another of the useful aspects of Phenomenological or Existential ways of thinking lies in appreciating the value of a greater degree of epistemological openness when doing research. And being epistemologically open, in the way we are using it here, is connected to a sense of epistemological 'nervousness'. Which is a good thing.

We have borrowed this notion of 'nervousness' from Peter Berger and Thomas Luckmann's book *The Social Construction of Reality*. In this book he talks about 'cognitive nervousness', by which he means the disjuncture between the experience of something and the lack of any deeper meaning of that thing, which often pervades contemporary culture.

We think something similar happens, or at least should do, within good research. It is all well and good deciding upon a clear research starting point, finding a good epistemological position, constructing tight research methods and pursuing them professionally. But don't run away with the idea that this will get you to some kind of *universal truth* that will:

- Last for ever and be the only time you will need to look at this research question.
- Be accepted by everyone else just because you have done the research really well.

Cognitive nervousness, when you don't really know what things mean is not good, and is 'dissonant'. But when it comes to epistemology, it can be healthy to be a little nervous, to have an *open hesitancy* about any research. It is healthy to have the kind of nervousness that comes from knowing the epistemological limitations of *any* research position. Epistemological nervousness is good for the creative soul and helps you to avoid making over-reaching statements and over ambitious creative business decisions based upon it.

It involves being open to:

- The constant movement of things.

- The difference between how things seem on the basis of your research and their real nature.
- The temporary nature of any plans you might make based upon that research.
- The inevitable incompleteness of any knowledge and, most fundamentally.
- The fact that you yourself as a creative person engaged in research are an on-going project.

These can all be a very useful for sustaining the act of being creative and innovative.
    Even though it doesn't always feel like that.

Theory

THEORIES OF CREATIVE INNOVATION: NO. 5 – THE EASTERN TRADITION

... creative thinking is the infinite movement of thought, emotion and action. That is, when thought ... is unimpeded in its movement, is not compelled or influenced or bound by an idea (for example, positivism's unity of method) *and does not proceed from the background of tradition or habit* (for example, a paradigm), *then that movement is creative. ... so long as thought is circumscribed, held by fixed idea, or merely adjusts itself to a background or condition and, therefore, becomes limited, such thought is not creative ... creative movement of thought never seeks a result or comes to a culmination, because result or culmination is always the outcome of alternate cessation and movement, whereas if there is no search for a result, but only continual movement of thought, then there is creative thinking.*

(from *To Be a True Human Being*, in *Total Freedom* by Krishnamurti)

What this means in more normal language is that good research is connected to creativity because both are ultimately about the *free and open flow of ideas*. And this is connected to innovation because that is also about the *free and open flow of ideas*.

We will come back to this in later chapters. But before we do that, let's try to pin down in more detail how you might put one or more of these epistemological positions into operation. That is, let's consider the *ins and outs* of actual research methods useful for creativity and innovation.

14 *Different Methods: Which Tools to Use, Why, When and How*

Story

HAVING TO TELL OFF CAROL

Kurt Lewin once wrote:

There is nothing so practical as a good theory.

I used to have to tell off my friend Carol. She was always saying that she was interested in practice, in doing stuff, in working with other people, so she didn't have much time for research, for theory.

She did do good work. But I had to tell her off, because there is a better relationship between theory and practice than that.

I didn't tell her off in a really angry way, we were only joking. But nevertheless researching *Behind, In/Though, For or In Front Of* your creative practice allows you to develop good theory, which allows you to develop better practice. And developing better practice will allow you to stand back from the details and see things from the outside: that is better theory. Sometimes Carol, there can be very useful dialectical dynamic between theory and practice.

One of the keys to sustaining this inter-relationship between what you are doing in practice and what you need to know more about in theory is knowing how to skilfully use the various tools out there for your own active research. The different methods that Mozart talked about (defining, crystallizing and enlarging creative practice) for researching creativity are the vital link between theory and practice.

After all the philosophical debate in the last chapter, we want this chapter to be more practical. We want it to be about putting concrete research methods at the centre of your creativity so that they can contribute to your *creative journey*. Knowing about concrete research methods can contribute to this journey by being:

- Part of the way you can read your *creative map* and make decisions about different ways to navigate.
- Part of your *creative fuel* to enable you to travel around this map. The research map we introduced above has arrows in it, indicating movement.
- Specific research methods can form the vehicles allowing such movement.

- In part your *creative passport* to enable you to enter new and undiscovered stop-offs and destinations as you make your journey.

The nature of the global cultural economy and the ever-present change and competition it brings suggests that building *regular research* into your creativity and innovation plan is not an optional extra. It is not a chore that has to be gone through at some time outside the main business of creative practice. It *is* the creativity.

You should find time for more reading Carol!

Most of the discrete research methods we will talk about in this chapter come from the social and cultural sciences. This is because the social and cultural sciences have done the most to devise tight methods with which to research what is going on in the society, economy and culture around you, or to get inside the heads of the people who make up that society, economy and culture. The Arts have obviously contributed to this, and there are lots of variations specific to the Arts that connect to certain research methods that we will not touch upon below. But as with the previous chapter, what we want to draw out in this chapter are the basic contours of well-established research methods. How you use them in concrete detail will be up to you at the end of the day, because it is still your thing.

The practical benefits of research methods mean they can help:

- Follow up on the epistemological discussions so that you can pin down a well-crafted programme of research that is commensurate.
- With your exploratory journey into any and all of the aspects of research you might have thought about whilst reading so far.
- Put into action the different research starting-points discussed above and obtain the different types of knowledge this might involve depending upon the What? Who? and Why? questions.

Reflective Practice as Research Method

Although science and social sciences have had established research methods for the past 150 years or so, Arts and Design disciplines have not consolidated core research methods within their disciplines to the same degree. So when it comes to specific research methods appropriate for Art and Design, there is still an emerging debate about which research methods can be developed or made appropriate for the central element of *practice*.

Bringing together elements of research and practice in a more consolidated way is what Gray and Malin, in their book *Visualizing Research* mean by the term 'reflective practitioner'. They point out that one of the key differences between research within the sciences and/or social sciences on the one hand, and research in/through creative practice on the other, is the way that the creative practitioner can often be the *object* of their own research (what it is about), as much as the person who is doing it. Because the personal and subjective is often central to creative practice, this kind of research chimes strongly with a phenomenological epistemology.

Gray and Malins suggest that because the interior meanings and perceptions of the practitioner sometimes *is* the research for the reflective practitioner, the relationship between research and practice has a highly multi-faceted character. The reflective practitioner's role can be one or more of the following:

- A generator of the thing that is being researched in/through the creative action itself.
- A self-observer through reflection back on creative action, which is simultaneously in creative action, and through creative discussion with others.
- An observer of the practice of others as the research into the broader context of practice and the gaining other perspectives.
- A co-researcher, facilitator and research manager of collaborative research.

These complicated inter-relationships between reflection and practice, interior meanings/ motivations and the creative acts that result from them mean that a new epistemological debate about new methods for practice-based research is emerging.

Quotation

This practice-based approach to research naturally prompts us critically to consider and evaluate methods used in practice as to their appropriateness as robust and rigorous methods for accessible and disciplined inquiry ...

... To date, there is no definitive published single source on research methods for artists and designers. Research methods development relies on researchers adding further detail and modifying as a method is tried and evaluated ...

... There are many parallels between the construction of an art/design work and the construction of a research argument, not least in the way that the form is proposed, critiqued, deconstructed, remodelled and resolved. Much of this process is evaluative and analytical, reflective and deconstructive, creative and synthetic. As practitioners we engage in these activities constantly and most of the time unconsciously. As reflective researchers we must make these activities explicit and accessible ... Art and Design research is a rapidly evolving activity. With each successful completion of a research degree along with a new contribution to knowledge it is likely that new and alternative research methodologies are proposed and validated.

(from *Visualizing Research*, by C. Gray and J. Malins)

You might not be interested in this methodological debate as such. Nevertheless, this new field of epistemological and methodological debates suggests that research methods appropriate for your creative practice might also include *research on how you research*. This can become a particular component of your thinking about how you do thinking in general terms, and your research in/through the creative practice itself in the more detailed sense. An important consequence of this is the need for evaluation, analysis and assessment of the 'results' of your research about how you do research. This can be key for reflective practice in that it helps you to be more aware of why your practice is the way it is, how it can be different and maybe better. In normal language, all this stuff shows the value of being constantly self-reflective back onto how you do what you do in practice, so as to be able to articulate it more clearly to yourself and thus maybe do it better.

Even this very brief, initial look at different research methods shows that a whole host of things might be needed if good research, leading to useful knowledge, leading the creative innovation is to be forthcoming. Knowing about different research methods for different research jobs enables you to make informed choices about which one to choose.

Commensurability

When trying to decide upon a specific research method, this is the place to start. As briefly mentioned above, commensurability is a fancy way of discussing the fit between the motivations behind your research agenda, the epistemological basis you are coming from, the detailed nature of the information you are trying to find, and the research methods you therefore adopt. And remember, in parallel to the key epistemological distinction between the Positivist and Interpretative Traditions, the key distinction when it comes to research methods is the one between quantitative and qualitative methods.

For instance:

- If you want to ask a large number of people some fairly simple questions to do with what they think about an aspect of the world, so that you can write a report on current trends to convince a funder/investor to finance your proposed project, then get into quantitative research methods. This will entail designing a questionnaire to cover lots of people, and if properly constructed and coded you will be able to generate statistical data, percentages and so on. Using such methods can help to keep your research 'real' in that it can say something about the world beyond your opinions or ideas of how it should be.
- However, if you want to know what these people really think and why they think as they do because you want this to inform a documentary film, or community art project, or some really good marketing, it will be pretty pointless asking them 'yes' and 'no' questions. So you will probably need to interview some of them to focus upon what they really believe, in the terms that they themselves think about it. This will entail getting into the different types of qualitative research methods.

Theory

THEORIES OF CREATIVE INNOVATION: NO. 6 – HUMANIST PSYCHOLOGY

Creativity always has the stamp of the individual upon its product, but the product is not the individual, not his/her materials, but partakes of the relationships between the two ... (it) is not, in my judgement, restricted to some particular content. I am assuming that there is no fundamental difference in the creative process as it is evidenced in painting a picture, composing a symphony, devising new instruments of killing, developing a scientific theory, discovering new procedures in human relationships or creating new formings of one's own personality as in psychotherapy.

My definition, then, of the creative process is that it is the emergence in action of a novel relational product, growing out of the uniqueness of the individual on the one hand, and the materials, events, people, or circumstances of his/her life on the other.

(from *Towards a Theory of Creativity*, by C. Rogers)

Nuts and Bolts, and also Brass Tacks

With the above discussion in mind, let's now turn to some of the discrete tools with which to put research into practice, the *nuts and bolts of actual research methods*. This also really takes us away from the philosophical debates of the previous chapters and gets us down to *brass tacks* – the why and how involved in the *craft* of doing research for creative innovation.

This is where it gets really practical.

Questionnaire Design

Questionnaires are the basic tool of quantitative research. They are for finding out what *other people think* and so will usually get used within research *Behind* and *In Front Of* starting-points. Questionnaires tend to be used for descriptive research of the world 'out there'.

The basic craft of questionnaire design involves the following key points:

Introduce Yourself – Write a short introduction to the questionnaire to tell people who you are, why you are doing the survey and to assure them about confidentiality.

Is It Big Enough? – make sure it is designed from the beginning to collect all the information you need. It will be very difficult to go back again afterwards. Think about what, in an ideal world the findings of the questionnaire would enable you to 'prove' so that you can make the argument you want to make, and then ask those questions.

Is It Small Enough? – keep it as short as possible. Most people will not actually want to do your questionnaire.

What's My Motivation? – sometimes it can be a good idea to give people some small rewards for filling in your questionnaire, in technical terms this is called incentivizing.

Keep It Simple – stick to simple straightforward language, no jargon, no fuzzy concepts, no big, long questions.

Got Any Filters? – think about filtering. For instance, where you have asked a 'yes' or 'no' question and the reply has been 'yes', design things to get them to carry on because you want more information on that. But if they have replied 'no', direct them to a question further down the questionnaire after the 'yes' section has finished. Otherwise they are being asked to answer questions that they have already told you are not relevant to them, and this gets irritating and looks unprofessional.

Rating and Scaling – think about *ratings and scalings*. This is the way to get a numerical value next to an opinion. *Rating* asks people to rate how 'important' or 'difficult' or 'successful' something has been. For instance, you ask them to choose between saying if something is 'very important' or 'fairly important' or 'not very important' or' irrelevant'. *Scaling* asks people to put things on a scale. That is, you ask them to rank things in order of importance by putting a '1' next to the most important, a '2' next to the next most important and so on. By allowing a number to be attached to an opinion, you avoid getting lots of answers that are a few sentences of dialogue. And this is good because such information can be very difficult and cumbersome to deal with when it comes to showing aggregated finding (averages, general spread of opinion, percentages etc). Rating and scaling allows for better *coding*.

Coding – when questionnaires are analysed, some version of *SPSS* (Statistical Package for the Social Science) will probably be used. This is the industry standard software for survey analysis. To do this some kind of 'data management' file is created, which is the file that tells the software what a particular number means in terms of the response to each question. For instance, the data management file will tell the software that for Answer 1, the presence of a '1' means 'female', and '2' means 'male'. Then there is some kind of 'data file', which contains all the actual answers for each completed questionnaire. This is then read by the data management file. The more times you can get a clearly coded answer the better as far as questionnaire design goes. Questions that involve rating and scaling allow the data to be read more effectively and statistical findings generated. This is better than dealing with 500 opinions that kind of say the same thing but in slightly different ways.

Who Do You Get in Touch With? – making sure that you have a representative sample for your questionnaire is important. If you are researching the population as a whole, then you will need 50 per cent males and 50 per cent female, and a good spread of ages, ethnicities and so on. But sometimes you will be researching a particular section of society, so you don't need to have a general sample, but a more precise one. Just so long as you are comfortable that your sample is *representative*.

Call Me, Write to Me, or Just Talk to Me – once you have designed your questionnaire you need to decide how you are going to get it to the people whose answers you want. This can be face to face, by (e)mail or by phone.

This largely depends upon how big a survey you want it to be. If you want it to be a really big survey, (say above 500, which is small for professional market research but big for most purposes) then a postal (email) campaign is probably best. The problem with this strategy is that the average return rate for postal surveys is around 20 per cent. So you can spend a lot of time and energy organizing a relevant address book, for little reward. If it is less than 500, think about a telephone strategy. This is obviously time consuming, and depends upon getting people's phone numbers, but it has the advantage of letting you know where you are up to in terms of numbers of responses all the time. So you can just stop when you have enough. Or sometimes, if your questionnaire is fairly short and sweet you could go to the event itself, or catch the users of your service, venues and so on, and ask to go through it with them there and then. This starts to become a structure interview, which we will talk about more below.

Keep an Eye on Things – it is good to keep an eye on the findings as you go along. If everyone is giving you very similar responses after you have completed a reasonable amount of questionnaires, you can see that there is little point carrying on just to re-prove the obvious again and again. This is another reason why telephone surveys can be good because you can keep an eye on things all the time.

Stages – you can think about stages within a survey. This can involve a *pilot phase* where you try out your questionnaire a few times to check it. This has the advantage of allowing you to tweak things before you have gone too far. You might also think about the possibility of an *interim* analysis, where you look at the findings at an intermediate stage to check progress and look at emerging themes, especially if you want to report back to someone else.

Users and Non-Users – an important issue to be aware of when using questionnaire-based research methods within the cultural and creative sector is the distinction between *users* and *non-users*.

Some people are just interested in the Arts and culture, they are users. And some are just not, they are non-users. What this can mean is that surveys on the Arts and culture can very easily become unintentionally biased towards the opinions of users.

Because users are already interested, they will already be interested in replying to your questionnaire. And because non-users are not, they will not, if you see what we mean.

This does not always matter. You might just want to evaluate your project by getting the opinions of those who came to it. But it might do, if your research wants to measure a broader spectrum of opinion. So you might need to deliberately seek out the opinion of non-users. This, however, is notoriously difficult because they tend to be difficult to identify, reach and then get interested enough to sit still long enough.

New Software and On-Line Quantitative Research – Developed in recent years, there are now a whole host of new data analysis software packages and on-line survey services out there which can take a lot of the hassle out of doing questionnaires and other kinds of quantitative research. This starts to get rather specialized now, however, so we will leave you to explore that world for yourself.

Warning

THE SOCIAL UNCERTAINTY PRINCIPLE

In the 1930s a series of research programmes were started at the General Electric's factory at Hawthorne in the USA. These Hawthorne Studies, as they became known, gave rise to The Hawthorne Effect which involved researchers realizing that, because they were seen as representatives of management, the act of actually talking to the workers meant that the research process itself was changing the perceptions of the workers being researched.

David Orne, another famous sociologist (they all have funny names) demonstrated this again in the 1960s by showing that when people were stopped in the street and asked questions, they often gave an 'answer' that they thought they should give, because it was 'respectable' or 'acceptable' rather than what they really thought.

The common point here is how the act of researching something can change the nature of the thing you are researching. This is one of the fundamental and perennial problems with researching anything that involves people, because people are complicated. But even within the strange world of sub-atomic physics, Werner Heisenberg encountered a similar problem. He referred to this as *The Uncertainty Principle*.

Remember epistemological nervousness from the previous chapter?

- Are you attaching too much Truth-with-a-Capital-T to your research?
- Are you therefore suggesting that other people should also see it as Truth-with-a-Capital-T too strongly?
- Is this appropriate? Does this bring too heavy an opportunity cost?
- Have you really tested your research to destruction enough?

When it comes to the practical activities of doing quantitative research, given its underlying Positivist epistemology, it can easily feel very safe and 'real'. After all, this is not your opinion. You have gone out there and really asked lots of other people what they think, so it must be right. Right?

Maybe not. This can sometimes encourage people to put too many creative business 'eggs' in one 'basket' that has not, and probably cannot ever be, proven to be really True-with-a-Capital-T. It is good to be nervous sometime because people don't always tell you what they really think!

Qualitative Research Methods

Because quantitative research methods are sometimes incommensurable with getting at what people really think, one might need to turn to more qualitative research methods. Related back to the Interpretative Tradition as they are, qualitative research methods can take many different forms. But the thing that they all have in common is the way they provide a research space so that the person being researched can articulate what they really think in a way that *makes sense to them*, rather than following the research agenda, mental boxes, priorities and issues set by someone else outside their own lives.

Quantitative research for creativity is good for covering the basic opinions of large numbers of people, it has *breadth*. But it is not good at really getting inside people's heads to find out what they really, really think about art, culture, your work, the information you might need for a documentary film or what they really think about your product. *Because* it has breadth, it tends to lack depth.

Qualitative research for creative practice can never cover as much ground as quantitative research. It is just far too time consuming to be interviewing people in such large numbers. Qualitative research does not have breadth but it more than makes up for that by having *depth*. Qualitative research takes far fewer people, but researches them in much more detail to get inside their heads, and this can bring the really useful information you need to develop new and innovative creative ideas.

But it doesn't have to be an either-or choice. Often professional researchers will start with quantitative methods to get a spread of opinion and draw out some interesting themes, and then switch to qualitative to go into them in more detail.

Qualitative research methods come in lots of varieties, with lots of different names and different slants.

Interviewing

A basic tool that is somewhere between quantitative and qualitative research is interviewing. Sometimes this can be as simple as talking to someone, and faithfully recording what they say to you. But there are more developed and professional techniques for this kind of research.

Doing professional interviews can involve different structures:

- **Structured** – sticking to a pre-arranged script that you use for each and every interview. This is only a little different from the face-to-face way of carrying out a questionnaire-based survey.
- **Semi-structured** – having a script with you, that you keep returning to so as to maintain some semblance of repeatability across all the interviews you do with various people, but also allowing space for the interviewee to go off on tangents or wandering away from *your* point. Remember you are trying to get them to tell you what they really think in the terms that make sense to *them*.
- **Open-ended** – completely open, with no script to structure the agenda of the interview. That comes solely from the person being interviewed.

- Being good at interviewing people also requires a certain level of commitment to the craft of research.
- You still need to think about getting a representative sample if you are intending to use your research to make those sorts of claims for it afterwards.
- Writing up findings straight away whilst it is fresh in your mind.
- Be as 'objective' and faithful as possible to what they said, not how you wanted it to be.
- Accept negative, difficult or contrary ideas and opinions.
- Even if you do not necessarily need a representative sample, still make sure you interview a proper cross-section of the group, population, customers you are interested in. It can include your mates, but it shouldn't be just your mates.
- Be aware that they might not be saying what they want to say, because it might feel embarrassing, non-respectable or silly to them.
- Assure them about confidentiality and other points concerning research ethics, discussed in below.

In a more general sense, be aware that your very presence will have an impact upon the people you are interviewing, and take control as far as possible of what that impact is going to be. For instance:

- Don't come across as representing authority if you are trying to get kids to tell you what they really think about authority.
- Don't dress or talk in a way that is going to piss people of because they see you as being 'posh' or 'snooty'.
- Don't try to 'sell them your product' when you are doing market research with them.
- Tell them what you are doing and why before you start so that they don't mistrust you from the off.
- Try as far as possible to speak their 'language'.

Sometimes there is just no way around these things. To get good depth from interviewing you might sometimes need to get someone else to do the interviewing for you. Someone who can more easily connect with the people being interviewed.

- Young/aged people to interview young/aged people.
- Men/women to interview men/women.
- People of whatever racial, ethnic, cultural or religious background to interview people from that racial, ethnic, cultural or religious background.

If you want the depth dimension you might need to recruit people to be your undercover agents, sometimes known as *field workers*.

Ethnography

- Ethno ... – the native, the ethnic, the things that make people as they are.
- ... ography – measuring.

Ethnographic research methods are towards the phenomenological end of the epistemological spectrum. It is about the search for the interior stuff that makes people what they are in their own terms, things like:

- perceptions
- meanings
- motivations
- aspirations
- expectations
- imagination
- memories
- personal relationships.

There are lots of variations of ethnographic approaches. One of the most historically well established and developed comes from cultural anthropology.

Although anthropology came from the rather patronizing, Euro-centric and patriarchal nineteenth century idea that people from a certain cultural and scientific background (usually white, Western men) could study people from a completely different cultural and scientific background (native cultures in 'primitive' societies) it has however become much more sophisticated since then. It is fundamentally based upon the idea that people from one social and cultural background are in an advantageous position to study other societies and cultures precisely because they are not immersed within the thing they are studying. Remember, the last animals to discover water will be fish, precisely because they are in it all the time. Being able to stand back from the details of living that cultural life and see things that those who are immersed within it find difficult to see, can be a very useful research method.

A particular technique for this kind of research is *participant observation*. As we saw above, there are problems associated with trying to do straight forward interview-based research by just going to ask total strangers what they think. Remember The Hawthorne Effect, The Social Uncertainty Principle and epistemological nervousness in general? It is not always easy to know what the best questions are, and people will not always tell you what they really think anyway.

Participant observation researchers try to get around this by immersing themselves into the group they are researching, to become a part of the group before they research it. This enables them to research the group from the *inside* more effectively. They are able to understand the cultural universe of the people they are interested in more effectively by observing people's actual lives as they are living them and not interrupt it by asking direct questions. By becoming part of the group, anthropologically oriented researchers are less visibly 'parachuted in' from the outside and their relative invisibility enables more authentic research.

This research technique is not just about Westerners studying 'primitive tribes' any more. Really interesting anthropological research has been done by Japanese people studying aspects of Western societies. Many creative professions routinely use this kind of research, although they often don't call it participant observation:

- The artist in residence goes to live within a community to understand it before beginning to work with it.

- The documentary film-makers tries to understand the group (s)he wants to work with by getting them to be part of the production.
- Method actors 'gets' the role by becoming it, by living in the context of the character they are to play.

However ...

Warning
WHO DO YOU THINK YOU ARE?

There are two problems associated with participant observation.

Problem 1 – It is very easy to not really, fully engage with the cultural reality of the group you are researching. There are natural tendencies to resist becoming part of the group's culture by keep hold of your own mental and cultural universe. This can lead to making judgements about what is going on which can get in the way. You have to know who you are and who you are not, and if you have not been accepted by the group as part of the group, then any such research can be flawed. In this case you have become a non-participating observer.

Problem 2 – It is very easy to become engrossed in the novelty and beauty of the group you are researching. This can mean you give up any distance you once had that could have helped you to see what is going on within the group. This can mean you are unable to make any useful statements or conclusions from the research because you are less able to 'stand back'. In this case you have become a non-observing participant.

So here, as with so many things, maintaining a skilful balance between being part the group you want to research on the one hand, and keeping a good distance to enable observation on the other, is needed.

You need to become one of the 'trees', but not so much of a tree that you cannot see the rest of the 'wood' for them. Knowing who you are, when and why, and adopting these various personas as needed is part of being good at participant observation.

This kind of research can be useful for creative innovation where the focus is upon working with other parts of the community or learning about overseas business cultures within the global economy. It can also contribute to personal exploration and the development of techniques for your practice itself through learning about the interior dynamics of other creative people. It can also provide very useful background and contextual research. So it can be a useful research method for each of the Behind, In/Through, For and In Front Of starting-points.

Audio-Visual Methods

We are very sorry, but we need to use a cliché: *a picture tells a thousand words*.

Taking a picture, or some music or some other artefact made by the group you want to research, or using these kinds of artefacts to say something about the research you have done with them can add nuance, subtly, pathos, beauty and loving insight to a piece of research that it is difficult to get through words alone, and impossible to get from a bar chart or graph.

However, when it comes to audio-visual material and its relationship to research methods, we need to make a basic distinction before we can go any further.

Audio-visual material can be related to doing research as:

- **The Object of Research** – that is, audio-visual material can be what you take as a particular manifestation of the world, and then study it. Audio-visual material is researched as a concrete manifestation of the meanings, motivations and aspirations of the people who created it. For instance, the formal techniques within the History of Art involve this approach.
- **The Vehicle for Research** – audio-visual research can be part of the way your research is framed, articulated and presented back to the world. This involves research in/through the making of audio-visual material as a way of disseminating what you have researched. Documentary film-making is an example of this.
- **The Culmination of Collaborative Research** – the audio-visual material created in partnership with the subjects of your research. This can be presented as a record of the creative and/or research process itself. This may include a combination of the previous two points. Collaborative Arts projects working with community groups are an example of this approach.

But using audio-visual material for *research*, rather than for the creative practice itself, is not an easy option. If you decide to use audio-visual material it still needs to connect to the professional practice of research as we have discussed it up to this point. That is:

- It needs to say something. Go right back to the beginning and Paul Ricoeur's idea of 'the text'. Any audio-visual material you use for research needs to be 'read as a text' if it is to say something.
- It needs to be able to say things to other people, not just you.
- It needs to be commensurate, credible, representative, and defendable as rigorous and planned research.

It is not easy to get right, and personally we would only use it as a complimentary addition to the words within a piece of research. Remember, it is research, not a photographic exhibition we are talking about here. If you want to be on an exhibition, then call it that and don't confuse people by making research claims that your use of the audio-visual material cannot follow through on.

But sometimes, using audio-visual material can lead to absolutely fantastic research. We want you all to put this book down now, and go out to get a copy of *A Seventh Man*, by John Berger and Jean Mohr to see this.

Semiotics

Now you are back, and continuing the theme of linking research methods to audio-visual material, all products of culture convey meanings through their shape, size, colour, form, materials and so on, over and above the content of what they are designed to say.

Semiotics sees all aspects of a society's material and visual culture as therefore being open to 'reading', in the same way that more orthodox texts can be read. This is because all such cultural artefacts are part of a broad process of cultural communication. This suggests that everything carries meaning and there can be no 'ground zero' of cultural meaninglessness. In common with some aspects of the use of audio-visual materials as the object of research, semiotics is concern with questions such as:

- What do the objects of culture mean and say?
- What message do they carry beyond themselves as objects?
- Is there a concerted visual language at work?
- What do these meanings tell us about the people who produced them?

They might not call it this, but actually many archaeologists adopt a research position very similar to this. It is also very similar to the branch of anthropology called visual anthropology. Alfred Gell's book *Art and Agency* is a good introduction to this.

Semiotics and the use of audio-visual material in general is connected to the general thrust of (visual) anthropology because they share common concerns with:

- How bits of material culture (objects, fashions) are produced by different groups for different reasons to articulate deeper meanings.
- How they are exchanged and used in different groups, again for lots of different reasons that can uncover deeper meanings.

So semiotics, within the broader context of anthropologically oriented research can be a useful research method for creative work that is attempting to uncover what people and communities are really thinking as it is articulated through their own material and visual culture. It can be a 'way into' understanding a social group or culture through its own cultural production. And this understanding can greatly improve the practice of working with such groups in concrete ways.

The Biographical Method

In recent years the biographical method has perhaps been less used in social science research. Within creative practice it is probably used all the time, but not necessarily recognized as a discrete and credible research method in and of itself. So it is useful to say a few words about the biographical method as a particular way of doing research and collecting 'data'.

Reflecting back upon our biography is probably something that we all do all the time. But as a creative person this is perhaps more intimately tied to your work than it is for most people – recording and collecting memories, thoughts, insights, plans, aspirations and inspirations wherever they come from.

The biographical method can obviously entail researching *yourself* by keeping some form of diary. But it can be equally useful research to get *other people* to keep a diary too. This still fits into qualitative research in general and ethnographic approaches in particular because it is still about getting people to articulate their own views, opinions, attitudes and interior monologues in their own terms. They can structure, record and present all this in a way that makes sense to them, and so it is another way to get at the depth of research into how people live and think.

Quotation

The biographical method can be defined as one which …

… presents the experiences and definitions held by one person, one group or one organization as this person, group or organization interprets those experiences. Life history materials include any record or document including the case histories of social agencies, that throw light on the subjective behaviour of individuals or groups. These may range from letters to autobiographies, from newspaper accounts to court records.

(from *The Research Act*, by N. Denzin)

Therefore we can imagine …

- a diary
- a personal log-book
- a reflexive journal
- a sketch book
- a blog
- an archive

… as places where the collection of research data can happen.

Theory

THEORIES OF CREATIVE INNOVATION: NO. 7 – FREUDIAN PSYCHOLOGY

Should we not look at the first traces of imaginative activity as early as in childhood? The child's best-loved and most intense occupation is with his/her play or games. Might we not say that every child at play behaves like a creative writer, in that (s)he creates a world of his/her own or, rather, rearranges the things of his/her world in a new way which pleases him/her? It would be wrong to think (s)he does not take the world seriously; on the contrary, (s)he takes his/her play very seriously and (s)he expands large amounts of emotion on it. The opposite of play is not what is serious but what is real. In spite of all the emotion with which (s)he cathects his/her world of play, the child distinguishes it quite well from reality; and (s)he likes to link his imagined objects and situations to the tangible and visible things of the real world. This linking is all that differentiates the child's 'play' from 'phantasying'.

… When a child has grown up and ceased to play, and after (s)he has been labouring for decades to envisage the realities of life with proper seriousness, (s)he may one day find him/herself in a mental situation which once more undoes the contrast between play and reality. As an adult (s)he can look back on the intense seriousness with which (s)he once carried in his/her games in childhood; and, by equating his/her ostensibly serious occupation of today with his/her childhood games, (s)he can throw off the heavy burden imposed on him/her by life and win the high yield of pleasure afforded by humour.

(from *'Creative Writers and Day-Dreaming'*, by S. Freud)

Yesterday: Historicism and Archives

It is always good to know history. It is useful to know about:

- The wider history of the society you live within and the way economic, social and political factors have impacted upon you and your work – mostly Research Behind.
- The specific history of your creative discipline or genre, and/or what the history of other disciplines can tell you; the history of (your) art – mostly Research In/Through and For.

Knowing history in general terms helps in understanding things in general terms. Knowing specifics history of your creative field helps you to know the details of where it came from and where it might therefore be going. This is because history is about understanding the *present*, where we, you, they came from. And because history is about the present, *history is about the future!* The future of where we, you, they, are all going. Because of this, it might be about the future of your creativity and lead you to innovation, which you need to know about. (Within the idea that *history is about the future*, we see another example of dialectical thinking.)

Archives can be a very useful and powerful source of research data. And this then immediately implies the need to keep your own archive of work up to date. Reflecting back upon your own history after you have gone so far down the line can be a vital part of research for developing your creativity and innovative future.

Research and the Web

This might be as good a place as any to mention the Web and its role in research. The relationship between the Web and research is increasingly like the relationship between gravity and human beings. It is so fundamental that it does not really need to be talked about.

However, the role of the Web in research does perhaps need a little more caution than that:

- The Web has little in the way of quality control other than on sites such as Wikipedia, which seem able to 'police' themselves. So caution as to the credibility of 'research' based purely on Web searching is needed.
- The Web can be very good for the collection of information, but information is not the same as knowledge. Something has to be done with information to turn it into knowledge (theory, synthesis, testing and so on).

As part of a discussion of creative networks, Benkler in *The Wealth of Networks* talks about the 'information economy environment' as the social and cultural space whereby people share time and effort to ensure a *quality and synthesis* of information that can create knowledge. This mutually created and tested *knowledge* can be more useful for getting you to innovation than pieces of free-floating information which can often have a very high flaky quotient.

This tends to suggest that researching the Web is best when it is researching what other professional researchers and potential collaborators out there are doing. As we will see below, Theodore Roszak has talked about the *cult of information* and has showed us how an obsession with collecting free-floating bits of it is not the same as research for the development of innovative knowledge. Information unsupported by background ideas of what to do with it is not always a good thing, because it can lead you down blind alleys and dead ends.

Which is partly why ...

Three is the Magic Number: Triangulation

Three is the magic number for several reasons. One of them is because of *triangulation*. Triangulation is a map-making and surveying technique that enables a particular point in space to be accurately fixed. It entails measuring the same things from three different angles. In its surveying context, it involves choosing three different angles from which to survey.

The line from the first angle measures the general direction towards the point we are interested in; the second line is drawn and where it crosses the first it pin-points where the point is; the third line confirms the accuracy of lines 1 and 2. The place where these three lines of direction cross each other shows the *point* for sure.

The idea of triangulation is useful for other kinds of research too. The idea of researching a particular topic from one angle by using one set of techniques can give us a certain insight; looking at things from a second angle by using a different method can help to pin down any findings; the third angle by using yet another method can really pin down the *point*. Triangulation gives you more assurance about your research findings. If your research has been triangulated and the three different methods are confirming each other, then you can probably rely upon it.

So, in terms of researching from different angles, a fairly standard way would be to:

- Look at the secondary literature and previous research.
- Carry out broad-brush survey research.
- Conduct more in-depth interviews with another set of people.

But you could perhaps imagine other, more imaginative ways to triangulate your research for creativity. It would depend very much on what the actual content of your research is.

Quotation

TRIANGULATION

Unfortunately, no single method ever adequately solves the problem of rival interpretations ... Because each method reveals different aspects of empirical reality, multiple methods of observation must be employed. This is termed triangulation ... multiple methods should be used in every investigation.

(from *The Research Act*, by N. Denzin)

This has been a short and quite brief introduction to the underlying logic of some concrete methods that might help you to carry out your research. If you look hard enough, you will come across lots of variations on these methods, with lots of fancy terminology. But the choice between quantitative and qualitative research methods in the context of commensurability, set against epistemological choices and the basic motivations within your research is the key thing here.

Having explored both the philosophy and methods for research that might help you with your creativity, let's now turn to how new ideas, techniques and processes might *flow* from research towards practical application.

That is, to innovation.

15 *The Flow of Ideas: Creative Business Innovation*

Story

'OH, BY THE WAY ...' – A STORY ABOUT SEX AND DRUGS

In 1985 the big pharmaceutical company Pfizer were thinking about high blood pressure. The size of the market associated with a treatment for the life-threatening condition of hypertension was (and is) vast. There were already products on the market, but a new one with improved activity would enhance treatment and be highly valuable to the company. In particular, the scientists had become aware of recent biochemical research into hypertension and thought it might fit in with some of their own chemical research. They set to work on it and in time a promising drug candidate emerged. A preliminary clinical trial was arranged but the results were rather disappointing in respect to lowering blood pressure. So another trial using higher dosages was carried out in an attempt to improve the activity of the drug, whilst keeping an eye on any emerging side effects as the dosages were increased. When the physician rang the development office with the progress report on the progress, he uttered the immortal words '… Oh, and by the way'.

For some unexpected reason the men taking part in the trials had experienced a much more pleasurable sensation than those predicted. Given this, the trial indicated an unexpected potential application, useful not just for the men on the trial. These results were interesting, but how should the project proceed? After all, everything was geared towards the dynamics of a relatively secure and predictable hypertension drug market. Would the other application for this new drug find a suitable therapeutic category? And what was the size of the market for something that could do this? Was there even a market out there?

Not withstanding these imponderables, the work was redirected and eventually Viagra was successfully launched.

There are many failed attempts at drug discovery, it is just that this one had a happy ending (in both senses). In this case research into a product designed for one known application found another in an entirely new area because of entirely peripheral and wholly unexpected observations. Being prepared to re-adjust to unexpected observations and reorder applications was the thing that brought these happy endings to fruition. No-one had set out to develop a drug to help men keep it up all night, but it works anyway! A great innovation.

Mr Big Stuff: Applied Science and Innovation

Science is very big stuff today because a whole business economy has grown up behind applied science that is geared towards finding market applications. This applied science is to a large extent the outcome of a selection process that business economics makes. You could make a convincing argument that the intimate relationship between research, business economics, potential applications and thus the innovations that actually get developed has been the main driver behind the last 300 years of history in Western societies, that is the Industrial Revolution and thus to a large extent the whole world. So it is big stuff.

But the central idea of *application* is also key to connecting research for creativity to ideas about innovation for creative business. As creative people, we all have new ideas, new inspirations and new aspirations all the time. How you bring these ideas to fruition needs to similarly include *researching applications* as much as researching the new ideas themselves.

The Creative Industries and Innovation

However, parallels with the big science approach to research and innovation only takes us so far when our concern is with the creative industries, because:

- The structure of the creative industries sector is different from most other industries. One aspect of this is the high percentage of micro-businesses (less the five people) and individual sole traders in the creative industries. It is unlikely that many creative industry companies would have the large dedicated R&D unit in the way big science has. The creative industries do not in the main do their own pure science nor invent their own technologies.
- For the creative industries informal networks often take the place of the dedicated R&D unit within large firms, and provide the innovation spaces that can be a consequence of cross-disciplinary and collaborative working/learning.
- Individual creative companies often work through very flexible processes, and where successful often benefit from economies of speed and cross-disciplines. Successful creative companies seem to be good at taking on board research, innovations and technologies from other industrial arenas, often developed for entirely different reasons, and turning them to their own innovative ends.

As we have noted already in several contexts, creative networks are good at finding innovative applications because they allow the *flow of ideas*. There is no point in having creative networks for the sake of them, and creative networks are only as good as the activities that people use them for. But when they are good, they can be very good for research and innovation.

Theory
THEORIES OF CREATIVITY: NO. 8 – A COLLABORATIVE VIEW

In reality, creativity has always been a highly collaborative, cumulative and social activity in which people with different skills, points of view and insights, share and develop ideas together. At root most creativity is collaborative. It is not usually the product of a flash of insight from a lone individual. The web gives us a new way to organize and expand this collaborative activity ... (which) *could make innovation and creativity a mass activity that engages millions of people ... Our preoccupation in the century to come will be how to create and sustain a mass innovation economy in which the central issue will be how more people can collaborate more effectively in creating new ideas.*

(from *We-Think: Mass Innovation Not Mass Production,* by C. Leadbeater)

but, also remember ...

Quotation

You have to choose such relationships carefully. The first thing we look for in a supplier or a contractor is the quality of their work. If the standards aren't high already, we don't delude ourselves into thinking they'll be raised for us ...

(from *Let My People Go Surfing,* by Y. Chouinard)

Why is Your Business Plan?

Looking briefly at the nature of innovation for creativity brings us to the question of *why is your business plan?* We have not stated this question incorrectly We do not mean *what* is your business plan, we mean *why?*

We have made some broad comments about the potential relationships between different types of research and different routes to innovation in previous chapters. When getting down to the details of your business and its planning, these broad questions can sometimes become crystallized into more specific questions about research and innovation. The questions useful for developing your *basic business plan* can also be questions useful for your *innovation plan.*

Research 'Behind' Your Business Plan – what is the context of your chosen industry? What is the current state of play within it, and perhaps more importantly what is its future? So, in what ways can you build innovation into your plan for the next few years?

Research In/Through Your Business Plan – what paradigm is your creative business within? Are you sufficiently aware of it? Is it the right one? Is it about to go through a 'scientific revolution'? So what new techniques, processes are you going to have to learn next?

Research For Your Business Plan – what are your business competitors doing, or planning to do? What are your potential creative collaborators doing, or planning to do? What can your suppliers do for your innovation? What potentially fruitful areas of business collaboration can you identify that will help with your innovation plan over the next few years?

Research In Front Of Your Business Plan – who are your customers today? Who are they going to be tomorrow? Have you tried to falsify your business plan with these audiences? Has it been tested by the awkward squad? What are they all telling you about your innovation needs?

Planning the *why* of your business so as to build innovation into the *what* and the *how* can enable you to have …

An Innovation Plan

In *Innovation Nation*, John Kao lays out some reasons why keeping a constant innovation agenda at the centre of business planning is an important facet.

Some of his arguments hark back to the famous economic philosopher Joseph Schumpeter and his notion of *creative destruction*. Creative destruction highlights how being able to 'kill', or in a more benign way leaving behind your 'normal' creative routine is necessary to keep the creativity fresh. But in recent years the space for 'pure research', which big business and universities used to allow for pure research not necessarily tied to immediate business application, seems to have been eroded. This institutional context means that an innovative mind-set can get left behind as an 'accountancy' or 'target-hitting' onus is placed upon things. This tends to demand more immediate concerns with commercial 'bottom lines' from the outset. Keogh bemoans the loss of this 'pure research' space, and thinks it is bad for business, because it is bad for innovation.

Within big business, lots of debate is about where innovation comes from, how it can be brought about and 'managed'. This can be to do with the 'hardware' of a particular industry – the technology, the machinery, the processes and the designs involved in making something in a new and better way. Or innovation can be more to do with the 'software' – changes in the way organizations are organized, managers manage, communicators communicate, and so on, which can lead to new and better ways of doing essentially the same thing.

Although it might not always necessarily seem like it when cash-flow is not great, working in a small creative company or a more fluid network-based project can be good for creative innovation precisely because it does not suffer from this over-institutionalization and its short-sighted, overly instrumental management. When it comes to research and innovation, you can have advantages over the big business if you put yourself in a position to grasp the potential advantages of *economies of speed*.

So how do you put yourself in a position to grasp economies of speed? Borrowing some ideas from Kao, it is useful to:

- Balance pure research (exploratory, Research Behind and For) with the applied (more instrumental and descriptive aspects of Research In/Through and In Front Of). Don't always go for a repetition of practice, the quick or the immediately obvious. Your creativity will need soul food, and pure research can be a good source of that.

- Keep an openness to your research and innovation plan. Think seriously about the mutual learning and development that networks can bring. Collaboration can bring innovation through mutual creativity that working alone can never bring. As we will explore in detail below, various forms of network orientations are often much more innovative than a closed-ness encouraged by over-competition.
- Seek ways of working that bring two or more previously unconnected branches of creativity, business, research and networks together. Kao calls this kind of brokering for innovation 'platform providing'. Make being a platform provider, or at least being a platform participant, part of your research and innovation plan.
- Finally, when it comes to research and innovation for your creativity, ask yourself what you really need. As in …

Do You Need a Discovery, an Invention or an Innovation?

In the context of research for creative business, Chouinard makes a useful distinction between:

- **Discovery** – finding something entirely new about the world that leads to new ideas and sets up the possibility of an invention.
- **Invention** – making something work from scratch through finding these new discoveries and following this through to new ways of doing things, new processes, new mechanical/technological stuff.
- **Innovation** – reconceptualizing the links between the way you currently do things, how they can be done differently and what is already out there elsewhere. In essence spotting new relationships between current *problems* and already existing *solutions* so that they can mutually inform each other.

As we have already mentioned, the creative business sector tends to be made up of small firms, individuals and networks-based projects. You are not big, so it is probably better if your research for innovation it is not big either, because it is:

- slow
- expensive
- of unknown practical benefit when you first start out on it.

It requires a lot of time, energy and investment to make an *invention*. Big corporations can benefit from inventions because of high *barriers to entry*. Often because the investment and set-up costs of moving into innovative markets are so high, it puts people off. So they have time to make money on the basis of their invention. Without these barriers to entry however, it is easy to find that after years of work and investment into innovation, a lot of people will be doing the same thing as you within a few months. Even with intellectual property protection, they will move into this market if the barriers to entry are low and it is lucrative enough.

So rather than being based upon invention, it is sometimes better for creative business to look for *innovations*, by finding ways to solve a problem with the tools that are already around. This means that being good at researching what is going on around you can be as important as being good at working everything out for yourself. If you are seeking to invent entirely new tools, maybe you are making things a little too complicated for yourself, especially if they already exist in a slightly different form out there.

Innovation can come from:

- A new application for established knowledge – much quicker.
- The use of 'intermediate technology', which can be the use of tools, software, equipment and so on in a new way – much cheaper than trying newly invented tools, software, equipment.
- Finding collaborative spaces with various people who already have the complimentary knowledge and skills that can lead you to innovation – you don't need to learn every new skill, process or technique out there, and you can get a very clear idea of the practical benefits of these new skills, knowledge and techniques right from the outset.

Case Study
USE A PENCIL, COMRADE

There is a story (which is not actually true but it makes a good point) from the Cold War and the Space Race between USA and USSR:

NASA spent lots and lots of time and energy, involving lots and lots of scientific research and technological invention developing a pen that would write in zero gravity, for astronauts to use whilst in outer space.

And the Russians used a pencil!

The common pencil becomes an innovation because it has a new 'killer application'. Heavy-duty invention of something new was not needed.

Which brings us to ...

Problems, Solutions and Killer Applications

This brings us to the strange, dialectical inter-play between *problems* and *solutions*, and the way that researching the potential inter-play between them can be fundamental to the logic of innovation. For instance:

- People routinely mistake problems for solutions and vice versa. Going back to the 'normal way' of doing things when under pressure is a common example of mistaking the behaviour that is the problem as the solution. Seeing change and new ideas as a threat to the normal way of doing things is an example of mistaking the innovative solution for the problem.
- The way things are normally done might not be perceived of as a problem until a new and better way is identified. It is the new 'solution' coming along which helps to identify that there is a 'problem'.

- A 'solution' might be out there, but is unaware of its solution-ness. It is a free-floating answer in search of a question. Only when someone comes along with the place to use it as an answer does it become apparent that it is the 'solution'.

Scientific research is sometimes described as *puzzle* or *problem-solving behaviour*. This might be good for research and innovation for creative business. But it might be equally useful to engage in *solution-searching behaviour* first. This is because the solution might already exist somewhere. You just need to *find* it.

Recognizing this complicated relationship between problems and solutions can help you innovate by seeing the new idea as a solution in search of *your* problem. You are providing the problem here, not the solution! This kind of innovation is about rethinking new ideas as an *opportunity in search of an application*. Which brings us to the *killer application*, another key concept for understanding innovation. The person who is good at innovation is often the one who sees the creative way of simply putting problems and solutions together in a way that completes the circle. Nothing actually 'new' need be discovered or invented to get you to a killer application.

The secret behind successful killer applications takes us back to the *application* bit, rather than the *discovery/invention of something new* bit. So maybe use your research time and energy to find out what is already out there, rather than trying to do it on your own. Find out what the rest of the creative network is up to and how they can help you. Find out how you can help them, and use a pencil rather than one of those complicated NASA space pens wherever possible.

Step outside the question and ask it differently, so that you can see it more effectively. Go back to lateral thinking.

For example ...

Game

WOULD YOU LIKE TO STEP OUTSIDE WITH ME

Another lateral thinking games might help with stepping outside the question as it is first presented to you.

QUESTION

Take all the numbers between 1 and 100 – and add them all together.

What is the answer? You have 30 seconds to work it out! And no calculators!

LATERAL THINKING ANSWER

Taking the first number, 1 and adding it to the last number 100 makes 101.

Adding 2 and 99, also to makes 101, as does 3 added to 98.

So within the question there are 50 pairs of 101s.

$101 \times 50 = 5,050$. Very quick and very easy, if you see the question differently.

As with all lateral thinking exercises, rather than trying to work out the answer with the tools given to you by the question, in this case simple addition, you can see how to use the much more efficient method of multiplication.

And this kind of imaginative recombining of problems and solutions can lead to great real world innovation.

Case Study

WHERE IS THE LOVE? PROBABLY THE BEST KILLER APPLICATION IN THE WORLD

When microbiologists were first researching genetic modification techniques, it is unlikely that they had the problem of unexploded landmines at the forefront of their thinking.

But nevertheless …

FLOWER POWER TAKES ON LAND MINES

A Danish biotech company has developed a genetically modified flower that could help detect land mines and it hopes to have a prototype ready for use within a few years. 'We are really excited about this, even though it's early days. It has considerable potential,' Simon Oestergaard, chief executive of developing company Aresa Biodetection, told Reuters in an interview on Tuesday. The genetically modified weed has been coded to change color when its roots come in contact with nitrogen dioxide evaporating from explosives buried in soil. Within three to six weeks from being sowed over landmine-infested areas, the small plant, a Thale Cress, will turn a warning red when close to a land mine.

(from *Wired Magazine*, at www.wired.com)

A truly great innovation stemming from a killer application. A Healing Application! Planting flowers to prevent kids from getting blown up! It doesn't get any more beautiful than that.

But the initial science (solution) was from one world, the detecting of land mines (problem) was from a completely unconnected world. The innovation came from putting the two things together. Sometimes when you put 2 and 2 together you get much more than 4!

So are there innovations from killer applications out there for you?

- Do you have a problem in search of a solution?
- Or maybe you have a solution in search of a problem?
- Maybe you should be researching people who know how to put these together?
- Maybe you should be researching other killer applications within your field to see what lessons they hold.

Market Research

Most of what we have said in this chapter so far has been about the relationship between research and the innovative use of new ideas for developing aspects to your creativity. But clearly, once you have done this and are ready, you will need to tell everyone else what you have and what you can do for them. Your ideas need to *flow out*, as well as *flow within* if your research is to take you to sustainable innovation.

So, in its broadest sense *market research* is a key component of any innovation plan. It will be really useful to research what other people are thinking and doing. It will also be useful to know how other people such as customers, collaborators and audiences are *receiving your ideas*. So this implies a whole new area of potential research that fits squarely within the *In Front Of* research starting-point.

Thinking about the various stages of business reminds you that you will potentially be working with lots of other people. And each one of these people, including suppliers and customers can be a source of research and innovation.

Let's return again to the stages involved in creative business:

- **Origination** – the 'light bulb' moment, the original creative idea that will form the basis of the creative business. This can involve working with collaborators and other like-minded people or companies.
- **Research and Development** – project planning, proto-typing or piloting something through a development stage. This can involve working with all sorts of experts who can advise on feasibility, technical know-how, and so on.
- **Production** – making it 'work' and producing it so that you can take it to market. This could be a product that you then get manufactured, a service that you get ready to deliver or a project or event that goes public. This is likely to involve working with all sorts of service providers and suppliers of all sorts of things that support your work.
- **Marketing and Distribution** – telling everyone else what you have and what you can do for them. Again this involves working with service providers and suppliers.
- **Customers and Consumption** – getting it to the customer and taking care of them. Working with the customer.

So, even this very brief sketch of the stages within business shows that lots of other people are probably going to be involved. Listening to them can be a good source of research and innovation for your company.

Market research can be broken down into several elements:

- What your suppliers can do for you.
- What your competitors are doing.
- What your collaborators are doing.
- What your customers, or potential customers are doing, or thinking, or thinking of doing.
- What your company personality is and how it is presenting itself to the world.

Researching Your Suppliers

It can be good to see your suppliers and service providers as people to be researched. They may know of much better and more efficient ways to do the things you do. Innovation can come from:

- Listening to advice and know-how other than the know-how you are buying.
- Buying a different service or component from them.
- Asking them to innovate for/with you by asking them different questions.

Case Study

THE GENIUS HAROLD LEFFLER

When I had my blacksmiths shop, I contracted out the tooling of our climbing gear, and some of the production, to Harold Leffler's machine shop in Burbank. Leffler was a draftsman and tool and die maker with fifty years' hands-on experience. We called him the genius as often as we called him Harold.

… Harold used to joke about blueprints he received from engineers; they were so over designed that the cost to produce them would be ten or twenty times higher than necessary, and in many cases they would be impossible to make at all. Because I had no training in engineering but did know what I wanted a carabiner or ice screw to do, I would show up with a simple sketch or a carved wooden model, or just an idea in my head, and we would work together to come up with a design that was feasible.

(from *Let My People Go Surfing*, by Y. Chouinard)

Researching Your Competitors

A good competitor analysis identifies who your competitors are and makes a comparison, broken down by:

- how much they charge
- what services or products they offer
- their target customers
- how they market themselves
- how customers access their service or product
- how they are perceived externally by their customers and within the sector by their industry peers.

This should tell you more about your own business than it does about anyone else's, by:

- identifying products, services or organizations that complement what you do
- opportunities for collaboration, growth or diversification.

Researching Your Collaborators

Remember emergent behaviour from the last section?

- **More/Different Is Better for Research** – The livelier and more diverse your creative network, the more often you will get to hear about new ideas and possibilities from a broader range of creative disciplines. It can get a little boring when everyone already knows what everyone already knows. Broadening your creative networks can help turn your whole world into your R&D lab.

- **Ignorance is a Useful Signpost** – One of the key reasons ignorance is useful is that it can show you very quickly and immediately what the gaps in your knowledge are. So if you take your ignorance seriously and grasp it as an opportunity when it becomes apparent to you, it can direct your research agenda into useful areas such as recognizing problems as problems, solutions as solutions and how to put them together.
- **Encourage Randomness in Your Research** – This is fundamentally about stumbling across new ideas, killer applications and collaborations. It is intimately connected with showing you your ignorance and how/why you can/should do something about it, as above.
- **Researching the Patterns in the Signs** – Researching killer applications, innovations rather than discoveries and generally doing something with ignorance and randomness will entail standing back from the details and looking *sideways* as well as forwards. Researching the creative garden around you as well as digging ever deeper into your small bit of it so as to spot similar patterns within what other people are doing is the mind-set that is needed for good innovation and finding killer applications.
- **Researching Your Neighbours** – Paying attention to your neighbours is the general social context within which all emergent behaviour occurs. But don't just research *them*, let them research *you* too. Like a lot of really good things, it needs to be mutual if it is really going to work.

But …

Warning
SEEING PRETTY PATTERNS

It is human nature to look for patterns and to assign them meaning when we find them … (Kahneman and Tversky) *dubbed these shortcuts heuristics. In general, heuristics are useful, but just as our manner of processing optical information sometimes leads to optical illusions, so heuristics sometimes lead to systematic error.*

(from *The Drunkards Walk*, by L. Mlodinow)

As we saw when considering emergent behaviour, it is good to look for patterns in the signs because it can show us similar themes and trajectories that we share with other areas of research.

But there can be dangers in overdoing this.

A heuristic is a kind of conceptual or mental template that we can apply to things – a kind of pattern we can use to make sense of the messy world out there. The danger comes in using the template too strongly to 'chop up' the world so that it fits the artificial heuristic more neatly. Think about the best relationship between carts and horses here.

The real world is usually much more random than that, but we seem to be hardwired to seek patterns rather than see randomness.

For instance, I used to sometimes think that when I thought about an old film I had not seen in ages, that it would appear on TV sometime over the next few days. This has happened to

---

me several times. The first time I didn't take any notice – it was just a coincidence. But then it happened again and again over the next few years. Maybe there is some spooky thing going on where I could predict the future TV schedule!

Of course, there is a fundamental problem with this – I did not remember the hundreds and hundreds of times over this period when I had thought of an old film and it had NOT appear of TV over the next few days.

I had only remembered the bit of pattern that I had remembered, not the whole thing. And it is all too easy to do this in situations where it really matters. To think we have spotted a pattern in your research when it is really just what we would expect from a normal random distribution of events.

In a way very similar to the more background idea of paradigms, heuristics can be good because they can help order our thinking. But they can be bad if we overdo them and start to mistake them for the real thing.

Researching Your Customers

Obviously another key part of market research for creative business is research into what the customer really thinks of you, your company and your stuff. This is why market research is much more than simple marketing, as in trying to sell something.

Good market research, like good social and anthropological research comes from getting to know your customers properly, understanding things in the way that they understand it themselves. At best, it entails asking them to be a genuine and on-going part of your creative project/business and using their input to continue developing your creativity. That is, good customer research is about more than just getting to understand them until they have bought your product or service.

Recent research (Chouinard 2006) has suggested that only 14 per cent of Americans get in touch with a company if they are *not* happy with it. The number is as little as 8 per cent in Europe. And in Japan it is only 4 per cent. However, other research suggests that if customers have a problem with a company, 66 per cent never buy from them again. They just don't tell you about it or about why. So *you* need to research *them* in some way.

Uncomfortable though it might be, it is useful to research what is wrong about you and what you are doing, rather than just focus upon what is right about you. Remember, you can learn more from failure than success if you have good falsificationist research methods and strategies to cope with the findings.

Researching Your Company Personality

A big part of the way the market perceives you and your company is your *organizational or company personality*. This is the image or reputation of your company. It is connected to, but broader than any specific logos, advertising or other public communications it might make. Because the creative industries are often made up of very small companies and/or sole traders, your company personality is often pretty much you yourself, your 'performance' (in both senses of the word) in talking to clients, customers or collaborators, and how you appear to them.

But it can come from other things. We don't want to imply that there is any 'one best way' of presenting your company personality, just that the following are factors you need to be aware of:

- **Your place** – Your building, your address, the interior design of your office, the fact that you don't have an office but work wifi. Working without an office can be an increasingly funky, interesting and cheap way of running a creative company whilst also having great contact with the creative network around you. So long as that is the company personality you think is best for you, you might not need an impressive office to impress clients. You see? No implications about 'one best way'.
- **Your product** – This kind of speaks for itself. If what you do and sell is very tightly linked to a particular product, then clearly your company personality will be too.
- **Your service** – Very similar to the previous point in some ways, but different in others. Providing a service is different from a product because there is usually more of an inter-personal and emotional aspect to it. So ways of being, talking and looking will figure up more in this aspect of company personality.
- **Your staff** – If you have staff they will form a big part of your company personality. The way they answer the phone, deal with people, get back to clients (or not) and so on. The customer will not make fine distinction in terms of your company personality just because (s)he is dealing with temporary staff, it will still have an effect.

You will have a company personality whatever you do. Even if you ignore the fact of company personality you will have a company personality, one that will probably be slightly schizophrenic. So it is probably best to research it as part of the general market research every so often, so you know what it is, where it comes from and make sure it is the one you want. It is a part of the broader idea of market research to know and therefore control better the factors impacting upon how you appear to the market out there, in terms of *all* the ways your company is presented to the world.

And then of course there is your Brand. This is one way of summing up all of what we have said. The problem with the idea of 'The Brand' is that the term has been so over-used, and in some uses contaminated with bullshit, that it is now a problematic term for a lot of people. That gets us into the politics (economics) of knowledge being put off for another time. But there is a relationship between The Brand and the Uncanny Valley.

Up to this point we have looked at what the different grounds for doing research can be, how to pin down research activity within specific methods and ways in which research can lead to creative innovations. But these new and innovative ideas and ways of working will probably entail all sorts of other changes as a consequence. They might require you to think, work, manage and get organized differently. This is especially the case if the innovative ideas are really to be fully developed and grown into something that you can protect, not get sued for, sustain and grow. So in the next chapter we turn to some of the associated skills involved in research and innovation for creative business.

16 'The Rules and Peculiarities of Various Instruments': Innovation Skills

---

Proverb

We can't go on together with suspicious minds.

(Elvis Presley)

They do say that you should be care-ful what you wish for, because it might just happen. And if it does happen, it is good to be ready.

So, having looked at some of the philosophy and methods for research, and begun to relate these ideas to creative business innovation, we now come to some of the associated skills that run alongside research and innovation. The common thread across all these skills is the way they can help in dealing with the consequences of your research, your innovations and changes to the context of your creativity. Indeed, it is important to note that some of the organizational skills discussed below can actually *be* the business innovation itself, if they contribute to finding different and better ways of doing what you do and how.

There are ethical, legal, managerial and organizational questions to consider when taking research into innovation, into managing and running a creative business, or just yourself. And as Elvis teaches us, it will be difficult to go on together if you get things wrong.

Research Ethics

First, going back to the initial question of research, we need to consider research ethics. As well as the broader question of ethics we looked at in Section 1, ethical issues are a key part of any professional research and an especially important factor when the research involves the real lives of other people. We do not have any off-the-peg answers. You will need to think about that for yourself, because constantly thinking about these things is possibly the best basis for any ethics.

General guidance on research ethics normally includes:

- **Consent** – ensuring that people actively agreed to participate, that they have not been deceived or coerced, that they are not too young or in some other way unable to give consent.
- **Withdrawal** – ensuring that people know they can withdraw from the research at any stage.
- **Confidentiality** – ensuring that any information stemming from the research is kept confidential, that findings are anonymized (it doesn't say anything about specific individuals) and that information is destroyed or at least kept secure once the research has finished.
- **Harm** – ensuring the protection of the people participating in the research from physical or mental harm to themselves, or from harming other people as a result of the research process.
- **Debriefing** – ensuring that the research process and any consequence of it has been discussed with the participants, that any help they might need as a result of being involved in it is offered, any concerns, stress or worries are overcome and the research findings are revealed to them.

In short, if you are reasonable about who and what you are asking, observing or recording and they've agreed, and you've given some thought to the potential problems, then you should be OK. But you do need to be care-ful and think about it first. Would you like it?

So in terms of professional skills, you might want to think about these questions before conducting the research:

- Do you have an honest appraisal as to whether there are any ethical risks, and if so does the proposed research activity need ethical approval?
- Can you provide information about the ethical quality of the proposed research activity?
- If so, what ethical issues are raised by the proposed research, and therefore how will you address them?
- Did you get consent from participants? For example, a signed consent form.
- How will you ensure confidentiality, security and retention of research data? Will all the information be kept confidential or left on a laptop on a train?
- Are they going to remain anonymous?
- Are you doing on-line and Internet research, and if so are there any specific problems associated with this? If there are, what are you going to do about them?
- Will you let the participants have a copy of the research?
- Are you sure that the participants know that they can withdraw at any time or have their data, responses, pictures withdrawn from the research?
- What kind of 'debrief' have you got planned?

Theory

Theories of Creative Innovation: No. 9 – An Ethical Note

Presumably few of us are interested in facilitating creativity which is solely destructive … Yet how is it possible to make the necessary discrimination such that we may encourage a constructive creativity and not a destructive one?

(from *Towards a Theory of Creativity*, by C. Rogers)

But this question of facilitating innovations that are constructive rather than destructive brings us very quickly to the concern that …

Knowledge Cannot Be Un-Invented

Because knowledge cannot be un-invented we all have responsibilities to each other to think about the care-ful attitudes advocated in Section 1. It is not true when people say 'All is fair in love and war', and 'the ends do not always justify the means' just because *you* have those ends in mind. If you hurt people you hurt them. And if your innovations allow other people to do the hurting, well the people are still hurt.

Nor is it good enough when people say 'business is business' as some sort of catch-all excuse for doing whatever nasty thing they want. Business is not exempt from wider social and ethical responsibilities, even though sometimes people try to claim it is. Nor does art or any other kind of creativity come with some kind of 'artistic licence' that exempts it from wider social responsibilities. Business is not *just* business. So research for business is not always just research for business. Mary Shelley's novel *Frankenstein* is not just a horror story. It is also an allegorical warning about how your inventions can come to have power over you.

The Uncanny Valley

Another reason for being care-ful about what you research and develop is the dangers of the Uncanny Valley. Sigmund Freud referred to the uncanny as the 'un-homely', as something out of place.

In a more specific sense, the Uncanny Valley refers to the revulsion, disjuncture or rift we experience between the hyper-realism of, for instance, the digital imagery within a computer game on the one hand, and the experience of this 'realism' as something we know instinctively is not real on the other.

> ## Quotation
>
> *The uncanny valley is a hypothesis that when robots and other facsimiles of humans look and act almost like actual humans, it causes a response of revulsion among human observers. The 'valley' in question is a dip in a proposed graph of the positivity of human reaction as a function of a robot's lifelikeness. It was introduced by Japanese roboticist Masahiro Mori in 1970 and has been linked to Ernst Jentsch's concept of 'the uncanny' identified in a 1906 essay, 'On the Psychology of the Uncanny' Jentsch's conception is famously elaborated upon by Sigmund Frued a 1919 essay, simply entitled 'The Uncanny' (Das Unheimliche). A similar problem exists in realistic 3D computer animation such as with the films The Polar Express and Beowulf.*
>
> (from Wikipedia)

In the wider cultural world, think about status symbols for a moment. None of us want to be perceived as too geeky for very long and we use fashion stuff to present a 'self' to the world so that others will see us as OK kind of people who 'get it'. But there is only so far you can go with this. It is not a never-ending ladder to 'better' status. The percentage of people we impress when we get into more and more specific labels designed to 'increase' our status is actually an ever-decreasing circle. And if we overdo it, it can flip over the edge very quickly and people start to see us as a bit of a fool As with a lot of these things, the behaviour, activity, strategy that was initially part of the solution becomes part of the problem.

So we can see a sense of innovative 'progress towards something' can easily reach the 'too much stage' and it becomes overstate and experienced negatively. It is good to make 'progress towards something' within research geared towards innovation. But if we over-reach the claims we make, if it gets too pat, too ordered a representation of the messy world out there, then it can easily be rejected as too 'perfect'. Again, too much of what used to be the solution becomes part of the problem. This can happen in lots of places, when pitching an idea and making too many claims, when designing an interior that is so perfect no one can live in it, when writing prose that is so 'purple' that the death scene becomes funny. Nervousness of the uncanny can be a useful self-corrective in lots of ways.

Managing the Flow of Ideas

We now come to those professional skills associated with finding the right business structure for the flow of ideas leading to innovation, and the corresponding 'management' of that flow.

A lot of what we have said so far, in this and previous chapters implies research and innovation comes from two inter-related things:

- developing new ideas
- talking to each other.

Historically, many medium-sized or large companies have not had an innovative culture because ideas have not flowed very well. Sometimes this is *because of* management. The very idea of management has always been underpinned, to a greater or lesser degree, by the *separation of conception from execution*. That is, some people (managers) do all the thinking, planning and having of ideas (conception), and other people (workers) do all the work (execution). This separation of conception from execution is the central facet that often really messes up the flow of new ideas, and therefore business innovation. This is not so much of a problem if you are running a business that just wants to do the same routine thing over and over again. But if you want to run a creative business that is operating in the ever changing environment of the innovation economy, needs to be responsive to the global cultural economy, that survives upon its ability to come up with creative business innovations and benefits from economies of speed, then such a style of management can be disastrous.

This is one of the main reasons to avoid suspicious minds. Trying, as far as possible to create a working environment in which all parties feel connected, feel that they are meaningfully contributing to, that they are valued and able to express themselves because the business space is creative and innovative is, in and of itself, good for creativity and innovation. As Elvis teaches us, trust is a better basis for creativity than suspicion and contemporary human-centred approaches to management (called various names) have tried to devise ideas of management that encourage this and the flow of ideas for innovation. Such approaches try to encourage:

- a greater sense of motivation, common purpose, commitment and team work;
- a better sense of two-way communication between management and staff so that ideas can flow 'up' as well as 'down';
- internal systems and processes that help the work to proceed rather than hinder it.

Of course, this kind of management is found in some industries and workplaces far more often than in others. Lots of people, indeed the majority still *suffer* from management rather than benefit from it, and experience work as something negative. However, that gets us into another dimension of the politics of knowledge that we keep putting off until another time.

In terms of managing the way a team works by encouraging the flow of ideas for innovation, Tom Kelley, in his book *The Art of Innovation* describes the five steps he uses:

- **Understand** – understanding the market, the client, the technology and the perceived constraints on the problem at hand. Later in a project, they often challenge those constraints, but it's important to understand perceptions.
- **Observe** – observing real people in real-life situations to find out what makes them tick. What confuses them, what they like, what they hate, where their latent needs are addressed by current products and services.
- **Visualize** – visualizing new-to-the-world concepts and the customers who will use them. For new product categories they sometimes visualize the customers experience by using composite characters and storyboard-illustrated scenarios.
- **Evaluate and Refine** – evaluating and refining the prototypes in a series of quick iterations. They try not to get too attached to the first few prototypes, because they know they'll change. No idea is so good that it can't be improved upon, and they plan a series of improvements.

- **Implement** – implementation of the new concept for commercialization. This phase is often the longest and most technically challenging in the developmental process.

As a manager, it is part of the job to deal with the other people in the team. Again we see another facet of the fundamental importance of *relationships* for creativity and business. If you want other people to contribute to the flow of ideas and generally *be there*, then it is *your responsibility* as a manager to create the right conditions for this to happen. If you don't, your business will miss out on the ideas and potential innovations.

Theory
THEORIES OF CREATIVE INNOVATION: NO. 10 – THE MANAGERIAL VIEW

Our 'secret formula' to (manage innovation) is actually not very formulaic. It is a blend of methodologies, work practices, culture and infrastructure. Methodology alone is not enough. For example … prototyping is both a step in the innovation process and a philosophy about moving continuously forward, even when some variables are still undefined. And brainstorming is not just a valuable creative tool at the fuzzy front end of products. It's also a pervasive cultural influence for making sure that individuals don't waste too much energy spinning their wheels on a tough problem when the collective wisdom of the team can get them 'unstuck' in less than an hour. Success depends on what you do and how you do it.

(from *The Art of Innovation*, by T. Kelley)

For example …

Closed and Open Innovation Paradigms

In his book *Open Innovation*, Henry Chesbrough makes a distinction between the 'closed innovation paradigm' and the 'open innovation paradigm' (paradigms can be good and bad). The open innovation paradigm takes us to a large extent back to thinking about creative networks.

The closed innovation paradigm is a way of thinking about business and innovation that is fundamentally based upon competition and therefore probably characterizes the norm in our society. Innovation is all supposed to come from *within* the firmly closed boundaries of the company. It is supposed to come from 'vertical integration' – the chain of vertical communication from the top, through the various departments of the firm, down through R&D and out through commercialization, marketing and distribution.

The closed innovation paradigm is characterized by the following corporate assumptions (or misapprehensions):

- The smartest people in our field already work for us.
- To profit from R&D, we must discover it, develop it and ship it ourselves.
- If we discover it ourselves, we will get it to market first.
- The company that gets an innovation to market first will win.

- If you create the most and best ideas in the industry, you will win.
- We should control our intellectual property, so that our competitors don't profit from them.

In contrast to this, the open innovation paradigm sees this approach as 'knowledge hoarding', as unnecessarily tight and closed, as overly competitive and therefore a mind-set that misses innovative opportunities that can come from collaboration. In a very strong parallel to the downside of formal rationality in general, if the established company system and culture is too closed it can become part of the problem rather than part of the solution.

This can be for a variety of reasons:

- If a system is overly closed it encourages an inward-looking focus upon R&D that can miss the innovations that have already happened out there. This encourages a focus upon new invention when an innovation (solution looking for a problem) already exists. As we have mentioned elsewhere, this can be unnecessarily slow and expensive.
- Because communications resulting from the Web are now much easier and quicker, other firms will probably be thinking about being more open, so an insistence on closed-ness can easily become the reason you are becoming less competitive, because of your focus on being too competitive.
- Workers have more mobility and no longer believe in, nor want, a job for life. Within this is an increased willingness of people 'to go it alone' and develop their own spin-off companies based upon innovations that could have stayed within your firm if it had been less tightly controlling because of its closed-ness. People are motivated to work for a variety of reasons, and money is only one of them. Creative rewards, interest, meanings and values are often more important, and an open innovation paradigm lends itself to a creative business culture that is better able to allow this, because …
- If the organizational culture parallels the closed-ness of the management and organizational processes, there will be less breathing space for research. Creativity, innovation and the flow of ideas will then be a flow *out of the company* as people seek creative and innovative spaces elsewhere.

These points have potential relevance for organizing creativity and innovation in any industry. But as see suggested in Section 2 creative business is based to a greater degree upon the collaboration, flexibility and innovation that brings economies of *speed* rather than *economies of scale*. Creative business also generally has lower barriers to entry so people can 'go it alone' quite easily at relatively low costs. Many people in the creative industries resist business growth purely in terms of numbers of employees because they intuitively feel this is not the kind of place they want to work. The development of spin-off companies within the creative industries is much more of the norm, and therefore creative businesses tend to be small and occupy creative networks rather than coalesce into big firms. Given all this, the potential problems associated with trying to apply a closed innovation paradigm can be that much more acute for pursuing innovation within a creative business.

The open innovation paradigm is characterized by the following assumptions:

- Not all the smart people work for us. We need to work with smart people from outside our company as well as inside.
- Whilst internal R&D is needed to claim some portion of the potential market value, external R&D can create significant additions to that value.
- We don't have to originate the research in order to profit from it.
- Building better, more collaborative business models is better than getting to market first.
- If we make the best use of internal and external ideas, we will 'win', maybe because everyone has 'won'.
- We should profit from others' use of our intellectual property, and we should buy others' intellectual property whenever it advances our own business models.

The open innovation paradigm sees working with others outside the tightly defined boundaries of the firm, and being less hung-up about the details of day-to-day competition as a useful component to developing better and more innovative businesses.

Warning

THE HOT-HAND FALLACY

We all like to think we are really, really good at what we do. Especially when we are enjoying some success and things are going well for a change. We like to think it is down to us being 'good' – creative, intelligent, skilful.

Obviously these things will be a factor, but it might also be that luck and chance are equally important. We are never as good, nor as bad as we think we are. Statistically, if you took all the thousands of people you have known since you started school, there will be at least one who has enjoyed great success due pretty much to luck, and someone else who has had no success whatsoever, even though they are really talented and hardworking:

Academics call the mistaken impression that a random streak (of success) is due to extraordinary performance the hot-hand fallacy ... In all aspects of our lives we encounter streaks and other peculiar patterns of success and failure. Sometimes success predominates, sometimes failure. Either way it is important in our lives to take the long view and understand that streaks and other patterns that don't appear random can indeed happen by pure chance.

(from *The Drunkards Walk*, by L. Mlodinow)

Epistemological nervousness and creative humility can be a useful component of your research and creativity. And anyway, it will probably help in being more ethical and graceful. And also anyway, remembering that you are not as 'good' as you think helps to remind you when you have a hang-over that you are not as 'bad' either.

It has taken Big Management theories of creativity and innovation until 2006 to fully recognize this alternative, collaborative, cross-boundary way of working towards mutually beneficial innovation. All this time, creative networks have tended to just live and work like this without any management guru telling us what a good idea it was! If you have lived and worked within a creative network over the past 10 years, you might ask: what is so new about this open innovation paradigm? And you would have a point. But at least the open innovation paradigm blows the gaff that the traditional macho-man-in-suit-paradigm of innovation for business is not all that the hype claims it to be. Maybe Alan Sugar and his Dragon's Den friends will catch up with us one day.

Case Study

AN OPEN INNOVATION FIELDTRIP: WORKING WITH *THE DO BOYS*

We have already mentioned Patagonia's business model several times. They are good at what they do in part because they use the products they are selling. Their research and innovation plan involves testing out product with the *Do Boys*, the extreme guys who are the leaders of the climbing, surfing and snowboarding scene.

This looks something like open innovation because:

- It is not easy to tell where the formal organization starts and ends, what is internal or external R&D or who is at work or at play, and so on.
- It is about the climbing first, then the market for climbing gear, then the business itself – in that order.
- There is a more organic relationship between the creators and the product, because the product is more of an expression of what the creators really are, rather than being what they do for a job.
- The relationships between 'management' and 'workers' is very different from the norm – there is no separation of conception from execution.

There is a different value system and a substantive rationality at work.

More Open Openness

The problems with the open innovation paradigm as it described by Chesbrough are associated with two key factors:

- Its logic is still very much located within the confines of the traditional firm, and within the economics of success through competition. But creativity and innovation often lie within a network of people who have a much broader list of motivations that 'winning'. As a result, the open innovation paradigm described by Chesbrough and others is not actually all that open in comparison.
- It tends to hold onto the idea that everything can still be rationally planned and managed. It therefore does not allow for the random, unexpected, spontaneous and *emergent*.

Recognizing a drunkard's walk can help open out your thinking about open innovation.

The Drunkard's Walk by Leonard Mlodinow shows how randomness plays a much more significant role in our lives than we like to think. Almost everything in our lives depends to some extent upon those unconscious gambles, unexpected turns and chance encounters that make up our lives. But this can be good news when it comes to creativity and innovation, if we know how to take advantage of it. This echoes what Johnson had to say about the 'natural history of innovation' in Section 2, and is something we will come back to in detail below.

Economists talk about the potential benefits of *diversification*. By this they mean the benefits of being involved in lots of different markets. This way, if their work in one market dries up, they can look to another one. Diversification is a fancy way of pointing out the benefits of 'hedging your bets', 'keeping your options open' and 'not putting all your eggs in one basket'. This makes sense if you are a big firm with the capacity for doing lots of different things at the same time, but what if you are a small firm looking to get something new going through research and innovation? Structuring the relationship between creativity, innovation and openness and grasping the usefulness of the diversification of creative entry points entails listening to others all the time. This entails being good at organizing collaboration if it is to culminate in doing something and become more than just 'pub talk'.

So ...

How T-Shaped Do You Need to Be?

Orthodox businesses tend to quickly develop very definite structures, hard and fast boundaries between 'inside' and 'outside' and lots of set rules about the relationships between employees and management. But as we have seen in Section 2 creative business is perhaps best pursued, and is sometimes more creative when it comes together within *organic networks* rather than *mechanical structure*. These creative spaces tend to be more informal, have less rigid structures and boundaries, no hierarchies to speak off and definitely no management. Because such creative networks are self-organized, the *flow of ideas for innovation* tends to happen 'naturally', at least if the network is vibrant and healthy. So collaborations and co-operation with people *outside* the formal boundaries of the company becomes more important as a source of research and innovation. So organizing this necessary collaboration within non-hierarchical and non-managed creative networks becomes an important issue for your business innovation.

Having lots of interesting conversations, making initial plans on the basis of excitement and inspiration, but then seeing the project fizzle out because there is no 'routine' is a very common failing of informal creative networks. They can be great for the origination and initial flow of new ideas, but absolutely frustrating for getting things done in a regular and sustained way. So, some degree of structure is needed if the ideas are to flow into *actual innovative work*.

One way of getting a hold on different structures for creative collaboration and the flow of ideas is the idea of *T-Shaped Teams* articulated by the David Garcia et al. in their book *(Un)Common Ground*. A T-shaped team has broad knowledge at one level. Its people can see how different things can fit together from different angles, from different creative disciplines. They understand several languages (creativity, business, technology, money, public sector priorities, legal stuff).

So they have *breadth across*.

But they also have their own creative specialisms that *go deep down*.

A broad line going across the top, a deep line going down, hence their T shape-ness.

Below are six structured shapes for developing creative business spaces that show *varying degrees of T-shaped*-ness and are relevant for thinking about different stages within open innovation. These six shapes need to be seen as points on a spectrum of T-shaped-ness. Back to commensurability again, you don't need to choose one of the six organizational shapes below and stick to it. The six shapes should be seen as a *reference library of structures* to which you can refer at various times depending upon what you are doing, rather than a list from which one should be chosen.

The different organizational shapes within the spectrum of T-shaped-ness are as follows:

Pragmatism: Focused Collaborations Directed towards Concrete Outcomes – the structure with the lowest degree of T-shaped-ness. Useful for organizing collaborations geared towards already clear and specific aims with a limited degree of open-ended-ness. Pragmatic structures organized in a way that echoes more traditional ideas of work and management, characterized by:

- a division of labour and clearly defined areas of individual responsibility;
- a team adherence to an overarching plan and the acceptance of some separation of conception from execution;
- clearly definable aims, objectives and ways of evaluating success;
- a relatively high degree of vertical communication from the top down to the bottom.

Such structures within specific creative projects are often time-limited and their T-shaped-ness lies in the variety of specific skills that individuals bring to the project to perform specific tasks. They are Pragmatic because they are more about people coming into an already organized creative structure and pursuing innovation by *getting on with it*, rather than being asked to engage in lots of talking about *what it is all about*. The assumption is that this has already been done.

Collaborative Experiments – to structure this kind of creative space you need to focus upon organizing inter-disciplinary or inter-business collaboration. This type of collaboration needs space for:

- more horizontal collaborations rather than relying upon already established Pragmatic plans and hierarchies;
- members to be drawn in from different creative and/or scientific disciplines to encourage experimentation and innovative dialogue;
- a plan or structure that can still stay focused upon a relatively specific creative outcome to underpin the open and experimental spirit.

This creative space needs to be less hierarchical than pragmatism, with less separation of conception from execution. It organizes creativity through a focus upon inter-disciplinary creative *processes* as much as upon creative *outcomes*. Creative experiments tend to be less time-limited and more focused upon on-going two-way innovation dialogues.

However, there still needs to be a clear demarcation between areas of expertise and responsibilities within a fairly high division of labour. So although creative experiments are more T-shaped than pragmatism there is still a relatively low degree of T-shaped-ness overall.

Inclusive Design: Innovation between creators and users – this is about forging new relationships between creators and end users to co-create and co-innovate. For instance, it can be about organizing openly democratic creative relationships such that innovation emerges between:

- members of the public and architects redesigning the area;
- product designers and potential consumers within 'design surgeries';
- performing artists and members of a participating audience.

This structure encompasses a high degree of T-shaped-ness because it is a very *open system*. Creative innovation can come from the multi-faceted social, political, economic and cultural facets the end users bring with them to the creative encounter. And these will probably be way beyond the specific creative act itself. Quite often it means resistance, the need for mutual listening rather than talking and diplomatic respect. But that is why they can be good. They are highly T-shaped structures because they open up the creative process to such a wide community of voices.

Lab Culture – this structure for creative innovation is a very free and open structure designed to bring people together to 'jump start' unforeseen innovative connections. Lab culture is very T-shaped because it encompasses lots of deep expertise which people bring together around broad themes of collaboration. It can be a good way of organizing a group of people to foster the emergent behaviour discussed above, in that it:

- is radically open to new and innovation dialogues forming out of the creative thinking of people with very different backgrounds;
- encourages randomness and the usefulness of recognizing ignorance for spotting innovation opportunities;
- offers a high level of *multi-* or *cross*-disciplinarity, the 'thinking outside the box' thing. This is different from the more straightforward *inter*-disciplinarity, whereby experts share their ideas but still from a position of 'thinking inside *their* box' which tends to characterize pragmatism and creative experiments.

Rather than being focused upon pre-established and specific creative aims, Lab Culture tends to be organized for *experimentation rather than delivery*. It is the journey rather than the arrival. Back the Krishnamurti.

The structure consequently has:

- a very 'flat' structure with little or no hierarchy up and down;
- little in the way of a 'master-plan' other than the encouragement of innovation as a basic premise;
- little or no separation of conception from execution or the management of creative direction;
- no defined areas of expertise or responsibility so that the creativity can move around and people can assume roles and responsibilities when they feel they have 'got that far'.

Once Lab Culture has done its work, you will probably need to go back towards the pragmatism end of the spectrum to get things done.

Partnerships and Placements – this structure for creative innovation is about encouraging and managing the placement of creative practitioners within other teams or business as a kind of *knowledge transfer or exchange space*. This can work in Pragmatic, Creative Experimental or Lab Culture ways.

New partnerships, innovative ideas, killer applications and business processes might flow in both directions as a result.

Cultural Brokers Facilitating Creative Encounters – as we saw above when we considered 'organizing coral reefs' this is about creating a structure to encourage emergent behaviour as a driver behind creative innovation. Cultural brokers facilitate creative encounters by becoming *ambassadors for emergence* and the *diplomats of creative networking*. Cultural brokers tend to run creative dating agencies and organize creativity spaces to connect and 'translate'.

They are people who '... drive and facilitate creative encounters connecting all domains and disciplines' as a structure for innovation.

We will come back to this in the next chapter. For now it might be useful to consider a fairly recent and world changing example of open innovation and T-shaped-ness.

From e2e to P-to-P: Open Source and the Flow of Ideas

If innovation comes from the flow of ideas, and if creative businesses are often individually small organizations that work within broader creative network of varying shapes, then getting the flow of ideas across networks could be key to creativity and innovation.

This requires a *network of networks*, which we might call the *Innovation Commons*, following the work of Lawrence Liang, Lawrence Lessig and Eric von Hippel and Yochai Benkler.

All these writers highlight in different ways how new digital networks have created new structures for collaborative innovation. In this sense, *the structures* are the innovations as much as the specific creative acts themselves and are intimately connected to a whole new attitude towards creative innovation that has only just begun to enable people to co-create in a non-hierarchical and non-proprietary way across the planet. This is why they are akin to *The Commons*, in the same way common land used to be an open, non-hierarchical space before they took it away from us with the Enclosure Acts. The Web has helped to create this *Innovation Commons* because it can only ever be a non-managed creative space. Whilst normal organizational spaces are controlled from *the centre*, the Web ensures that ideas and creativity is kept at the *ends of the wires*. The structure of co-creation on the Web is end-to-end, or *e2e*. No one is in control and the centre is relatively simple, containing not much more than the pipe that allows connectivity. This plastic *e2e* architecture of innovation has the fundamental impact of increasing the freedoms of people to create and distribute.

Theory

THEORIES OF CREATIVE INNOVATION: NO. 11 – THE OPEN SOURCE TRADITION

We can see how the end-to-end principle renders the Internet an innovation commons, where innovations can develop and deploy new applications or content without the permission of anyone else. Because of e2e, no one needs register an application with 'the Internet' before it will run; no permission to use the bandwidth is required. Instead, e2e means the network is designed to assure that the network cannot decide which innovations will run ... Because of e2e, innovators know that they need not get the permission of anyone – neither AT&T nor the Internet itself – before they build a new application for the Internet. If an innovator has what he or she believes is a great idea for an application, he or she can build it without authorization from the network itself and with the assurance that the network can't discriminate against it.

(from *Commons on the Wires*, by L. Liang)

And *e2e* structures enable innovative processes to happen though direct Peer-to-Peer (P-to-P) working.

In lots of contemporary ways P-to-P is proving to be a very successful form of 'industrial relations' for increasing the flow of ideas and producing highly innovative products.

So, in the light of the preceding discussion of degrees of T-shaped-ness, perhaps the most innovative aspect of e2e and P-to-P is the fact that it appears to have very little structure at all. In that sense it is an anti-structure structure organization, because it:

- enables a community of creative people to come together to be each other's R&D department, without boundaries, fear of failures and hard and fast divisions of labour, so increasing the *flow* of ideas;
- enables a self-selection of work, so increasing the sense of commitment and meaning of those tasks, and increasing the flow of *quality* ideas;
- is usually *non-proprietary in its processes*, in that it emerges out of voluntary and non-financial working relationships;
- is often *non-proprietary in its outcomes*, in that it leads to Copylefted creative output.

Within this chapter on organizing and managing innovation and associated creative business skills, it might ultimately be a bit out of place to be discussing *e2e*, P-to-P and Open Source ways of working because no one 'organizes' or 'manages' them. The words 'organize' and 'manage' are always difficult words because they imply that someone is in charge and making decisions. In contrast to this, these new innovative structures and their 'industrial relations' happen because they happen. Because the people who take part in them want their bit of them to happen.

But clearly most of the cultural economy does not happen this way, at least not yet. Most of it happens within either the commercial sector of creative business or the more publicly funded sector of cultural organizations. We have discussed some ideas concerning the theme of innovation within creative business, so let's now turn to consider the same theme within the context of cultural organizations and the professionals who run them.

What can the different agendas within the public sector of cultural organizations do when it comes to supporting innovation for/by creative business?

17 *Houses of Learning: Cultural Organizations for Cultural Innovations*

Story

... in addition to the academies of Syriac learning, Muslims had also incorporated Harran into their realm during the Caliphate of 'Umar ... Situated on the small river Jullab, at the intersection of important caravan routes to Asia Minor, Syria and Mesopotamia, the town is believed to have been the birthplace of Abraham. According to al-Biruni, the town resembled the shape of the moon and it was a community of star worshippers ... The Arabic translations from the Pahlavi, Sanskrit and Syrian texts preceded the translations from the Greek ... The translation activity quickly gained momentum and by the time of al-Ma'mum the internal dynamic of the Islamic tradition of learning had clearly displayed a need for a more systematic, organized and larger-scale translation movement. Al-Ma'mum and several influential personages of his court responded positively to this need and established the famous 'House of Learning' which became the hub of one of the most fascinating cross-cultural movements of transmission of knowledge ... This brief account of the translation movement helps us to construct the environment in which the Islamic tradition began to take shape ... It received its kinetic flow from the reflection on nature and the human condition by the early Qur'an exegetes and, starting in the middle of the eighth century, it came upon a rich harvest of scientific texts, concepts, theories and techniques from Greek, Persian and Indian sources. What came into the body of Islamic thought from outside was neither accidental, nor marginal. It was as sustained, deliberate and systematic effort that actively sought manuscripts, books and personages to satiate its internal needs ...

(from *Islam and Science,* by M. Iqbal)

The organization of knowledge into 'Houses of Learning' means that 'translations' can stimulate a 'kinetic flow' of ideas that is systematic, organized and large in scale. Within the broad theme of research and innovation for creative business, this central idea suggests certain tasks for the cultural professional who wants to provide support that is also systematic and large in scale. As we explored in Section 2, connections made between two or more 'somewhere elses' is what often leads networks to innovations. Bringing knowledge together into 'Houses of Learning' and translating for different voices could become part of the support that public organizations could give to creative business. This can be seen in two overlapping but distinct ways:

- certain aspects of the creative business sector is under-researched – more translations between the creative, business and organizational worlds are needed;

- the research and information that is at hand within cultural organization is often not used to its full extent – there is too little 'kinetic flow' of knowledge within cultural organizations, between cultural organizations and out to the creative ecology and public realm as a whole.

But this can be a mutually beneficial relationship if the public organization gains its own internal research and innovation back from the broader creative ecology. For contemporary cultural organizations to become 'Houses of Learning' and support research and innovation then relationships between the organizational 'inside' and the creative ecology 'out there' is a key factor. It shows a particular facet of the idea of organizations as open systems that respond to their environment. And this may ask cultural professionals to develop ways of thinking and acting that are quite counter-intuitive to the normal routines of organizational life.

This is the central theme of this chapter.

One of Us Must Know: Finding Serendipity

The first facet of professional counter-intuitiveness comes from the recognition of serendipity – happy accident within creative innovation. As we explored in Section 2 creative business and its innovations do not always come in through the 'organized' routes that characterize other industrial sectors. Creative businesses do not tend to have large 'R&D' settings, the research tends to be fragmented and about disparate pieces of research by individual creative businesses or sole traders for their own particular, often time limited projects. It happens too often to be called disorganized in a pejorative sense, but it is unorganized in the sense that it is often formed through unplanned and non-routinized research processes whereby people seem to pick things up by 'osmosis' within informal creative networks.

And we do have a word for this rather haphazard character …

Story

The English language is blessed with a wonderful word that captures the power of accidental connection: 'serendipity'. First coined in a letter written by the English novelist Horace Walpole in 1754, the word derives from a Persian fairy tale titled 'The Three Princes of Serendip', the protagonists of which were 'always making discoveries, but accident and sagacity, of things they were not in quest of'. The contemporary novelist John Barth describes it in nautical terms, 'You don't reach Serendip by plotting a course for it. You have to set out in good faith for elsewhere and lose your bearings serendipitously.

(from Where Good Ideas Come From: A Natural History of Innovation, by S. Johnson)

Serendipity often seems to enable the slow hunch to find adjacent possibles so that they can grow into firmer ideas. But serendipity is likely to make the world of formal organizations – with its plans and strategies; management and organizational charts; and clearly defined areas of responsibility rather nervous. Organizations do not like the feelings of 'leaving things to chance'. But there are key things a cultural professional can do. Let's consider some of them in more detail.

Steven Johnson's ideas about how serendipity works might be useful. It can happen as:

- **Combinatorial Serendipity** – as those happy coincidental combinations emerge from more scatter-gun thinking that lead to a clearer configuration of ideas.
- **Generative Serendipity** – as new ideas develop and appear in parallel and then cross-fertilize each other so that the sum grows into something greater than the parts initially that generated it.
- **Chaotic Serendipity** – it just happens through chance and no one can remember very clearly what actually happened and where it all came from, they are just very glad that it did.

For cultural professional to support creative business innovation through serendipity they may need to act as business agents and brokers within T-Shaped structure so that they can work to combine and generate. The chaotic is likely to take care of itself. But for cultural organizations to themselves benefit from serendipity they may need to embrace 'looser' organizational spaces and allow spaces of 'organizational error'. A second facet of professional counter-intuitiveness is required when we recognize that error is a key facet of innovation.

Accidents Will Happen: Embracing Error

We have already noted that 'ignorance is useful' if we embrace it to inform us of what we need to learn. The history of innovation is full of examples of how initial error based upon such led to World-changing innovation. Being wrong in our problem-solving searches helps us to frame better questions and sometimes re-see the often two-way relationships between problems and solutions. Being wrong in one research trajectory can open up whole new trajectories if we learn from error. As we saw earlier in this section, Karl Popper built his whole idea of scientific method upon the notion that we should embrace errors and ignorance as a positive by trying to disprove our ideas, theories and propositions.

Finding errors can be very useful.

But formal organizations can find it difficult to embrace error as much as serendipity because they have traditionally been built upon organizing for clarity, precision and accuracy. As we have already noted with the 'upside' of bureaucracy, this may be very beneficial if your organization is working within a predictable environment.

However, we have also already noted that the creative world seeking new innovation is not such an environment. Change, novelty, the unpredictable and exciting are more valued. If cultural professionals are too concerned with avoiding error and do not sufficiently embrace the unpredictable or the experimental then their organization may become very *efficient* – able to follow its own rules well, but it may become much less *effective* – able to get the job of supporting creativity and innovation done.

Cultural organizations may need to incorporate, indeed encourage, spaces for creative error. But of course, it is better if this error is *constructive error* that achieves a positive outcome by enabling broader creative innovation rather than the *simple error* of making mistakes over and over again. That just creates unnecessary problems.

We can develop this point by making a distinction between 'relevant information' and 'background noise'.

Learning from Noise

More professional counter-intuitiveness. Rather than the organizational concentration only on 'relevant information' in the name of efficiency, it might at times be useful to find organizationally relevant ways to research the 'irrelevant' because creativity and innovation can come from sifting for new knowledge combinations within what you originally thought was 'irrelevant information'. This is where the new adjacent possibles might lie.

And the 'irrelevant' is often thought of as organization 'noise' – the informal chatter, the coffee-break moment, pet projects and information held 'on the shop floor' that might not seem important, but one day becomes really creative. Why not grasp it now instead of waiting until the moment has gone? Sometime it is these organizational space that most resemble the creative coral reefs 'out there' and should be cultivated as part of the emergent behaviour attitude that we have touched on in previous chapters.

We can compare the orthodox approach to organization with the professional counter-intuitiveness suggested by embracing serendipity, error and 'noise' by considering the basic hallmark of industrial management with more open approaches.

Towards the end of the nineteenth century, Fredrick W. Taylor was busy inventing 'Taylorism' or what he liked to call 'scientific management'. His basic idea was that the methods of industrial management at the time were inefficient because they were too reliant upon 'rule of thumb' and 'muddling through' approaches. He felt that management had not collected all the relevant information involved in the thing they were managing. Too much of this information was held 'on the shop floor'.

Taylor built 'scientific management' upon three basic principles:

- collect all information previously held on the shop floor;
- centralize it within the hands of management;
- use this information to devise specific ideas telling each specific worker what they were to do and how they were to do it for each moment of each working day.

This central control of information was thus able to remove the background noise of each worker having opinions. It was able to take that confusion out of the organization by separating the conception of work – forming ideas and plans which should be by management, from the execution of work – the actual doing of the work carried out by workers who are now reduced, symbolically and almost literally to 'hands' (separated from their brains as thinking human beings).

Scientific management quickly became central to virtually all theories of management, and it is still with us today. Anyone who has done any factory work will have experienced its consequences and what it has done to the relationships between 'management' and 'workers' through its insistence on centralizing 'relevant information and removing organizational 'noise'.

It has been good for organizational efficiency, but has been very bad for:

- the ability of organizations to learn, recognize the creative talents within it, or innovate;

- the experience of work which as a result has been greatly de-humanised for large numbers of people.

By trying to remove the contamination of 'noise' and only concentrating upon 'relevant information' such approaches to management and organization have often achieved accuracy and clarity at the expense of creativity and innovation. This is because creativity and innovation do not, indeed sometimes cannot happen in the overly controlled, overly sterilized noise-free environments.

It is all very well us suggesting that cultural professionals embrace serendipity, error and 'noise' in this counter-intuitive way, but the organizational mind-set that tries to drag people into conformity to the 'norm' is not always so easily resisted.

Houses of Non-Learning: The Problem of Organizational Culture

All organizations *have* a culture in the sense that they have internally accepted views and ways of doing things that are shared by its members. And these norms can be very powerful because they are re-asserted in subtle and informal ways.

All these things can be good for the organization because they can help to create internal harmony, generate a sense of meaning, belonging and commitment and deepen the sense of common purpose. But organizational culture can be a facet of the Dark Side by severely restricting the organizations ability to be self-learning and innovative. Resisting the Dark Side of organizational culture is another facet of organizational counter-intuition, and the broader theme of personal awareness and authenticity we touched upon in Section 1.

We have touched upon how groupthink can have a negative impact upon individuals already. But it can have the same negative impact upon organizations and professional life. Organizations are often defined by their sense of group-ness, and as social animals, human beings tend to form and maintain this group-ness by:

- declaring through all sorts of subtle or not so subtle informal means our membership (opinions, dress, where you sit in the canteen, and so on);
- declaring through all sorts of informal means our hostility to other groups.

Groups are formed by making distinctions between 'in groups' and 'out groups' which can lead to all sorts of irrational behaviours, blind spots, goal displacements within organizational life and other symptoms which are not good for organizational learning and innovation.

Organizational groupthink can lead to:

- **Over-estimations of the group's 'rightness'** – an illusion of universal correctness and an unquestioned belief in the group's existing beliefs.
- **Closed-mindedness** – collectively reinforced rationalizations to discount negative views and ignore contrary information.
- **Self-generated pressures towards uniformity:**
  - Self-censorship of deviations from group norms and opinions.

- A shared illusion of unanimity concerning new decisions (augmented by the silence within meetings due to last point).
- Direct pressures put upon group members by rest of group if they express dissent (the shooting the messenger syndrome).
- The emergence of self-appointed 'mind guards' who work to protect the group from non-comfortable news and opinions.

These pressures can become the on-going processes of the unlearning organization due to:

- bias in dealing with the information and incomplete surveys of alternatives ideas – not good for *how* questions.
- incomplete surveys of objectives and risks associated with preferred plans – not good for *why* questions.
- failures to re-appraise systems and outcomes – not good for *if* questions.

All these factors amount to an organizational inability to hear and listen to new information, take it on board and use it.

Quotation

The deficiencies about which we know the most pertain to:

Disturbances in the behaviour of individuals in a decision-making group – temporary states of elation, fear or anger that reduce a person's mental efficiency; shortcomings in information processing that prevent a person from comprehending the complex consequences of a seemingly simple policy decision.

(from *Groupthink*, by Irving Janis)

Instead of groupthink, maybe consider ...

Exercise

GOING ON AN 'ORGANIZED WALK'

Many innovators report that going for a walk to remove themselves from their immediate task environment has enabled them to stumble towards new creative avenues. Going for a walk seems to allow people to enter a more open, associative state of mind. Make it part of your everyday professional practice to take your organization for a walk (actual or figurative) so as to find Serendipity and resist groupthink.

For instance:

- What have you done to make sure all staff meet for a coffee all together to talk about nothing much at all?
- When was the last time you spoke to the cleaning staff and found out what they think about the latest organizational problem?
- How do the people outside your organization, the ones that are not part of the group, think of you?

And taking your organization for a walk implies ...

Memories Are Made of This

Earlier in this chapter we read of John Barth using the nautical metaphor of sailing to Serendip by not looking for it. Johnson talks about going for a walk. But journeys towards serendipity need eventually to 'end up' somewhere. Eventually a focus will be needed. Whichever type of serendipity occurs, whatever the error leads you to, and however much you might learn from organizational 'noise', it needs to be brought to fruition if it is not to slip through your fingers. To revive John Barth's nautical metaphor, we will need an anchor when our meandering journey to Serendip is done, otherwise we might drift right past it. And a good anchor is the development of organizational memory, because memory is a fundamental aspect of learning.

Cultural organizations have a potentially key role in supporting research and innovation not so much by doing research and innovation but by being the anchor point that brings the research and innovation occurring somewhere else into a consolidated cultivation of co-research and co-innovation. Cultural professionals, organizations, business mentors, creative business support programs of all kinds – formalized or informal network advocates, have a key role as these anchor points to achieve real world innovation by remembering who is doing what and who needs to speak to whom. The challenge is to create environments of shared memory.

David Byrne had it down as *Once in a Lifetime*, but maybe organizational memory suggests it can be more often than that, if we learn to remember and revisit ideas and information within 'Houses of Memory', that can become 'Houses of Learning' that actually cultivate serendipity.

The 'organizations as brains' metaphor which we touched upon in Section 2 recurs here when we recognize the importance of organizational memory as the basis for better retention of useful information, internal communication and intelligence feedback loops'. It might be useful to try to mirror the neural networks that enables the brain to talk to itself as an organizational 'architecture of serendipity'. This also suggests a specifically professional aspect to the emergent behaviour discussed in Section 2.

Remembering what you have already done before, and why you did it is the basis for another aspect of 'Houses of Learning'. Which is ...

Organizing for Exaptation

Johnson refers to the process of exaptation as the process whereby adaptations originally created for one use get recycled for something else. The feather originally adapted for warmth gets reused for flight. Again we see that chance is central, that error can be useful and that serendipity can lead from one adjacent possible to another.

So organizational tools, knowledge, processes and relationships that were originally good for one thing can become even more useful for organizational innovation in anther way, if they are re-seen, re-communicated and re-opened.

Strong organizational communication leading to a shared memory can help with this by enabling everyone to know what everyone else knows. This will enable information and ideas developed in one organizational space become useful in other organizational space for other reasons. Proactively opening the store of organizational information and memory will allow greater mutual exploration of adjacent possibles, both within the organization itself and between the organization and the creative ecology. Informal creative networks can be good at exaptation, but given their informal nature this process can be very haphazard. Cultural organizations can be key hubs for exaptation if they organize themselves as a 'central intelligence bureau' of cross-disciplinarity, mutli-disciplinarity and T-shaped-ness. This might facilitate the exaptation that can find new relationships between problems and solutions.

'Houses of Learning' could invite people in for a creative 'coffee'.

Analogy

'TALKING TO STRANGERS IN THE FREE SCHOOL OF INGENUITY'

Coffee-house conversations, (Samuel) Pepys had discovered, presented a fascinating panoply of philosophical puzzles. The attractions of the place was never simply coffee, which Pepys did not seem to like much, but rather the potential he found there for social intercourse and companionship with one's fellows ... a coffee-house only really exists when it is full of people ... The emergence of the coffee-house transformed the social organization of the city, bringing with it a new principle of convivial sociality based on conversation and discussion. From the first, coffee-houses attracted particular coteries of men, who enjoyed the opportunity presented there by the free and unregulated nature of debate. But though it was free and unregulated, it was not completely unstructured, because many coffee-houses became associated with specialized discourse on tightly defined matters.

(from *The Coffee-House: A Cultural History*, by M. Ellis)

And the process of free and unregulated debate is still with us, and still intimately connected to creativity and innovation. For instance, rather than relying upon traditional chains of expertise from designer, through to manufacturing engineer to marketing in a linear way, Apple's product development is a messier form of exaptation that allows joint discussion of the core idea to ensure a sustained, shared understanding of the projects innovative excitement. This helps to prevent the common problems of 'design by committee' and the emptying out creative innovation due to 'death by compromise'.

As we have already noted in Section 1 when we considered what John Holden has called the 'cultural system', the instrumental values of politicians and cultural policy-makers and the institutional values of cultural professionals tends to encourage a 'closed conversation at the top'. This tends to neglect open dialogues between the organizational 'inside' and the public 'outside'.

So, taking the ideas of serendipity, error, noise and organizational memory at the heart of 'Houses of Learning' forward, what about opening a few more doors. Remember that creativity and innovation stems from the adjacent possible of opening doors for others, to others. What about issuing ...

Day Tripper: An Open Invitation to the 'House of Learning'?

Theory

THEORIES OF CREATIVE INNOVATION: NO. 12 – A NEW CULTURAL POLITICS OF INNOVATION

Innovation is rapidly becoming democratized. Users, aided by improvements in computer and communications technology, increasingly can develop their own new products and services. These innovating users – both individuals and firms – often freely share their innovations with others, creating user-innovation communities and a rich intellectual commons. In Democratizing Innovation, Eric von Hippel looks closely at this emerging system of user-centred innovation. He explains why and when users find it profitable to develop new products and services for themselves, and why it often pays users to reveal their innovations freely for the use of all ... Von Hippel argues that manufacturers should redesign their innovation processes and that they should systematically seek out innovations developed by users. He points to businesses that have learned to assist user-innovators by providing them with toolkits for developing new products. User innovation has a positive impact on social welfare, and von Hippel proposes that government policies, including R&D subsidies and tax credits, should be realigned to eliminate biases against it. The goal of a democratized user-centred innovation system, says von Hippel, is well worth striving for.

(from *Commons on the Wires*, by L. Laing. You can download this book under a Creative Commons licence at: http://books.google.co.uk/books?id=BvCvxqxYAuACanddq=Eric+von+Hippelandsource=gbs_summary_sandcad=0)

Cultural professionals have a key role to play by using their central positions within local cultural economies to create open innovation settings and re-vitalized cultural governance. Open invitations to the 'Houses of Learning' given out to the ecology of creative practitioners and businesses, and the public as a whole could help to co-innovate in many different ways. In no particular order of importance, it could help to:

- generate better mutual understanding between the policy-making, organizational, business, 'artistic' and public cultural constituencies;
- overcome existing social and cultural capital boundaries and other class divisions;
- develop better outreach spaces and include a broader sense of proactive public cultural authorship in partnerships with the formal cultural organizational settings;
- create mutually understood cultural languages and voices;
- sustain on-going relationships between the professional, independent creative and public worlds;
- articulate alternative agenda-setting exercises with which cultural professionals could influence public policy and spending decisions;
- enable the unused or 'left over' information and research they currently hold to be used by others for public co-innovation;
- enable cultural professionals understand and enjoy their civic role as representatives of something broader than themselves and thus be revalued by the public they serve in much deeper and more profound ways;

- delve into the 'terra incognito' of the unrepresented and non-participating parts of their cultural ecology.

Cultural professionals and the organizations that they represent have a lot to gain from adopting a broader research and innovation commons and allowing it to inform internal organizational strategy and tactics.

Quotation

In every sphere the expert by definition will be operating at a level of greater sophistication and depth than the laity. But in every sphere that relationship is being renegotiated. In science, for example, the unquestioning acceptance of expert opinion is a thing of the past, and there are currently hot debates about the public understanding of, and agenda-setting in, science ... In the cultural world, the undermining of respect for the role of expert opinion has been lamented as 'dumbing down', but it is wrong to think that increased participation in, and enjoyment of, culture must be at the expense of quality ... Professional and the public have an interest in the best and not the worst of intrinsic value; they should be natural allies against the dominance of instrumental values in culture.

(from *Cultural Value and the Crisis of Legitimacy*, by John Holden)

The spatial metaphor of 'Houses of Learning', along with David Garcia's idea of protecting 'Uncommon Ground' and the corollaries of 'frontiers and bridges' might therefore help cultural professionals to better consider co-creation and co-innovation with those 'outside' the formal structures of the organization as moments of creative:

- (un)invitation
- (dis)engagement
- (dis)inclination
- (re)alignment
- (dis)estrangement
- (re)invention
- (de)articulation
- (mis)translation

of public culture beyond the formal 'cultural system'. Because Open 'Houses of Learning' and 'Memory' could be the way that cultural organizations can contribute to better democratic cultural governance and the shaping of a broad cultural commons as a form of open innovation, and suggest the possibility of a broad cultural commons for mutual learning, creativity and innovation, they bring us back to the theme we started this book – the question of values and ethics.

Marvin Gaye once asked us 'What's Going On?'

But he didn't ask us this in an off-hand way, as a way of simply saying hello. He asked us this in a much more heartfelt way – what is going on? How is it that we cannot see what we are doing, that we are failing to protect our children, failing to support each other?

Perhaps the ultimate point of open invitations to the 'Houses of Learning' lies in its contribution to cultural organizations being able to pay as much attention to their culture and values on the inside as they do to the doing of culture with, and all too often to those on the outside, so as to create an ethical environment and release the (probably) natural capacity of (organizational) individuals to be good and do right. But perhaps for the same reason that hairdressers always seem to have a bad haircut and car mechanics always drive around a wreck, it is remarkable how often attention to internal cultural values is lacking within cultural organizations.

Thinkpiece

Thinking of (culture) as complex, living systems rather than a machine has important implications for the conduct of public policy ... the delusion of control which it offers, diverts resources and debate away from more important matters ... It is this which should be the focus of discussion rather than the frenzy of intervention which passes for policy most of the time.

(from *Butterfly Economics*, by P. Ormerod)

Good cultural governance is:

... a co-operative effort for sustainable development ... (and) creative answers to local needs, using local resources, creating organizations and institutions which co-ordinate a multitude of efforts integrating community organizations, private companies and government action.

(from *Urban Future 21: A Global Agenda for Twenty-First Century Cities*, by P. Hall and U. Pfeiffer)

Cultural organizations can do more things to encourage broad value choices as part of their learning. It can work to create an internal environment whereby the individual professional feels able to represent and personify the values of the organizational as a whole. Conversely, if the individual professional feels that the organization as a whole does not represent ethical values, they can be discouraged and their individual behaviour can collapse back into the care-less and non-learning. Perhaps open public invitations to 'Houses of Learning' for co-creation and co-innovation of a public realm that cultural organization could issue is another facet of creating new spectacles for Juliette. Perhaps it is a facet of the *Ultimate (Organizational) Choice*.

A necessary choice, because ...

Quotation

We must build, in hope and joy and celebration. Let us meet the new era of abundance (or now the falsely created 'austerity') *with self-chosen work and freedom to follow the drum of one's own heart. Let us recognize that a striving for self-realization, for poetry and play, is basic to man once his needs for food, clothing and shelter have been met – that we will choose those areas of activity which will contribute to our own development and will be meaningful to our society ...*

(from *Celebration of Awareness*, by I. Illch)

> *People need not only to obtain things, they need above all the freedom to make things among which they can live, to give shape to them according to their own tastes, and to put them to use in caring for and about others ...*
>
> (from *Tools for Conviviality*, by I. Illich)

So now we have discussed the basis for research, the epistemological choices and methodological tools out there for activating it in a smart way, some of the key skills for turning research into innovations and what the organizational world of cultural professional might do to help with this.

Let's now turn to Mozart's own game plan for innovation with which we started this section. Let's think about how we might make a good dish out of all these ingredients, before we end by saying how these themes of values and ethics; networks and innovation might be the basis for a new approach to creative business that fits with our radically unequal post-crash economy and ecologically unsure future.

PART IV *Summary*

CHAPTER 18

Making a Good Dish of It: Where is Creativity?

Proverb

The oven has to get hot before you can bake any bread, and you can't make an omelette without breaking some eggs.

It is supposed to be difficult and complicated. That is why it is interesting and useful.

THE CREATIVE VOICE

He who learns must suffer, and, even in our sleep, pain we cannot forget falls drop by drop upon the heart, and in our own despair, against our will, comes wisdom to us by the awful grace of God.

(Aeschylus)

Derive happiness in oneself from a good day's work, from illuminating the fog that surrounds us.

(Henri Matisse)

Having looked at ideas concerning research planning and routes to innovation, we now want to return to the ideas of Mozart which started all this. He talked about how he brought things together to 'make a good dish' out of the ingredients that his thinking helped him collect. No discussion of innovation could be credible without some consideration of the processes of thought, action and development by which we all put new ideas into new combinations to make new things.

This brings us to issues of the nature and processes of creativity itself. That way of thinking that enables us to take the new information we collect through research and combine it into new combinations that can lead to innovation. We have touched already on the ideas of people and perspectives that we hope have already given you food for thought about this. So this chapter is in some ways a 'conclusion' to all that. But we are quite nervous of the idea of 'conclusion'. This implies we have said everything that needs to be said and we can now 'sign off'. This is obviously not the case. So we offer this last chapter in Section 3 as a kind of summary.

But we still want to be playful and creative ourselves. So rather than approaching this question head on by asking *what is creativity?* which is a big question and possibly the wrong one to ask, let's approach things in a slightly more tangential way, by thinking about *where is creativity?*

Where is Creativity?

Our culture overemphasizes the idea that creativity comes from that mysterious touch of genius that only some people (that is, not you) have. Because this idea sees creativity as ineffable it already militates against discussing and sharing it. It encourages people to believe creativity is 'out there' somewhere, outside us and only to be found in the officially selected visual arts, designs, fashions, music, literature and architecture that surround us. This view encourages us to just stand in awe and passively *consume feelings* created by Official Cultural. This view also tends to encourage a false distinctions between the 'Arts' (with a Capital A) which are designated creative and other activities – engineering, cookery, educating your children, boat-building, gardening and making each other laugh as somehow belonging to another type of human endeavour. The whole notion of creativity as 'out there' is unhelpful for an active cultural community and the future of our children, which is the future of our society.

On the other hand, there is the view that creativity is 'in here'. Psychological theories of creativity and the biographies of creative lives tend to discuss how and why specific bits of creativity come about through innate creative qualities, personal inspirations, inherent drives, touches of 'genius' or 'madness'. This overemphasizes the 'in here' feelings of the Creative Self and underemphasizes the collective and collaborative nature of creativity.

So which is it?

Maybe that is another wrong question. Rather than being 'out there' or 'in here' it might well be that creative is most often found in the spaces that are formed by relationships *between* people, that then affect and change those very people. What we as individuals experience as creativity is maybe 'out there' and 'in here' at the same time!

But recognizing this 'third space' of creativity begs some rather complicated questions about these relationships. Does creativity emerge from your lifetime of experiences of other people and the World or from the 'hardwiring' of your personality? How does the creativity you get from talking to other people connect with what is going on inside you own head? Does creativity come from your understanding of this particular point in history or from your memories of being a child? Is creativity about clearly combining objective research and innovation for others, or is it necessarily a personal and emotional experience that you have for yourself?

We will come back to this later.

No Set Menus for Making a Good Dish

Part of this 'emotional' view is the common experience that the initial creative inspiration just *comes*. We are not sure why and perhaps we don't really want to know. There is the fear that if we analyse it too much it might not come any more. Is creativity best left at the emotional level so that we can simply respond to our experiences? We might not need nor want to routinize our creative thinking to make it 'rational' or systematized. After all we are not philosophers or scientists, we are artists and for good reasons we are quite deliberate in preciously defending our particular approach to the World.

The Creative Voice

Rules and models destroy genius and art.

(William Hazlitt)

Theories are patterns without value. Only action counts.

(Constantin Brancusi)

You cannot acquire experience by making experiments. You cannot create experience. You must undergo it.

(Albert Camus)

Photographers deal in things which are continually vanishing and when they have vanished there is no contrivance on Earth which can make them come back again.

(Henri Cartier Bresson)

Examine nature accurately, but write from recollection, and trust more to the imagination than the memory.

(Samuel Taylor Coleridge)

So we need to be cautious about thinking that this food for thought can enable us to arrive at an *à la carte menu* for being creativity.

But nevertheless, a philosophy of creativity might be of intermediate use for:
- talking about the specifics of our creativity to others and so that we can talk about it to ourselves more clearly;
- being self-reflexive about our creative selves so as to understand ourselves, our values, where we are going and where we want to go in a more fully rounded way;
- developing professional strategies to stimulate and hold onto creativity when it does arrive;
- contributing to the building and growing of creative relationships and environments which can help to sustain co-creative practices.

So although there are no set menus, it might be useful to consider the 'logic' behind creativity.

Under My Skin: Creative Logic

As we have already touched upon, a lot of Western(ized) thinking is underpinned by *formal logic* that tends to most value internal consistency and logical coherence characterized by well-defined and fixed meanings that support clear ideas, propositions and plans. On the whole, Western culture tends to favour this kind of logic because it helps us to avoid contradictions, emotional responses and the 'woolly' thinking that confuses one thing with another.

This tends to be what we mean with our everyday sense of 'being logical'. It often gets played out within behaviour geared towards a specific, predetermined ends. Max Weber has called it *instrumental rationality* …

Definition

instrumental rationality (zwerkrational) … (is) *determined by expectations as to the behavior of objects in the environment and of other human beings; these expectations are used as 'conditions' or 'means' for the attainment of the actor's own rationally pursued and calculated ends.*

(from *Economy and Society*, by M. Weber)

Business-oriented discussions tend to equate instrumental rationality with innovation because they tend to focus upon the 'calculated' actions of the business plan, an approach that seeks something outside and beyond the creative act itself. But instrumental rationality is not the only kind. Weber also discusses value-rationality, effectual rationality and traditional rationality …

Definition

value-rationality (wertrational) … (is) *determined by a conscious belief in the value for its own sake as some ethical, aesthetic, religious, or other form of behavior, independently of its prospect of success* …

affectual (especially emotional) rationality … (is) *determined by the actor's specific affects and feeling states* …

traditional (rationality) … (is) *determined by ingrained habituation.*

(from *Economy and Society*, by M. Weber)

Instrumental rationality may play a part in each of these stages as each concrete bit of action is made. A clear instrumental purpose might be the final stage of the creative act as an innovation is 'taken out there'. But it would be superficial to suggest that the whole process of creativity and innovation is defined by (business or market) instrumentalism. Other types of rationality or logic are equally prevalent within creativity. As well as instrumental rationality, it is pretty clear that creativity also involves something:

- guided by the expression of ethical, aesthetic or other values within creative act rather than a calculation for pursuing something outside creativity;
- more akin to an ineffable feeling which sparks emotional and aesthetic reactions rather than a clearly stated ideas and concepts;
- that happens out of a sense of tradition or responsibility to that traditional, other people or the culture at large.

Something like this might explain why creativity does not always flow from clear, rational purposes that are amenable to clear, rational descriptions. Sometimes we can only say that creative ideas are things-in-themselves that grow and develop from within their own skin, according to what we experience as 'their' agenda, pace and trajectory. As we will explore in this chapter, it is probable that creativity involves non-rational factors such as vagueness, wanderings, visceral reactions, non-goal oriented play and other experienced unknowns that propel us to work within an intellectual space that is *between* these different kinds of logic. So logical 'confusion' is OK, indeed it might be necessary for the making of a good dish.

But I Get a Kick out of You: An Anatomy of Creativity

David Bohm's anatomy of creativity echoes a lot of what we have already said. It seems we all:

- get a kick out of solving a puzzle, playing with sometimes arcane ideas, connections and details until we 'come up with something';
- enjoy the feeling of discovering something new and stepping into the unknown, even if it is only new and unknown to us;
- value the feeling of 'oneness' and connection between our self and the World when do this kind of stuff;
- experience our self more fully when we demonstrate this 'oneness' because it involves an inevitable self-reflection and therefore greater self-awareness.

For instance, creative practitioners often articulate versions of a 'research and development' process that exhibits features such as:

- exploring tenuous paths, hidden circles, hints at routes to unknown destinations;
- cherishing the sometimes arcane details these tenuous paths contain and lessons they promise for the future;
- finding a way to express the poetics within these tenuous paths and arcane details;
- experiencing a sense of wonder in the 'meanings' they represent;
- broadening meanings and purposes out so the creative process becomes crystallized and new connections are made;
- developing a sense of location for one's relationship with the wider World;
- distilling meanings into increasingly clear statements to the rest of the World;
- offering this self-finding for other peoples' appreciation;
- folding these reactions into further circles of development and concocting yet newer recipes within the general cultural kitchen;
- repeating new versions of the process again and again – Creative Practice (sense of career) as creative practice (doing the same thing over and over).

Creativity and innovation is sometimes for nothing other than the pleasure of creativity and innovation. A heightened sense of self-reflection and self-awareness is often its own *purpose*. The purpose of creativity, maybe the purpose of life lies not in an arrival at the destination at ones creative 'aims and objectives' but in the journey that has its own purpose.

But this is beginning to sound like we have the answer to the meaning of life, which is very pompous of us. Let's talk about something else.

The Long and Winding Road: Creativity as Movement

Virtually all of this 'kind of' thinking and idea of *between spaces* suggests that the *fixing* characteristics of formal logic and instrumental rationality cannot fully understand the underlying logic of creativity, because it is *movement*. This brings us back to the *dialectical* idea of creativity we introduced earlier in this section, whereby opposites create and shape each other through moving interrelationships. Dialectics is another kind of logic that is perhaps a better way to understand the movement at the heart of creativity and the way new things seem to emerge from out of those very things themselves.

It is likely that a big part of creativity comes from an *interpenetration of opposites* which sets up the moving interplay between:

- **Your Brain and You** – the way your brain functions to take in information whilst simultaneously reflecting back upon its own brain-ness. This process selects certain ideas and information in terms of what is important to this thing you call 'You'. As we will explore below, being aware of this selection process is a good way of getting better at doing it. Being good at creativity entails being good at self-awareness.
- **You and Others** – the way this thing called 'You' – your personality, experiences, motivations and skills are shaped by the relationships you have with everything that is 'Not-You', that is everyone else. And then the way the 'Not-You' is shaped in turn by their experiences of you. 'You' are 'Not-You', and 'Not-You' is 'You'. Being good at creativity often entails being good at relationships.
- **Now and the Past** – what you are working on 'Now' is the culmination of a long series of 'Not-Now' events from your own past that have formed your current perceptions. The present is a culmination of the past, and your sense of creativity for the future is made from the idea you have of the present. Being good at creativity entails recognizing the historical context within which your creativity is situated.
- **What You Do and What You Don't Do** – the way you define what your creativity 'is' against ideas of what you 'don't do'. The 'presence' of your creativity is made up partly from what is 'absent'. Connecting these 'presences' to 'absences' is what sometimes makes new bits of creativity move. Being good at creativity sometimes entails knowing about what you 'don't do', so that you can then 'do it'.
- **Your Imagination and the Real World** – the way your inner, subjective experiences are shaped by the objective social, political and economic realities of the World, which you then in turn shape with your inner imaginings of other possible Worlds. Being good at creativity can entail being good at thinking about 'what is' and 'what ought to be'.
- **Working and Not-Working** – the way creativity involves researching, thinking and planning something so that you can forget about it, go for a walk, do something else, get drunk so that you can arrive at a solution without appearing to have thought about it. Many creative people report that the flash of inspiration comes when they are relaxed, comfortable, taking time off from work. Being good at creativity often entails taking a bath.

In *Consciousness Explained*, Daniel Dennett offers an evolutionary facet to this idea of dialectical creativity. He discusses the 'multiple drafts' model of consciousness to explain the relationship between the brain and the brains reflection back on its brain-ness as what creates all the possible different paths we can take between experience to perception to action. According to his view we do not simply take in signals from the World around us and process them in some kind of centralised 'Head Office' which then 'publishes' our perceptions to us. Rather, there are multiple versions of a perception forming or half-forming within us as we experience and perceive. So rather than creative consciousness being analogous to a camera-printer set-up that points out to the World and 'prints' what it sees, it is analogous to the various drafts of a book that get read at different times, edited and republished. It might be that the ability to see new and interesting connections between things that no one has come up with yet, what we tend to call creativity or innovation, is connected to the ability to be looser about the process of editing these various drafts so that more diverse and unusual versions can get 'published'.

It is truly amazing that this whole creative interplay between initial experience, formation of various possible perceptions, choice of one perception to be 'published', ideas or feelings that result from the 'publication' and subsequent responses takes around 200 milliseconds, which is about the time it takes to pronounce the first syllable 'B' of 'Bang'. This is so quick that we do not experience it as an active, moving creative process but as a *sensation* (sometimes in both sense of the word). But even at the level of brain function it appears that creativity is at work through an active process of movement and flux *between* possibilities.

It seems that the evolution of language has played a central role in the evolution of this creative consciousness because it allows movement in the experiences of, and with others. Talking to others becomes talking to yourself, which becomes a route to understanding and developing your creativity. Talking to yourself and others becomes 'thinking to' yourself, which becomes creative 'thinking for' yourself.

In technical jargon this process is called *vocal autostimulation*, and it does not rely just upon the spoken word.

Quotation

This private talking-to-oneself behaviour might well not be the best imaginable way of amending the existing functional architecture of one's brain (as it is evolving), but it would be a close-at-hand, readily discovered enhancement, and that could be more than enough ... Talking aloud is only one possibility. Drawing pictures to yourself is another readily appreciated act of self-manipulation. Suppose one day one of those early hominids idly drew two parallel lines on the floor of his cave, and when he looked at what he had done, these two lines reminded him, visually, of the parallel banks of the river that he would have to cross later in the day, and this reminded him to take along his vine rope, for getting across. Had he not drawn the 'picture', we may suppose, he would have walked to the river and the realized, after quick visual inspection, that he needed his rope, and would have had to walk all the way back. This might be a noticeable saving of time and energy that could fuel a new habit, and refine itself eventually into private diagram drawing 'in one's mind's eye.

(from *Consciousness Explained*, by D. Dennett)

Certain aspects of the psychology of creativity have echoed this sense of movement as the basis of creativity by emphasizing the shapings and selections we make within our interior mental lives as we move between:

- **Deliberate or Non-Deliberate** – actions deliberately chosen by 'paying attention', and the things that happen even though we are not fully aware of them and have not chosen that particular attention.
- **Continuous or Discontinuous** – internal mental processes which we experience as continuous, and those that are intermittent and haphazard intervals within our life.
- **Goal-Defined or Non-Goal-Defined** – attention to a specific things for a specific reason to achieve a specific goal, and mental activity without any of these specific things, reasons or goals.
- **Subjectively or Objectively Novel** – individual responses that are experienced as new, and individual responses that leads to novelty of which we are unaware.

Which brings us to …

I Don't Want to Go to Chelsea: Creativity as Idle Play

Sometimes creativity can come from playing rather than working. It can come from hanging out with your family, friends or whoever rather than going to the (metaphorical) 'London' of trying to earn lots of money from creative business success and all the stresses that often entails.

In his book *In Praise of Idleness*, Bertrand Russell has discussed the relationship between developing new knowledge and having the time to do nothing, or what appears to be nothing. Idleness gives us the time to remember why we are doing what we are doing and the 'head space' to fit bits of creative movement together …

The Creative Voice

… in the case of the more difficult forms of creative thought, the making, for instance, of a scientific discovery, or the writing of a poem or play or the formulation of an important political decision, it is desirable not only that there should be an interval free from conscious thought on the particular problem concerned, but also that that interval should be so spent that nothing should interfere with the free workings of the unconscious or partially conscious processes of the mind. In those cases, the stage of incubation should include a large amount of actual mental relaxation.

(from *The Art of Thought*, by G. Wallas)

So far as I am concerned, they (happy ideas) *have never come to me when my mind was fatigued, or when I was at my working table … They came particularly readily during the slow ascent of wooded hills on a sunny day.*

(Helmhotz, ibid)

Children play by doing the same thing over and over again. They love using routines as a form of play and learning. This connects us back to the idea that creativity is often found in and through the *practice* of doing the same thing over and over until you get good at it, until it is satisfactory. Creativity is often found in the repeat iterations that play can help you develop.

In Part 2 we touched upon the play ethic discussed by Pat Kane, which in different ways seeks the freedom for open-ended exploration. Play can be:

- for education as a basis for healthy development
- for imagination
- for as a sense of happiness.

But play can also be about 'joining in and taking part' – as in 'are you coming out to play'. This version of play is more about sharing and devising the rules within which the other forms of play take place. Play can be practised as:

- contest
- rituals
- exploring one's chances just through taking part
- frivolity.

Play is not the waste of time away from 'work' that some people think it is:

The Creative Voice

I do not know what I may appear to the world; but to myself I seem to have been only like a boy playing on the seashore, and diverting myself in now and then finding a smoother pebble or a prettier shell than ordinary, whilst the great ocean of truth lay all undiscovered before me.

(Isaac Newton from *The Life of Sir Isaac Newton*, by D. Brewster)

The creation of something new is not accomplished by the intellect but by the play instinct acting from inner necessity. The creative mind plays with the objects it loves.

(Carl Jung from *The Myth of Analysis*, by J. Hillman)

More Than a Feeling: Creativity as Serious Urgency

On the other side of the coin we need to recognize that creativity often comes from a felt need to express something that holds deep meaning. A sense of seriousness, urgency and struggle is often vital if creative work is to be taken through to fruition. Sometimes it needs to make you cry.

The Creative Voice

I have often thought that if photography were difficult in the true sense of the term – meaning that the creation of a simple photograph would entail as much time and effort as the production of a good watercolour or etching there would be a vast improvement in total output. The sheer ease with which we can produce a superficial image often leads to creative disaster.

(from *A Personal Credo*, by Ansel Adams)

You can approach the act of writing with nervousness, excitement, hopefulness, or even despair (about) the sense that you can never completely put on the page what is in your mind and heart. You can come to the act with your fists clenched and your eyes narrowed, ready to kick ass and take down names. You can come to it because you want a girl to marry you or because you want to change the world. Come to it any way but lightly. Let me say it again: you must not come lightly to the blank page.

(from *On Writing: A Memoir of the Craft*, by Stephen King)

And this suggests that creativity is often connected to a wholehearted *visceral need* to express oneself, something often reported by creative people:

The Creative Voice

I have never thought of writing for reputation and honour. What I have in my heart must come out; that is the reason why I compose.

(Ludwig van Beethoven from *Recollections from my Life*, by Carl Czerny)

I paint my own reality. The only thing that I know is that I paint because I need to, and I paint whatever passes through my head without any consideration.

(Freida Kahlo from *Frida: A Biography of Frida Kahlo,* by Hayden Herrera)

What really counts is to strip the soul naked. Painting or poetry is made as we make love; a total embrace, prudence thrown to the wind, nothing held back.

(Joan Miro from *Theories of Modern Art*, by Herschel Browning Chipp)

A balance between play and seriousness, relaxation and urgency, free time and work appears to be needed for creativity. And this question of balance between often contradictory elements brings us to the question of self-awareness within one's creative processes.

Don't Stop Me Know: Creativity as On-Going Process

Obviously a concentration upon our creative outcomes – what gets exhibited beyond the studio, editing room or rehearsal space comes with the creative territory. But before that it is equally obvious that may we need creative processes. No matter how much success and public acclaim one might get, a continued concentration upon what happens inside the studio, editing room or rehearsal space is going to be necessary if your creativity is going to be long-term and innovative. Continued and repeated concentration on the processes is probably going to be necessary.

The Creative Voice

On action alone be thy interest,

Never on its fruits.

Let not the fruits of action be thy motive,

Nor be thy attachment to inaction.

(Bhagavad Gita)

Our main business is not to see what lies dimly at a distance but to do what lies clearly at hand.

(Thomas Carlyle)

This concentration upon creative process implies the efficacy of the self-awareness and authenticity we touched upon in Part 1, not only of *what* one does, but also *how, why* and *if*.

The Creative Voice

My destination is always the same but I work out a different route to get there.

(Henri Matisse)

When I paint my object is to show what I have found and not what I have been looking for. In art intentions are not sufficient and, as we say in Spanish: love must be proved by facts and not by reasons. What one does is what counts and not what one had the intention of doing.

(Pablo Picasso)

And within their on-going reflections upon their creative processes, many creative people report on the way they pay conscious attention to establishing their own idiosyncratic routines:

The Creative Voice

The problem of creative writing is essentially one of concentration, and the supposed eccentricities of poets are usually due to the mechanical habits and rituals developed in order to concentrate ... Schiller liked to have a smell of rotten apples, concealed beneath the lid of his desk, under his nose when he was composing poetry. Walter de la Mare has told me that he must smoke when writing. Auden drinks endless cups of tea. Coffee is my own addiction, besides smoking a great deal, which I hardly ever do except when writing. I notice also that as I attain a greater concentration, this tends to make me forget the taste of cigarette in my mouth, and then I have a desire to smoke two or even three cigarettes at a time, in order that the sensation from the outside may penetrate through the wall of concentration which I have built round myself.

(Stephen Spender)

> *I find if I drink two or three brandies, or a good bottle of claret, I'm far better able to write. I also find that if I listen to music, that loosens me up.*
>
> (David Ogilvy)
>
> But, also remember:
>
> *Always do sober what you said you'd do drunk. That will teach you to keep your mouth shut.*
>
> (Ernest Hemingway)

I Want to Break Free: Creative Autonomy as Intrinsic but Contextual

Whilst many creators have emphasized the idea of individual creative processes, we should still remember that these individual processes exist within a broader context. In earlier chapters we discussed how this broader context can help you shape and plan your creativity and innovation when we discussed the role of paradigms. But as we also noted paradigms can also be bad for creativity if they become restrictions. Particularly in the twentieth century, many artists have avoided, or in more strongly worded terms attacked, any sense of tradition that seems like the 'rules' for the preceding agenda or creative paradigm.

The Creative Voice

I never go to museums. I avoid their odour, their monotony and severity. In them I rediscover my grandfather's rages when I played hookey. I try to paint with my heart and my loins, not bothering with style. I never ask a friend how he makes love to his wife in order to love mine, nor what woman I ought to love, and I never worry about how women were loved in 1802. I love like a man and not like a schoolboy or a professor.

(Marice Vlamnick)

This view places *autonomy* at the centre of any understanding of what creativity is, where it comes from and how it can be used to make a good dish. There are no set menus remember. And this often entails deliberately rejecting existing conventions in favour of seeking autonomous expressions of the ineffable and the intrinsic rather than seeking 'success' according to some external scale – money, status, fame, notoriety.

Quotation

Assume man to be man and his relationship to the world to be a human one; then you can exchange love only for love, trust for trust, etc … If you love without evoking love in return – that is, if your loving as loving does not produce reciprocal love; if through a living expression of yourself as a loving person you do not make yourself a beloved one, then your love is impotent – a misfortune.

(from *The Economic and Philosophical Manuscripts*, by Karl Marx)

'A Robust Generalization': The Who and How of Creativity

Having briefly looked at some of the ways in which creativity is experienced, let's now start to bring this together to make some general points. In *Creativity: Flow and the Psychology of Discovery and Invention*, Csíkszentmihályi sees three types of people who usually get to be recognized as 'creative':

- those who seem to stand for the unusual, the novel, those who do 'unexpected thinking';
- those who seem to 'experience the World differently';
- those who have had a big, commonly recognized impact upon our common culture, who have 'changed things'.

For Csíkszentmihályi the first two types of people are seen as 'brilliant', whilst the third is seen as 'important'. For him at least, the first two types of creativity are different from the third. This distinction can perhaps be best summed up with the distinction between creativity-with-a-small-c – the stuff we all have to some degree but some people seem to have more of (maybe) on the one hand, and Creativity-with-a-Capital-C – given its impact upon Culture-with-a-capital-C on the other. This type of 'important' creative person has importance ascribed to them by a much broader social, economic and political selection process that stands to some extent outside and above the creative act itself. You might be as good a musician as Damon Albarn, but not everyone knows that yet. Mary Boden makes a similar distinction between the *P-Creative person* who is impelled by their own psychological drives (hence P) and inner talents on the one hand, and the *H-Creative person* who is earmarked by their reception and location within the broader historical (hence H) context.

Policastro and Gardener echoes some of this discussion in their article *From Case Studies to Robust Generalizations*, found in Sternberg's *Handbook on Creativity*. For them, creative people tend to exhibit a range of common characteristics:

- **A holistic involvement in work** – creative people usually get more immersed in their work than the norm, and work in/through it to the exclusion of more aspects of social life (often to the exclusion of family life and stable relationships with loved ones).
- **Links to specific domains** (or the paradigms we touched on earlier) – creativity is often located by a thorough inculcation into a particular set of skills, priorities and agendas upon which the new adherent builds.
- **A generative cognitive style** – creative people all seem to exhibit 'divergent thinking' and 'ideational fluency', which means they tend to be good at imagination and other ways of playfully unpacking thoughts to take them beyond the normal logical rationalities through which we tend to conduct our everyday lives. Creative people seem to more often start with the 'what if' types of question.
- **Domain relevance** – some creative people seem to have a flair for distinguishing what 'has legs', what might 'go somewhere' within their chosen field of activity, to take imaginative play through to actual creative output that can be well received by others ready to listen.

- **Interpersonal intelligence** – some creative people seem to be good at simultaneously seeing themselves from the 'inside' and the 'outside' so as to make subtle judgements about the 'who' and 'why' of their work. That is, creative people seem to have an abundance of the self-reflexivity we touched upon in Section 1 as the hallmark of human consciousness.

Policastro and Gardener than develop their robust generalization by speculating about certain 'patterns of creativity' and the people who engage in them, which involves two spectrums of difference:

- **Kinds of creativity** – creative people sometimes focus upon the practical *problem solving* activities we have touched on throughout this book so far; they sometimes focus more on upon *theory building* activities that seek to generate novel ways of thinking and seeing; and they sometimes focus upon *symbolic systems* that seek to perform, exhibit and ritually explain something through abstraction as their way of engaging with the World.
- **Kinds of creators** – different types of creative person seem to predominate within different kinds of creativity. Some creative people accept and work within the *traditions of their chosen field*, whilst others *challenge their own parameters* as their creative work. Some creative people are more concerned with *practical considerations* (which includes commercial considerations) whilst others seem more concerned with *abstract representations*.

For Policastro and Gardener, these two spectrums of difference culminate in four archetypes of creative person (and they are archetypes, in the real World most creative people will navigate between and across these different emphases). They point out:

- **The master** – the person who accepts the current domain (paradigm) they are working within to become the master exponent of it – for example, Mozart or Shakespeare.
- **The maker** – the person driven to challenge the basic assumptions of the current domain, using their creativity to create a new domain – for example, Darwin or Freud.
- **The introspector** – the person devoted to exploring their own interior meanings and motivations, through developing their own symbolic abstractions regardless of what the World thinks – for example, Proust and Woolf.
- **The influencer** – the person who uses creative explorations of their own world to derive broader ideas, plans and arguments designed to change the world around them through cultural politics – for example, Gandhi and Mandela.

So this generalization starts to pin down the 'who' and 'how' of creativity by exploring the often complex interplay between the creative person and the context of their creativity.

Which brings us to …

Thinkpiece

'PUTTING IN THE HOURS', OR 'BEING IN THE RIGHT PLACE AT THE RIGHT TIME'?

In *Outliers: The Story of Success*, Malcolm Gladwell offers insights into 'how' the creative person comes about. On the one hand it might just be about 'putting the hours in', on the other hand it might just be about 'being in the right place at the right time'.

On the one hand, creative success might stem from the ten thousand hours rule:

The idea that excellence at performing a complex task requires a critical minimum level of practice (doing it over and over again) surfaces again and again in studies of expertise. In fact, researchers have settled on what they believe is the magic number for true expertise: ten thousand hours.

(from *Outliers: The Story of Success*, by M. Gladwell).

On the other hand, Gladwell shows how successful people get to be successful by being in the right place at the right time, and how getting selected because of this happy positioning can have a massive impact. One example, in the context of professional sports in the USA, he shows why a disproportionate number of people born between January and March become professionally successful:

... the eligibility cutoff for age-class (ice) hockey is January 1. A boy who turns ten on January 2, then, could be playing alongside someone who doesn't turn ten until the end of the year – and at that age, in preadolescence, a twelve month gap in age represents an enormous difference ... coaches start to select players for travelling 'rep' squads – the all star teams – at the age of nine of ten ... and what happens when a player gets chosen for a rep squad? He gets better coaching, and his team mates are better, and he plays fifty or seventy-five games a season instead of twenty ... and he practices twice as much ... by the age of thirteen of fourteen, with the benefit of better coaching, and all that extra practice under his belt, he really is better ...

(from *Outliers: The Story of Success*, by M. Gladwell).

Whilst the variable of age might not be the big one for many creatives, other variables that affect 'being in the right place at the right time' will be significant. Having the right contacts to keep exhibiting, having enough money not to have to work and be able to concentrate solely upon one's creative work, not to mention broader issues of class, race and gender are all going to have a similar 'selection' impact. It might even be down to just luck, plain and simple.

But either way, the ten thousand hours rule or the selection process both show in their different ways that the 'how' of creative success is not always what we think it is. At the very least, both ideas tend to debunk the notion that creative success simply comes on the back of innate 'genuis'. It is more complicated than that. So if you are a success, have a little humility for the rest of us. If you're not, keep at it, You will get there one day!

So all in all, creativity might just be about working hard, or it might be about being in the right place; it might have its own logic, perhaps a dialectical logic of movement; it might require strange balances between idle play and serious urgency; it may require a focus upon processes that temporarily ignore outcomes; it might lie in an autonomous space that allows for its intrinsic nature to come out in opposition to broader cultural contexts and traditions. Using research to make a good dish with these tools of creativity is a complicated thing. So complicated it may be beyond any attempt to 'systematize' it.

It is for this reason that we have a slight sense of foreboding as we come to the next point of discussion, ideas that have offered 'systems' for thinking about the stages that allow initial research to become amenable to creativity so that it can culminate in innovation.

Stairway to Heaven: 'Stages' Within Creativity

George Wallas suggests we can learn to be more creative if we develop our ability to be more self-reflexive about the processes behind the sensation we experience as creative inspiration. He presents this as four successive stages:

- **Preparation** – the stage during which the problem is investigated.
- **Incubation** – the stage where one is not consciously thinking about the problem.
- **Illumination** – the stage where the flash of inspiration seems to appear as if from nowhere.
- **Verification** – testing the conclusions that one reaches.

Similarly James Webb-Young, in his book *A Technique for Producing New Ideas* suggests there are four principles and two methods involved in relating research to the creativity that can produce innovation:

- **Principle 1 – Combining Old Elements** – *'an idea is nothing more nor less than a new combination of old elements'*. This first principle asks us to consider that generating creativity is the search for a new fit between existing ideas.
- **Principle 2 – The Ability to See Relationships** – *'to some minds each fact is a separate bit of knowledge. To others it is a link in a chain of knowledge. It has relationships and similarities. It is not so much a fact as it is an illustration of a general law applying to a whole series of facts'.*

After explaining these two principles, Webb-Young discusses the key methods for producing new ideas.

Method 1 – Gather Raw Materials – this is not as simple as it may sound. Indeed you may find it a big problem to be constantly looking for new information that re-problematizes what you thought you could comfortably take for granted and 'know'. Often, rather than getting down to the 'job' of gathering new materials (research) we find it easier to sit around waiting for 'inspiration'.

But Webb-Young suggests that gathering raw materials for producing new ideas might be:

- **Specific** – information about those factors that impact upon the internal dynamic of creativity such as the tools, techniques and other aspects of material production.
- **General** – the history and context within which one is working, and the potential for learning relationships with other traditions of knowledge.

Method 2 – The Mental Digestive Process – '... the process of masticating (chewing over) these (newly gathered) materials, as you would food that you are preparing for digestion ... What you do is to take the different bits of material which you have gathered and feel them all over, as it were, with the tentacles of the mind. You take one fact, turn it this way and that, look at it in different lights, and feel for the meaning of it.'

This is the best way of seeing new relationship and finding new combinations. But strangely it is often the case that new ideas and combinations are arrived at more quickly, and perhaps more effectively, when one does not scrutinize the newly gathered materials too directly or consciously. It seems that a degree of *incubation* similar to that presented by Wallas' is present within Webb-Young's account of the genesis of new ideas. Both suggest a period where the newly gathered material is left to the unconscious or preconscious mind and no direct effort is made.

Travel to Serendip by not looking for it.

It is important to note that this apparently inactive stage is actually an *active stage* necessary for creativity. It seems it is important to turn the creative process over to the unconscious mind and *deliberately* do something else – walk, listen to music, make love, do sport, go for a drink.

Method 3 – Constantly Thinking About It – '... out of nowhere the idea will appear. It will come to you when you are least expecting it – while shaving, or bathing, or most often when you are half awake in the morning. It may wake you in the middle of the night.'

Sometimes we need to stop trying so hard and let creativity happen to us. And it will if we have prepared ourselves and the ground for it well.

Method 4. The Final Stage – '... might be called the cold, grey dawn of the morning after (when) ... take your little new-born idea out into the world of reality'.

This requires a different mind-set to the previous stages, a more methodical, patient, practical mind-set. One which will help in dealing with the frustrating and boring aspects of actually getting it done and 'out there'. This will probably require an element of compromise and adaptability whereby one tailors ones original idea into something achievable and viable '... do not make the mistake of holding your ideas close to your chest at this stage. Submit it to the criticism of the judicious. When you do, a surprising thing will happen. You will find that a good idea has, as it were, self-expanding qualities. It stimulates those who see it to add to it.'

The 'True Art of Thinking'

Information is not knowledge. In his book *The Cult of Information and the True Art if Thinking*, Theodore Roszak shows how our ability to define, evaluate and discriminate between the myriad bits of information we get from our experiences requires us to form ideas if that information is to become knowledge useful for innovation.

As we touched upon in Section 1, our distinctive human capacity for creativity probably lies in our advanced abilities in self-reflection and self-awareness. We can think about how and why we are thinking as we actually do that thinking. Roszak's version of events in the true art of thinking echoes this when he places the interplay between *experiences* and *memory* at the centre of *insight*.

Experience – '... *we ordinarily take in the flow of events as life presents it – unplanned, unstructured, fragmentary, dissonant. The turbulent stream passes into memory where it settles out into things vividly remembered, half remembered, mixed, mingled, compounded.*'

Memory – '... *the register of experience where the flux of daily life is shaped into the signposts and standards of conduct.*'

We actively shape, select and mould our experiences and so actively choose what our memories are to be on the basis of importance, usefulness, warmth, fear and all the other emotions that make us what we are. Memory is not made up of information bits downloaded from the World as some kind of faithful record. They are more like a stew of strange mixtures made from unexpected cooking ingredients than they are a filing system.

And according to Roszak it is this active creation of strange mixtures that produces ideas in the form of:

Insights – which can be:

*   very fleeting, or they can stay with us for the rest of our lives;
*   very personal and idiosyncratic, or they can confirm what turn out to be very widely shared beliefs;
*   encounters that radically change our previously held beliefs;
*   but the active shaping and deliberate use of such insights seem to be at the very heart of the curiosity, novelty, imagination, thirst, experimentation and challenge that drives creativity forward as an un-ignorable aspect of creative lives.

Quotation

Perhaps this volatility of mind is what saves human society from the changeless rigidity of the other social animals, the ants, the bees, the beasts of the pack and the herd. We are gifted as a species with the crowning tangle of electrochemical cells which has become an idea-maker. So spontaneously does this brain of ours make ideas and play with ideas that we cannot say much more about them then that they are there, shaping our perceptions, opening up possibilities. From moment to moment, human beings find new things to think and do and be: ideas that erupt seemingly out of nowhere.

(from *The Cult of Information and the True Art of Thinking*, by T. Roszak)

Without the 'true art of thinking' that generates ideas then information is merely a series of free-floating informational bits. Insights produce knowledge by giving it:

*   meaning
*   focus
*   interpretation
*   extension
*   adaptation
*   use.

It generates broader and firmer ideas is based upon:

Generalizations – that order experiences coming from the outside World into patterns that give a sense of continuity to other bits of information by adding things like *coherence* and *connection*.

The degree of generalization has implications for how informational bits can be used by creative thinking:

- **Cautious Generalizations** – those based upon a close reading of information bits as 'facts' and care about saying *too much* too quickly, too stridently.
- **Riskier Generalizations** – those guesses, hunches and feelings that become the 'buzz' behind on-going creativity.
- **Hazardous Generalizations** – those large, sweeping statements that we all make about the World which turn out to be embarrassingly reckless cases of 'overdoing it'. But nevertheless such statements can still be a vital basis for creativity. As we have already said – the types of question you ask shape the types of answers you get, and you learn more from failure that success if you are able to recognize failure as failure.

Risky and hazardous generalizations show how over-cautiousness can be a barrier to creativity and sometimes needs to be overcome.

Enlargements – that goes beyond initial pattern-giving generalizations to develop reworked ideas that give bigger, broader or deeper *meanings* and *direction*.

Integration – into patterns they start to satisfy our minds and feel like *viability* and *'answer'*.

The common view that simply collecting informational bits through research is for Roszak the current 'cult of information' in the Web-age. In contrast to this he argues that new knowledge that aids creativity and innovation has to be 'sculpted' out of new combinations of informational 'raw material' which are not *already within* the informational bits themselves. The ingredients of generalization, enlargement and integration have to be added to make the good dish.

Quotation

(the true art of thinking comes) … *not from data, but from absolute conviction that catches fire in the mind of one, of a few, then of many as the ideas spread to other lives where enough of the same experience can be found waiting to be ignited.*

(from *The Cult of Information and the True Art of Thinking*, by T. Roszak)

And perhaps that is the ultimate point of all this, the creative convictions that catch fire in our mind and grow to become shared experiences for others. In the end perhaps it is this that defines creativity. The ignition. The oven needs to be hot to bake bread.

The World needs your creative ignitions as much as you need them yourself.

We have already quoted Carl Rogers several times, so let's end this chapter with another one, from his brilliant essay *Towards a Theory of Creativity*. His eloquence is greater than ours and the fact that this was originally written in 1954 does not detract from it, but rather shows just how brilliant and relevant it still is.

Theory

THEORIES OF CREATIVE INNOVATION: NO 13 – TOWARDS A CREATIVE FUTURE

Only in a very general way can we say that a creative act is the natural behaviour of an organism which has the tendency to arise when that organism is open to all of its inner and outer experiencing, and when it is free to try out in a flexible fashion all manner of relationships. Out of this multitude of half-formed possibilities the organism … selects this one which most effectively meets an inner need, or that one which forms a more effective relationship with the environment, or this other one which discovers a more simple and satisfying order in which life may be perceived …

(from *Towards a Theory of Creativity*, by C. Rogers)

We can explore the nature of creativity all we want, and we hope the ideas and schemas we have discussed in this chapter have given you food for thought as you consider making a good dish out of your research. But in the end the actual cooking is up to you.

Go light the cooker.

19 *Creative Business at a Transformative Moment?*

Story

CREATING DHARMA

In his book *Gem in the Lotus: The Seeding of Indian Civilization*, Abraham Eraly tells the story of Asoka, Emperor of India some time around 270 BC. In the early years of his reign Asoka had a reputation for cruelty and vindictiveness. But one day he witnessed a sage emerge unscathed from a fire he had had him thrown into. This led to Asoka's conversion to Buddhism, a renouncing violence and the setting for himself more noble aims concerning the welfare of all people:

Work I must for the welfare of all the folk, and for that energy and dispatch of business are essential. It is hard to obtain happiness in this World and the next without utmost love for dharma (duty and personal knowledge as enlightenment), *utmost self-examination, utmost obedience, utmost fear of sin, and utmost effort …*

He insisted that all his officials adopt a similar outlook if they were to represent him:

You are in charge of thousands of living beings. You should win their affection. Reflect on it well. You should strive to practice justice. But this is not possible for one who is envious, lacks perseverance, is cruel and heedless, wants application, is lazy and slack. Ill performance of duty can never gain my regard …

Rather than holding to a belief in what we would today call an established ideology, Asoka turned a humane face to all people, went to other kingdoms to spread his word and asked all people to live simply, sensibly and responsibly:

… medical services have been instituted by Asoka, for the treatment of man and for the treatment of beasts. And wherever they were now herbs that are beneficial to men and to beasts, everywhere they were cause to be brought and planted; similarly, roots and fruits, wherever lacking, have been planted. On the highways I have had banyan trees planted, to give shade to beasts and men, and I have had mango-groves planted, and I have had wells dug and rest houses built at every half-kos (about 4 km). And numerous watering-places have been provided by me here and there for the comfort of man and beast …

(from *Gem in the Lotus: The Seeding of Indian Civilization*, by A. Eraly)

How do we respond to Asoka's examples? How do we apply the ideas we have discussed so far to the specifics of creative business? Can we use his ideas about dharma to sum up what we have said so far about values, networks and innovation? Can we find contemporary examples of creativity that Asoka would recognize as dharma?

But before we get into the details of that, let's stand back and recognize that we are living, working and doing business within the context of the Big Economy and the fact that it is a time of dramatic change.

What Is, and What Ought to Be?

Since 2008:

- The continued failures of the Big Economy and Big politics to adequately address ecological problems become more and more obvious as the need for solutions become more and more urgent.
- The continued, unnecessary poverty in the developing world continues to show that some of the basic assumptions of the Big Economy are overblown, and in some cases false.
- The fetishized belief in markets as the only tool of social, economic and cultural decisions-making has culminated in an 'age of austerity'.
- The banking sector and related economic technocrats, for years the most gung-ho representative of the Big Economy have become a basket case because of its internal irrationality and greed.
- Establishment social, economic and religious institutions and the power elites who occupy them have been shown to be inept, untrustworthy and in many cases corrupt.
- As corporate pay and bankers bonuses increase exponentially, the professional politicians who bailed them out claim 'fairness' as they 'balance the books' through cuts to welfare spending that the poorest in society rely upon the most.

The poor all around the World continue to subsidize the lifestyles of the rich, and politicians seem intent on creating a new type of welfare state – what Joe Stiglitz in his book *Freefall: Free Markets and the Sinking of the Global Economy* has called the *corporate welfare state*. The welfare of the World's richest corporations and the people who occupy them has become the main concern of governments around the World. The inauthenticity, bad faith and ethical bankruptcy of the Big Economy and Big Politics seem to know no limits.

There is very, very little dharma here.

On the other hand:

- Ecological consciousness continues to grow and increasing numbers of people put the search for ecological solutions at the top of their list of social and political priorities.
- Micro-experiments in alternative economics, new forms of solidarity and conviviality are being developed, especially in the developing world.
- Western cultural values are shifting such that many people are thinking about their quality of life in terms of cultural, spiritual and emotional factors rather than their standard of their living measured purely through the consumerist trappings of affluence.
- A black man has become President of the USA, which 10 years earlier would have seemed utterly impossible.
- Arab people all over North Africa and the Middle East are beginning to challenge the corruption and political oppression that has been their lot for 30–40 years.

- The Web allows people to co-create and distribute their own politics and culture(s) independently, away from the technocrats and gatekeepers of Big Politics and the Big Economy.

It is far too early to know what the outcomes of these challenges to the Big will be. It is difficult for people to realize concrete solutions to the problems of the Big Economy and ecological issues through community action alone, and no doubt Establishment institutions will work tirelessly to contain fundamental change. But nevertheless, as the Big Economy continues with 'business as usual' after their dramatic collapse of Reason, the everyday lives of many people seem to be heading in the opposite direction. Everywhere people are turning more consciously to questions of values and ethics, seeking to develop self-organized networks of convivial, practical Reason and looking for real-world innovations to improve their lives, their relationships with each other and Nature.

Quotation

There are:

... two contradictory hypotheses: (1) that advanced industrial society is capable of containing qualitative change for the foreseeable future; (2) that forces and tendencies exist which may break this containment and explode the society.

(from *One Dimensional Man*, by H. Marcuse)

We may have reached a transformative moment.

And at the heart of this is the question we raised at the beginning of this book – *what do we want this thing called the economy, and by extension our business, to be **for**?* We are not interested in the question of how the Big Economy is going to get back to 'business as usual', or how can the latest shonky statistics on the last quarters economic growth are going to be used by professional politicians to justify themselves – *what it is all actually for*.

The collapse of Reason we have just witnessed within the Big Economy has shown that this question cannot be answered by yet more standard business economics. It needs some new thinking because it raises questions about how we are going to organize ourselves to produce and distribute the basic wherewithal for life, pursue social responsibility and justice, relate to each other in more humane ways and create common culture.

Creative business could ask itself specific questions like:

- What gets produced?
- How and why?
- Who gets it?
- Who doesn't get it, and why not?
- What proportion of creative business is to be about the Public Good?
- What relationship does creative business want to have with social responsibility, usefulness and justice?
- What character of human relationships do you want your creative business to operate with and express?

- What relationship does creative business want to have with Nature?
- Is creative business going to be just about personal profit, or is it going to be about devising new types of social and economic interaction?
- Can creative business envisage innovations that contribute to human welfare?

If we think about such questions then trade, exchange and other human interactions can return to trust (which is actually part the fundamentals of business despite what the gung-ho brigade now say) and we can contribute in our specific ways to the transformative moment.

Do you want your creative business to have dharma?

All this might seem rather big and grand for someone running a small creative business. But we believe that asking such questions will help give your creative business more purpose, a better vision of relationships with other people and generate a greater flow of ideas. In short, we believe that asking these big questions will help to make your business practices more creative and more innovative.

There are no easy answers to such questions, at least we do not have any. It is still your choice, your relationships and your creativity.

We just wanted to ask the question.

Case Study

Do we do what someone in power tells us to do if we think it is wrong, or do we refuse to carry out the command, even if it means that we personally pay for such a decision ... the real change will happen with a change in our thinking and in our actions on a daily basis ...

- *Instead of superfluous form, make everything count.*
- *Instead of quantities, focus upon qualities.*
- *Instead of throwing away, reuse or recycle.*
- *Instead of ignoring sources, attend to the source of everything.*
- *Instead of consuming things, treat everything as sacred.*
- *Instead of wanting more, seek doing with less.*
- *Instead of expensive, focus upon affordability.*
- *Instead of exclusivity, provide everyone a space.*
- *Instead of cutting us off from Nature, connect us to it.*
- *Instead of reducing ecological diversity, improve it.*
- *Instead of creating objects, build community.*
- *Instead of specialized things that can only have one use, make them multi-functional.*
- *Instead of radical experiments, see everything in evolutionary terms.*
- *Instead of focusing on abstractions, attend to what is real.*

(from *Architectural Design and Ethics*, by T. Fisher)

Autonomous Thinking

Socrates thought that 'intrinsic knowledge' was the particular kind of knowledge that led to authenticity and awareness because it was underpinned by self-questioning and self-criticism. Central to this is knowledge of one's own limitations.

Quotation

Now that you know that you do not know, we can begin to make progress.

(Socrates)

This probably requires ethical, networked and innovative creative businesses to engage in what Cicero called 'autonomous thinking'. As we have already suggested, the Big Economy and its ideas of Business and Markets tends to come with ready-made pronouncements about what is 'real, 'normal' and 'necessary'. Authenticity and awareness for creative business in the transformative moment asks that we question these ready-made 'truths' and choose the creative and business lenses most appropriate for the job.

We have come back to the spectacles thing.

Thinkpiece
MAYBE YOUR LENS IS TOO SCRATCHED?

Are you 'marooned in your own selfhood'? The poet John Donne thinks you are. He thinks we all are.

To make this point he talks about a mirror which after years of use has millions of tiny scratches all over, all pointing in every direction. If you bring a candle close to the mirror's surface, these millions of scratches disappear and the light that you bring beautifully re-arranges itself into a series of orderly, concentric circles. And your reflection, the very light of you being will appear at the centre of this 'little universe'. The light that you bring will make all the disorder of the Universe, represented by the millions of haphazard scratches disappear. How very beautiful and benevolent you are to bring this light to bear upon the World:

Of course, we are being a little sarcastic. You are not the centre of the Universe and the light of your Being cannot really make the millions of scratches on the face of the mirror/World disappear.

This asks you to consider whether putting yourself and your 'light' at the centre of things is to mistake yourself for the Universe. If you are doing this it is not the answer, it is the problem. Putting yourself at the centre of the Universe is what creates 'limits to sympathy' and shows that the degree to which you have become unaware of your real self:

... if a man entertains false opinions regarding his own nature, he will be led thereby to courses of action which will be in some profound way immoral and ugly ...

(from *Steps to an Ecology of Mind*, by G. Bateson)

Autonomous thinking about values, networks and innovations within your creative business might thus involve:

- **A deeper look into yourself** – through constant self-examination, self-honesty and skill in reflection when dealing with your own fundamental creative business values.

- **A broader perspective about others** – through better empathic insight into people and situations that your creative business wants to work with.
- **A sharper vision of possibilities** – through reconsidering what your ideas, creativity and talent could actually lead to in terms of practical innovations.

And when navigating across these reflections about deep values, broad network relationships and innovative destinations for the future it might good to have a map.

Analogy
YOUR CREATIVE BUSINESS MAP

In his book *A Guide to the Perplexed,* Ernst Schumacher talks about how all Russian maps during the Soviet period had the churches removed for ideological reasons. He uses this as an analogy to point out the continued need for spiritual reference points over and above purely practical information. The sanitation of these maps is often paralleled within traditional business studies rhetoric.

We should not let an overly economic mentality distract us from the necessity of everyday ethical skill within creative business.

We should not let it distract us from the character of the relationships we want for our creativity and business.

We should not let it distract us from away from where we want to go with our creative talent for future innovations.

To protect your creativity you will probably need 'churches' as well as 'factories' and 'offices' on your creative business map.

Which then leads us to …

The *If, Why, With Whom* and *How* of Your Creative Business

If, Why, With Whom and *How* questions for creative business can be considered across various *facets of choice*:

- **Strategic choices** – what kinds of work you undertake, for whom and why? Ethical choices about the kinds of creative projects and relationships you are willing to engage with.
- **Aesthetic choices** – the concepts, look and design choices related to issues of broader responsibilities and usefulness and authenticity.
- **Relationship choices** – choices about the character you want to bring to all the relationships your creative business will entail.
- **Action choices** – the degree to which your creative business will be *reactive* to issues of ethics, relationships and needs compared to the degree that it is a *proactive* attempt to find more ways to do more good within innovative creative business.

- **Public choices** – choices about the relative degrees of open authenticity and conviviality on the one hand, and the degree of closed-ness and competition on the other.
- **Ecological choices** – what kinds of impact, 'carbon footprint', and 'cultural carbon footprint' are you going to allow for yourself? The ecology includes the social, cultural and emotional relationships within the creative ecology too.
- **Integration Choices** – the degree to which values, networks and innovation considerations are integrated and therefore intrinsic to your creative business, or left extrinsic and 'dealt with' when someone else raises a complaint.

A case study that seems to represent useful intrinsic spectacles across all these facets of creative business is …

Case Study

ETHICS FOR BUSINESS SUCCESS

Patagonia has grown directly out of an environmental sensibility, ethical commitment to its customers and convivial relationships between everyone who works at the company. It seems to embody ecological, relational, public and integration choices within a highly successful business. Its strategic, aesthetic and action choices seem to stem from deeply help values of the people within the company. Their business strategies:

… are an expression of our values as they apply to different parts of the company. Our philosophies for design, production, distribution, image, human resources, finance, management, and the environment are each written specifically to guide Patagonia through the process of designing, manufacturing and selling clothes. But they can be applied to any other kind of business as well …

And these business values are expressed through their design principles:

- *Is it Functional?*
- *Is it Multi-functional?*
- *Is it Durable?*
- *Does it Fit Our Customer?*
- *Is it as Simple as Possible?*
- *Is the Product Line Simple?*
- *Is it an Innovation or an Invention?*
- *Is it Global Design?*
- *Is it Easy to Clean and Care For?*
- *Does it Have Added Value?*
- *Is it Authentic?*
- *Is it Art?*
- *Are We Just Chasing Fashion?*
- *Are We Designing for Our Core Customers?*
- *Have We Done Our Homework?*
- *Is it Timely?*
- *Does it Cause Any Unnecessary Harm?*

To find out more and unpack the details of these design principles go to *Let My People Go Surfing* by Yvon Chouinard.

We are coming to the end now, and we need to find a good way of wrapping things up.

The Public Good – Broad Front: Small Changes

We have decided to refer to the work of Nabeel Hamdi and his book *Small Change: About the Practice and the Limits of Planning in Cities*, because we think he represents a position that brings together the three themes we have been considering – an ethical dimension, a concern to develop new ways to work with the 'informal city' and an attitude of open, publicly engaged innovation. This will also enable us to wrap things up by interspersing these ideas with concrete examples form all sorts of creative people who have put their money where our mouth has been to actually produce ethically oriented work through he relationships of various creative ecologies to come up with truly innovative outcomes for the public good.

It is helpful to think on a broad front when considering the debates we have touched upon. But making small changes within this broad front might be a useful tactic. Hamdi sees the non-institutional spaces and processes that make up the public sphere as a route towards 'network governance' whereby people work together to devising mutually supportive and respectful dialogue, more authentic joint actions and forge innovations for themselves. He offers ideas.

This involves:

- recognizing the organic processes through which cultural and economic activity occurs within relationships that are simultaneously social, business and emotional– *a diversity of creative business meanings requiring that we are good at values.*
- finding sensitive and inclusive ways of engaging with these processes as the people themselves understand them – *a diversity of creative business means requiring that we are good at relationships.*
- ways of working that are sensitive to the nature of the needs and tasks in hand – *a diversity of business ends requiring that we are good at innovative solutions.*

Hamdi suggests 14 practical points, that might help in finding the 'churches' of your the creative map and growing value-based meanings, relationships-based means and innovative ends. This list might help pin down routes to the value-based creative purpose, a 'this Worldly 'attentiveness', a practical Reason and the expansion of care within creative business, which is where we came in.

1. Recognize Convergence

Institutional boundaries between creative, economic, political and environmental concerns; and between different agencies, networks, businesses and communities are probably overblown. They should be avoided and/or broken down as much as possible. Creative businesses can become more 'open systems' if they are to be better at encouraging and supporting 'associations of difference' that an authentic public sphere needs to enable articulate innovative ideas about the public good.

2. Keep it to a Minimum

Use the minimum of Big Plan and Big Management thinking to allow a maximum of flexibility, innovation and creativity to emerge out of the *daily doing* of your stuff. Over-planning and over-management encourages an egocentric, mechanistic and personally unaware approach to creativity and business that can easily misunderstand the organic and relationship-based nature of the creative business World. This puts creative means on a par with business ends.

Case Study

REINSTATING THE DRINKING FOUNTAIN

Design for voluntary simplicity and sustainability asks us to re-see simple and elegant design solutions that have worked for time immemorial, but have been discarded for weak reasons. This re-seeing can replace overblown and wasteful technologies with more graceful creative business solutions.

For instance:

Say 'no' to bottled water – and 13m plastic bottles sold in the UK every year (just 3m of which are recycled) – is catching on but still hard work. This begs the question of what happened to all the beautiful fountains, many donated by philanthropists in the 1880s that were once dotted around civic centres and parks, and when are they coming back?

(from *The Observer* ,10/1/09)

3. Understand Your Paradigm

Understand that everyone operates within a particular (self)-selected World-view which is never the only way to see things. They are not set in concrete and can be re-seen, re-chosen. Put another way, all creative businesses have an internal culture that impacts upon the way it responds to the World.

A healthy creative business is aware of its own ignorance and embraces:

* lateral thinking

- emergent behaviour
- cyclical rather than linear thinking
- mutualism and joint growth
- growing new collaborations
- seek joint authorship and intelligence feedback loops from both inside and outside the business.

To a large extent this is the theme of Sections 2 and 3.

Quotation

... in practice, we need often to act spontaneously, to improvise and to build by small increments. First, spontaneity, as a quality of practice, is vital because most problems and opportunities appear and disappear in fairly random fashion and need to be dealt with or taken advantage of accordingly. Sometimes problems appear all at once and not according to predictable patterns. One therefore has to be selective, knowing that once a problem has been dealt with another will appear equally randomly. When you have run out of resources but not out of problems, you improvise – inventing rules, tasks or techniques as you go along. Improvisations then become a means of devising solutions to solve problems which cannot be predicted, a process full of inventive surprises that characterize the informal way in which many poor people gain employment, make money and build (creative) houses ... The question is, to what extent are these changes inhibited or supported? And, having answered that question, what kind of intervention is appropriate at each of the various developmental stages?

(from *Small Change*, by N. Hamdi)

---

4. Holism and Ecological Sensitivity

Work in a wholehearted, humble, dignified and simple way *with* the environment (social, cultural, economic or natural) rather than trying to master it. A broad point that suggests that the Alan-Sugar-Dragon's-Den mind-set at the heart of traditional business agendas is sometimes deeply inappropriate for creative business because it is inherently egocentric and obsessed with *maximums*.

For instance ...

Case Study
SLOW WARDROBE

Fashion designers seem to be grasping the 'eco' label, but are still intent on over-producing more and more garments. Maybe they still haven't really sorted out the problem from the solution. Maybe we just need less of it. As they say, 'less is more', but in this case this is not simply a style thing, but actually, really just 'less would be better'. Which some people think is more stylish anyway. Without this, 'eco' fashion runs the danger of being figuratively and maybe literally the 'window dressing' for traditional Big Economy self-obsessions with maximum sales and profits.

But the Slow Wardrobe Movement proposes a more ecologically sensitive mind-set. For example:

How big is your fashion footprint? From 2003 to 2007, garments fell in price by an average of 10 per cent, and over the past five years the rate of frenzied buying has accelerated. We make room for the new by discarding some 2m tones of old every year, which goes into landfill. The Slow Wardrobe extends the useful lifespan of the threads already hanging in the national wardrobe while redistributing stockpiled fashion to those who will wear it, with the aim of reducing today's average consumption of 35 kg of clothing per season to a more sustainable 7 kg. Consumers prioritize longevity by buying trans-seasonal garments (such as a classic jacket) rather than pure fashion and by purchasing as far up the material food chain as they can afford (higher durability so it lasts longer). We also learn to wash and dry-clean more sparingly (both decrease the lifespan of clothes) and to use specialist services to refashion and/or mend older garments (just 2 per cent of the annual fashion budget goes on mending or servicing clothes, so this needs to be increased). Meanwhile a 2008 YouGov poll found that there are an amazing 2.4bn pieces of clothing unworn for an entire 12 months (many possibly brand new) cluttering up the national wardrobe. This needs to be redistributed via a system of clothes swap parties and targeted donations before it is chucked in landfill.

(from *The Observer*, 10/1/09)

5. Bottom-Up

For too long the Big Economy has fetishized economic growth no matter what the immediate costs of pursuing it have been to the public good, because they argued that eventually the benefits will 'trickle down'. The problem is that they never really do, at least not fully enough. Innovations, ideas, inputs, community voices, the power to make decisions and put real World practical improvements in place often need to start at the bottom. This is what the organic intellectual would do within creative business. Maybe then values, relationships and innovations will *trickle-up*. This is particularly important for any creative businesses wishing to avoid a 'democratic deficit' and engage in the felt needs and experiences of other people. At the very least this asks creative businesses to become the 'bridges', the 'choreographers', the 'conductors' between:

- the bottom-up voices
- the more unified and established voices
- the Institutional voices
- the Big Politics voices.

whilst also contributing in some way to practical improvements.
    For instance …

Case Study
THE HOMELESS VEHICLE BY KRZYSSTOF WODICZKO

There is a significant group of homeless who work day and night collecting bottles and cans in New York … So Wodiczko thought that the best way to make the situation clear to the non-homeless would be to help the 'bottle men' by providing them with a tool which would not be associated with stolen objects, such as shopping carts, but something that would be especially designed for them (and with them). The vehicle can be used both for personal shelter and can/bottle storage. Through the increased presence and mobility of this object it would become both communication and transport, articulating the real conditions of work and life and the resistance of this group.

6. Work Backwards, Move Forwards, Start Where You Can

Work backwards by starting with small changes geared towards making practical differences rather than trying to devise an overall 'master plan' too far ahead of time. On-going creative analysis and evaluation within each small business step can be a good basis for on-going decision-making. This is better for public authenticity and personal awareness. Big Institutions find it nearly impossible to turn around to see from the other direction, but as a creative business you can easily and quickly devise new spectacles. You just need to choose them.

Quotation

I and many others, known and unknown to me, call upon you:

To celebrate our joint power to provide all human beings with the food, clothing and shelter they need to delight in living.

To discover, together with us, what we must do to use mankind's power to create the humanity, the dignity and the joyfulness of each one of us.

To be responsibly aware of your personal ability to express your true feelings and to gather us together in their expression.

(from *Celebration of Awareness*, by I. Illich)

7. Recognize Your Own Ignorance

It is perfectly understandable for us all to believe that the view from our spectacles is the clearest and most developed. The only trouble with this is that it is incorrect! The best creative spaces are the ones that exist *between* people, groups, agendas, and so on. Ignorance can be a useful thing if it is recognized and embraced. Recognizing your ignorance is but a small, everyday sub-set of the wider notion of recognizing the limitations of your paradigm. Recognizing one's ignorance '... leaves space to think creatively in search of alternatives' and is helpful for finding good everyday contact lenses for your creative relationships.

Thinkpiece
LOOKING WHOSE TALKING ... AND HOW

In his book *I and Thou*, Martin Buber suggests that the 'between' space created by two or more people through dialogue is key for pursuing the common good. But not all dialogue is neutral.

Buber makes a distinction between:

- **Technical Dialogue** – that tends to be purely instrumental aimed only at getting information to or from the other person rather than arriving at mutual understanding.
- **Monologues** – that are guided by pre-established agendas and already taken decisions that masquerade as dialogue between people.
- **Genuine Dialogue** – guided by intentions to establish on-going, living dialogue between mutually respectful people to develop mutual understanding and care.

You might not be right this time! You might be engaging in technical dialogue that is bamboozling people. You might simply be engaging in a monologue.

Paying attention to this might help with the If, Why and With Whom of a creative business dialogue so it can demonstrate grace, empathy and expanded care. Your preferred ideas, theories and ways of talking might not be the best available. You might need more genuine dialogue.

8. Never Say Can't

Findings various ways of saying 'can't' should be resisted. Rather than focusing upon 'what's in it for me ...' focus upon 'why not ...' aspirations. This encourages proactively doing more good unless there is a reason not to. Move from reactive ideas of 'I can't because ...' to proactive ideas of 'I should because ...'. Such a 'this Worldly' attentiveness asks you to search for ways to recombine your knowledge with character, your science with humanity, your commerce with morality, which is probably necessary because ...

Thinkpiece
THE SEVEN SOCIAL SINS

For Gandhi's *Seven Social Sins*,

knowledge without character

science without humanity

wealth without work

commerce without morality

politics without principles

pleasure without conscience

worship without self-sacrifice

9. Let Your Imagination Wander, Reason Later

Try thinking the unthinkable as this is at the heart of creativity. If it is combined with judgement, awareness and skill, imagination can be as central as knowledge for engaging with the felt experiences of others and unlocking ideas for proactively care-ful creative business.

Case Study

THE HIGH LINE

The High Line grew upon the derelict structure of a raised railway line going through the West Side of Manhattan. Until the 1980s this raised railway had been used to ship meat from New York's meat-packing district up through Chelsea and Soho. Once closed down it quickly became an eyesore and a break on regeneration.

In 1999 it was slated for demolition. But then Robert Hammond and Joshua David formed Friends of the High Line because they saw other possibilities. They did not know at first what the space could be used for, they just knew they wanted to save it. Eventually they came up with an idea that local residents got behind. They would transform the old railway line into a raised linear park that would weave its way above the city.

The High Line is now both a green space in the heart of the city and an elegant architectural reuse of what was previously nothing but a problem. It has become an organic, social and cultural benefit to the city all in one.

It was more important to have some commitment from like-minded people, some imagination and some hard work than a clear plan from the outset.

---

10. Be Reflective

Taking time to stop, to be as personally aware as often as possible, to think about what just happened, what went right and wrong is always good.

Exercise

A BUDDHIST 'CODE OF PRACTICE' FOR CREATIVE BUSINESS?

To become fully skilled in Buddhist practices is a lifetime journey, which would probably need to be a thing in its own right. But we can bring this 'down to earth' by remembering the lessons of Buddhism in our daily creative business lives.

- **Right Viewing** – offering your creativity to potential clients in a way that avoids any delusions for either party in a way that is able to truly deliver.
- **Right Intentions** – working with people through intrinsic good intentions even though you may have no emotional investment with the business client.
- **Right Speech** – being aware of treating people in business dealings through graceful and gentle interactions.

- **Right Action** – seeking to do work and business that ensures your own ethical peace of mind.
- **Right Livelihood** – trying to act in ways that proactively increases the good between yourself, your business clients and the rest of the World.
- **Right Effort** – seeking work that allows you to hold feelings of virtue whilst conducting business.
- **Right Mindfulness** – bringing a compassionate mindfulness to the real people involved in your business dealings.
- **Right Concentration** – bringing yourself wholeheartedly to creativity and business to keep a clear focus.

Reflecting upon how to help make these co-operative conditions allows competitiveness and aggression to be removed. This 'Buddhist economics' helps to guide creative business relationships within creative ecologies of co-operation and contributes to solidarity and conviviality that speaks to the mutual needs of people. These kinds of action based upon personal awareness might help with your general expansion of care.

11. Embrace Serendipity

Don't necessarily try to sort out the ambiguity. Maybe try to engage with it. Allow for messiness, uncertainty and change because that is how the World is. Having a clear, well-ordered creative business plan is not always the same as actually getting things to happen. And anyway, trying to impose such order might actually be counter-productive. A plan that points out signposts, progress milestones and achievement targets is not the same as having a good map. It is probably fundamental to creative behaviour that we see the patterns across random encounters and pay attention to the haphazard and unplanned message we get from unexpected quarters. If we do not 'plan-out' haphazardness and spontaneity but embrace it, then it can help with creative business values, relationships and innovations in lots of so far unknown ways.

Case Study
TWO PROBLEMS BECOME ONE SOLUTION

On witnessing the problem of homelessness, the artist Michael Rakowitz used his creative energies to solve two problems with one solution. He created the ParaSITE, a small inflatable 'tent' structure that the homeless can attached to the warm air escaping from the heating, ventilation and air conditioning (HVAC) system of public buildings to both inflate and warm their 'home'.

Two problems – homelessness and the waste of energy are brought together through serendipity into one solution.

12. Challenge Consensus

Groupthink is the natural tendency for groups of people to congregate around their mutually shared idea of the 'Truth'. But it is often a creative blindfold and not new spectacles. And our culture does precisely that, blindfolds us with received ideas about what is 'right', what 'everyone does, knows, thinks'. Whilst we probably need something shared, a social contract, it is also good to check this 'everyone' and think for yourself by challenging the supposed consensus sometimes. It is not comfortable to be the one person that challenges the group consensus, especially if it is a group you like being in. But it is probably necessary for creative thinking. Consensus-centredness has a strong tendency towards reducing all possible options down to the one that fits best with the existing group mind.

For instance, maybe challenge the biggest consensus of all, the link between consuming more, feeling better, being happier and living peacefully. We in the West consume lots and are at war. Embracing Ivan Illich's idea of 'voluntary simplicity' might be a good antidote to this supposed consensus and might contribute to authenticity, awareness, creative skill and the expanded care that cam come from simplicity.

Quotation

The optimal pattern of consumption, producing a high degree of human satisfaction by means of a relatively low rate of consumption, allows people to live without great pressure and strain and to fulfill the primary injunction of Buddhist teaching: 'Cease to do evil; try to do good'. As physical resources are everywhere limited, people satisfying their needs by means of a modest use of resources are obviously less likely to be at each other's throats than people depending upon a high rate of use. Equally, people who live in highly self-sufficient local communities are less likely to get involved in large-scale violence than people whose existence depends on World-wide systems of trade.

(from *Buddhist Economics*, by E. F. Schumacher)

---

13. Look for Multipliers

Sometimes 1+1 equals 3. Working through different creative business relationships and networks of mutual care for greater solidarity can create synergies so that the sum of energy is greater than the individual parts. This can sometimes mean that social, economic and cultural benefits can be multiplied so that everyone benefits. Traditional business strategies that favour competition and individualism often miss this potential. Ethical creative business strategies can sometimes be found through initial ideas that enable people to use and re-develop things in their own way and so multiply the benefits for themselves.

For instance …

Case Study

SOLAR POWER AS PEOPLE POWER

Portable solar powered re-chargers can help to re-power anything from an electric light to a mobile phone. In that sense it is a good example of a piece of care-ful design that can perform multiple functions.

But it goes much further than merely technical considerations. In areas of the developing World:

- It replaces people's reliance on the Big Grid – which is easily controlled by Big Politics and is therefore usable as a weapon of political control – with something that enables people to be more autonomous.
- It gives these people access to something that is relatively cheap to replace their reliance on candles – which are expensive and burn out, and kerosene lamps – which are more expensive and very bad for their health.
- It enables electric light after dark which thereby enables more cultural life, more education (kids can do homework after the farming day) and better communication in all sorts of ways.
- It brings mobile phone technology within their use so that they can call a doctor or check local market prices so that they don't get ripped off by the local merchants, and so on.

One small, simple piece of technology allows for a multiplicity of developments to improve political freedoms, health, education, economic knowledge and culture.

14. Feel Good about Yourself

It is not always easy or comfortable to be working within this messy, unpredictable way, embracing your own ignorance, searching for personal awareness and trying to be authentic. But don't be defensive, don't feel guilty or stupid, don't patronize and don't dismiss. Try to inspire and from that take inspiration yourself, about yourself.

Story

Jean Demenico de Pico was the UN Emissary who helped to broker the peace to end the Iran – Iraq war in the 1970s, a war which had up until then killed 1,000,000 people. But he is just as committed to what he calls the 'footnotes of history'. He put his own life at risk to save the hostages taken by the Iranian regime, which included John McCarthy and Terry Waite.

When describing why he did this, he suggests that '… *you should take your chance to be helpful*'.

Encourage small changes. And then we can maybe make big changes.

We would like to end our small book with one last case study. It is one that we believe encapsulates everything we have tried to say about values, network relationships and innovation within creative business. It shows with great beauty how creative business that combines an expanded care, an ability to forge networks of collaboration and a creative, innovative mind can lead to truly great work. It shows that with attitudes of simplicity, dignity, humility and empathy creative work can bring great benefits to people's lives. It shows the power of co-creation that networks make possible when ideas are allowed to flow. It shows the power of the adjacent possible, of serendipity, of error and the slow hunch. It hints at what formal organization can do to support such creativity. It shows that researching the real needs of people can bring a sense of creative purpose and practical Reason. It shows what we can do together for the public good even with minimal finance if we have good values, good networks and innovative ideas.

We hope you like it.

Global Lesson

THE JAIPUR FOOT

In the northern Indian town of Jaipur lived a doctor called Pramod Karan Sethi and an artisan worker called Ram Chandra. Together they built The Jaipur Foot, an artificial limb that has transformed the lives of thousands of people who have lost limbs in accidents or because of unexploded land-mines left in ex-war zones.

Western artificial limbs are expensive to make and difficult to fit, but The Jaipur Foot is light and mobile, can be easily fitted and cost much less. It is a beautifully low-tech design using materials – rubber, wood or metal that can be easily sourced locally.

Dr Sethi was working as an orthopaedic surgeon when his path first crossed that of Ram Chandra. Dr Sethi was fitting his patients with unsatisfactory and expensive artificial limbs whilst Ram Chandra was helping lepers learn handicrafts so they could make their own stuff.

The artificial limbs that Dr Sethi was working with were far too expensive for most people, and anyway did not work well. Common people in India sit, eat and sleep on the floor and do not often wear shoes. But the Western style artificial limbs got in the way of this lifestyle and all came with the 'shoe' already attached. They marked the wearer out as a cultural oddity, which only added to their stigma. The Western style artificial limbs also used a heavy sponge that made it prone to become water logged, making it useless for rural people who were often the ones in most need.

When he saw Dr Sethi patients, Ram Chandra became convinced he could use his craftsman skill to find a solution. Dr Sethi explained to the barely literate Ram Chandra the nature of human movement and the problematic pressure point involved with artificial limbs, and for two years the two men experimented. 'We made all kinds of silly mistakes', said Dr Sethi afterwards.

But when Ram Chandra ran his bike over a nail and got a flat tyre, he wheeled his bike to a roadside stall to get it fixed. Here he watched a repairman re-treading a truck tyre with vulcanized rubber. After consulting Dr Sethi, Ram Chandra returned to the repairman and asked if he could use the cast from an amputee to make a rubber foot. The repairman agreed, '… and refused to accept any money once he found out why we were doing it', explains Dr Sethi.

This formed part of their solution, but the rubber alone shredded after a few days. It was only after Ram Chandra added a hinged ankle joint wrapped in lighter rubber to the foot, and began casting it in flesh coloured rubber that they were truly successful.

The resulting Jaipur Foot now takes around 45 minutes to fit, last for around 5 years and costs £28 in India.

Since it was developed The Jaipur Foot has gone on to be used throughout the World, whilst Dr Sethi and Ram Chandra continue their work:

At his Delhi workshop, where he has been developing above-the-knee artificial limbs, Chandra points out a little girl whose leg was severed in a bus crash. 'People said I would be a rich man if we had patented the Jaipur foot, but it's enough satisfaction for me to see the joy on that girl's face when she walks again.' He adds, 'I'm still learning from my patients. I haven't done anything yet.' …

He dresses in a simple white dhoti and lives frugally. 'I only need money for the barber and occasionally the tailor,' he says, laughing. He rises at 4:30 a.m., milks his cow and prays until breakfast time. Only then does he resume his ongoing effort to improve the Jaipur foot and create new artificial limbs that will be as real and useful as humanly possible.

(from *Ram Chandra and the $28 Foot*, by T. McGirk)

References

Adams, A. (1944) 'A Personal Credo'. In *American Annual of Photography*, Vol 58.

Ball, P. (2004) *Critical Mass: How One Thing Leads to Another*. London: Arrow Books.

Bateson, G. (1978) *Steps to an Ecology of Mind: Collected Essays in Anthropology, Psychiatry, Evolution and Epistemology*. London: Aronson.

Begley, S. (2009) *The Plastic Mind: New Science Reveals Our Extraordinary Potential to Transform Our Lives*. London: Constable.

Benkler, Y. (2006) *The Wealth of Networks: How Social Production Transforms Markets and Freedoms*. New Haven, Mass: Yale University Press.

Berger, J. and Mohr, J. (1982) *A Seventh Man: A Book of Images and Words about the Experiences of Migrant Workers in Europe*. London: Writers and Readers Association.

Berger, P. L. and Luckmann, T. (1975) *The Social Construction of Reality*. London: Penguin.

Bohm, D. (1998) *On Creativity*. London: Routledge.

Brewster. D (2009) *The Life of Sir Isaac Newton*. BiblioBazaar.

Brookes, D. (2011) *The Social Animal: A Story of How Success Happens*. London: Short Books.

Buber, M. (2004) *I and Thou*. London: Continuum.

Capra, F. (1996) *The Web of Life: A New Synthesis on Mind and Matter*. London: Harper Collins.

Carey, J. (2006) *What Good Are the Arts?* London: Faber.

Chesbrough, H. (2008) *Open Innovation: Researching a New Paradigm*. Oxford: Oxford University Press.

Chipp, H. B. (1968) *Theories of Modern Art*. University of California Press.

Chouinard, Y. (2006) *Let My People Go Surfing: The Education of a Reluctant Business Man*. London: Penguin.

Coyle, D. and Quah, D. (2002) *Getting the Measure of the New Economy*. London: iSociety, The Work Foundation.

Cropley, A.J. (1972) *Creativity*. London: Penguin.

Csíkszentmihályi, M. (1990) *Flow: The Psychology of Optimal Experience*. New York: HarperPerennial.

Csíkszentmihályi, M. (1996) *Creativity: Flow and the Psychology of Discovery and Invention*. New York: Harper Collins.

Czerny, C. (1956) 'Recollections from my Life'. *Music Quarterly*, XLII(3), 302-317 doi: 10.1093/mq/XLII.3.302

de Bono, E. (1992) *Serious Creativity: Using the Power of Lateral Thinking to Create New Ideas*. London: Harper Collins.

Deakin, R. (2007) *Wildwood: A Journey through Trees*. London: Hamish Hamilton.

Dennett, D. (1993) *Consciousness Explained*. London: Penguin.

Denzin, N. (1989) *The Research Act*. London: Prentice Hall.

Dissanayake, E. (1995) *Homo Aestheticus: Where Art Comes from and Why*. London: University of Washington Press.

Durning. A. (1995) '*Are We Happy Yet?*' In *Ecopsychology: Restoring the Earth, Healing the Mind*, ed. T. Roszak et al. San Francisco: Sierra Club Books.

Eco, U. (1989) *The Open Work*. Cambridge, Mass: Harvard University Press.

Ellis, M. (2004) *The Coffee-House: A Cultural History*. London: Pheonix.

Epictetus and Dobbin, R. (2008) *Discourses and Selected Writings*. London: Penguin Classics.

Eraly, A. (2000) *The Gem in the Lotus: The Seeding of Indian Civilisation*. London: Orion.

Esteva, G. and Prakash, M.S. (1998) *Grass Roots Post-Modernism: Remaking the Soil of Culture*. London: Zed Books.

Feyerabend, P. (1993) *Against Method*. London: Verso.

Fisher, T. (2008) *Architectural Design and Ethics: Tools for Survival*. Oxford: Oxford University Press.

Flew, T. (2005) 'The Cultural Economy'. In *The Creative Industries*, ed. John Hartley. Blackwell: Oxford.

Fraser, S. et al. (2008) *The Critical Practitioner in Social Work and Health Care*. Oxford: Oxford University Press.

Frazer, J.G. (1998) *The Golden Bough: A Study in Magic and Religion*. Oxford: Oxford University Press.

Freire, P. (1972) *The Pedagogy of the Oppressed*. Harmondsworth: Penguin.

Freud, S. (1972) 'Creative Writers and Day-dreaming'. In *Creativity*, ed. A.J. Cropley. London: Penguin.

Fromm, E. (1976) *To Have or To Be*. London: Continuum.

Gambrill, E. (2005) *Critical Thinking in Clinical Practice: Improving the Quality of Judgments and Decisions*. London: John Wiley and Sons.

Garcia, D. et al. (2007) *(Un)Common Ground: Creative Encounters Across Sectors and Disciplines*. Amsterdam: BIS Publishers.

Gell, A. (1998) *Art and Agency: An Anthropological Theory*. Oxford: Oxford University Press.

Gladwell, M. (2008) *Outliers: The Story of Success*. New York: Little, Brown and Company.

Gray, C. and Malins, J. (2007) *Visualizing Research: A Guide to the Research Process in Art and Design*. London: Ashgate: London.

Gray, L. (1995) 'Shamanic Counselling and Ecopsychology'. In *Ecopsychology: Restoring the Earth, Healing the Mind*, ed. T. Roszak et al. San Francisco: Sierra Club Books.

Grayling, A.C. (2003) *What is Good? The Search for the Best Way to Live*. London: Weidenfeld and Nicholson.

Hall, P. and Pfeiffer, U. (2000) *Urban Future 21: A Global Agenda for 21st Century Cities*. London: E and FN Spon.

Hamdi, N. (2004) *Small Change: About the Art of Practice and the Limits of Planning in Cities*. London: Earthscan.

Handy, C. (1993) *Understanding Organizations*. London: Penguin.

Harth, E. (1995) *The Creative Loop: How the Brain Makes a Mind*. London: Penguin.

Herrara, H. (1983) *Frida: A Biography of Frida Kahlo*. New York: Harper & Row.

Hillman, J. (1992) *The Myth of Analysis*. New York, Harper and Row.

Holden, J. (2006) 'Cultural Value and the Crisis of Legitimacy'. Available at www.demos.co.uk/publications.

Hyde, L. (2006) *The Gift: How the Creative Spirit Transforms the World*. London: McMillan.

Illich, I. (1973) *Tools for Conviviality*. London: Calder Boyars.

Illich, I. (1976) *Celebration of Awareness: A Call for Institutional Reform*. Harmondsworth: Penguin.

Iqbal, M. (2004) *Islam and Science*. London: Ashgate.

Janis, I.L. (1982) *Groupthink: Psychological Studies of Policy Decisions and Fiascos*. Boston: Houghton Mifflin.

Johnson, S. (2002) *Emergence: The Connected Lives of Ants, Brains and Cities*. London: Penguin.

Johnson, S. (2010) *Where Good Ideas Come From: A Natural History of Innovation*. London: Allen Lane.

Kane, P. (2005) *The Play Ethic: A Manifesto for a Different Way of Living*. London: Pan Books.

Kant, I. (1996) *Kant: The Metaphysics of Morals (Cambridge Texts in the History of Philosophy)*. Gregor, M. J. ed, Cambridge University Press.

Kao, J. (2007) *Innovation Nation: How America Is Losing Its Innovative Edge, Why it Matters, and What We Can Do to Get It Back*. Cambridge, Mass: Harvard University Press.

Kelly, T. (2004) *The Art of Innovation: Lessons in Creativity from IDEO*. London: Profile Books.

King, S. (2001) *On Writing: A Memoir of the Craft*. London: New English Library.

Krishnamurti (1996) *Total Freedom: The Essential Krishnamurti*. San Francisco: Harper.

Kuhn. T. (1970) *The Structure of Scientific Revolutions*. Chicago: University of Chicago Press.

Laing, R.D. (1997) *Knots*. London: Routledge.

Laing, R.D. (1999) *Self and Others*. London: Routledge.

Lama Surya Das. (1993) *Awakening the Buddha Within: Tibetan Wisdom for the Western World*. New York: Broadway Books.

Leadbeater, C. (2008) *We-Think: Mass Innovation Not Mass Production*. London: Profile Books.

Levi, P. (1987) *If This Is a Man*. London: Abacus.

Liang, L. (2005) *A Guide to Open Content Licenses*. Amsterdam: Piet Zwart.

Liang, L. (2005) 'Commons on the Wires'. In *The Creative Industries*, ed. John Hartley. Oxford: Blackwell.

Marcuse, H. (1964) *One Dimensional Man: Studies in the Ideology of Advanced Industrial Society*. London: Routledge and Kegan Paul.

Marcuse, H. (1969) *An Essay on Liberation*. Boston: Beacon Press.

Marx, K. (1977) *Economic and Philosophical Manuscript*. London: Lawrence Wishart.

McIntosh, A. (2001) *Soil and Soul: People versus Corporate Power*. London: Aurum.

Merton, R. (1952) *Bureaucratic Structure and Personality*. In *Reader in Bureaucracy*, ed. R. Merton et al. London: Collier Macmillan.

Mintzberg, H. (1983) *Power in and around Organizations*. London: Prentice Hall.

Mishra, P. (2006) *An End to Suffering: The Buddha in the World*. New York: Farrar, Straus and Giroux.

Mlodinow, L. (2008) *The Drunkard's Walk: How Randomness Rules Our Lives*. London: Allen Lane.

Morgan, G. (2006) *Images of Organizations*. London: Sage.

Nussbaum, M.C. (2007) *Frontiers of Justice: Disability, Nationality and Species Membership*. London: Belknap.

Omerod, P. (1998) *Butterfly Economics: A New General Theory of Social and Economic Behaviour*. London: Faber and Faber.

Orsi, C. (2006) *The Value of Reciprocity: Arguing for a Plural Political Economy*. Roskilde: Federico Caffè Centre.

Papanek, V. (1985) *Design for the Real World: Human Ecology and Social Change*. London: Thames & Hudson.

Papanek, V. (1995) *The Green Imperative: Ecology and Ethics in Design and Architecture*. London: Thames & Hudson.

Parrish, D. (2007) *T-shirts and Suits: A Guide to the Business of Creativity*. Merseyside ACME.

Policastro, P. and Gardener, H. (1999) *From Case Studies to Robust Generalization*. In Handbook of Creativity, ed. R.J. Sternberg. London: Cambridge University Press.

Popper, K. (2002) *The Logic of Scientific Discovery*. London: Routledge.

Rahnema, M. and Bawtree, V. (1997) *The Post-Development Reader*. London: Zed Books.

Robinson, J. (1964) *Economic Philosophy*. Harmondsworth: Penguin.

Rogers, C. (1980) *A Way of Being*. Boston: Houghton Mifflin.

Rogers, C. (1972) 'Towards a Theory of Creativity'. In *Creativity*, ed. A.J. Copley. London: Penguin.

Rogers, R. (1997) *Cities for a Small Planet*. London: Faber and Faber.

Rorty, R. (1982) *Consequences of Pragmatism*. Minneapolis: Minneapolis University Press.

Roszak, T. (1981) *Person/Planet: The Creative Destruction of Industrial Society*. London: Granada.

Roszak, T. (1986) *The Cult of Information: The Folklore of Computers and the True Art of Thinking.* Cambridge: Lutterworth Press.

Russell, B. (2006) *The Conquest of Happiness.* London: Routledge.

Sahlins, M. (1974) *Stone Age Economics.* London: Routledge.

Sartre, J.-P. (1995) *Being and Nothingness.* London: Routledge.

Schumacher, E. (1993) 'Buddhist Economics'. In *Small Is Beautiful: A Study of Economics as If People Mattered,* ed. E. Schumacher. London: Vintage.

Sen, A. (2009) *The Idea of Justice.* Harvard: Harvard University Press.

Sennett, R. (2008) *The Craftsman.* London: Penguin.

Singer, P. (1997) *How Are We to Live?: Ethics in an Age of Self-Interest.* Oxford: Oxford University Press.

Steare, R. (2009) *Ethicability: How to Decide What's Right and Find the Courage to Do it.* Roger Steare Consulting Limited.

Sternberg, R.J. (1999) *Handbook of Creativity.* London: Cambridge University Press.

Stiglitz, J. (2010) *Freefall: Free Markets and the Sinking of the Global Economy.* London: Penguin.

Taleb, N. (2010) *The Bed of Procrustes: Philosophical and Practical Aphorisms.* Harvard: Harvard University Press.

Teilhard de Chardin, P. (1965) *The Phenomenon of Man.* London: Collins.

Tillich, P. (1986) *The Courage to Be.* London: Fontana.

Tudge, C. (2006) *The Secret Life of Trees: How They Live and Why They Matter.* London: Penguin.

von Hippel, E. (2006) *Democratizing Innovation.* London: MIT Press.

Wallas, G. (1972) 'The Art of Thought'. In *Creativity,* ed. A.J. Copley. London: Penguin Books.

Ward, C. (1996) *Talking to Architects.* London: Freedom Press.

Wasserman, B. et al. (2000) *Ethics and the Practice of Architecture.* New York: Wiley.

Webb-Young, J. (1965) *A Technique for Producing New Ideas.* New York: McGraw-Hill.

Weber, M. (1975) *Economy and Society: An Outline of Interpretative Society,* ed. G. Roth and C. Wittich. Berkley: University of California Press.

Weber, S. (2005) *The Success of Open Source.* Harvard University Press.

Weintraub, L. (2003) *Making Contemporary Art: How Today's Artists Think and Work.* London: Thames & Hudson.

Zeldin, T. (1995) *An Intimate History of Humanity.* London: Minerva.

Zohar, D. and Marshall, I. (1994) *Quantum Society: Mind, Physics and a New Social Vision.* London: Bloomsbury.

Index